# HARVARD ECONOMIC STUDIES

## HARVARD UNIVERSITY PRESS

### CAMBRIDGE, MASS., U.S.A.

# HARVARD ECONOMIC STUDIES

## VOLUME XLII

AWARDED THE DAVID A. WELLS PRIZE FOR THE YEAR 1931–32 AND PUBLISHED FROM THE INCOME OF THE DAVID A. WELLS FUND. THIS PRIZE IS OFFERED ANNUALLY, IN A COMPETITION OPEN TO SENIORS OF HARVARD COLLEGE AND GRADUATES OF ANY DEPARTMENT OF HARVARD UNIVERSITY OF NOT MORE THAN THREE YEARS STANDING, FOR THE BEST ESSAY IN CERTAIN SPECIFIED FIELDS OF ECONOMICS

LONDON : HUMPHREY MILFORD

OXFORD UNIVERSITY PRESS

RAILROAD MAP
OF
ILLINOIS
1857

ILLINOIS IN 1857
(Prepared from map in Gerhard's *Illinois in 1857* and other contemporary sources by the Illinois Central Railroad)

# The Illinois Central Railroad and Its Colonization Work

BY

## PAUL WALLACE GATES

ASSISTANT PROFESSOR OF HISTORY, BUCKNELL UNIVERSITY

CAMBRIDGE

HARVARD UNIVERSITY PRESS

1934

PRINTED AT THE HARVARD UNIVERSITY PRESS

CAMBRIDGE, MASS., U. S. A.

*To*

FREDERICK MERK

# PREFACE

THE glamour and romance in the early history of American railroads have led to the writing of many volumes dealing with its more spectacular features. These accounts have been devoted largely to two phases of the story, construction and the battles of the financial giants, Fiske, Gould, Vanderbilt, Huntington, Hill, and Harriman. The more important social and economic results of the laying down of the railroad net have been little touched. We know far more about the conflict between Daniel Drew, Jay Gould, and Commodore Vanderbilt over the control of the Erie Railroad than we do about the effects which the construction of this road had in providing rapid transportation facilities for the southern counties of New York, in making it possible for previously isolated farmers to get their commodities to market easily and cheaply, and in giving greater mobility to the people living along its line. The Crédit Mobilier scandal in connection with the construction of the Union Pacific Railroad, because of its political complications, has also been treated at length, but little attention has been paid to the more important contribution which that railroad made in opening up great regions previously so isolated as to prevent their settlement except by hardy and venturesome pioneers. Likewise the conflict between Hill and Harriman over the possession of the Northern Pacific Railroad, which led to the organization of the Northern Securities Company, has received much attention but, until recently, the sale and settlement of its princely 40,000,000 acre land grant has been barely mentioned.

Another feature of the railroad histories so far produced which it is difficult to explain is that they have been based largely on published documents such as the annual reports and other company pamphlets, state and federal documents, newspapers, and reminiscences. The search for manuscripts which has led historians to delve deeply into government archives has not attracted the railroad historian. This cannot be accounted for by the fact that the records do not exist, since this does not appear to be the case. The archival materials of three great American railroad systems, which have recently been explored, have proved both extensive and valuable, and there is little reason to suppose that other railroads are less well off in this respect.

Nor can it be said that historians have not had their attention called to the value of railroad archives. As far back as 1913 Professor William E. Dodd, speaking of the desirability of someone's making a study of the Illinois Central Railroad, said: "There are rich files of papers and collections of manuscripts in Chicago awaiting the right man. Such a work would certainly change some 'fixed opinions' of American history for the years just preceding the War." In an earlier article in the *American Historical Review* in 1911, Professor Dodd had suggested the importance of the colonization work of the land grant railroads in Illinois and Iowa, indicating their political importance with reference to the election of 1860.

The suggestion of Professor Dodd and the hints thrown out by other writers who have recognized the importance of the railroads in affecting the social and economic development of the United States had to wait until Dr. James B. Hedges began his valuable studies of railroad strategy and colonization which have done much to show the real significance of the railroads in American history. Dr. Hedges encouraged the writer to undertake the study of the colonization work of the Illinois Central Railroad, and his inspiration and criticisms have been of much assistance.

It was the original intention of the writer to limit his study of the Illinois Central Railroad to its land policies and colonization activities. As the work progressed, however, it was found necessary to examine the question of the land grant and the charter, and, because the financial history of the road is inseparable from its land policies, some attention had to be paid to the former. Consequently the study is not devoted simply to land policies and colonization but endeavors to deal with those phases of the early history of Illinois and the Illinois Central Railroad which supplement and help to explain the colonization work, the encouragement of agriculture, town-site promotion, and the political significance of the immigration resulting from the advertising of the road. It was also found necessary to study the operation of the federal land system in Illinois in order to understand the competition which the railroad had to face in disposing of its land grant.

During the preparation of this study the writer received assistance from numerous people to whom grateful acknowledgements are due. Professors Fish and Paxson, then of the University of Wisconsin, Professors Dodd, Jernegan, and Craven and Miss Pierce of the University of Chicago, the late Professor Frederick Jackson Turner, and Professors Gay and Merk of Harvard University have all given him encouragement and helpful suggestions.

His greatest obligation is to Professor Frederick Merk, who, by suggestions as to form, content, organization, and style, by patient advice and friendly encouragement, and, most of all, by the example of his own critical and careful scholarship, has placed the writer under a lasting obligation.

The officials of the Illinois Central Railroad were most generous in giving the writer access, without restrictions, to everything in their extensive archives, including both the financial and the land and colonization records. To Mr. C. J. Corliss, Associate Editor of the *Illinois Central Magazine*, whose interest in the early history of the railroad led him to delve into and to preserve many of its early records, the writer's most cordial thanks are due. Through his assistance missing material was found, inaccessible records were made available, and everything possible was done to facilitate the work. Mr. Corliss's last kindness was in supplying the map which is reproduced as the frontispiece. Other officials of the railroad, too numerous to mention, were equally courteous in aiding in the search for material.

Miss Edith Rantoul, of Salem, Massachusetts, kindly gave the writer access to the family manuscripts dealing with the Associates Land Company, recently deposited in the Baker Library of the Harvard Graduate School of Business Administration. Mr. T. Hasselquist, of Rock Island, recalled many interesting facts concerning the early development of the Swedish settlement at Paxton. Miss Anna Olsson, likewise of Rock Island, aided the writer in translating some of the Hasselquist correspondence and the Swedish newspaper, *Hemlandet*. Mr. E. P. Skeene, last Land Commissioner of the Illinois Central, supplied some missing links concerning the work of the Land Department.

Thanks are due to Professor Harlan H. Barrows of the University of Chicago for permission to republish the glacial map and the prairie and woodland map which are taken from his *Geography of the Middle Illinois Valley*. The editors of the *Journal of Economic and Business History*, *Agricultural History*, and the *Studies and Records* of the Norwegian-American Historical Association have kindly consented to the republication of material which first appeared in those publications.

Acknowledgements should also be made to the many library officials for their kind cooperation. Special attention was given by Mr. Herbert Kellar of the McCormick Library, Miss Margaret Norton of the Illinois State Archives, and Mrs. Oscar Nelson of the Illinois State Auditor's office.

My most recent obligation is to Professor A. P. Usher, who has assisted a novice in preparing this manuscript for the press.

Finally to my wife, Lillian Cowdell, who has delayed her own plans to assist me in organizing the material, in writing, in weeding out many awkward phrases, and in checking for accuracy, my most heartfelt thanks are extended.

P. W. G.

WASHINGTON, D. C.
March, 1934

# CONTENTS

CHAPTER VII

CHAPTER VIII

CHAPTER IX

CHAPTER X

CHAPTER XI

## CHAPTER XII

## CHAPTER XIII

## CHAPTER XIV

# MAPS AND ILLUSTRATIONS

# THE ILLINOIS CENTRAL RAILROAD AND
## ITS COLONIZATION WORK

# CHAPTER I

## THE SETTLEMENT OF ILLINOIS TO 1850

ILLINOIS, like most American states, is not a geographic unit. Its boundaries cut through the center of prairies and its watersheds are common to Wisconsin and Indiana. The geographic districts into which the State may be divided differ markedly from one another as to climate, rainfall, topography, and soil characteristics. The prairies of central and northern Illinois are more like the prairies of Indiana and Iowa than like the wooded area of southern Illinois; the latter section, in turn, has more in common with western Kentucky and the southern part of Indiana; finally, the northwestern part of the State resembles southwestern Wisconsin more than any other part of Illinois.

Geographic factors have been of profound importance in conditioning the settlement of Illinois, and in determining the character of the settlers, the regions wherein they have settled, and the pursuits which they have followed. Moreover, these factors have helped to mold political opinion, to influence the social outlook, and to change religious views. As a preliminary to this study it is therefore important to understand the topography of the State, the geographic sections into which it may be divided, the drainage systems, and the variations in types of soil.

The surface of Illinois is quite level, the total relief being only 973 feet.[1] The most rugged and broken sections are the Ozark Plateau of southern Illinois, the unglaciated region of northwestern Illinois, and the bluffs along the Illinois River. The remainder of the State is gently rolling or level, broken only by small valleys and the terminal moraines deposited by the glaciers.

Illinois is fortunate in the number of navigable rivers located within or on its boundaries. Along its western border flows the Mississippi River, which is navigable for the entire length of the State, except during the winter months. The Ohio and Wabash

---

[1] Douglas Clay Ridgley, *The Geography of Illinois* (Chicago, 1921), p. 37.

Rivers on the southeastern border of the State are likewise navigable. The Illinois River — next to the Ohio the most important eastern affluent of the Mississippi — drains the central part of the State and its watershed extends into Indiana and Wisconsin.[2] This river was destined to become part of one of America's greatest waterways because the low barrier which separates it from the watershed of Lake Michigan could be pierced by a canal with comparative ease. In the southwestern part of the State the Kaskaskia River, with its numerous tributaries, flows into the Mississippi. The Kaskaskia River, the Illinois River, and to a less extent the Rock River were the main avenues of approach into the interior of Illinois, and their importance in the early history of the State cannot be overemphasized.

The lands of Illinois may be classified in three groups, the bottom lands of the Mississippi and its tributaries, the timbered lands, and the prairies. The last two are the most important, both in area and influence, and will be given the most consideration.

The bottoms of Illinois were the first lands to which the early voyager came when making his way down the Ohio and up its tributaries and those of the Mississippi. These bottoms extend back some distance from the rivers and, because of their low, flat nature, are periodically flooded. By deposition the floods have built up an immensely rich soil which is extremely productive. The Great American Bottom, a broad flood plain — in places seven miles wide — which extends along the Mississippi from Alton to the mouth of the Kaskaskia River, was early considered the most fertile section of the State.[3] The Wabash, Kaskaskia, and Illinois River valleys likewise contain many thousand acres of such lands. Along the lower course of the Illinois River the bottom in places extends back from the stream for a distance of five miles.[4]

[2] Harlan H. Barrows, *Geography of the Middle Illinois Valley*, Division of the State Geological Survey, *Bulletin*, No. 15 (Urbana, 1925), p. 3.

[3] (S. A. Mitchell), *Illinois in 1837* (Philadelphia, 1837), p. 101. Its total area was estimated at 288,000 acres (*ibid.*, p. 18). One writer called it the richest agricultural land in the United States. Elias Pym Fordham, *Personal Narrative* . . ., F. A. Ogg, ed. (Cleveland, 1906), p. 105, note.

[4] University of Illinois Agricultural Experiment Station, *Soil Report* (1915), No. 11, "Pike County Soils."

The timbered areas of Illinois are the southern section, the northwestern corner, and the narrow fringes along the streams in the predominantly prairie regions. Southern Illinois was the most heavily wooded, but its lumber was in less demand during the pioneer period than that of the narrow fringes of timbered land along the rivers. These latter lands, located beside the treeless prairies, were in great demand because of the high prices for which their timber sold. Indeed, the possession of a small patch of timbered land in the midst of a prairie was a great asset to the fortunate owner. The existence of forests in northwestern Illinois was also fortunate for that region because it made possible the development of the lead-mining industry there in the early nineteenth century. With the opening of the railroad era in the Northwest and the movement of population into the prairies, the demand for lumber increased tremendously and its production soon became one of the State's major industries.

The feature which most attracted the attention of early travellers in Illinois was the broad expansive prairies.[5] These great stretches of level or gently rolling land, bare of trees, with long thick grasses billowing and blowing in the breezes, were magnificent to behold and rarely failed to impress the visitor. The prairies were located back from the streams, being separated from them by the narrow fringes of timbered land mentioned above.

In the early part of the nineteenth century it was the more obvious physical characteristics of the land which either attracted or repelled the settler. Among these were the presence or absence of timber, the drainage of the land, and its proximity to transportation routes. Little consideration was given to the quality of the soil. This is not surprising, however, as there existed then little knowledge of soil composition problems which have since received much attention. Nevertheless, soil composition, though little understood at the time, had a great effect upon the development of Illinois.

Almost the entire area of Illinois was covered by one or more of the glaciers which swept down from the north in past geologic

---

[5] Charles Dickens devotes a chapter entitled "A Jaunt to the Looking-Glass Prairie and Back" to his visit to the prairies near Belleville. *American Notes* (Boston, 1867), ch. xiii.

ages. These glaciers, by leaving rich deposits of till to great depths, laid the basis of Illinois's preeminence as an agricultural state.[6] Because the successive glaciers did not cover the same areas, and because each glacier varied its deposits in different locations, wide variations in types of soil resulted. The soil quality in the driftless areas of southern and northwestern Illinois, which were untouched by the glaciers, is much lower than that of land in the glaciated territory. A comparison of the soils in Johnson County in the driftless area with those in Will, Logan, and Woodford Counties in the glaciated region indicates that the latter are much richer in organic carbon, nitrogen, sulphur, potassium, magnesium, and calcium.[7] A similar comparison of lands in southern Illinois covered only by the Illinoisian drift with lands covered by the Wisconsin or Shelbyville drift reveals an equally marked variation. The accompanying map shows the terminal moraine which divides these two regions. The Wisconsin glacier which deposited its till north of the moraine brought with it rich chemical compounds which have made the Grand Prairie one of the richest agricultural areas in the United States. The till of the region covered by the Illinoisian drift is much poorer, as shown by crop yields and land values.[8] This difference helps to explain why southern Illinois has been more backward in economic and social development than the northern and central portions of the State.[9]

The main routes which immigrants to Illinois followed in the first half of the nineteenth century were (1) the Wilderness Trail through Kentucky, across Ohio and Indiana to Illinois; (2) over-

[6] Ridgley, *op. cit.*, p. 36.

[7] This comparison is made on the basis of soil analyses given in the *Soil Reports* of the four counties named above. For purposes of comparison Upland Soils Nos. 1034 and 1035 were used. The *Soil Reports* were Nos. 30, 35, 36, and 39. For a discussion of the disadvantages of Jo Daviess County see B. H. Schockel, "History of Development of Jo Daviess County," Illinois State Geological Survey, *Bulletin* (1916), No. 26, pp. 206–207.

[8] G. D. Hubbard, "A Case of Geographic Influence upon Human Affairs," American Geographical Society, *Bulletin* (March, 1904), XXXVI, 152.

[9] The prices which the Illinois Central Railroad received for its lands in northern and southern Illinois clearly indicate this difference in the land values of the two sections. North of the moraine, the lands sold for prices ranging from $6 to $20 per acre, while south of it the prices were much less.

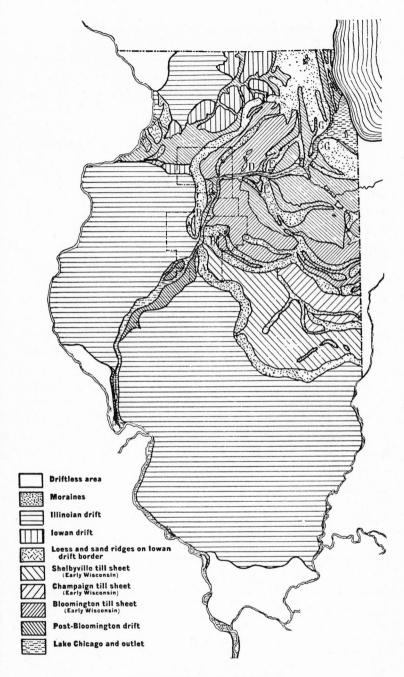

| | Driftless area |
| | Moraines |
| | Illinoian drift |
| | Iowan drift |
| | Loess and sand ridges on Iowan drift border |
| | Shelbyville till sheet (Early Wisconsin) |
| | Champaign till sheet (Early Wisconsin) |
| | Bloomington till sheet (Early Wisconsin) |
| | Post-Bloomington drift |
| | Lake Chicago and outlet |

GLACIAL MAP OF ILLINOIS

(Reproduced by permission of Professor Harlan H. Barrows from his
*Geography of the Middle Illinois Valley*)

land to the headwaters of the Ohio, down it either to the mouth of the Wabash or to the Mississippi, and then up one of these rivers to the place of destination; (3) a third possible route by way of the Maumee River and portage to the Wabash. The opening of the Cumberland Road in the 'thirties provided an all-land route which was followed by many. After 1825 the most important route was the Erie Canal and thence by steamboat through the Great Lakes or overland.[10]

The pioneer settlers in Illinois were, for the most part, from the southern states. The so-called southern uplanders, who had come originally from Virginia and the Carolinas to Kentucky and Tennessee and had then resumed their westward trek to southern Indiana, Illinois, and Missouri, opened up southern Illinois, and were the dominant element in the State until the 'thirties.

These immigrants settled on the first land which was available, the bottom lands bordering on the rivers. A fringe of settlements was thus established on the banks of the Ohio, Mississippi, and Wabash Rivers. The Great American Bottom was the goal of many of the migrants. On this bottom the French had made settlements at Cahokia and Kaskaskia, the latter being the first capital of the Territory of Illinois. Around these centers grew up the densest settlements of that section,[11] and by 1815 there was not an acre of government land for sale along the entire stretch of the Bottom.[12] At one time it was even estimated that three-fourths of the population of Illinois resided in this area.[13] Its palmy days were from 1790 to 1810, but even then forces were at work which were to destroy its prosperity. The Mississippi River was constantly encroaching on the banks of the Bottom. In 1772 the area was completely inundated and twelve years later it was flooded again. The frequent floods, together with the unhealthy character of the region, which was caused by the existence of

[10] For a discussion of the routes to the west see William V. Pooley, *The Settlement of Illinois from 1830 to 1850* (University of Wisconsin, *Bulletin*, "History Series," vol. I, 1908), ch. iv, pp. 352–374.

[11] Solon J. Buck, *Illinois in 1818* (*Illinois Centennial Publications*, Introductory Volume, Springfield, 1917), pp. 75 ff.

[12] *Ibid.*, map opposite p. 52.

[13] John Reynolds, *Pioneer History of Illinois* (Chicago, 1887), p. 202.

swampy and poorly drained land, led to the gradual abandonment of this rich area. After 1810 the region no longer attracted
settlers.[14] The flood of 1844 completely blighted the prospects of
Kaskaskia, and in 1858 it was reported to be a "recluse" of a
town accessible only by country roads.[15] Not until adequate
drainage facilities were provided did this section of the State
again become attractive.

The bottom along the lower course of the Illinois River was
considered forever impracticable for settlement because of the
difficulty of draining it.[16] Along the upper reaches of the river the
bottoms were settled at an early date, but as these lands were considered less desirable than the terraces or woodlands their population was scanty.[17] The Wabash River bottom was avoided by
incoming settlers because of the frequent floods, and furthermore
it was not as broad as some of the others.

The prevalence of the ague or malarial fever in the poorly
drained sections of Illinois, including the prairies, deterred many
immigrants from settling in those districts, rich as the soil un-
deniably was. Schoolcraft, in 1821, wrote of the bottom lands of
the Illinois River: "The insalubrity of the climate . . . must be
considered as presenting a formidable impediment to its speedy
settlement." [18] A year later another traveller pronounced the
American Bottom "almost uninhabitable by its unhealthiness." [19]
When the settlers were induced to abandon the bottoms in favor
of the woodlands back from the streams they were still subject to

[14] *Ibid.*, pp. 113-115, 201 ff. Cf. Mitchell, *op. cit.*, pp. 17-19; W. B. Cowan, *A
Description of Grand Tower on the Mississippi* (New York, 1839); Arthur Clinton
Boggess, *The Settlement of Illinois, 1778-1830* (Chicago Historical Society's *Collection*, vol. v, 1908). The last two mention the large amounts of cattle, swine, and
horses raised on the Bottom. For an account of the activities of a prominent resident
of the Bottom from 1817, when he arrived there, until 1833, when he finally abandoned the location, and the reasons for the change, see J. F. Snyder, *Adam W.
Snyder and His Period in Illinois History, 1817-1842* (Virginia, Ill., 1906), pp. 23,
58-67, 150. The author finds it incomprehensible why Snyder "remained so long in
that location, remote from his professional interests, and so insalubrious as to endanger his life and that of each member of his family."
[15] *L'Occident* in *New York Tribune*, August 17, 1858.
[16] Barrows, *op. cit.*, p. 6.          [17] *Ibid.*, pp. 76-77.
[18] Henry R. Schoolcraft, *Travels in the Central Portions of the Mississippi Valley*
(New York, 1825), p. 300.
[19] (W. N. Blane), *An Excursion through the United States and Canada during the
years, 1822-23* (London, 1824), p. 181.

the dread disease. There was much marsh and swamp land in southern Illinois, some counties having more than a third of their area under water.[20] The early pioneers did not understand health and sanitation problems. They settled near these low wet areas and quickly acquired the "seeds" of the ague. Subsequent periodic visits of the "chills" sapped their vitality and made them listless and unambitious. Thus was the hardy southern uplander transformed into a shiftless and lazy character who only desired to be let alone by the later immigrants whom he despised.[21]

Southern Illinois early acquired the reputation of being an unhealthy locality and was spurned by thousands of immigrants who, in the 'forties and 'fifties, went farther west to the healthier regions of Wisconsin, Minnesota, and Iowa.[22] The more ambitious residents of southern Illinois were much distressed by the unfavorable opinion of their section which was held by many people and which was broadcast by rival sections. They wrote frequent letters to the newspapers and agricultural journals of the day in an attempt to combat this opinion.[23] As will be seen later, the Illinois Central Railroad had to contest this same unfavorable reputation which southern Illinois had gained.

[20] In Saline County 35.46 per cent of the lands were swampy and in Randolph County 22.64 per cent. It is true that some of the northern counties such as McHenry, Kane, Lake, and Rock Island likewise had large amounts of swamp land, but the worst areas were in the south. The figures are taken from the *Soil Reports* of the University of Illinois Agricultural Experiment Station.

[21] For a graphic picture of the "shakes," see Hans Mattson, *Reminiscences. The Story of an Emigrant* (St. Paul, 1891), pp. 29–31. Schoolcraft, *op. cit.*, pp. 300–301, describes the results of the constant attacks of fever upon the people of the lower Illinois valley. See Dorothy A. Dondore, *The Prairie and the Making of Middle America: Four Centuries of Description* (Cedar Rapids, 1926), opposite p. 206, for a reproduction of a contemporary cartoon depicting the horrible results of the Illinois climate.

[22] See letter of Steffan Steffanson of October 9, 1849, in Swedish Historical Society of America, *Yearbook*, 1926, XI, 93–95, 97, for an example of a Swedish immigrant who followed this course.

[23] The files of the *Illinois State Register*, the *Chicago Democratic Press*, the *Prairie Farmer* and the *Country Gentleman* contain many of these letters. The Land Department of the Illinois Central Railroad published two letters in its pamphlet of 1856, *The Illinois Central Rail-Road Company offers for Sale over 2,000,000 Acres . . .*, pp. 19–26, 46–47, 52–54. In this same pamphlet appears a letter from an inhabitant of Wabash County who turned the tables on the north by remarking, "That scourge of the North, consumption, is almost unknown here" (p. 53). Other examples of this sectional jealousy may be found in Theodore C. Pease, *The Frontier State, 1818–1848* (*Centennial History of Illinois*, vol. II, Springfield, 1918), p. 386.

Cholera, the great scourge of the frontier settlements, seemed to strike all sections of the State alike. Thus, in 1854 and 1855, cholera was reported along the Illinois Central Railroad at Galena, Chicago, Shelbyville, Salem, Cairo, and La Salle.[24] Because it was found indiscriminately in most sections of the West, cholera retarded settlement less than the constantly recurring, though less fatal, fever and ague.[25]

Northern Illinois suffered on account of the general reputation for an unhealthy climate which the entire State had acquired. It is true that the ague was prevalent here, but this was so to a less degree than farther south.[26] Residents of this section sought to correct the prevailing opinion by pointing out in the public press the differences between northern and southern Illinois, always to the detriment of "Egypt." [27]

When the fertile bottom lands of southern Illinois had been settled, population began slowly moving into the timbered areas along the many branches of the Kaskaskia, Big Muddy, Illinois, and Wabash Rivers. These river valleys were all heavily wooded for the greater part of their length, the width of the timbered areas being from 1 to 5 miles.[28] It was these lands which were attracting settlers rather than the solidly timbered areas in the extreme southern part of the State. On the bluffs near the rivers town sites were laid out by ubiquitous and optimistic speculators. In the early part of the century, practically all the towns of importance were to be found in such locations, and not until internal improvements were made did prairie towns rival them in population.[29] As immigration to Illinois increased, settlers were forced

[24] Letters of W. P. Burrall to Jonathon Sturges of May 1, 18, 28, 31, June 22, 1854; B. F. Johnson to Osborn, August 15, 1855, Presidents' Correspondence, Magazine Office, Central Station. This archive is hereafter cited as M. O. See also the *Chicago Democratic Press*, July 20, August 3, 1854. The papers tried to minimize the cholera epidemics which occurred in their cities while exaggerating the misfortunes of rival cities.          [25] Letter of Steffanson as in note 22.

[26] Gjerset and Hektoen, "Health Conditions and the Practice of Medicine among the early Norwegian Settlers, 1825–1865," Norwegian American Historical Association, *Publications*, "Studies and Records" (Minneapolis, 1926), I, 19 ff.

[27] A term of contempt applied to southern Illinois.

[28] The timbered areas along the rivers which flowed through the lands of the Illinois Central are well indicated, as they were in the 'fifties, on the plates in *Sectional Maps Showing the Location of over 2,500,000 Acres* . . . (1867).

[29] A glance at the maps in Mitchell's *Illinois in 1837* will confirm this. Of the

to push farther into the interior in their search for forest lands. Except in southern Illinois, the timbered areas were only narrow finger-like protrusions extending into the prairies. They were soon exhausted, and then settlers found they must either move into the much dreaded prairies or go farther west.

It is not difficult to understand why the early settlers avoided the prairies. These settlers came from wooded areas in Kentucky, Tennessee, and the coastal states. The Illinois prairies were the first great timberless areas with which the pioneers came in contact.[30] Their treeless expanse seemed to indicate that the soil was too poor for heavy growth. The thick forests and swamp lands which separated them from the rivers would make it difficult to bring in lumber for the construction of houses, barns, and fences, and for fuel. For the same reason, the exportation of surplus products would be impossible. A good deal of prairie land, being poorly drained, was covered with water during part of the growing season. Furthermore, such districts were unhealthy owing to the miasma arising from the dampness. As the individual pioneer did not possess the means to drain the land and as, by going a little farther west, dry lands could be secured, he was not interested in the prairies. The absence of drinking-water was another factor which made the prairies less inviting.[31] A final factor of real significance was the difficulty with which the tough prairie soil was plowed. The prairie grasses, with their interlaced roots, formed a compact mass of dense sod which was not easily broken. The early plows were crude and ill-adapted to such tough soil. From three to six yoke of oxen were required to operate them on account of their awkward construction,[32] and few pioneers possessed so many draft cattle.

twenty-nine towns and cities discussed in this guide, eighteen were directly on the rivers or creeks, Chicago was on the Lake, six were located in close proximity to streams, and only four were situated at any real distance from water courses.

[30] See map of virgin forests in the United States in W. B. Greeley, "The Relation of Geography to Timber Supply," *Economic Geography* (March, 1925), I, 4.

[31] Professor Joseph Schafer has an interesting chapter entitled "The Selection of Farm Land" in *Four Wisconsin Counties* (*Wisconsin Domesday Book*, "General Studies," vol. II, 1927), pp. 107–139. See also Bidwell and Falconer, *History of Agriculture in the Northern United States, 1620–1860* (Washington, 1925), ch. xxi.

[32] Mitchell, *op. cit.*, p. 14; Bidwell and Falconer, *op. cit.*, p. 283.

The prairies were not to remain without settlement, however. The completion of the Erie Canal in 1825 and the construction of the Cumberland Road made available new routes into central and northern Illinois whereby an ever-increasing volume of settlers reached the State.[33] These new transportation facilities, together with the introduction of steam navigation on the Great Lakes, changed the character of the immigration. In place of the southern upland stock of which the immigration prior to 1825 had been largely composed, there came the New York-New England element. They, too, came from wooded agricultural regions and were likewise ignorant of the superior qualities of the prairie lands. They therefore followed the example of those who had preceded them and settled first in the timbered areas. As these areas were by no means extensive they were soon exhausted, and then, under the pressure of necessity, the newcomers were forced to turn to the prairies.

This shift from forested to prairie land was not made suddenly. Early writers observed the beginnings of this change, which was under way at least by the second decade of the nineteenth century.[34] Settlers would locate on a prairie near a timbered section from which they could secure lumber and fuel. The cattle and other stock would be turned loose on the prairie and perhaps a small corner of it would, by dint of much labor, be broken for cultivation.[35] Another settler would follow shortly at a different location on the same prairie, and before long there would be a circle of farms around the open area. This process would continue until the entire prairie had been taken up.[36] It should be noted that

[33] For a suggestive study of the effects of the construction of the Erie Canal upon western settlement see L. K. Mathews, "The Erie Canal and the Settlement of the West," Buffalo Historical Society, *Publications*, 1910, XIV, 189–203. For the Cumberland Road see A. B. Hulbert, *The Cumberland Road* (*Historic Highways of America*, vol. x, Cleveland, 1904).

[34] John Wood, *Two Years Residence in the Settlement on the English Prairie in the Illinois Country, United States* . . . (London, 1822), pp. 145 ff., 162 ff. A map showing the location of Morris Birkbeck on the English Prairie is included in *Fordham's Personal Narrative*, p. 112 f.

[35] John Bradbury, *Travels in the Interior of America in the Years 1809, 1810, and 1811* . . . (Liverpool, 1817), p. 308, observes the use of prairies for feeding cattle.

[36] Mitchell, *op. cit.*, p. 14. Further study may show that foreigners had less aversion to the prairies than the American pioneers had. It is certain that Morris Birkbeck and Richard Flower, pioneer English settlers in southern Illinois, had located

such a process took place generally on the smaller prairies located not far from the rivers. The settler always had to keep in mind transportation facilities. Settlements at a distance from the navigable rivers were undesirable because the cost of transporting agricultural products was more than the price for which they would sell. This consideration necessarily prevented any extensive settlement of the great prairies south of Lake Michigan until the Illinois Central Railroad had opened up the country.

The southern uplander had pushed northward along the rivers into the interior of the State until his advance was checked by the diminishing supply of timber land. After 1830 his place was taken by the sturdy New York-New Englanders who were pressing westward in ever-increasing numbers. These newcomers, being more adaptable, began moving into the smaller prairies,[37] as has been explained. This led to a peculiar juxtaposition of the two diverse elements: the southern uplanders occupied the narrow tongues of timbered land along the rivers, while the New York-New Englanders pushed down between these tongues into the smaller prairies.[38] In only one section in the northern part of the State did the southern uplanders predominate after 1830. This section was the unglaciated lead-mining district around Galena. Mining operations on a large scale had been commenced here in the 'twenties and had attracted the migrating southern uplanders. With the later influx of New York-New England immigrants agriculture began to develop, and after the lead industry lost its tariff protection replaced mining as the chief occupation.[39]

on the English Prairie, a small opening 4 miles in width and a half mile in length. Their homes were constructed not far from timber and their locations included small stands of timber. *Fordham's Personal Narrative*, p. 115. Both Flower and Birkbeck in 1818 expressed their preference for the prairies over the timbered land. Richard Flower, *Letters from Lexington and the Illinois* . . . (London, 1819), pp. 19–22; Morris Birkbeck, *Extracts from a Supplementary Letter from the Illinois* . . . (London, 1819), p. 17. Most of the English travellers spoke of the prairies as the future homes of a large agricultural population and expressed surprise that they had been so neglected. Invaluable for a study of this nature are the accounts of foreign travellers who visited Illinois in this period, reprinted in Thwaites, *Early Western Travels*.

[37] Pooley, *op. cit.*, p. 383.          [38] Barrows, *op. cit.*, p. 74.

[39] B. H. Schockel, "Settlement and Development of the Lead and Zinc Mining Region of the Driftless Area with Special Emphasis upon Jo Daviess County, Illinois," *Mississippi Valley Historical Review* (September, 1917), IV, 169–192; Boggess, *op. cit.*, pp. 150–153, 172.

The cultivation of the prairies was rendered possible by improvements in the plow which made easier the task of breaking the prairie sod. The wooden moldboard plow,[40] in use until 1825, was gradually replaced by the more efficient cast-iron plow. Even this plow failed to give satisfaction on prairie soil, for it would not scour and was too cumbersome to operate. The demand for a better plow was frequently voiced. Agricultural societies offered prizes for improved plows, the rural journals opened their pages to persons making suggestions for improvements,[41] and many inventors experimented with different types. In 1837 the first steel plow was made by John Deere, and within a few years his plow and the rod plow had quite revolutionized prairie breaking.[42]

The next obstacle to the cultivation of the prairies to be removed was the lack of transportation facilities. Prior to the construction of the railroads, the Mississippi and Illinois Rivers were the main arteries of commerce. Down the former were carried the lead products of the Galena district [43] and down the latter the agricultural output of central Illinois. To a lesser extent the Wabash, Kaskaskia, Rock, and Big Muddy Rivers, with their tributaries, provided means of transportation for the settlers located in their valleys. On the Mississippi and Illinois Rivers there developed, in the 'twenties and 'thirties, a large steamboat traffic. Regular schedules were maintained between the more important cities such as St. Louis, Peoria, Galena, and Alton. At Beardstown, a small town on the Illinois River, there were, according to report, 450 arrivals and departures of steamboats in 1836.[44] Peoria, destined to be the chief port on this river, had 694 arrivals of steamboats in 1845, 871 in 1846, about 1116 in 1848, and 1286 in 1850.[45] One river captain reported that in 1839 he had

40 For a cut of this plow see Bidwell and Falconer, *op. cit.*, p. 124.

41 The files of the *Prairie Farmer* for the 'forties are replete with items, communications, and notices of plow contests and new improvements.

42 *Prairie Farmer* (1844), IV, 146, 227; Bidwell and Falconer, *op. cit.*, p. 283. This work discusses the various improvements in plows and gives a number of valuable cuts. *A Guide to the Illinois Central Railroad Lands* (1859), p. 27, presents a cut of a plow drawn by three yoke of oxen and another drawn by two horses.

43 See Schockel, *loc. cit.*, p. 181. Attempts to transport the lead overland to the Lake proved to be impractical.

44 Mitchell, *op. cit.*, p. 34; Pooley, *op. cit.*, pp. 358 ff.

45 Barrows, *op. cit.*, p. 91.

made 58 trips from St. Louis to Peru and had carried 10,000 pas-
sengers.[46] Many river towns enjoyed a rapid growth in the heyday
of steam navigation, only to suffer a decline when, in a later decade, the railroads passed them by.[47] The effect of the development of steam navigation is shown by the growth of the principal
river counties during the decade of the 'thirties. Adams County
had the largest increase in population of any county in the State,
while Fulton, Hancock, La Salle, Peoria, Pike, and Scott Counties
also had large increases.[48]

Between the numerous towns a system of stage roads and common roads provided means of communication of a very poor sort.
The road map of Illinois in 1837 [49] seems to show a well developed
system of roads connecting the principal points. Most of these
roads, however, were nothing more than old Indian trails, and
were hardly passable by wagons except when the ground was
frozen.[50] The stage roads were somewhat better, and over them
regular stage service was maintained. Thus, in 1831, the stage
left St. Louis for Vincennes three times a week, once a week a
stage went to Vandalia, and once a week to Galena.[51] These
routes were mostly for mail and passenger traffic and, except for
short hauls, were little used for freight. A charge of 50 cents a
hundredweight for every 20 miles prohibited long hauls.[52] The
stages aided in opening up the regions back from the rivers, but
they served as mere tributaries to the river and lake commerce.
They did not solve the transportation problem, but they pointed
the way to a solution. In a later decade the railroads were to follow in many cases the routes marked out by these stages.

The sixty-mile frontage on Lake Michigan provided the State
with excellent water transportation facilities, which, however,

---

[46] Mrs. [E. R.] Steele, *A Summer Journey in the West* (New York, 1841), p. 164.
[47] Barrows, *op. cit.*, pp. 85-92.        [48] *Ninth Census*, 1870, I, 23.
[49] See map in Mitchell, *op. cit.*
[50] N. Matson, *Reminiscences of Bureau County* (Princeton, Ill., 1872), pp. 345-
346.
[51] Pooley, *op. cit.*, p. 357. The journey from Vincennes to St. Louis required three
days. Seymour Dunbar, *A History of Travel in America* (Indianapolis, 1915), III,
762. A stage route from Chicago to Galena was established in 1839, the 160 miles
being covered in two days. Pooley, *op. cit.*, p. 359.
[52] Boggess, *op. cit.*, p. 161. This work contains a discussion of transportation in
the State in the 'twenties (pp. 157-164).

were not not utilized until the 'thirties. In 1833, the year that Indian uprisings ceased to menace the State, Chicago was incorporated. Chicago's early growth was largely dependent upon its fine harbor facilities on Lake Michigan and the development of its rich hinterland. The hinterland of Chicago drained into the Mississippi, but this fact did not hinder the development of the city's export and import trade because of the advantages of its water connections with the East.[53] Places as far distant as Ottawa carried on their trade through this port, which became by 1837 the largest city in the State.[54]

With the development of the hinterland came the need for better means of communication. The cry was raised for internal improvements: canals, plank roads, railroads, and the dredging and deepening of rivers. Chicago in particular needed railroad or canal connections to replace the inadequate system of roads over which its commerce was hauled. Galena desired a quicker and more certain means of getting its lead to market. Its river transportation route was closed in the winter months because of ice and frequently in the summer because of low water. Other rival towns such as Peoria, Alton, Quincy, Shawneetown, and Rock Island, which were all jealous of each other and together jealous of the more rapid growth of Chicago, looked upon railroads as their means of outdistancing all rivals. Interior towns such as Shelbyville, Bloomington, Vandalia, Freeport, and Springfield believed that lack of transportation facilities alone prevented them from becoming great cities. Finally the land speculator advocated internal improvements as a means of increasing the value of his holdings.

The first internal improvement scheme for which there was any real support provided for the construction of a canal from the head of navigation on the Illinois River to Lake Michigan. For this purpose the Second General Assembly asked the Federal Government for authority to build such a canal through the pub-

[53] Mitchell, *op. cit.*, p. 119; A. T. Andreas, *History of Chicago* (Chicago, 1885), I, 179.
[54] Judson Fiske Lee, "Transportation. A Factor in the Development of Northern Illinois Previous to 1860," Illinois State Historical Society, *Journal* (April, 1917), vol. x, No. 1, pp. 17–85. See especially ch. i.

lic lands and further requested a donation of public lands to aid in its construction.[55] In 1822 the right-of-way was granted, and in 1825 a company was incorporated to dig the canal. Finally, in 1827, the Federal Government donated alternate sections of land in a strip 5 miles wide on either side of the proposed route of the canal, to aid in its construction.[56] Even this generous grant was insufficient to interest eastern capitalists in the project. They were suspicious of investments based on the wild lands of the West, and required a pledge of the credit of the State before they would make a loan. The loan was ultimately secured in 1836 and construction work commenced at once.[57] Subsequently the credit of the State became strained owing to the large debt incurred in the canal and other internal improvement ventures. Consequently, when the disastrous Panic of 1837 occurred, work on the canal was retarded and in 1841 suspended altogether. In 1845, after the original plans had been modified to a considerable extent, work on the canal was resumed, and thereafter the undertaking was rapidly pushed to completion in 1848.[58]

The construction of the canal, as was expected, gave a great impetus to the development of northern Illinois and, in particular, to the region through which the canal extended. Population poured into Cook, La Salle, Will, and Du Page Counties. The first three of these, unorganized in 1830, reached first, ninth, and eleventh places respectively in 1850, in the State's population.[59] Towns such as La Salle, Utica, Ottawa, Joliet, and Lockport sprang up along the canal route and soon became thriving communities. Settlers moved into the prairie regions more and more rapidly.. By 1850 approximately 80 per cent of the land of La Salle County, over four-fifths of which was prairie soil,[60] was under

---

[55] James William Putnam, *The Illinois and Michigan Canal; A Study in Economic History* (Chicago Historical Society's *Collection*, vol. x, 1918), pp. 11–12.

[56] *Laws of Illinois*, 1824–1825, pp. 160–165. The charter was repealed in the following year to make way for state construction. *Laws of Illinois*, 1826, p. 64. 4 *United States Statutes-at-Large*, 234.

[57] *Laws of Illinois*, 1835–1836, p. 145; Putnam, *op. cit.*, p. 34.

[58] Putnam, *op. cit.*, ch. ii, "Finance and Construction"; Andreas, *op. cit.*, I, 165–173; Rufus Blanchard, *Discovery and Conquests of the Northwest with the History of Chicago* (Chicago, 1900), II, 163–171.

[59] *Ninth Census*, I, 23.

[60] *Soil Report*, No. 5, "La Salle County," pp. 4–5.

cultivation. Grundy and Will Counties likewise had a high percentage of lands under cultivation.[61] The land sales of the government land offices at Dixon and Chicago show how rapidly the region was being settled. These offices, which were opened in 1835,[62] showed surprisingly large sales in the first year, and from 1841 to 1849 they led all the other land districts of the State in the amount of land sold.[63] So rapidly were the lands sold that by 1851 practically all the area within 15 miles of the Illinois Central route, in the region where it crosses the canal, had been taken up and the railroad company was forced to look elsewhere for its sections.[64] It should not be supposed that all of these lands were sold to settlers; thousands of acres had passed into the hands of speculators, who were holding them for higher prices.[65]

The rapidly growing metropolis on the lake shore received the greatest benefit from the canal. The increased demand for building material in the canal counties aided in developing the lumber trade of Chicago.[66] Wheat and surplus farm products were shipped by way of the canal, via Chicago, to eastern markets. The growing hinterland also made its purchases through that port.[67] In short, the canal enabled Chicago to supplant St. Louis as the export and import center for a large part of Illinois, a process which was to be carried further by the railroads. Chicago in the 'forties was one of the most rapidly growing cities in the coun-

[61] Pooley, op. cit., p. 388.

[62] See map of Illinois land districts in volume of transcripts and photostats in Harvard College Library entitled "Purchase Money Received and Acreage Transferred by the United States Government, 1806–1860," prepared under the direction of A. H. Cole.

[63] The Dixon office was originally located at Galena. See the Reports of the Commissioner of the General Land Office, 1835–1850.

[64] Along 16 miles of the route of the Illinois Central, south of Chicago, and along 27 miles of the main line above and below La Salle, the Company received only 5360 acres of the 165,000 to which it was entitled. In their place indemnity lands were in part secured within the fifteen-mile limit in other regions where government land was still available. See Sectional Maps, plates 16, 17, 23, A.

[65] Pooley, op. cit., p. 385. The State Legislature had limited the sale of canal lands to one section to a purchaser, but there was no limit upon the purchase of federal lands.

[66] Barrows, op. cit., p. 94.

[67] Elmer A. Riley, The Development of Chicago and Vicinity as a Manufacturing Center prior to 1880 (Chicago, 1911), ch. iii.

try,[68] and by 1850 it bid fair to become the great metropolis of the Middle West.

It is easy to exaggerate the significance of the canal in the economic life of northern Illinois. Not six years had passed after its completion before the Rock Island Railroad was competing with it along its entire route and absorbing a good share of its traffic.[69] Furthermore, the Galena and Chicago Union Railroad, the Chicago, Burlington and Quincy, and the Illinois Central tapped as rich territories for the benefit of Chicago as did the canal.[70]

North of Cook County, and extending along the Wisconsin border, was a tier of counties which were growing rapidly. These counties were Jo Daviess, Stephenson, Winnebago, Boone, McHenry, and Lake. The lead-mining region in Jo Daviess County was in its heyday; its chief center, Galena, was even thought to be rivaling Chicago; trade and navigation were expanding and immigration continued. These regions, together with the hinterland of Chicago which comprised Du Page, Kane, and Kendall Counties, were the most rapidly growing sections in the State. They attracted both the New York-New England and the foreign immigrant because they possessed extensive prairie lands, none of which were far from timber.[71] They were well

---

[68] The growth of population in Chicago from 1830 to 1850 was as follows:

| 1830 ..... 70 | 1844..... 10,864 | 1847..... 16,859 |
| 1840 ..... 4,853 | 1845..... 12,088 | 1848..... 20,023 |
| 1843 ..... 7,580 | 1846..... 14,169 | 1849..... 23,047 |

Chicago Board of Trade, *Annual Report*, 1865, p. 12.

[69] Putnam, *op. cit.*, p. 110.

[70] *Ibid.*, pp. 92–125; Barrows, *op. cit.*, pp. 92–106; Pooley, *op. cit.*, pp. 375–395.

[71] The following table, showing the percentage of prairie and timber land and density of population in these counties, explains why the land was so desirable in this period. One should also see the soil content maps for these counties.

| County | Prairie land Per cent | Timber land Per cent | Population per square mile | County | Prairie land Per cent | Timber land Per cent | Population per square mile |
|---|---|---|---|---|---|---|---|
| Jo Daviess .. | | | 29 | Lake ......... | 29 | 49 | 31 |
| Stephenson .. | | | 21 | Du Page ...... | 60 | 22 | 26 |
| Winnebago .. | 42 | 29 | 22 | Kane ......... | 46 | 29 | 31 |
| Boone ...... | | | 26 | Kendall ....... | | | 24 |
| McHenry ... | 25 | 29 | 25 | State of Illinois | | | 15 |

Blank spaces indicate that figures are unavailable. The percentages of timber and prairie lands were compiled from *Soil Reports* of the University of Illinois Agricultural Experiment Station. These reports are not available for all the counties. It is obvious from the timber and prairie map that these counties were well supplied with timber. The density per square mile was computed from the *Seventh Census*, 1850.

drained for the most part and therefore healthier than the south-ern counties. The settlement of this region may be said to mark the transition or intermediate stage from pioneer farming in the timbered areas to the exploitation of the prairies, which was fully under way in the 'fifties and 'sixties.

As late as 1850 settlers had not advanced into the larger prairies to any great extent. The construction of the Illinois and Michigan Canal had increased interest in prairie lands, to be sure, but chiefly in those lands which were situated in the canal zone itself. The lands within 15 miles of the canal had been taken up by 1850, but the larger prairies beyond were still neglected.[72] The Grand Prairie, from Urbana north to the canal zone near Chicago, was quite untouched with the exception of two small settlements at Bourbonnais — on a wooded slope — and at Spring Creek.[73] It was said that south of La Salle one could travel 40 miles without seeing a house of any description.[74] The objections to the prairies, however, had largely disappeared by 1850. Settlers had already moved into the smaller prairies and only required means of trans-portation to induce them to take up lands in the larger prairies. Canals and rivers were inadequate; railroads alone could satisfy their needs.[75]

[72] See plates in *Sectional Maps*. See also manuscript diary of John Davis in Har-vard College Library, entitled "Diary of a journey to Illinois in 1843 and 1844, etc."

[73] Letter of R. B. Mason in Andreas, *op. cit.*, I, 253–254. Mason travelled over the route in 1851. The region around Monee was described as late as 1853 as being "wild" with deer, and wolves were plentiful. Communication of D. J. Benton, August 16, 1857, in *New England Farmer* (1857), IX, 517.

[74] Mason in Andreas, *op. cit.*, I, 254.

[75] In the late 'forties and 'fifties, plank roads were advocated in lieu of railroads. Some were constructed and proved to be profitable for a short time. A traveller ob-served in 1851, after making a trip up the Illinois River, that almost every town and landing along the river was engaged in constructing plank roads into the interior. He mentioned the following projected roads: Florence to Griggsville and Pittsfield; Beardstown to Virginia; Frederic to Rushville and Macomb; Copperas Creek to Canton; Liverpool to Canton; Pekin to Bloomington, while Peoria, Peru, La Salle, and Ottawa were contemplating several each. *Chicago Tribune* clipped in *Illinois State Register*, March 13, 1851. Plank roads could not compete with railroads and were used largely to supplement the latter. For this phase of transportation history see C. E. MacGill, *History of Transportation in the United States Before 1860* (Wash-ington, 1917), pp. 299–305; Lee, *op. cit.*, pp. 29–35; Arthur C. Cole, *The Era of the Civil War* (*Centennial History of Illinois*, vol. III, Springfield, 1919), p. 28.

## CHAPTER II

### THE FIRST RAILROAD LAND GRANT

AFTER the United States had recovered from the effects of the Panic of 1819, there set in a period of rapid expansion and speculation which had its wildest manifestations in the West. Here speculation in lands and the scramble at the government land offices for choice locations led purchasers to pay ridiculously high prices for wild lands or town lots on the open prairie. Land sales increased enormously until the middle of 'thirties, when they reached their highest peak in American history. The land business was only one manifestation of the rapid economic expansion. Partly as a result of the success of the Erie Canal and of the recent invention of the steam locomotive, there developed at this time a demand for internal improvements which swept like wildfire over the western states. Hardly a state in the Mississippi Valley was immune from the demands of its citizens that it undertake a program of railroad and canal construction and river improvements. The states responded with legislation providing for complete transportation networks so planned as to bring every section of their areas within easy reach of markets.[1] Although these visionary schemes met with an almost uniform lack of success, they played an important part in the history of the West, and in many cases they were later carried out in part by private capital.

Illinois was not the first of the western states to be affected by the craze for internal improvements, but when its citizens once realized their possibilities they demanded a most elaborate construction program. After the Illinois and Michigan Canal had been provided for the benefit of northern Illinois, the residents of other sections of the State demanded their share of state and federal aided improvements. They wanted railroads and, because there was little capital available for such ventures, government

[1] John W. Million, *State Aid to Railways in Missouri* (Chicago, 1896), pp. 15 *passim*.

aid in their construction. In response to this demand, the State Legislature enacted the Internal Improvement Bill of 1837.[2]

This measure provided for the expenditure of $10,250,000 on fifteen different projects, in addition to the millions which had already been appropriated for the Illinois and Michigan Canal. All parts of the State were to benefit by this omnibus bill, either by specific appropriations or by the general clause which authorized the expenditure of $200,000 for the "improvement of roads, constructing bridges and other public works . . ." in those counties which did not share in the specific appropriations. These appropriations provided for the improvement of the Rock River in the northern section of the State, the Illinois River in the central part, and the Kaskaskia, Little Wabash, and Great Wabash Rivers in the south. In addition there were to be built three cross-state railroads, with four branches of no small size and, most important of all, a great central railroad which was to extend the entire length of the State from the northwestern corner to the southernmost point. This last line, if completed, would be the longest railroad in the country. With a population of less than 400,000 people, most of whom were pioneer farmers struggling to make farms for themselves out of the wilderness, Illinois proposed to carry out this huge program.

It would be interesting, were the records of the committees of the Legislature and a full report of the debates available, to study the steps by which this program was prepared. Undoubtedly the study would remind one of the way in which our tariff laws are enacted. The act was the result of a long process of logrolling between the representatives of various sections, each of which desired certain specific improvements. Coupled with the manoeuvring of the different sections for railroads and river improvements was the pulling and hauling of several towns to be chosen as the capital of the State. The "Long Nine," — among whom was Abraham Lincoln, — who were fighting for Springfield, played no unimportant part in the struggle. One disgusted contemporary aptly described the situation as follows: [3]

[2] *Laws of Illinois*, 1836–1837, pp. 121–152.
[3] Thomas Ford, *A History of Illinois from its Commencement as a State in 1818 to 1847* (Chicago, 1854), p. 187.

By log-rolling on the canal measure, by multiplying railroads, by terminating three railroads at Alton, that Alton might become a great city in opposition to St. Louis, by distributing money to some of the counties, to be wasted by the county commissioners, and by giving the seat of government to Springfield, was the whole State bought up and bribed, to approve the most senseless and disastrous policy which ever crippled the energies of a growing country.

Work was soon begun on this program of construction, but it did not continue for long. The scheme was obviously too burdensome for a frontier state such as Illinois to undertake, and it was doomed to failure even without the intervention of outside factors. Fraud and collusion existed on all sides; [4] little actual work was done for the money expended; too many high salaried officials were employed and no consideration was given to economic factors in the choice of routes.[5] The Panic of 1837, the resulting depression, and the inability of the State to borrow additional money because of its near approach to bankruptcy brought about the abandonment of the program.

As a result of the Internal Improvement Bill of 1837 Illinois acquired little railroad mileage, since nothing of importance was accomplished in this way, but it did incur a huge debt, the interest on which exceeded its entire revenue. This debt, the crippled credit of the State, and the resulting high taxes had the effect of discouraging immigration to Illinois. Throughout the 'forties immigrants avoided the State for more distant communities, such as Wisconsin and Iowa, which were relatively free from debt.[6] Illinois did not recover from the evil effects of the Internal Improvement Bill for nearly a decade, and thenceforth its people were cured of any desire to have the State undertake a program of internal improvements.

The history of the central railroad project antedates the Internal Improvement Bill of 1837. It is intimately connected with that of the city of Cairo, which was located at the confluence of the Ohio and Mississippi Rivers. The site of this city, at the junc-

[4] D. B. Holbrook to the Hon. John Davis, May 16, 1844, Baring MSS.

[5] In the various reports of the Committee on Internal Improvements to the General Assembly there is a great deal of information on this saturnalia of fraud and corruption. See *Illinois Reports*, 1839–1841.

[6] Ford, *op. cit.*, pp. 222–223, presents a doleful picture of conditions in the State.

tion of two of the most important river routes in the country, was early recognized as valuable. The location was entered in 1818 by a group of promoters who secured a liberal charter from the State Legislature, but they accomplished little and the lands reverted to the Federal Government. In 1835 another group of politicians and speculators, headed by Darius B. Holbrook, "a shrewd Boston Yankee," [7] reentered the land and again laid plans for the establishment of a city there. These promoters conceived the idea of constructing a railroad from Galena, then the chief city in the State, to their site, in order to make of the latter a center for the transfer of goods brought to and shipped from central Illinois. At this time Cairo was only a mud flat, frequently flooded to a depth of 3 feet or more and extremely unhealthy. [8] Its advantage over competing towns in the same locality was that both within and without the Legislature it possessed a vociferous and power- ful lobby, consisting of such men as ex-Lieutenant-Governor Jenkins, John Hacker, and Sidney Breese. [9] To these men the railroad was of secondary importance; the growth of the city of Cairo, which the railroad was to further, was their chief interest. Thus the central railroad project was originally a grand scheme conceived by speculators to increase the value of their lands. At first the Cairo promoters planned to construct the railroad from Cairo to Galena themselves, and were granted a charter for this purpose in 1836. [10] They accomplished little before the Internal Improvement Bill of 1837 was passed, and then they were quite willing to permit the State to shoulder the burden of providing the funds for construction. [11]

The Internal Improvement Bill was thus the second plan for building a central railroad for Illinois. This time the road was to

[7] So styled by J. F. Snyder in "Charles Dickens in Illinois," Illinois State His- torical Society, *Journal* (October, 1910), vol. III, No. 3, p. 21.

[8] See letters of Wilson Abel, George Cloud, and John S. Hacker in *Prospectus of the Cairo City and Canal Company* . . . (1838), p. 5 of appendix.

[9] Jenkins and Hacker were directors of the Cairo City and Canal Company. *In- corporation Laws of Illinois*, 1836–1837, pp. 302–307. Breese was a director and pro- moter of the central railroad as incorporated in 1836. *Laws of Illinois*, 1835–1836, pp. 129–135.       [10] *Ibid.*

[11] John Reynolds in his *Pioneer History of Illinois* (p. 388, note), states that Jen- kins "cheerfully surrendered" the charter of the central railroad company in 1837 when the State proposed to construct the road.

be financed by the State. To secure sufficient legislative support for that part of the Internal Improvement Bill which provided for the central railroad it was necessary to specify five towns besides the termini through which the road was to run: Vandalia, Shelbyville, Decatur, Bloomington, and Savannah. The inclusion of some of these towns necessitated wide divergencies from an air line.

There were many unsound features about the plan for the central railroad. In the first place, the terminus at Galena could have been dictated only by expediency. True, this enterprising city was the center of an important lead-mining district and was exporting quantities of its chief product, but its prosperity was extremely unstable, dependent as it was upon one industry. Nor was it well located to become a commercial city, as its site was some distance from the Mississippi. Even before the railroad reached Galena its prosperity was declining, owing to the drop in lead production.[12] Furthermore, the proposed route avoided all the more populous towns and localities of the State, and ran instead through a region which was largely unsettled. There was little likelihood of any great industrial development taking place in the prairie regions through which it passed, and an agricultural population could not supply sufficient traffic to warrant a line which was not to connect two or more important points. The more practical route by way of Pinckneyville, Hillsboro, Springfield, and Peoria did not seem to appeal to the legislators, perhaps because these towns had already been satisfied with other projected railroads. Even better would have been a line to Chicago, a town which was already becoming an important commercial center. This would have made possible the importation of lumber, — the great desideratum on the prairies, — and would thereby have assisted their further development. A central railroad might be a powerful factor in opening up the great prairie regions of central and northern Illinois, but if this were to be its main purpose, a more eastern route through the Grand Prairie, which was then almost entirely unsettled, should have been chosen.

---

[12] B. H. Schockel, "History of the Development of Jo Daviess County," *Illinois State Geological Survey, Bulletin* (1926), No. 26, pp. 192–196.

For a brief period construction was pushed rapidly on the central railroad. A large corps of officials and engineers was placed on the payrolls, high prices were paid for rights-of-way and for damages, dam sites, and terminal facilities. Contracts were made with a lavish hand and elaborate stations and office-buildings were erected. In the brief period of three years, more than $1,000,000 was expended.[13] With the collapse of the State's ambitious program of internal improvements, construction work on the central railroad ceased.

Holbrook and the Cairo promoters did not become discouraged by the period of depression in the late 'thirties and by the abandonment of railroad construction by the State. Instead, they undertook to revive the central railroad project. In 1843, they secured from the State a charter incorporating the president and directors of the Cairo City and Canal Company as the Great Western Railway Company. All lands, materials, rights-of-way, and work done on the central railroad were to be turned over to the new company at a fair valuation and were to be paid for in bonds of the State. The charter provided that when all obligations of the Company should have been paid, the State should thenceforth receive the annual net income of the road. It also provided that all donated lands which the Company received from any source, which had not been sold at the end of five years after the completion of the road and which were not required for railroad use, should revert to the State.[14] This charter safeguarded the interests of the State more effectively than the subsequent charter given in 1851 to another group for the same purpose. Indeed, so carefully did the charter protect the interests of the State that it seems not unlikely that it prevented the Holbrook group from raising adequate capital to carry their project to completion.

At this time Holbrook was planning to construct the entire 450 miles of the road from Cairo to Galena on piles at an estimated cost of $3,150,000. With the aid of Sidney Breese, who had a direct financial interest in both the Cairo City and Canal Com-

---

[13] *Reports to the House of Representatives*, 1840–1841, p. 112.
[14] *Laws of Illinois*, 1843, pp. 149–203.

pany and the railroad, and who had been elected to the United States Senate in 1843, and of John Hacker, a director of the road and a member of the State Legislature, he attempted to induce Congress to assist the Great Western Railway Company in financing construction by a grant of preemption rights. Holbrook proposed that the railroad should have the right of preempting four sections of land for each mile of its line at the minimum price of $1.25 an acre and ten years time in which to pay for the grant, which would amount to 1,152,000 acres. He estimated that the lands would be worth at least $5 an acre after the road was completed, and that they would more than pay for the cost of construction. In the meantime the road was to be financed by a bond issue secured by an indenture on the lands. Holbrook anticipated that there would be no difficulty in raising adequate capital for the venture once the preemption grant had been passed.[15]

In spite of the powerful support which the preemption bill received, it failed of passage more than once between 1844 and 1849. One reason for its failure was Stephen A. Douglas's opposition to it. Douglas was not in favor of making the proposed railroad a feeder to the city of Cairo, as Holbrook visioned it, nor was he in favor of making a direct grant of land to the Great Western Railway Company. He wanted the lands turned over to the State. Furthermore, Douglas favored an outright grant of lands, while Breese favored a grant of preemption rights. It was apparent to Douglas that a mere grant of preemption rights would be insufficient to ensure the construction of the railroad, and consequently he favored a donation on a larger scale than the preemption bill provided.[16]

[15] Holbrook to John Davis, May 16, 1844, Baring MSS.

[16] J. Madison Cutts, in *A Brief Treatise upon Constitutional and Party Questions, and the History of Political Parties, as I Received it Orally from the late Senator Stephen A. Douglas, of Illinois* (New York, 1866), sets forth what purports to be Douglas's story of his participation in the fight to secure the passage of the land grant. The entire story is unreliable in general outline and must be used with great care. Cf. John Bell Sanborn, *Congressional Grants of Land in Aid of Railways* (*Bulletin*, University of Wisconsin, No. 30, 1899), p. 129. In his newspaper controversy with Sidney Breese over the relative share of each in securing the grant, Douglas displays more political acumen than historical accuracy. These letters, first published in the Springfield papers, were reproduced in William K. Ackerman, *Early Illinois Railroads* (*Fergus Historical Series*, No. 23, Chicago, 1884). The letters were published in the *Illinois State Register*, December 28, 1850, January 20, February 6, March 13, 1851.

In the meantime much criticism had been directed against the Holbrook plan for the construction of the central railroad. The feeling existed that Holbrook was promoting the road entirely for the benefit of his land investments in Cairo and that he did not visualize it as a means of building up the great undeveloped central portion of Illinois. Furthermore, the indifferent success of the Cairo group did not promise well for the future. Their previous financial arrangements in England had not improved the credit of Illinois and had been partly instrumental in calling forth the burning satire of Charles Dickens.[17] Moreover, it would be difficult for this group to secure additional capital, and there may have been some justification for Douglas's later accusation that Holbrook merely hoped to secure a land grant and charter in order that he might peddle them out to the highest bidder. Holbrook's own popularity in the State was waning until, in 1850 and 1851, he became the object of a bitter campaign of vilification, much of which was political in its origin.

The old route of the central railroad was no longer satisfactory to many people. Sectional rivalry was always keen in Illinois, and Egypt at this time was very unpopular with the central and northern parts of the State. Moreover, since 1840, New York-New England immigrants by the thousands had been pouring into the northern and central counties, which were as a result threatening to assume a position of predominance in the State. During the past decade Chicago had definitely displaced Galena as the chief city of the North. With a population of 29,963 [18] it was already in 1850 the largest city in the State, and its claims to railroad connections could no longer be ignored. There was now even less reason for a railroad to Galena than in 1837. Foreseeing the future importance of Chicago, Douglas moved there in 1847 from his home in central Illinois. The same year he was elected to the Senate, thereby becoming a colleague of Sidney Breese. Hence-

---

[17] Dickens apparently had invested in the securities of the Cairo Company and when dividends were not forthcoming his resentment was created to a marked degree. This was expressed in *Martin Chuzzlewit*, a book which aroused much feeling in the West. J. F. Snyder, *loc. cit.*, p. 21. But see John M. Lansden, *History of the City of Cairo, Illinois* (Chicago, 1910), pp. 31–39.

[18] *Seventh Census*, 1850, p. 705. The population of Galena in 1850 was 6004.

forth Douglas favored making Chicago the northern terminus of the road.

Aside from Senator Douglas, Holbrook was undoubtedly the most ardent supporter of and the most efficient lobbyist for the passage of the land grant. Ever since he had secured a new charter for the Great Western Railway Company in 1843, he had sought to induce Congress to make some sort of land grant to aid in the construction of the central railroad. Naturally he favored Breese's preemption bill, which would give preemption rights to his own company, but his eagerness to have the road constructed for the benefit of Cairo, by some other group if need be, led him also to support an outright donation to the State of Illinois. In 1844 Holbrook had even seemed willing to accede to Governor Ford's suggestion that the holders of the Internal Improvements bonds be permitted to finance and construct the railroad.[19] He was not discouraged by the action of the Illinois Legislature in repealing the charter of the Great Western Railway Company in 1845, because there seemed no prospect of the road being completed, nor by the inability of the Illinois delegation in Washington to secure the much coveted grant. He continued lobbying, both in Washington and in Springfield, using the funds of the Cairo City and Canal Company lavishly for this purpose. The completion of the central railraod, with its southern terminus at Cairo, would be of immense benefit to that city, and large expenditures to secure the land grant seemed justified. In 1847 Holbrook published a pamphlet setting forth the claims of the Great Western Railway Company to public consideration should a land grant be received by Illinois.[20] He still retained sufficient public confidence in his ability to complete the central railroad so that, in 1849, the Legislature of Illinois rechartered the Great Western Railway Company, granting it the right to receive any lands which the State might obtain for the central railroad. As Holbrook would now profit equally from the preemption bill of

---

[19] Holbrook to Davis, May 16, 1844, Baring MSS.
[20] *Great National Thoroughfare From the West and South-West into New England, by the Northern, or Lake Route, from New Orleans to New York, Boston and Portland,* December, 1847.

Breese or the donation bill of Douglas, he was ready to support either measure.

During the years 1843 to 1849, the advocacy by Breese and Douglas of the preemption bill and the land donation bill respectively kept the question of a central railroad for Illinois before Congress, where added support for some such measure was slowly being won. Success could not be secured, however, until the Illinois delegation was unitedly in support of a single bill. Breese's preemption bill elicited little support from other members of the Illinois delegation. Although it passed the Senate, partly as a matter of courtesy to Breese, it was defeated in the House. Breese himself failed of reelection in 1849, which fact indicates the shift in the political balance of power from southern to central and northern Illinois. His place was taken by General Shields, who favored the donation plan. The Illinois delegation was now solidly in favor of this plan.[21] Nevertheless, it was plain that additional support must be secured or a grant could never be obtained. Precisely how this additional support was gained is a question which has aroused much controversy.

As a frontier people Illinoisians had few or no constitutional scruples against the employment of the public domain to aid internal improvements. Their Legislature was constantly importuning Congress for grants of land to aid local projects such as canals, river improvements, and railroads. Thus on October 24, 1849, the State Senate, after communicating the proposal for a Pacific railroad and recommending Council Bluffs as an eastern terminus, requested the Illinois representatives and senators to secure liberal land grants to aid in constructing four branches from the eastern terminus of the road: one to Chicago, one to Quincy, one to St. Louis, and one to the mouth of the Ohio River or to Memphis.[22] In the next session of the Legislature a joint resolution was passed instructing the Illinois congressmen to advocate grants of land for the construction of a road from Alton, via Mt. Carmel, to New Albany, and for another from Quincy to the Indiana line.[23]

[21] Ackerman, *op. cit.*, p. 73.

[22] *Journal of the Senate*, 1849, pp. 19, 26. These resolutions as a rule passed unanimously.

[23] *Journal of the House*, 1851, p. 40.

Again, the Senate requested a donation to aid the Warsaw and Rockford and the Peoria and Warsaw Railroads.[24] More vociferous and frequent were the demands for a central railroad, the darling of so many special interests.

In the late 'forties the press of the State, particularly of those towns which were located along the proposed route, took an active interest in the subject. The Chicago papers, after Douglas had included in his bill a branch line to that city, fairly shrieked their support of his measure.[25] The plan for a central railroad was also strongly supported by John S. Wright, land speculator, editor of the *Prairie Farmer*, and pamphleteer. According to his own account, Wright distributed in 1848 6000 copies of petitions for a grant of land to Illinois, which were sent to Washington with numerous signatures. Furthermore, in 1850, he spent three weeks in Washington working for the same end.[26] Numerous public meetings were likewise held to draw up petitions to the Federal Government for the project. This constant agitation aroused local interest in the proposed railroad and may have won some support in Congress.[27]

As long as the central railroad could be considered a local affair it was difficult to overcome the constitutional objections of congressmen from the South and East. Douglas, in realizing the importance of these objections, and the basis of sectional selfishness upon which they really rested, showed himself a more astute politician than his colleague. He either introduced or supported a number of changes in the original measure which facilitated its passage. It was seen that Galena, with its declining lead trade and unfavorable location, was not a suitable terminus for the road. Dubuque, Iowa, which was more favorably situated on the Mississippi, was therefore made the western end of the main line.[28]

---

[24] *Journal of the Senate*, 1851, p. 217. A donation was also requested to aid in the improvement of the Kaskaskia River. *Ibid.*, p. 144.

[25] John Wentworth's *Democrat* was particularly ardent in this matter.

[26] John S. Wright, *Chicago; Past, Present, Future* (Chicago, 1868), pp. 22, 138.

[27] *Herald of the Prairies*, January 26, 1848; *Chicago Democrat*, January 23, 1850. Lansden, *op. cit.*, pp. 101–102. Cf. *House Journal*, 31st Cong., 1st Sess., 1850, pp. 544–632.

[28] The inhabitants of Galena were tremendously aroused by this action for they feared it meant the death-knell of their city. The change in terminus later became a

At this point the central railroad would meet the roads which were then projected to the West and which would provide important feeders for it.

A more important modification of the original bill was the addition of a provision for a branch line to Chicago.[29] Breese later accused Douglas of adding this provision because of his own financial interest in Chicago real estate,[30] the value of which would be much enhanced by the building of such a branch. This consideration may have had some weight with Douglas, but it is probable that political reasons were of more importance. Like most westerners, Douglas was not averse to speculating in lands, but that was not his chief interest as it was with many Illinois politicians. His first interest was politics. Nothing could win greater popularity for Douglas in northern Illinois, and especially in Chicago, than to champion the Chicago branch. It was, then, his desire to strengthen his political position in northern Illinois rather than his personal financial interests that induced him to support the Chicago branch. Moreover, the addition of this branch to the original line made of the latter something more than a project for the benefit of Cairo. At Chicago the railroad would connect with lines already being built to that city from the East. By the construction of the central railroad a considerable portion of Illinois would become tributary to the East as much as to the South, which previously had been the only market for its surplus products. This consideration, Douglas reasoned, would win support for the measure among eastern Congressmen.[31]

subject of much controversy between Douglas and Senator Jones of Iowa. Douglas accused Jones of forcing the change in terminus by withholding his support until it was granted. Jones denied this accusation, declaring that he had supported the land grant consistently from the beginning, and in turn accused Douglas of bringing the matter up in 1858 to secure the vote of the Galena population. For Douglas's accusation and Jones's response see John C. Parish, *George Wallace Jones* (Iowa City, 1912), pp. 189–205. The two men were permanently estranged by this quarrel. Letter of George W. Jones to W. K. Ackerman, February, 1892, Ackerman MSS., Newberry Library.

[29] Allen Johnson states that the bill introduced by Douglas provided for a branch line from Centralia to Chicago. Douglas did not care to determine the diverging point and furthermore Centralia was not in existence at the time the bill was passed. *Stephen A. Douglas: A Study in American Politics* (New York, 1908), p. 170.

[30] Breese to Douglas, January 25, 1851, Ackerman, *op. cit.*, p. 80.

[31] Sanborn, *op. cit.*, p. 36. Douglas later maintained that this provision, which

The addition of the Chicago branch to the central railroad was not original with Douglas, although he was its most urgent supporter. Some years before it had been suggested that the road might well be laid out through eastern Illinois, which was then the most neglected portion of the State. This plan had won little support, however, because the eastern section was not strong politically. When it was realized that eastern Illinois must be tributary to Chicago, and as that city grew in commercial and political importance, many of the local politicians came to favor enlarging the original project for the central railroad to include the eastern branch.

The object of the original promoters of the central railroad, to develop the city of Cairo, was by the addition of this branch line thwarted; commerce, instead of going south to Cairo, was to go north to Chicago. True, this was not altogether obvious in 1850, and it even failed to dampen the ardor of the Cairo Company's support of the land grant. Indeed, when the charter of the Great Western Railway was renewed in 1849, it included the right to build to the city of Chicago.[32] That Holbrook did not actively oppose this addition is apparent.[33]

A third and politically more important modification of the original plan was a provision for the extension of the central railroad to the Gulf of Mexico at Mobile, Alabama. The road was thereby made an interstate as well as an intersectional line. Probably Douglas had some share in including this extension. He could easily see the importance of securing the votes of southern members for the bill. Furthermore, the extension would increase

would connect the main line with the various roads building toward Chicago, secured the 38 votes of the eastern members of the House of Representatives which were so necessary for the passage of the bill. Douglas to Breese, January 5 and February 22, 1851, Ackerman, *op. cit.*, pp. 65–98. It is interesting to note that Breese looked upon Charleston, South Carolina, as a port which possessed greater advantages for trade with the West than New York or other northern cities. Commerce between Charleston and Illinois would go by way of railroads to the Tennessee River, thence by the same and Ohio River to Illinois. See letter of John C. Calhoun to Sidney Breese, July 27, 1839, "Calhoun Correspondence," American Historical Association, *Annual Report*, 1899, II, 430–431.

[32] Act of February 10, 1849, *Private Laws of Illinois*, 1849, pp. 89–90.

[33] Holbrook to Douglas, June 17, 1850, Douglas MSS. Mr. George Foote Milton kindly supplied the writer with a copy of this letter.

his own popularity in the South, and this was already a factor worth considering. At any rate, this provision was successful in securing sufficient additional support among the representatives of Mississippi and Alabama to reverse the previous vote and ensure the passage of the land grant.[34]

Earlier writers have maintained that the land grant of 1850 was won for Illinois by an exchange of votes with eastern members on the tariff. The Illinois delegation, so the story runs, promised to support a tariff bill, the pet measure of the eastern representatives, in return for their support of the land grant. John Wentworth, member of Congress from the Chicago district, has perpetuated this story in his reminiscences, and incidentally has taken for himself the chief credit for arranging the bargain. According to his account, the members of the Illinois delegation, while keeping Douglas entirely ignorant of the scheme, determined to employ this means to secure their end. Wentworth writes, "As Douglas was then looking to the Presidency, we wanted him to be able to say that he knew nothing of any trade with the tariff men." [35] Wentworth went to Webster and then to George Ashmun,[36] representative from Massachusetts and sup-

---

[34] Sanborn, *op. cit.*, p. 35. Cf. Cutts, *op. cit.*, pp. 193–195, and William E. Martin, *Internal Improvements in Alabama* (Johns Hopkins University, *Studies in Historical and Political Science*, vol. xx, No. 4, 1902), pp. 65–67. The latter accepts the view expressed in Cutts's work.

The importance of this extension of the road is shown by a comparison of the votes in the House on the bill of 1848 with that of 1850, which included the southern extension. By sections the votes were as follows:

| Section | Vote of 1848 For | Against | Vote of 1850 For | Against |
|---|---|---|---|---|
| New England | 10 | 5 | 10 | 11 |
| Middle States | 25 | 22 | 28 | 22 |
| South Atlantic States | 7 | 31 | 8 | 23 |
| Gulf States | 3 | 4 | 13 | 0 |
| Western landed States | 27 | 9 | 34 | 12 |
| Western non-landed States | 1 | 8 | 8 | 7 |
| Totals | 73 | 79 | 101 | 75 |

These tables were compiled by Sanborn, *op. cit.*, pp. 29–33.

[35] Wentworth to Ackerman, January 21, 1883, Ackerman MSS., Chicago Historical Society Library.

[36] Albert J. Beveridge seems to think that the chief credit for the passing of the land grant bill belongs to Douglas and Ashmun. He writes that Douglas got the "bill through the Senate and . . . Ashmun secured its passage through the House. . . ."

porter of Webster, to secure aid for the bill. He implies that the members of the Illinois delegation agreed to help Ashmun on the tariff as much as possible, and when they thought they could go no farther they were to "dodge." [37]

This story has sounded so plausible that it has never been questioned. The congressional debates on the tariff during the sessions of 1850 and 1852, however, give little support to it. There was no tariff legislation enacted in the three years following the passage of the land grant,[38] in spite of the frequent efforts of George Ashmun and other representatives from the East to secure such legislation. There were, however, constant discussions and manoeuvrings by tariff advocates which enable one to discover the sentiments of the Illinois representatives towards such efforts.[39] Two weeks before the land grant was passed, a resolution was introduced into the House providing that the Committee on Ways and Means should be instructed to report a bill to increase the tariff rates on foreign goods which were in competition with domestic goods. Upon this resolution Baker of Illinois, the lone Whig in the delegation of that State, voted favorably; McClernand, Wentworth, Young, and Richardson opposed it, with Harris and Bissell not voting.[40] Seven days after the passing of the land grant,

Abraham Lincoln, 1809–1858 (Boston, 1928), I, 584. For this view he relies on William K. Ackerman, Historical Sketch of the Illinois Central Railroad (Chicago, 1890), pp. 15–17.

[37] John Wentworth, Congressional Reminiscences, Adams, Benton, Calhoun, Clay, and Webster (Fergus Historical Series, No. 24, Chicago, 1882), pp. 40–42. Howard Gray Brownson states, "Among the eastern members secured by this agreement were Daniel Webster and Mr. Ashmun of Massachusetts." History of the Illinois Central Railroad to 1870 (University of Illinois, Studies in the Social Sciences, vol. IV, Nos. 3 and 4, Urbana, 1915), p. 30, note. But Webster had previously supported the bill and, furthermore, was not in the Senate when it was passed. Moreover, Webster advocated a liberal land policy, and even went so far as to favor free homesteads in 1852. Webster to D. A. Neal, March 12, 1852, Fletcher Webster, ed., The Writings and Speeches of Daniel Webster (National Edition, Boston, 1903), XVI, 647–648. Brownson is in error in saying that Ashmun was "interested in the Illinois Central," or that a town of the same name was named after him (p. 30, note). He has confused Ashkum with Ashmun.

[38] Edward Stanwood, American Tariff Controversies in the Nineteenth Century (Boston, 1903), II, 93–94.

[39] As tariff bills have to originate in the House and as none were passed there during the Taylor-Fillmore administrations, there was little chance for discussion on this subject in the Senate.

[40] Congressional Globe, 31st Cong., 1st Sess., 1850, part 2, p. 1728.

on another test vote of tariff advocates and opponents, Harris, McClernand, Richardson, and Young voted negatively, while the others refrained from voting.[41] Perhaps Wentworth's abstention from voting might be considered a means of "dodging," but if so it was of no value because the bill was easily defeated. The following February, Harris delivered a strong free-trade speech in the House in reply to a speech of Hampton of Pennsylvania advocating a higher tariff.[42] Finally in February, 1852, another attempt to pass a tariff resolution was defeated, with four Illinois representatives voting against it and the others absent or not voting.[43] It is evident, therefore, that little credence can be given to Wentworth's story. Furthermore, it is ridiculous to maintain that Wentworth could have convinced Ashmun of his ability to deliver the votes of such strong anti-tariff men as Harris, McClernand, Young, and Richardson.[44] Nor does an examination of the votes for the land grant bill give any support to the story. The habitual tariff areas of the middle states and New England gave altogether 35 votes for and 27 votes against the bill in 1848 and in 1850 38 votes for and 33 votes against. Thus there was more opposition in the East by 6 votes in 1850 than in 1848 and a gain of only 3 votes for the land grant.[45] Other reasons must be found for the 19 New York, 5 Pennsylvania, and 4 Massachusetts votes for the land grant.[46]

A reason of first importance, and one which has been largely neglected, is to be found in Wentworth's reminiscences. Wentworth suggests that an influential factor in winning support for the land grant among representatives and senators from the northeastern states was the fact that a large amount of money from that section had been invested in Illinois securities. Several million dollars had been invested by easterners in the internal improvement bonds of the State. These bonds had greatly depreciated in

[41] *Ibid.*, p. 1951.

[42] Appendix to *Cong. Globe*, 31st Cong., 2nd Sess., 1850–1851, XXIII, 234–237.

[43] *Cong. Globe*, 32nd Cong., 1st Sess., 1851–1852, part 1, p. 506.

[44] All writers agree that Ashmun was influential in pushing the bill through the House. See Wentworth, *op. cit.*, pp. 41–42; Wright, *op. cit.*, p. 138; *Chicago Democrat*, July 23, 1851.

[45] Sanborn, *op. cit.*, p. 29. See above, note 34.

[46] *Cong. Globe*, 31st Cong., 1st Sess., 1850, part 2, p. 1838.

value, and their holders were anxious to recover their losses. They saw in the proposed grant of land to Illinois a means of doing so. They hoped either to have the grant turned over to them to construct the road, as Governor Ford had earlier suggested, and as had been done with the Illinois and Michigan Canal lands, or that a certain percentage of the profits of the proposed railroad would be returned to the State to liquidate its bonds, as the charter of the Great Western Railway provided.[47] In either case they stood to gain and therefore they favored the grant.[48]

Among those holding Illinois securities were Jonathon Sturges and Ketchum, Rogers & Bement of New York, Franklin Haven, Thomas Ward, and Abbott Lawrence of Massachusetts, and the Baring Brothers and Magniac, Jardine & Company of England.[49] These bondholders were among the most intimate friends and supporters of Daniel Webster. Indeed, the intimate contact between Webster and these people, especially the two British firms, is notorious in American history, and it can hardly be doubted that their influence helped to win his support for the land grant. John Wentworth — himself an owner of Illinois bonds — tells us that he and a committee of the bondholders composed of Caldwell of Philadelphia, Hiram Ketchum of New York, brother of Morris Ketchum, and Franklin Haven interviewed Webster to secure his support for the land grant.[50]

The support which Webster, Ashmun, and other eastern representatives gave to the land grant bill can be further explained by the fact that a considerable amount of eastern money had been invested in the Cairo City and Canal Company. This company had issued between one and two million dollars worth of securi-

---

[47] Wentworth, *op. cit.*, pp. 40–41.

[48] It is interesting to note that upon the passage of the land grant bill the quotations on Illinois bonds advanced sharply. Wadsworth & Sheldon to Governor Augustus C. French, September 21, October 8 and 11, 1850; Julius Wadsworth to French, September 23, 1850, Greene & Thompson, *Governors' Letter-Books, 1840–1853* (Illinois State Historical Library, *Collections*, vol. vii, "Executive Series," vol. ii, Springfield, 1911), pp. 342–344, 354–355; *Statement and Replies in Reference to the Compensation for the use of the Road of the Illinois Central . . .* (1860).

[49] *Illinois State Register*, March 25, 1851; John Davis, "Diary of a journey to Illinois in 1843 and 1844, etc.," Harvard College Library.

[50] Wentworth to Ackerman, January 17, 1883, Ackerman MSS., Chicago Historical Society Library. Cf. Wentworth, *op. cit.*, p. 45.

ties, which had been purchased by people in the eastern part of the United States and in Great Britain.[51] These securities had depreciated in value after the Panic of 1837, and any value which they might acquire seemed to depend upon the construction of the central railroad.  In the summer of 1850, Holbrook, who was at that time cooperating intimately with Douglas in the fight to obtain the grant for Illinois, advised the latter to urge upon the Pennsylvania and New England congressmen the importance of the project for the "interests."[52]  In addition to Holbrook, Hiram Ketchum and Samuel Jaudon were prominently connected with this company, and all three were close friends of Webster.[53]

Besides the many millions of eastern money which had been sunk in the securities of the State of Illinois and in the Cairo City and Canal Company, additional millions from the same section had been invested in Illinois lands.  From the beginning of the century eastern capitalists had invested money in Illinois lands in constantly increasing amounts.  The Acts of 1811 and 1812, which granted bounty lands to soldiers who served in the War of 1812, had enabled speculators to acquire huge holdings of land in the Military Tract of Illinois at comparatively low prices.  Thus by 1819, the Berrian Brothers of New York had acquired 140,000 acres, and Col. Joseph Watson had secured 127,000.[54]  By 1837 practically one-fourth of these military bounty lands had passed into the hands of the New York and Boston Illinois Land Company, which offered for sale in that year over 900,000 acres.[55]  In the same year Romulus Riggs, a prominent Philadelphia capitalist, offered for sale 40,000 acres of Illinois land.[56]  Another Phila-

---

[51] *Cairo Business Mirror and City Directory for 1864–1865*, p. 19.

[52] Holbrook to Douglas, June 17, 1850, Douglas MSS.  Douglas's later break with Holbrook seems to have been largely political in origin and should not be permitted to hide the effective work which the latter did in securing support for the land grant.

[53] Holbrook had paid Webster a large fee for services in 1838.  Furthermore he knew Ashmun very well.  *Engineer's Reports and other Documents relating to the Cairo City Property, at the Confluence of the Ohio and Mississippi Rivers, Illinois* (New York, 1848); *Cairo, Illinois, 1856; The Past, Present and Future of the City of Cairo in North America*, 1858; *Cairo Business Mirror and City Directory for 1864–1865.*

[54] *House Executive Documents*, 26th Cong., 1st Sess., vol. VII, doc. 262.

[55] *For Sale, The Following Parcels of Land, Situate in the Military Tract of Illinois and belonging to the New York and Boston Illinois Land Company*, n. d.

[56] Pease, *The Frontier State*, p. 175.

delphia financier, John Grigg, owned over 100,000 acres in the Springfield land district, which he purchased during the years 1836 and 1837.[57] The American Land Company, organized by a number of New York and Boston capitalists, among whom was Franklin Haven, owned nearly 9000 acres of land in Illinois, the majority of which was near Chicago in the vicinity of the proposed line of the central railroad.[58] Webster himself was at an early date interested in land speculation, and purchased a large quantity of land in the vicinity of La Salle which, in 1839, he valued at $100,-000.[59] In 1850 he still possessed this property,[60] which was certain to increase in value with the construction of the central railroad. Senator Jones of Iowa, likewise an ardent advocate of the grant, owned lands along the proposed route, and from them he hoped to secure a good return.[61] Many smaller eastern investors had purchased town lots either in projected prairie towns or in the more substantial cities.[62] Their hopes for quick fortunes were shattered by the Panic of 1837, but those who retained their land remained boosters for Illinois and naturally favored the land grant.[63]

Another factor worth consideration is the attitude of eastern capitalists who had surplus funds for investment. This surplus capital was partly the result of the decline in the shipping industry occasioned by the introduction of steam navigation, which

[57] Compiled from Tract Brooks, Springfield land district, State Auditor's Office, Springfield, Illinois. This office is hereafter referred to as S. A. O.

[58] *Catalogue of lands in the Northwestern States Belonging to the American Land Company* (New York, 1847).

[59] Webster to Samuel Jaudon in C. H. Van Tyne, ed., *Letters of Daniel Webster* (New York, 1902), pp. 723–726.

[60] *Illinois State Register*, January 17, 1853; Webster, *Writings and Speeches of Daniel Webster*, XIII, 587.

[61] *Cong. Globe*, 34th Cong., 1st Sess., 1855–1856, p. 1188.

[62] W. R. Sandham, "A Lost Stark County Town," Illinois State Historical Society, *Journal* (April, 1920), XIII, 109–112. Justin Morrill of Vermont, while visiting relatives in Illinois in 1841, was impressed with the opportunities for investment in lands and purchased some prairie land. William Belmont Parker, *Life and Public Services of Justin Smith Morrill* (Boston, 1924), p. 47. Morrill was not in Congress until 1854. Asahel Gridley sold between $20,000 and $30,000 worth of Bloomington lots in Philadelphia in 1836. *History of McLean County, Illinois* (1879), p. 343.

[63] Holbrook's Great Western Railway Company had pointed out, in 1847, that the construction of the central railroad would enable the northern capitalists to sell their Illinois lands at a substantial profit. *Great National Thoroughfare from the West and South-West into New England. . . .*

gave English ship-owners an advantage over American. The China trade was also losing its importance for eastern traders. Much of the capital withdrawn from shipping was invested in textile and shoe manufacturing.[64] These rising industries, however, did not absorb all the capital available and, indeed, provided more wealth which sought investment. Increased business and manufacturing required improved transportation facilities. Altogether, the result was that surplus capital was rapidly invested in railroads. This movement gained great momentum in the late 'forties and 'fifties, and roads were constructed from eastern centers in all directions.

Representative of the men who had made their fortunes in the China trade and who later became interested in railroad promotion are John Murray Forbes of Boston, David A. Neal of Salem, and the Griswolds of New York. These men, with a number of other eastern capitalists, some of them retired ship-owners, had purchased the Michigan Central Railroad in 1846. This road, which had been begun by the State of Michigan during the internal improvement era of the 'thirties, extended from Detroit to Kalamazoo, a distance of 145 miles. The Forbes-Neal-Griswold group were able to purchase the road from the State for less than the cost of its construction. The new company planned to extend the road to New Buffalo on Lake Michigan, but competition with the Michigan Southern Railroad, which was likewise building westward, forced the directors to change their plans. They determined to extend their line to Chicago, where it would connect with the proposed Galena and Chicago Union Railroad, the rival line having adopted the same plan some time before. Both roads desired wider railroad connections at Chicago than the Galena road would provide.[65] It is easy to see, therefore, why their directors should favor the land grant to Illinois. The central railroad, if constructed as planned through the great prairie regions of

[64] Henry Greenleaf Pearson, *An American Railroad Builder, John Murray Forbes* (Boston, 1911), p. 28.

[65] John Murray Forbes to Joshua Bates, May 10, 1848, Baring MSS.; Autobiography of D. A. Neal, Neal-Rantoul MSS.; *Laws and Charters in Michigan, Indiana, and Illinois, under which the Michigan Central Road and its Connections with Chicago, have been constructed* (Detroit, 1856), charter.

Illinois, would supply a substantial amount of traffic to eastern roads running into Chicago. The directors of the Michigan Central were a most aggressive and resourceful group, and it is not unlikely that they came to the support of the land grant before it was finally passed by Congress.

The land donation bill, being supported by so many influential elements in the East, consisting of the bondholders of the State and of the Cairo City Property, the stockholders in other land companies, the individual land owners, and the different groups which were hoping to secure from the State of Illinois the right to construct the central railroad, at length won considerable support among eastern congressmen. The usual constitutional objections to donations of federal lands were made by representatives and senators of the southern and some of the eastern states and had to be met. The disagreement between Douglas and Breese in regard to the kind of grant to be made and the Illinois delegation's lack of interest in a preemption grant delayed the measure, as we have seen.[66] The replacement of Breese by Shields in 1849 gave Douglas the support he needed, and quick action followed. He added to the original proposal a branch line to Chicago; Senator King of Alabama added an amendment to extend the railroad and land grant to Mobile, Alabama;[67] and Senator Jones of Iowa further amended the bill to extend the main line to Dubuque.[68] In this form the bill passed the Senate on May 3, 1850, by a vote of 26 to 14[69] and the House, with vigorous opposition, on September 17, by a vote of 101 to 73.[70]

The details of the land grant bill are as follows: the states of Illinois, Mississippi, and Alabama were granted a right-of-way through the public lands for the construction of a railroad to extend from the western end of the Illinois and Michigan Canal to

[66] Sanborn, *op. cit.*, pp. 26–27.

[67] *Cong. Globe*, 31st Cong., 1st Sess., 1849–1850, part 1, p. 845.

[68] *Ibid.*, p. 852; Jones to Ackerman, February 18, 1892, Ackerman MSS., Newberry Library. The attitude of Douglas on this amendment is not clear. See above, note 28.

[69] *Cong. Globe*, 31st Cong., 1st Sess., part 1, p. 904.

[70] *Cong. Globe*, 31st Cong., 1st Sess., part 2, p. 1838. The bill was approved on September 20, 1850. 9 *U. S. Stat.*, 466–467.

Mobile, Alabama, via Cairo, with a branch to Dubuque via Galena and another branch to Chicago. Alternate even sections of land on each side of the road for a distance of 6 miles were granted to the three states, and, in cases where such sections had already been taken up, the states were given permission to go 9 miles farther to secure indemnity lands. The odd numbered sections within 6 miles of the line of the road, which were still in the hands of the Government, were to be sold at double the government minimum price. The purpose behind this clause was, of course, to provide constitutional objectors with some acceptable excuse for supporting the bill. It permitted them to maintain that, by granting one section of land, the Government was enabled to sell the next section for the same amount which it would have secured for the two single sections. This grant, unlike many of the later railroad grants, was made directly to the states.[71]

It is evident from the foregoing discussion that, with all the various interests which stood to profit from the passage of the land grant bill, there must have been a good deal of lobbying, log-rolling, and political bargaining among the friends and foes of the measure. The congressional debates are, as usual, quite barren of interest and give little or no indication of the issues at stake.[72] The final vote in both houses was no longer a sectional one; it was a national vote with support from all sections. It should be remembered in this connection that the passing of such a bill over the protests of constitutional objectors was a landmark which opened the way for a continual stream of similar measures.[73] It

[71] The act provided that the road should be completed in ten years or the lands would be forfeited.

[72] It does not seem necessary to discuss the congressional debates on the act as they are adequately treated in Sanborn, *op. cit.*, ch. ii. It appears that most of the actual work was done in the committee rooms and lobbies, and the debates are quite barren of interest.

[73] Section 4 of the bill provided that the road should be free from toll or other charges upon the transportation of any property or troops of the United States while section 6 of the act provided that United States mail should be transported over the road at such prices as Congress might direct. General Nathaniel Banks later maintained that the act was passed only because of these provisions, by which constitutional objections were removed. Banks to Osborn, April 17, 1861, "Osborn Letter Book," 1860–1861, M. O.

broke down the barriers, and henceforth the public lands were granted lavishly to groups of sufficient influence who desired assistance in the matter of constructing railroads.

The passing of the land grant shifted the center of activity from Washington to Springfield, where the various forces interested in the road shortly converged.

# CHAPTER III

## THE STRUGGLE FOR THE CHARTER

PROBABLY no Legislature in the history of Illinois has had more special interests appealing to it for charters, rights-of-way, and other privileges than the Seventeenth General Assembly, which met in Springfield in 1851. At the first session of this Legislature there were passed 21 bills granting ferry monopolies, 4 bills incorporating insurance companies, 5 bills incorporating coal companies, 13 plank road bills, and 28 measures incorporating railroads or amending charters of existing railroad companies.[1] The mere enumeration of the bills which were passed does not give an adequate picture of the business of this Legislature, for there were three major conflicts during the session between rival groups fighting each other for railroad concessions.

The first of these conflicts was between the representatives of the Michigan Central and the Michigan Southern Railroads, both of which were seeking the right to construct lines from the Indiana-Illinois border to Chicago. Bitter rivals in their fight to be the first to connect Chicago with the East, each fought the other's attempt to secure a charter from the Illinois Legislature, hoping thereby to monopolize, at least for a time, the traffic which entrance into Chicago would give and, if possible, to prevent its rival from reaching the lake port at all. Prominent among the promoters of the Michigan Central were John Murray Forbes, George Griswold, and John Thayer. James F. Joy, destined to become one of America's great railroad promoters, presented their demands to the Legislature and was assisted, according to his own account, by Abraham Lincoln. The evidence seems to be almost as good, however, for believing that Lincoln was lobbying for the Michigan Southern, though in either case he was appearing merely

[1] Compiled from *Private Laws of Illinois*, 1851.

as associate council.[2] The promoters of the Michigan Southern, John Stryker and John B. Jervis of New York, Edwin C. Litchfield of Detroit, and George Bliss of Springfield, Massachusetts, likewise had powerful financial support.[3] The fight between these two groups for a time produced a stalemate and led both to look around for railroad connections in Illinois by means of which they might gain the much desired entrance into Chicago.

The promoters of the Michigan Central had already begun to extend their interests into Illinois. They had purchased control of a small line, the Aurora Branch Railroad, extending 13 miles from a point on the Galena & Chicago Union Railroad to Aurora, and they now wanted the right to build westward to connect with the Central Military Tract Railroad, which they were also promoting.[4] Not to be outdone in the struggle for railroad domination in northern Illinois, Stryker, Jervis, and Litchfield were seeking the right to construct a railroad from Chicago to Rock Island, which would give them a shorter and quicker connection with the Mississippi River than the other group would enjoy. Furthermore, if Stryker, Jervis, and Litchfield failed to secure a right-of-way and

[2] "James F. Joy tells how he went into the Railroad Business," *Detroit Free Press*, May 1, 1892, reprinted in Michigan Pioneer and Historical Society, *Historical Collections* (1894), XXII, 297–304. Robert S. Rantoul, son of Robert Rantoul, Jr., has perpetuated a curious story of Lincoln's opposition to the plan of the eastern capitalists led by Forbes, Neal, and Griswold, for the construction of the central railroad. *Personal Recollections* (1916), pp. 27–28. He states that Lincoln was retained by a local group of magnates to fight the Rantoul proposal, discussed below. The only local group which was taking any interest in the central railroad, as far as construction was concerned, was the Holbrook company. This company was bitterly denounced by the *Illinois State Register*, and if Lincoln had appeared in its behalf, this paper, which disliked him because he was a Whig, would surely have mentioned it. There is not a shred of evidence for the story except that offered by Rantoul, who had the account from his father. Nor is there any better basis for the story that Lincoln was associated with Rantoul in lobbying for the grant and charter. For these two dubious stories see John William Starr, *Lincoln and the Railroads* (New York, 1927), pp. 40–45. Joy's story may have been the origin of these two accounts. If, on the other hand, Lincoln had represented the Michigan Southern, he would have been in the opposite camp from Rantoul, thus bearing out in part the latter's story. See the letter of William Jervis in the *New York Times*, May 19, 1853, originally published in the *Chicago Democratic Press*.

[3] *Exhibit of the Condition and Prospects of the Michigan Southern Railroad*, New York, 1850.

[4] W. H. Swift to Thomas W. Ward, December 9, 1850; Ward to Baring Brothers, November 19, December 28, 1852; John Murray Forbes to Ward, December 27, 1852, Baring MSS.

charter for their Michigan Southern Railroad, as seemed possible in 1850, they might be able to use the Rock Island as a means of entrance into the city of Chicago.[5]

The conflict between these two groups for charters and rights-of-way was further complicated by the fact that they were seeking charters for railroads which would more or less parallel the Illinois and Michigan Canal and would thereby be in direct competition with it for traffic of which it had enjoyed a monopoly for only two years. The canal company sent an agent to Springfield to oppose both the Rock Island Railroad and the extension of the Aurora Branch, or at least to secure some guarantee that the canal would not suffer from loss of traffic resulting from the construction of these two lines.[6] As the canal company was strongly entrenched in Illinois, its representative was sure of considerable support against the railroad promoters.

The most important problem to be decided during the 1851 session of the Legislature was the disposition of the grant for the central railroad which Illinois had just received from the Federal Government. There were three influential groups of capitalists, representing some of the wealthiest merchants, bankers, and railroad men in the country, striving to secure this land grant and railroad charter which together would be worth millions. A minor problem which had to be decided was the route which the central railroad should follow. As the Act of Congress granting land to the State had stipulated only the termini and Galena, so far as Illinois was concerned, the selection of the route was left to the Legislature. This brought to Springfield a motley crowd of representatives from many towns in the central part of the State who hoped to secure either the main line or the branch line for their communities. With all these special groups and their lobbyists seeking concessions, the situation was comparable to the mad scramble for internal improvements in 1837, and provided an unrivalled opportunity for logrolling among the different interests.

After the costly experience of the failure of the State's program

---

[5] *Report,* Board of Directors of Michigan Southern & Northern Indiana Railroad (New York, 1853), p. 22.

[6] Ward to Baring Brothers, December 11, 1850; copy, letter of W. H. Swift to Ward, February 3, 1851, Baring MSS.

of internal improvements in 1837 and 1838, there was little demand for State construction of the central railroad. James Holford, the largest creditor of the State, did urge upon Governor French the propriety of the State's undertaking the project as part of a program to rehabilitate its credit.[7] His plan called for a reassessment of all the property in Illinois which, he estimated, would increase the tax lists by 500 per cent; next he would have a slightly higher tax rate. These measures, together with the revenue from the sale of the federal grant, would, he thought, yield sufficient funds not only to construct the road but also to resume full interest payments upon the outstanding State securities. Holford's proposition received no support in Illinois, where eager bidding for the right to build the road was already under way between two private groups. As Governor French pointed out, "The constitution having wisely debarred the state from again involving its credit in wild and visionary schemes of internal improvements, their chance of success rests upon individual skill, capital, and enterprise."[8] The Legislature was therefore left to select one of three other proposals for the construction of the road.

The first proposition which came to the fore was that the Cairo interests should be given the land grant and the right to construct the road. It will be remembered that in 1843 this group, incorporated as the Great Western Railway Company, had received a charter to construct a central railroad from Galena to Cairo, and had taken over the route begun by the State in 1837. By an act of 1845 this charter had been repealed, as there then seemed little likelihood that the road would be completed.[9] However, when in 1849 it seemed more likely that Illinois would receive a land grant from the Federal Government, the Cairo interests had secured from the State Legislature a new charter which, in addition to including all the privileges contained in the previous one, authorized the Company to receive any lands granted by Congress to the

[7] Copy, letter of James Holford to Governor Augustus C. French, December 10, 1850, Baring MSS.

[8] Annual message of Governor French to the Illinois Legislature, January 6, 1851, *Illinois Reports*, 1851, p. 18.

[9] Act of March 3, 1845, *Laws of Illinois*, 1844–1845, p. 253.

State to aid in constructing the central railroad.[10]  Pressure had been brought to bear upon the Great Western Railway Company to give the State a release from this charter.  After a bitter campaign full of vilification, in which the press and leading politicians participated, Holbrook had been induced to surrender the charter on December 24, 1849,[11] the release being conditional upon the continuance by the State of the old route of 1837.

The Great Western Railway Company did not give up hope of securing the lands from the State in spite of this release, which Holbrook seems to have considered only tentative, especially as it had not yet been accepted by the Legislature.[12]  He continued his efforts to secure the grant for the State, and after it was passed recommenced work on the road,[13] a privilege which the release had permitted.[14]  Holbrook was determined and aggressive, and had powerful support in southern Illinois both in the press and among politicians.  Furthermore, because of the money and work which he and his group had already expended on the project it was natural that they should expect to receive the grant.  But the Cairo interests did not play their cards well.  They incurred the dislike and distrust of other sections of the State by subordinating the railroad project to their Cairo interests.  Their opponents, although divided in their advocacy of different plans for the construction of the road, were quite united in combating any move to give the lands to Holbrook and his associates.

The second or bondholders' plan for the construction of the central railroad was drawn up by Julius Wadsworth, the financial agent of Illinois.  This plan was prepared with the idea of protecting the interests of the holders of the internal improvement bonds and of establishing more firmly the credit of the State.  Unlike Holford's proposal, it did not provide for state construction.  Wadsworth proposed that the bondholders put up additional money to construct the road in the same way that they had pro-

[10] *Private Laws of Illinois*, 1849, pp. 89–90, Act of February 10, 1849.

[11] *Illinois House Reports*, 1851, pp. 29–30.  The release was not acted upon by the Legislature until after the charter had been granted to the Illinois Central Railroad Company.

[12] The release is in *Illinois House Reports*, 1851, pp. 29–30.

[13] *Illinois State Register*, January 2, 1851, quoting *Chicago Argus*.

[14] Breese to Douglas, January 25, 1851; Ackerman, *Historical Sketch*, p. 89.

vided additional capital to complete the Illinois and Michigan Canal, and that the road be turned over to them until the State and railroad obligations had been paid, when it should revert to the State.[15] Wadsworth was aware that other groups were manoeuvring to secure the grant, and consequently had to proceed with haste. As the bondholders were scattered throughout the eastern states and Great Britain, it was difficult to present the matter to them all before it was submitted to the people of Illinois.

Wadsworth's plan received but indifferent support from the various holders of Illinois securities. The Baring Brothers, representing the largest group of foreign bondholders, felt it would be impossible to win support for the plan within the limited time remaining before the Legislature convened.[16] James Holford bitterly opposed it, and attacked it with a great deal of vehemence.[17] In general the plan did not arouse much enthusiasm among the security holders. Nevertheless, believing that he had the support of Governor French and Senator Douglas, Wadsworth submitted his plan to the State Legislature.

The third group seeking the right to construct the central railroad, some of the members of which were likewise bondholders of Illinois, had first become interested in the project through their work in promoting the Michigan Central. David Neal, George Griswold, John Murray Forbes, and John Thayer,[18] all heavy investors in the latter road, together with Jonathon Sturges, Robert Schuyler, and a number of other prominent eastern capitalists, determined to secure the right to construct the road. Neal was connected with the Reading and Eastern Railroads, Griswold was director of the Great Western, now the Wabash, Sturges had been one of the original promoters of the New York and New Haven Railroad,[19] and Robert Schuyler, probably the most prominent

---

[15] Wadsworth & Sheldon to Governor French, October 8, 11, 1850, Greene and Thompson, *Governors' Letter-Books, 1840–1853*, pp. 353–355.

[16] Baring Brothers to James G. King & Sons, November 15, 1850, Baring MSS.

[17] James Holford to French, December 10, 1850, *ibid.*; Wadsworth to French, January 9, 1851, *Governors' Letter-Books*, p. 369.

[18] There is considerable information on the railroad activities of Neal, Griswold, Forbes, and Thayer in the Baring MSS.

[19] Mrs. Jonathon Sturges, *Reminiscences of a Long Life* (New York, 1894), *passim; Complimentary Dinner to Jonathon Sturges* (1867), p. 11.

railroad man of his day, was president of five railroads, among which were the New York and New Haven and the Harlem companies.[20] Some of the other men who were drawn into the group were Morris Ketchum, member of the locomotive manufacturing firm of Rogers, Ketchum and Grosvenor and director of the New York and New Haven; [21] Franklin Haven, president of the largest bank in New England and for many years a director of the Eastern Railroad,[22] and J. W. Alsop and G. W. Ludlow, organizers of the Panama Railroad and of the Pacific Mail Steamship Company.[23] This imposing array of business, banking, and railroad talent could not fail to make a strong impression on the rustic legislators meeting in Springfield.

Shortly after Congress passed the land grant act, this group began laying plans to secure the grant and a charter from Illinois. Its members did not take any half-way measures, but drew up their plans with care. They induced a number of prominent people to lobby for them in Washington and Springfield, and provided them with all the money they needed for their work. George W. Billings, former agent of the Cairo City and Canal Company, was made leader of the group with authority to spend money without vouchers and to employ anyone whose assistance he

[20] *New York Times*, July 3, 1854.

[21] Ackerman, *Historical Sketch*, p. 73. Though one of the most influential promoters of this group, Ketchum was not an incorporator.

[22] *Boston Transcript*, May 9, 1851. For sketch of Haven see *New England Historical and Genealogical Register* (1894), XLVIII, 474–475.

[23] Other prominent men who were among the incorporators of the Illinois Central were Gouverneur Morris, Robert Rantoul, Jr., John F. A. Sandford, Henry Grinnell, Leroy Wiley. None of these men were at all important in the history of the Company. But cf. William E. Dodd's inference that the same group of men controlled the Illinois Central, the Mobile and Ohio, the Panama Railroad, and the Pacific Mail Steamship Company. *American Historical Review* (1911), XVI, 774–788. It is true that Ludlow, Alsop, and Aspinwall were associated with three of these companies but at no time did they control the Illinois Central. By 1855 Aspinwall and Ludlow were no longer directors of this Company. Furthermore Aspinwall was not one of the original promoters of the Illinois Central and it appears that his name was later added by mistake. *Journal of the Senate*, 1851, p. 103. There was a closer connection between the Illinois Central and the Michigan Central and also between the former and the Great Western, now the Wabash Railroad. George Griswold, Morris, and Schuyler were directors in the Great Western and the Illinois Central; Schuyler was president of both, Morris Ketchum was treasurer of both and S. Alofsen was secretary of both. *Annual Reports* of the Illinois Central and the Great Western Railroads, 1853.

desired.[24] Billings perceived that the support of some of the Illinois politicians would be necessary if his group were to be successful at Springfield. Accordingly he approached Mason Brayman, John Wentworth, and William H. Bissell, and won their support by promises of generous rewards of one kind or another if they were successful in securing the charter for the powerful group of capitalists which he represented. Brayman was a well known lawyer who had won renown as special commissioner to settle the Mormon difficulties.[25] He was chosen to attend to the legal details in Chicago and Springfield and to assist in drawing up and securing the charter. "Long" John Wentworth, representative in Congress of the Chicago district, was one of the most prominent Democrats in the State. As owner of and contributor to the *Chicago Democrat* he had a wide influence on public opinion in northern Illinois. Bissell, at this time a member of Congress, was one of the most popular politicians in the State, and his task was to secure the support of other Illinois politicians for the plan.

Bissell felt that the chief obstacle to the success of his group was the Wadsworth plan. He wrote to his political opponent, Joseph Gillespie, "Be prepared for God's sake, to stamp the *impudent* proposition in the dust! Better a thousand times, let the effete Cairo Company do anything or nothing." [26] In his correspondence, while omitting to mention his own connection with the Neal-Griswold group, Bissell raised numerous objections to the Wadsworth proposal, many of which were valid criticisms. This plan [27] provided for an extremely cumbersome organization with two boards, one of which was to have charge of the lands and the other of construction, which meant, according to Bissell, "an army of agents and officeholders costing $30,000 a year;" it re-

[24] Schuyler, Griswold, and Ketchum to Billings, January 5, 1851, M. O.

[25] The Brayman MSS. in the Chicago Historical Society Library contain much information on Brayman's early connection with the Illinois Central.

[26] Bissell to Gillespie, December 22, 1850, Gillespie MSS.

[27] Copies of the proposed Wadsworth charter are in the Baring MSS. and in the Ackerman MSS., Chicago Historical Society Library. The plan was published in full in the *Chicago Democrat*, January 11, 1851, was summarized in a letter of Wadsworth to French, December 20, 1850, *Governors' Letter-Books*, p. 366, and was partly given in the annual message of Governor French, January 6, 1851, *Illinois Reports*, 1851, p. 19.

quired a change in the constitution of the State; it did not ensure adequate capital; no actual work was to be done on the road for sixteen months, but the preliminary expenses, which would be heavy, were to be borne by the State; the bonds of the project were to be made the basis for banking privileges; and finally the lands would, under the plan, be withheld from sale for years, whereas the people wanted the railroad constructed at once and the lands offered for sale as rapidly as possible.[28]

During the course of the controversy support came to Wadsworth in the person of John S. Wright, editor of the powerful *Prairie Farmer*, the leading agricultural paper in the Northwest. After the passing of the land grant, to which he had contributed much, Wright published in the *Chicago Journal* an extended article on the advisability of the State's creditors' using the land grant to construct the road themselves. Like Wadsworth, he believed that this was a plan which would enable the State to meet its obligations and to remove the stain of repudiation which still clung to it. This article, with an additional letter, was republished in pamphlet form and widely distributed throughout the State.[29] Wright observed:

> But from what I can learn, so many conflicting plans will be proposed, and such extraordinary and powerful efforts made to get the grants of land and the railroad into the hands of scheming speculators, there is much reason to fear that neither this nor any other that looks well to the public good, and to that of our creditors, will be successful.

He likewise used the columns of the *Prairie Farmer* to win support for Wadsworth's plan. Knowing Illinois legislatures, Wright had little confidence in the present one and warned the people to be on the lookout that in the disposal of the lands "no scheme of villainy and corruption" be permitted.[30]

Wright's support of the Wadsworth plan only served to arouse still further the rival group which now, under the leadership of

[28] Bissell to Gillespie, December 22, 1850, Gillespie MSS.
[29] John S. Wright, *Grants of land to Illinois. Plans for using the lands donated by Congress to Illinois under the "Chicago & Mobile Railroad Bill," and the "Swamp Land Bill;" and while in the most effectual manner securing the speedy construction of Railroads, at the same time providing amply to pay the Public Debt, and the Debt to the School Fund* (Chicago, 1850).
[30] *Prairie Farmer* (November, 1850), x, 353.

John Wentworth, began a press campaign full of bitter denunciation of Wadsworth, Wright, Holbrook, and the creditors of the State. This was not a difficult task, as it has always been easy in the rural West to raise the anti-monopoly cry against eastern and foreign security owners. The material, first published in the *Chicago Democrat*, was widely copied in the newspapers of other sections of the State. Wentworth, with the support of Douglas, Shields, Bissell, and other politicians, soon succeeded in killing Wadsworth's proposal. The latter, finding it impossible to interest the chief bondholders in the East and in Great Britain, and embittered by the opposition of James Holford and by the unfavorable reception which his measure had received, retired precipitately from the field early in January, 1851.[31] Henceforth the struggle was between the Cairo and the Neal-Griswold groups.

While Bissell felt that the main obstacle to be removed was the Wadsworth plan, Billings looked upon the Holbrook interests as the chief enemy. After the land grant was passed Holbrook had resumed work on the railroad, thinking that by so doing he would commit the State to his program. He began by making surveys and letting contracts, and it appears that some work was actually done.[32] Billings therefore redoubled his energies to counteract Holbrook's activities.

On December 1, 1850, when Brayman was lobbying in Springfield, Billings wrote him asking if he thought it would be expedient to bring to Illinois the Honorable Robert Rantoul, Jr., of Massachusetts, to present to the Legislature the petition of the Neal-Griswold group for the land grant and charter. Most of the promoters, including Franklin Haven, George Griswold, Morris Ketchum, and Jonathon Sturges, were Whigs, and Billings evidently felt that it would be difficult to secure a charter from the partisan Democratic-controlled Legislature of Illinois unless the Whig element remained in the background. This accounts for his retaining Wentworth, Bissell, and Brayman as lobbyists and also for the selection of Rantoul to present the matter to the Legisla-

---

[31] Wadsworth to French, February 11, 1851, *Governors' Letter-Books*, pp. 376–377.

[32] *Illinois State Register*, January 2, 1851, quoting *Chicago Argus*.

ture.[33] Rantoul was a prominent Massachusetts Democrat whose views on the tariff and on slavery had won for him a considerable reputation.[34] In addition he had had some experience in railroad matters. Brayman recognized that he could not handle the situation in Springfield alone, and he was glad to have Rantoul's assistance. The latter was received with open arms by the Democratic press of Illinois and highly acclaimed. The *Illinois State Register* and the *Chicago Democrat* led the applause, and did much to smooth the way for the passage of the charter.

It was next felt that additional support was necessary from the Whig press of the State, and consequently Rantoul made an arrangement with Simeon Francis, editor of the *Springfield Journal*, by which that paper was to be "particularly devoted" to the interests of the group which Rantoul represented. In return for his support Francis was to be granted a "loan" of $2000 which was to run for two or three years.[35] Not only was this agreement successful in winning the support of the *Springfield Journal* but, because its editorials were widely copied throughout the State, it gave a great deal of additional publicity to Rantoul's proposition.

The representatives of the eastern capitalists had no lack of funds to secure their ends,[36] but they were careful in employing them. Money was not as essential as astute generalship and clever manipulation on the part of the promoters and their representatives. At this session of the Legislature there were so many special interests working for concessions, charters, and laws that the proper amount of logrolling and wirepulling would be more effective than mere money. It was here that Bissell and Brayman excelled, for well did they know how to handle such a situation. Bissell, always a popular character in Illinois, had a special advantage because he was given the freedom of both the House and the Senate.[37]

[33] Wentworth, *Congressional Reminiscences*, p. 41.

[34] Merle E. Curti, "Robert Rantoul, Jr., The Reformer in Politics," *New England Quarterly* (April, 1932), v, 274–275.

[35] Francis to Brayman (copy), May 10, 1851; Brayman to Schuyler (copy), June 10, 1851, Brayman MSS.

[36] Schuyler, Griswold, and Ketchum to Billings, January 6, 1851, M. O.

[37] *Journal of the House*, 1851, p. 26; *Journal of the Senate*, 1851, p. 7.

Soon after the opening of the session it appeared that there were two major groups lined up against each other in a struggle for railroad concessions. The Forbes-Neal-Griswold group were seeking a charter for the Michigan Central, the right to connect the Aurora Branch with the Central Military Tract Railroad, and the land grant and a charter for the Illinois Central. By combining the local groups interested in each of these projects, and by promises of support for other bills and of positions to influential members of the Legislature, a supporting block was built up for the Neal-Griswold plan for the construction of the central railroad.

Opposing them were Stryker, Jervis, and Litchfield, who were seeking a charter and right-of-way to Chicago for the Michigan Southern Railroad and also a charter and right-of-way for a railroad to connect Rock Island with Chicago. They likewise had powerful support in the Legislature as the result of a combination of local capitalists and farmers who would benefit from the construction of the two lines. There is no evidence that this group had any intention of including the central railroad in their system, but it was natural that its members should oppose awarding the land grant and charter of the central railroad to the Neal-Griswold group because of their conflict with the latter over other railroad concessions. The opposition of these men delayed the success of the Neal-Griswold group, but was offset by the supporting block which Bissell, Brayman, Wentworth, and Rantoul had organized.

The *Journals* of the House and the Senate indicate little of the wirepulling and backscratching which was taking place in this session of the Legislature over the central railroad. Two measures were introduced early in the session: the first provided that the State should accept the release of the Great Western Railway Company;[38] the second, probably sponsored by Billings and Rantoul, provided that the charter of this company should be amended so as to include the new group of eastern capitalists.[39] The latter bill was introduced apparently with the idea of includ-

---

[38] *Journal of the House*, 1851, pp. 60–64; *Journal of the Senate*, 1851, p. 35.
[39] *Ibid.*, p. 35; Brayman to Ackerman, August 12, 1891, Brayman MSS.

ing the Cairo interests in an enlarged company, control of which would be in the newer element.[40] This second measure passed the Senate on January 10 but made no further progress. Billings, Brayman, and Rantoul were feeling their way slowly, not knowing just how strong the Holbrook opposition would prove to be and not desiring to bring their proposal to a decision too early in the session.

The greatest obstacle to the success of the Neal-Griswold group in their fight for the charter was the opposition of Darius Holbrook and all those persons interested in the Cairo City Property and the Great Western Railway Company. There was no overlooking the fact that Holbrook had first popularized the idea of a central railroad and that he and his short-lived companies had spent considerable money on the project. Before the session had proceeded far, both Holbrook and the Neal-Griswold group saw the necessity for compromise. Holbrook feared that if he remained adamant in his demands the rival group might obtain sufficient additional support to secure the charter by an agreement to make Metropolis — a rival of Cairo — the southern terminus. Thus he would lose not only the right to construct the railroad but also the benefit which would come to his land investments in Cairo if that city were retained as the southern point. Billings, on the other hand, recognized the strategic position which Holbrook held, and consequently came to favor a compromise with the latter and with the trustees of the Cairo City Property. An agreement was finally reached according to which 1000 shares of Illinois Central Railroad Company stock were to be reserved for Holbrook with the understanding that the stock was not to be assessed.[41] In addition the new company agreed with the Cairo City Property to make extensive improvements in Cairo, the most important of which was a levee to keep out the flood waters of the Mississippi.[42]

In connection with this compromise there is an intriguing letter

---

[40] *Ibid.*

[41] Robt. Schuyler to Dana, November 8, 1852, "Treasurers letters," No. 1, box 48, 63rd St. archives, Illinois Central Railroad.

[42] These were later embodied in an agreement of June 11, 1851, and in subsequent agreements and contracts of 1853–1855. *The Past, Present, and Future of Cairo in North America*, pp. 85–89.

of December, 1853, from Billings in the Brayman manuscripts in which the former explains that Holbrook had agreed to pay him expenses and $20,000 of Cairo city stock. One cannot but wonder whether this is a reward for the compromise which Billings arranged between Holbrook and the promoters of the Illinois Central Railroad.

With the bondholders' plan submerged by the clamor against it, and with Holbrook and the Cairo interests induced to give up their opposition, there was little further trouble in the way of the Neal-Griswold group, except for the question of the route. The group could now safely show its hand. Accordingly, the previous half-way measures mentioned above were dropped and a memorial, dated December 28, 1850, was presented to the Legislature on January 15, 1851, by Rantoul. This memorial stated that the signers, who were experienced railroad promoters and capitalists, were prepared to construct the central railroad on the terms laid down in the federal act and to complete it by July, 1854.[43] The day before the memorial was presented Asahel Gridley, who was friendly to the Rantoul proposal, had introduced a bill into the Senate entitled "An Act to Incorporate the Illinois Central Railroad," [44] which replaced the second act mentioned above providing for an amendment to the Great Western charter.

Between January 14, when the Gridley measure was introduced, and February 10, when it was finally passed and signed, the principal problem in connection with the central railroad was what route, if any, should be prescribed for it. The Act of Congress had provided that the central railroad should extend from the "southern terminus of the Illinois and Michigan Canal to a point at or near the junction of the Ohio and Mississippi Rivers, with a branch of the same to Chicago on Lake Michigan, and another *via* the town of Galena in said state to Dubuque in the state of Iowa. . . ." [45] The only definite points which it was necessary for the State to retain, therefore, were Chicago, Galena, Peru, or La Salle at the end of the Canal, a point opposite Dubuque on the

<hr/>

[43] *Illinois House Reports*, 1851, p. 31.
[44] *Illinois State Register*, January 16, 1851. Gridley was in touch with the agents of the eastern capitalists and this measure probably met their wishes.
[45] 9 *U. S. Stat.*, 466–467.

Mississippi, and some place near the junction of the Ohio and Mississippi Rivers. Some nearby place might well have been substituted for Cairo, as that site was not specifically mentioned in the act, nor was any route specified. The Legislature accordingly had to determine first, whether to designate a route, and second, if a route were to be designated, what it should be. These questions were hotly debated before the Legislature convened, and during the session they were the cause of a great deal of discussion and delay.

Assuming that the route was to be prescribed there were two further questions to be decided, first whether or not the old line of 1837 by way of Vandalia, Shelbyville, Decatur, Bloomington, and Savannah should be retained, and second, from what place on the main line the Chicago branch should diverge. Prior to the convening of the Legislature, it was generally thought that the old line would be retained; advocates of other routes, however, had become active and persons who owned property along the old route were much alarmed. Many of them, in anticipation of the maintenance of the old route, had bought lands along it, and under the leadership of Sidney Breese, who was himself financially interested and was planning shortly to move to Cairo,[46] they began an active campaign against any change. In a long speech before the House, Breese warmly defended the line of 1837, maintaining that the State should keep faith with the people who had invested their money in lands and had settled along that route.[47] Mass meetings were held and petitions drawn up for presentation to the Legislature demanding the retention of the old line. Ames of the Woodford district and Miller of the Carroll and Ogle districts each presented four such petitions from their constituents, and other interested representatives followed their example. Of the sixteen petitions dealing with this matter which came before the House, twelve asked for the continuance of the old route, two

[46] Sidney Breese to Col. Wm. J. Brown, April 22, 1851, Chicago Historical Society Library.

[47] *Illinois State Register*, January 30, 1850. Senators Douglas and Shields had both favored the retention of the old line and had advocated a provision in the Act of Congress granting the lands to ensure such retention. *Cong. Globe*, 31st Cong., 1st Sess., p. 852.

dealt with particular points on the branch line, and two asked that the southern terminus be Metropolis rather than Cairo.[48]

More practical advocates were doing something more than drawing up petitions. On the floor of both houses, in the committee rooms, and in private interviews bargains were struck, votes were exchanged, and support was promised. The manoeuvring on the floor of both houses reflects the selfish desires of each locality and the bitterness which was aroused. Thus in the House, on January 29, Mr. Martin moved an amendment to the proposed charter to strike out all points in the bill except Shelbyville and the northern and southern termini. In retaliation, Ames moved to strike out Shelbyville and insert Bloomington as the junction of the Chicago branch. When both were defeated, Casey moved to substitute Mt. Vernon for Shelbyville and this was likewise defeated.[49] In the Senate, Caldwell moved that the branch line should diverge at Charleston in Coles County.[50] Somewhat later, Parker of the Champaign district moved that the branch should go through Sullivan in Moultrie County and Urbana in Champaign County. After this was tabled, he moved, likewise unsuccessfully, to have the branch take off from the main line at its junction with the Terre Haute and Alton road.[51] Most of these measures were futile and were easily defeated.

Probably the most effective of all the lobbyists and legislators who were fighting for the location of the route of the central railroad was Asahel Gridley, senator from the district comprising Tazewell, McLean, Logan, Dewitt, and Macon Counties. Gridley was a typical representative of that group so frequently met with in Illinois history, the speculator-politicians. Not only was he interested in land investments to the amount of over 15,000 acres,[52] but his chief supporters were likewise large investors. David Davis, Jesse Fell, and Isaac Funk, together with Gridley, composed a very active and influential group. Each of them owned

[48] *Journal of the House*, 1851. But four petitions on this question were noted in the *Journal of the Senate* for the same session.
[49] *Illinois State Register*, January 30, 1851.
[50] *Ibid.*
[51] *Journal of the Senate*, 1851, p. 215.
[52] Tract Books, Danville district, S. A. O.

large amounts of land in and around Bloomington,[53] and not only were they determined that the main line should go through their town, but they also hoped to secure the western terminus of the Chicago branch for it.  Moreover, Gridley feared that the branch line would benefit only Chicago, and therefore wanted its construction delayed until the main line was completed and Bloomington had thereby obtained a good start as a growing city.  At this time it was greatly feared that the Illinois Legislature would locate the line by way of Springfield and Peoria.  This would have kept Bloomington off the line entirely.  The Peoria route was through territory already well developed, and would have provided more business in the early days than the central route.  Its selection would, however, partly defeat the purpose of the land grant, which was to aid a railroad which would open up the great prairie region of the central counties.  To Gridley is due much credit for preventing this change.[54]  He was elected largely for the purpose of securing the old route,[55] and worked untiringly for this end.  On the third day of the session he introduced in the Senate an amendment to a resolution concerning the incorporation of the central railroad company, which provided that the main line should follow the old route "*via* Bloomington, Clinton, Decatur, Shelbyville, etc., to . . ., and that the Central Railroad be completed before the branches are commenced; and that the Chicago branch railroad be constructed from Bloomington, *via* Joliet, to Chicago." [56]

The shortness of the session and the desire for speedy construction of the road made haste essential, and the Legislature consequently decided to leave the choice of the route to the Company with certain exceptions.  The old route, for which there had been the most support, was retained in a modified form.  Instead of laying down a hard and fast rule the Legislature provided that the road should at no point diverge more than 17 miles from a straight

[53] Francis Milton I. Morehouse, *Life of Jesse W. Fell* (University of Illinois, *Studies in the Social Sciences*, vol. v, No. 2, Urbana, 1916), p. 32.

[54] Fell to Duis, in E. Duis, *The Good Old Times in McLean County, Illinois* (Bloomington, 1874), pp. 44, 269–270.

[55] Fell to Duis, *op. cit.*, p. 269.

[56] *Journal of the Senate*, 1851, p. 31.

line drawn from Cairo to the southern terminus of the Canal, and in particular should not pass "more than five miles from the northeast corner of township 21 north, range 2 east of the third principal meridian." [57] With regard to the branch line it was stipulated that it should diverge "from the main track, at a point not north of the parallel of thirty-nine and a half degrees north latitude, and running on the most eligible route into the City of Chicago. . . ." [58] The first provision virtually ensured the road for Bloomington, while the latter required that the Chicago branch should diverge from the main line at some point considerably south of Clinton and Bloomington. The charter also required that construction should first begin on the main line.

With the question of the route settled there was little else to delay the charter which, under the able guidance of Gridley, Judd, and Roundtree in the Senate and Murphy [59] in the House, was passed and signed by February 10, 1851.[60] The question of the percentage of the gross income of the road which was to be paid to the State does not concern us here, nor do the other financial obligations need discussion. The federal land grant was turned over to the newly incorporated company with a charter far more liberal than that granted to the Great Western Railway Company in 1843. Indeed, Rantoul considered the value of the charter and grant together to be five or six million dollars.[61]

[57] Just why this point was chosen it is difficult to say, as it was 12 miles south of Bloomington and near no other town of any importance. This provision practically ensured the road for Bloomington and may have been included in this disguised way to allay the ill-feeling of other sections which were unsuccessful in their efforts. See letter of A. Gridley to *Western Intelligencer*, February 6, 1851, reprinted in *History of McLean County, Illinois* (1879), p. 363.

[58] *Incorporation Laws of Illinois*, 1850–1851, pp. 61–74; *Charter of the Illinois Central Railroad Company, and other documents* (Chicago, 1878), p. 23. This compilation is hereafter cited as *Charter*.

[59] Murphy had been friendly to the plan since December and his aid was counted on by Bissell. Bisell to Brayman, December 12, 1850, Brayman MSS.

[60] *Journal of the Senate*, 1851, pp. 215, 237, 266.

[61] Robert Rantoul, Jr., to Robert S. Rantoul, February 22, 1851, copy sent by Pres. Fish to Bruen in 1902, in box; "W. R. Head, 1," 16th St. archives, Illinois Central Railroad. The question as to the author of the charter has attracted much attention. Because of Rantoul's position as the most outstanding incorporator, most writers have maintained, in spite of much evidence to the contrary, that he drew up the charter. It is natural that the Illinois Central officials should support this view, and their stand has largely influenced unattached writers. The grounds

The charter was not granted without leaving a certain amount of ill-feeling in the State. Every region which had failed to secure the road for its principal towns was aggrieved. Especially was this true of the Galena district, whose representative in the Senate voted against the bill.[62] In this case the action of the Legislature was not accepted as finally determining the western terminus, and further steps were taken by the inhabitants of the lead-mining metropolis to prevent the road from building beyond their city.

Elsewhere the way was left open for different localities to bid against each other for the location of the line. As the charter had not stipulated any definite locations for stations, the Company was privileged to lay them out on its own lands at distances from towns. This would spell the doom of town sites located a few miles off the road. The danger was foreseen by Senators Morrison and Gridley; the former introduced into the Senate an amendment to the charter, the purpose of which was to prevent the Company from laying out any towns in the interior of the State.

on which the Company's president, Stuyvesant Fish, based his argument are as follows: (1) Because the "Great Western Railway" of Massachusetts was mentioned in the charter and Rantoul was at one time connected with this road; (2) because of his distinguished position as a member of the United States Senate; (3) because of his experience as a lawyer and railroad promoter; (4) such an important assignment as drafting an incorporation charter would not have been left to Brayman, an insignificant Illinois lawyer. Stuyvesant Fish to W. G. Bruen, February 2, 1902, *ibid.* That these reasons carry little weight is easily demonstrated. In the first place the mention of the "Great Western Railway" was not in the original bill, but was added by the committee on internal improvements. *Illinois State Register*, January 30, 1851. In the second place, Rantoul did not become a member of the Senate until after the charter was drawn and in any case this point has no value. The third point proves nothing, and finally the confidence which was later placed in Brayman and Billings leaves little to the entire argument.

John Wentworth later said that Hiram Ketchum drew up the charter. This is not unlikely as he was connected with the Neal-Griswold group some time before Rantoul was brought into it. Wentworth, *Congressional Reminiscences*, p. 41. Brayman seems to have felt that the credit belonged to him and probably he had some share in drawing up the charter. Brayman to Ackerman, August 12, 1891, Brayman MSS. See also in the same collection a manuscript copy of the charter which purports to be *the* original final draft. Bissell later stated that Morris Ketchum, Griswold, Neal, and Sturges were the chief men in organizing the Company, and does not mention Rantoul's name. Message to Illinois Legislature, January 5, 1857, *Illinois Documents*, 1857, p. 21. Whoever drew up the charter, it was, when finally completed and adopted, an entirely different instrument, for it had been so amended that one could trace little resemblance to the original.

[62] *Journal of the Senate*, 1851, p. 215. Plato of the Ogle-Lee-Dekalb-Kane district likewise voted against the bill.

The future of the town of Bloomington lay in the balance, for if some such action were not taken by the Legislature the Company could establish a new town a few miles away to secure the high prices for which its lands would sell in the form of town lots. Many other towns were likewise threatened. Although introduced late in the session, this bill was jammed through by Gridley [63] on the same day it was introduced, and a week later it passed the House, though with considerable opposition.[64] The amendment, which was in effect for only four years, was a wise measure, as it prevented the establishment of stations in poor locations merely for the benefit which would accrue to the Company from the sale of town lots.

One is naturally interested in the rewards which came to the lobbyists who had secured the charter for the Neal-Griswold group. Rantoul, the best known of the lobbyists, became a charter member of the Illinois Central Railroad Company, although he had not been one of the first to become interested in the project and had invested little or no money in it. Bissell and Brayman received plums in the nature of appointments as solicitors for the road with salaries reputed to be $4000.[65] Bissell also received 100 shares of stock in the Illinois Central Railroad Company.[66] John Wentworth desired no office from the railroad but received, according to his story, the right to subscribe to one-fortieth of the capital stock of the Company.[67] In addition, his paper, the *Chicago Democrat*, was thereafter known as the "official" paper of the Illinois Central because all advertisements, notices, and accounts were published in it, and it frequently received advance notice of developments which were to take place concerning the road. For his support in connection with the act of incorporation Gridley later received an appointment as sales agent of the Illinois Central Land Department. As will be seen, Gridley was able to make use of this position to his own advantage. Douglas did

---

[63] Duis, *op. cit.*, p. 44.
[64] *House Journal*, pp. 515–516. The bill is available in *Charter*, pp. 37–38.
[65] *Illinois State Register*, May 31, July 31, 1856.
[66] Ackerman to Bissell, June 26, 1860, "Ackerman Letters," 1858–1861, box 48, 63rd St. archives.
[67] Wentworth to Ackerman, December 14, 1882, Ackerman MSS., Chicago Historical Society Library.

not do badly for himself by his support of the land grant in Congress and of the eastern capitalists' petition for a charter before the Illinois Legislature. He was able to sell 16 acres of his Chicago property, 13 of which were under water, to the Illinois Central for its right-of-way for the sum of $21,310.[68]

George W. Billings, who was the one most responsible for securing the charter for the Neal-Griswold group, was generously repaid for his efforts. What financial return he received in money or shares is not clear, but practically all the $51,229 listed as "charter expenses"[69] went through his hands, and he may have retained some of it as his share. Certain it is that his expenses were paid while he was lobbying in Washington and Springfield. In addition, Billings was retained as a sort of financial adviser to the newly organized Company, and was later sent to England to market the mortgage bonds. What promised to be the most valuable return for Billings's work is revealed in a circular which he issued in 1852:[70]

> For services to the aforesaid Railroad Company [Illinois Central], the Agent of this Association has been acquainted with the precise route fixed by the Directors, and which will not be made known to the public until October next. He has also been furnished with a certified map of the lands, together with accurate surveys of each section of the grant, which gives him a key to make choice selections in advance of public entry.

Billings planned to buy alternate sections in the vicinity of the road, as soon as the lands were brought back into the market and before people generally had learned the route of the road. He expected that as soon as the railroad was put under construction the price of the alternate sections would advance rapidly, and that he would thus reap a handsome profit from his advance knowledge of the route.

The State of Illinois also expected to benefit from the valuable land grant and charter which it had granted to the Illinois Central Railroad Company. At this time the credit of the State was so

[68] Brayman to Schuyler, September 27; Burrall to Brayman, December 24, 1852, Brayman MSS.

[69] *Annual Report*, Illinois Central Railroad Company, 1854.

[70] Circular in Baring MSS.; Billings to Brayman, February 22, 1852, Brayman MSS.

low that it could not have secured sufficient capital to construct
the road itself, especially as the new line was to run through undeveloped territory where there was no likelihood of immediate
profits from traffic. The building of the road would open this
territory to settlement and would thereby increase the amount of
taxable property. The increased revenue from taxes, together
with the anticipated income from that clause of the charter which
required that 7 per cent of the gross revenue of the railroad should
be paid to the State [71] would, it was thought, make it possible for
the State to repay its obligations and to re-establish its credit on
a stable basis.

Furthermore, there is good reason for thinking that the State
secured the best bargain possible at that time. Certainly Holbrook and his supporters could not compare in financial soundness
and backing with the successful competitors, and the Wadsworth
proposal, as Bissell so aptly pointed out, was too cumbersome and
unwieldy to meet the hopes of quick construction. The rapidity
with which this, the longest railroad then projected in America,
was constructed argues well for the sagacity and judgment of the
Legislature.

[71] According to this clause, 7 per cent of the gross revenue from the charter lines
of the Illinois Central were to be paid annually into the State treasury. Sections 18
and 22 of charter, *Charter*, pp. 27–31.

## CHAPTER IV

### EARLY FINANCIAL DIFFICULTIES

THE Illinois Central Railroad Company was organized in March, 1851, with Robert Schuyler as president.[1] Schuyler was perhaps the most outstanding railroad executive and promoter in the United States, and his selection for the position seemed logical, but it was to prove most unfortunate. Although Schuyler was prominently connected with such important lines as the Great Western, the New York and New Haven, and the New York and Harlem Railroads, he had not shown himself to be a safe and conservative business man and was consequently distrusted by the more cautious bankers. Schuyler was more of a gambler than a railroad builder and, like Fiske and Gould of a later day, was more interested in playing the Wall Street game than in devoting his time to working out the problems of railroad construction and operation. He was selfish, unscrupulous, and dishonest, and his election as president did more to damage the credit of the newly organized company than any other possible action.[2]

David A. Neal, who was made vice-president, was in many respects quite the opposite of Schuyler. In his past business relations Neal had won the confidence of the banking world. His selection was intended to give an air of solidity and conservatism to the new company, and was received as favorably as Schuyler's was unfavorably.[3] The *New York Times* spoke of it as "most judicious,"[4] and one of Barings' correspondents in the United States wrote of Neal: "He has always been honorable and true and he seems to have grown and to have been prudent himself and kept safe and is independent and is now believed to be a man of handsome property."[5] For some years Neal, like Schuyler, had been

---

[1] *Charter*, pp. 35–36.
[2] Ward to Baring Brothers, June 4, November 19, 1852, Baring MSS.
[3] Same to same, August 30, 1851, and November 19, 1852.
[4] *New York Times*, August 21, 1851.
[5] Ward to Baring Brothers, August 30, 1851, Baring MSS.

actively interested in a number of prominent railroads in which he had substantial investments. He was one of the largest investors in the Illinois Central and was prepared to give it much of his time. Because he devoted more time to the affairs of the Company than did Schuyler or any of the other directors, Neal was the one who was the most influential in the period from 1851 to 1855, and most of the policies which were adopted emanated from him.

The first important task to which the promoters of the Illinois Central had to turn their attention was the matter of securing funds with which to construct the railroad. This was a task of great magnitude and one which had of necessity to be handled with care. There had been four previous attempts to build the road, and each had failed because of the difficulty of raising the necessary capital. The promoters estimated that the cost of constructing the 700 miles of road would be approximately $16,500,000,[6] which was a large sum to be invested in a prairie railroad.

Practically all of the men interested in the new company possessed considerable means, and some of them were rated as being among the wealthiest people in the country, but it was out of the question for them to attempt to finance the construction of the Illinois Central themselves. Nor did the promoters seem anxious to put much of their own money into the road at the start. They did, indeed, pay an assessment of 20 per cent on the first million dollars worth of stock, as their charter required;[7] and in September, 1851, to indicate their confidence in the project, the directors and a few other parties subscribed to approximately $2,000,000 worth of the bonds of the Company.[8] They were careful, however, to provide that the payments on these bonds should extend over a considerable period of time, so that they were not immediately liable for the full payment.

The funds provided by the stock assessment and the first bond issue were insufficient to do more than to establish the new company and to begin surveying the lands and the line of the road.

---

[6] *Report* of President Schuyler to Board of Directors, September 12, 1851.
[7] *Charter*, p. 19.
[8] Copy of contract dated September 12, 1851, M. O.

Actual construction could not be undertaken until additional money was made available. This need was met by a secret agreement entered into by the Illinois Central and the Michigan Central Railroads early in 1852, according to which the latter undertook "to carry" $2,000,000 worth of the bonds of the Illinois Central for two years, in return for which the Michigan Central was to have the use of the line of the Illinois Central from the junction of the two roads into the city of Chicago.[9] The money secured in this way made it possible for construction on the branch line from Chicago southward to be begun even before a foreign bond issue had been sold.

The promoters of the Illinois Central planned to finance the construction of the railroad by the sale of bonds secured by a mortgage upon 2,000,000 acres of the donated lands and the entire right-of-way with all improvements on it.[10] Under this plan they thought it would not be necessary to make assessments upon the stock,[11] which was issued largely to themselves as their compensation for carrying the project to completion. The promoters recognized, however, that sufficient capital could not be obtained in America for what appeared to be a speculative enterprise, and therefore planned to secure aid from abroad. To find purchasers for their bonds they turned first of all to English capitalists.

During the 'forties and early 'fifties, American investments had a none too savory reputation in England and on the Continent. Many of the states had repudiated their obligations, and as a result foreign security owners had suffered severely. Illinois in particular had sinned in this respect, both by State and private action.[12] From 1841 to 1846 the State had failed to pay the interest on the huge debt incurred in the internal improvement program of 1837.[13] Furthermore, it had impaired its credit by giving preference to some of its bonds at the expense of the holders of

[9] Ward to Baring Brothers, November 22, 1852, Baring MSS. This agreement was made necessary by the failure of the Michigan Central to gain permission to build through Illinois to the city of Chicago.

[10] Copy of mortgage in Baring MSS. and republished in *Charter*, pp. 79–96.

[11] This fact was constantly stressed in the financial prospectuses.

[12] See Leland Hamilton Jenks, *The Migration of British Capital to 1875* (New York, 1927), ch. iv, for a discussion of this question of state repudiation.

[13] Greene and Thompson, *Governors' Letter-Books*, p. lii.

its other securities.[14] Finally the failure of the Cairo City and Canal Company, which had a large bonded debt, had caused the credit of Illinois to decline still further. As the State securities and the bonds of the Cairo Company were held to a large extent by British investors the people of that country looked upon Illinois as faithless and untrustworthy. The Baring Brothers expressed this feeling as follows: "Illinois is under a cloud here on account of her state debt . . . & her name is against any new negotiations connected with that state."[15] Because of this foreign antagonism toward Illinois, many financial authorities in the United States feared that the Illinois Central would be unsuccessful in disposing of its bonds abroad.[16]

Nevertheless, the promoters of the Illinois Central were confident of their ability to secure a loan abroad. Many of them were well known and respected in England, not only as experienced railroad men but also as individuals of character and financial standing. They considered the proposed railroad with its potentially valuable land grant of two and a half million acres to be one of the best speculations in the country, and hoped to convince the British capitalists that their money would be safe in it. The returns from land sales alone, they optimistically estimated, would more than pay for the cost of constructing the road and the traffic income would ensure additional safety for the investor.

Excellent representatives were chosen to negotiate a loan.[17] Robert J. Walker, Secretary of the Treasury under President Polk, was placed in charge of the negotiations in England. He was considered a very able man, and it was felt that he could present the proposition most favorably to the London bankers. If he was unsuccessful, David Neal was to try his hand at securing a loan.[18] As a result of his previous railroad connections, Neal had formed

[14] James Holford was particularly incensed at this action. Holford to Governor French, December 10, 1850, Baring MSS.

[15] Impression copy, Baring Brothers to Thomas W. Ward, April 29, 1852, Baring MSS.

[16] *American Railroad Journal* (1851), XXIV, 792. Cf. *New York Tribune*, June 28, 1852.

[17] See extract of resolution of Board of Directors, September 12, 1851, instructing Neal to proceed to England, Ward's office, Illinois Central archives.

[18] The account of Neal's negotiations abroad is largely based on Neal's Autobiography and the Baring MSS.

many acquaintances among the industrialists and bankers of England and the Continent, and there was good reason to believe that he could do more than any other director.[19]

Upon arriving in England in September, 1851, Walker opened negotiations with the Barings, the Rothschilds, and other London firms. At the same time Neal visited Amsterdam and Rotterdam, where he attempted to induce the Dutch bankers to take part of the bonds. To place the Illinois Central Railroad before investors, an edition of Robert Rantoul's pamphlet *Letter on the Value of the Public Lands of Illinois* was published for distribution,[20] and Walker and Neal both wrote and published pamphlets describing the project of the Illinois Central, its land grant, the rapid growth of Illinois, and the prospects of the Company.[21]

Walker was aided in his negotiations with the Rothschilds by August Belmont, who "strongly recommended" the bonds.[22] For a time it appeared that this firm would underwrite the loan. Indeed, negotiations were proceeding so encouragingly that reports were published in American newspapers that Walker and Neal had already negotiated a loan.[23] The reports were premature, however, for with the coup d'etat of Napoleon in December all hope of inducing the Rothschilds to underwrite the loan vanished.[24]

In the meantime, both Walker and Neal had approached the Barings in the hope that they might be induced to accept an agency for the sale of Illinois Central securities.[25] The Barings at this time were less interested in American railroad securities than were the Rothschilds, and were loath to make any ventures in this field. Nevertheless, for a number of reasons they watched with

[19] Neal was likewise seeking a market for the bonds of the Michigan Central Railroad.

[20] Walker to Schuyler, October 31, November 7, 1851, Ward's office.

[21] Robert J. Walker, *Examination of the Value of the Bonds of the Illinois Central Railroad Company* (London, 1851); D. A. Neal, *The Illinois Central Railroad. Its Position and Prospects.*

[22] Walker to Schuyler, November 14, 21, 28, 1851, M. O.

[23] It was reported in the *New York Tribune*, November 8, 1851, that Neal and Walker had met with success in their negotiations, $11,000,000 of the bonds having been subscribed. The *New York Tribune*, January 7, 1852, denounced these rumors as false.

[24] Walker to Schuyler, December 5, 1851, M. O.; Neal Autobiography.

[25] Ward to Baring Brothers, August 30, Neal to Joshua Bates, October 26, November 5, 1851; Neal to Baring Brothers, Dec. (n. d.), 1851.

much interest the progress of the Illinois Central. The success of this railroad and the payment by it of 7 per cent of its gross income to the State of Illinois would aid that State in resuming full interest payments upon its bonds. As the Barings and their clients had a large investment in these securities they naturally stood to gain from the success of the Illinois Central.[26] Furthermore, many of the Barings' American correspondents and friends were interested in the Company and the Barings were inclined to look favorably upon it for this reason.[27] Finally, if the Illinois Central should prove successful, the opportunity for profit in its securities was immense. These factors kept the Barings from turning Neal and Walker down at once.[28]

There were, on the other hand, a number of considerations which were working against the success of these two so far as the Barings were concerned. The latter were unutterably disgusted with the State of Illinois for its partial repudiation of its debts, and had no confidence in its representatives.[29] They feared that the State might repudiate or change the provisions of the charter of the Illinois Central at some future date in such a way as to affect seriously its financial standing.[30] The Barings had no confidence in Schuyler and would not take an interest in any company of which he was president. They mistrusted the action of the directors in not making assessments upon the stock, and they also felt that it was a mistake for them to monopolize the stock and profits while asking the purchasers of the bonds to take all the risk.[31] They were of the opinion, too, that the market was saturated with American railroad securities and that there was little hope of floating more bonds not of the first grade.[32]

[26] The Barings were receiving correspondence from both sides of the controversy over charters described in the preceding chapter. See the letters of Ward & Co., W. H. Swift, and J. M. Forbes. The letters clearly indicate the Barings' interest in Illinois securities.

[27] Baring Brothers to Thomas W. Ward, April 29, 1852, impression copy, Baring MSS.

[28] Baring Brothers to Ward, October 10, 1851, impression copy, *ibid.*

[29] Same to same, April 29, 1852, impression copy, *ibid.*

[30] W. H. Swift to Ward, September 8, 1851, copy, *ibid.*

[31] Ward to Baring Brothers, September 12, 1851, January 7, 1852, *ibid.*

[32] Baring Brothers to Ward, September 16, October 24, 1851, April 29, 1852, impression copies, *ibid.*

Probably the most important reason why the Barings finally determined to remain aloof from the enterprise was that they received most unfavorable news concerning it from their American correspondents. The source of most of this unfavorable news was William H. Swift, Trustee of the Illinois and Michigan Canal. From the start Swift seems to have been hostile to the Neal-Griswold group, which was promoting the Illinois Central, and his judgment was affected by this hostility. His letters were filled with unfavorable news about the Company, its management, and its plans. He was particularly critical of what he considered the ridiculously high valuation placed upon the railroad lands.[33] Inasmuch as Swift was later retained by the Barings as their adviser upon American railroad matters, his opinion of the Illinois Central must have been influential in determining their refusal to handle the securities of the Company.[34]

With the doors of both the Barings and the Rothschilds closed to him Neal felt that it was useless to remain longer in England. Before leaving he induced the Rothschilds to send to their correspondents on the Continent a circular on the Illinois Central in French, German, and English. He also arranged with Fox, Henderson & Company to send an agent to America to investigate the prospects of the Company, in the hope that the agent's report might favorably influence British investors.[35] Leaving Walker to continue negotiations, Neal returned to America to take charge of the lands.[36]

Walker was no more successful in London during Neal's absence than he had been before, and the task of arranging for a loan was then turned over to three other men, Billings, W. W. Gilbert of Gilbert and Johnson of New York, and a man named Winslow. In March, 1852, these three men reported that negotiations had proceeded so far that they required Neal's presence again.[37] Neal

[33] Frequent quotations from and sometimes the entire letters (copies) of W. H. Swift were sent to London by the Barings' American correspondents, Thomas W. Ward and Sam G. Ward.

[34] Ward to Baring Brothers, November 19, 1852, Baring MSS.

[35] *New York Tribune*, January 22, 1852; Neal Autobiography.

[36] *New York Tribune*, February 25, 1852.

[37] The *New York Tribune* speaks of the "utter failure" of Walker and gives the credit for negotiating the bond issue to Gilbert and Billings. Neal, in his Autobiog-

returned to London in the same month, and by May succeeded in completing arrangements with a British syndicate headed by Devaux & Company for a loan of £1,000,000. This firm had recently made a great deal of money in French railroads, and it looked upon the Illinois Central as an excellent speculation. To secure the loan, the promoters of the Illinois Central had to extend to each purchaser of a $1000 bond the right to subscribe to five shares of stock, thus reversing the policy they had hitherto adhered to of retaining the stock for themselves. The subscribers were told in the prospectus for the loan:

> There is every probability that the railroad will be constructed without any call on the Share Capital. A small deposit may be required on the Shares, and these Shares will thus become an actual bonus, and entitle the holder to a participation in all the profits of the line.

The bonds were to be paid in ten quarterly installments extending from July, 1852, to October, 1854.[38] As a result of this bond issue English capitalists acquired $5,000,000 in bonds and a possible 25,000 shares of stock.[39] The English bondholders decided to pay up on their bonds at once, thus providing the Illinois Central with an adequate supply of capital for a time.[40] It was this British loan, rather than the earlier American loan, which was being paid slowly,[41] that enabled the Illinois Central to proceed with construction and established the credit of the Company on a fairly stable basis.

This loan of $5,000,000 was the only important one which the Illinois Central raised abroad in the first years of its existence, but it does not represent the total foreign investment in the Company.

raphy, takes most of the credit for this success for himself, merely mentioning the assistance of Billings and Winslow. He does not mention Gilbert. George Griswold in a letter of January 10, 1853, to Baring Brothers, speaks of the $5,000,000 loan "negotiated by Mr. Gilbert with Messers Devaux & Co."

[38] The prospectus for the loan, originally published in the *London Economist* (June 12, 1852), x, 668, and elsewhere, was reprinted in the *New York Tribune*, June 26, 1852.

[39] *American Railroad Journal*, 1855, pp. 35, 119, states that 23,905 shares had been issued in London by January 1, 1855.

[40] *New York Tribune*, July 5, 1852. From later reports it is apparent that not all the London bondholders paid in full at this time.

[41] Only 30 per cent had been paid by April 20, 1853. *New York Times*, April 11, 1853.

The loan gave the British investing public a large enough stake in the railroad so that henceforth it took much interest in the Company's affairs. The *Railway Times* of London, the *London Times*, and other British financial papers published quantities of information on the Illinois Central and its lands, much of which was excellent advertising for the Land Department. From time to time the British investing public bought bonds and stock of the Illinois Central in the open market, until eventually it was largely owned in Great Britain and on the Continent.

The $5,000,000 loan and the slow returns from the earlier issue were soon exhausted, and it was necessary to seek a number of later loans, both at home and abroad. The Barings persisted in their refusal to take any interest in the Company,[42] and as the British investors did not show any further inclination to take loans at par it was necessary to induce American capitalists to subscribe to them. On a number of occasions the promoters themselves were forced to take large portions of otherwise unsubscribed loans. By 1855 the Griswolds, Neal, Ketchum, and a number of other directors had taken large blocks of bonds, and consequently it is not fair to assume that none of the directors had sufficient faith in the Company to risk their money in it.[43] It is true that they unloaded their securities on the market as conditions permitted, but nevertheless a relatively large portion of the funds with which the railroad was constructed was first supplied by its directors.[44]

Throughout the period of the 'fifties the Illinois Central Railroad, as Swift had once suggested, was considered a speculative enterprise, and its securities were rated below those of the best-grade railroads. Aside from the nature of the project, which certainly was speculative, the management did not always have the

[42] S. G. Ward to Griswold, February 14, 1853; James G. King & Sons to Baring Brothers, March 1, 1853, copies.

[43] *New York Times*, June 16, 1853. In a letter to the Barings of February 14, 1854, Sam G. Ward wrote: "Our friend Mr. Griswold & others interested must be very heavily loaded."

[44] In the Journal of D. A. Neal may be found the record of Neal's frequent sales of his Illinois Central securities. It also appears that the other promoters were unloading their securities in the period prior to 1857 for it is difficult otherwise to understand the heavy sales of these securities.

confidence of either the State or the country. These factors not only depressed the securities but also made it difficult for the Illinois Central to float new loans, except at prices below par. One loan even had to be sold at 70 per cent.[45]

The choice of Robert Schuyler as president prejudiced many people against the Illinois Central and weakened its financial standing. Schuyler was either not willing or not able to give much attention to its business because of his multifarious railroad activities, and consequently there was no strong hand at the helm. Neal, who was spending most of his time in Illinois supervising construction and organizing the Land Department, was not the man to take charge of the road. In 1853 Schuyler resigned as president,[46] and there was no suitable person to take his place. The position was offered to Neal, who, because he was becoming deeply involved in a large land company operating in Illinois, refused to accept it.[47] The position was then given to an understudy of Schuyler, William P. Burrall, who was connected with the Great Western and the New York and New Haven Railroads. His election was only a temporary expedient which would continue only until some person with real executive ability could be induced to take the place. To strengthen the standing of the Illinois Central and to cement the relations of this road with the Michigan Central, James F. Joy was made resident director in Chicago with supervisory powers. At the same time Joy was acting in a similar capacity for the Michigan Central.[48]

Early in July, 1854, the defalcation of Schuyler in connection with the New York and New Haven Railroad was discovered.[49] Although Schuyler had resigned the previous year as president of the Illinois Central, he had not severed his connection with the road. The situation was most damaging to the interests of the Illinois Central, and it was forced to publish a notice in the New York papers stating that Schuyler had previously resigned

---

[45] *New York Tribune*, February 22, 23, 1855.
[46] *New York Tribune*, July 10, 1854; Stuyvesant Fish to Ackerman, December 30, 1896, Ackerman MSS., Newberry Library.
[47] Sturges to Brayman, July 28, 1853, Brayman MSS.
[48] W. P. Burrall to J. F. Joy, January 31, 1854, photostatic copy, M. O.
[49] *New York Tribune*, July 3–6, 1854.

as president, that he had nothing to do with its stock or bonds, and that there was no fraud in connection with its securities.[50] This notice did not remedy the situation, but seemed to indicate that the officials were on the defensive. The bonds which had been declining on the stock market for some time now fell more rapidly, till in August they were selling for less than 62 cents on the dollar.[51] American holders were unloading their bonds and stock at a rapid rate.

The declining quotations on the bonds and stock were precisely the opportunity for which the British investors were looking. Having arrived at the conclusion that the Company's securities were a desirable and reasonably safe speculation, they now began to pour money and orders into Wall Street to snap up the bargains in its bonds and stock. The financial editor of the *New York Tribune* in 1854 and 1855 was constantly alluding to the orders which were taking large amounts of these securities abroad. Thus on September 2, 1854, $85,000 worth of Illinois Central bonds were purchased for foreign accounts, and a steamer which arrived that day from abroad brought such large orders for the securities that their price advanced sharply.[52] By August, 1855, foreign purchasing had raised the price of the bonds to nearly 90.[53] This foreign purchasing continued until well into the 'sixties, by which time the control of the Illinois Central had actually passed into the hands of foreign investors. In February, 1856, over 40,000 shares of the stock were held in Europe [54] and six months later this amount had more than doubled, while $12,000,000 worth of the bonds was held abroad, mainly in Great Britain.[55] In 1864 over three-quarters of the stock was held by British investors.[56] Henceforth until nearly the end of the century the Illinois Central was largely owned by English and Continental financiers.[57]

[50] *New York Tribune*, July 10, 1854.     [51] *Ibid.*, August 25–30, 1854.
[52] *Ibid.*, September 4, 1854.     [53] *Ibid.*, August 10, 1855.
[54] J. N. Perkins to Franklin Haven, February 6, 1856, Haven MSS.
[55] *New York Times*, September 6, 1856.
[56] Minutes of meeting of shareholders, June 25, 1864, Ward's office. Cf. *Chicago Press and Tribune*, June 17, 1859. See also *Annual Report*, Illinois Central Railroad, 1876.
[57] Stuyvesant Fish said, in 1902, that when he entered the employ of the Company less than one-seventh of its stock was owned in the United States, while over

It was essential for the Illinois Central to gain the confidence of the banking world in order that it might be able to raise on favorable terms the additional capital necessary to complete construction. The resignation of Schuyler and the election of Burrall had not provided the necessary leadership, and Joy was devoting most of his time to the Michigan Central and to the other Illinois railroads in which he was interested. Neal, although admittedly a man of great ability and uprightness, had not proved himself well suited to the West. His tactlessness and inability to conciliate opposition had made not only himself but his company unpopular in Illinois. George Griswold was the mainstay of the road in this trying period, but he had too many irons in the fire to permit him to become president and furthermore was too old for the position.[58]

The need for stronger leadership was met in the latter part of 1854 by the election to the Board of Directors of two young men who had previously been engaged in the China trade. John N. A. Griswold, son of George Griswold, who probably had the largest single investment in the Illinois Central, was made director, and early in 1855 was elected president to succeed Burrall. William H. Osborn, son-in-law of Jonathon Sturges, was made director and placed in charge of affairs in New York. Both of these men were aggressive, capable, and possessed of imagination. They set about reorganizing the Company and establishing its credit on a firmer basis.[59]

In December, 1855, Griswold was replaced as president by Osborn, who for the next ten years gave practically all his time to the duties of his new position. No man in the entire history of the railroad has been more closely identified with its interests than Osborn. He virtually directed the finances and policies of the Land Department, did much to promote the agricultural development of the Northwest, and settled many problems in connection with the operation of the road. Osborn was a man of indomitable

one-half was owned in England and nearly 30 per cent by a company in Holland. *Address of Stuyvesant Fish at a banquet at the Union Club*, Philadelphia, February 27, 1902.

[58] Sam G. Ward to Baring Brothers, July 5, 1853, Baring MSS.

[59] *Annual Reports*, Illinois Central Railroad, 1855, 1856.

will, initiative, and strong character. From the start he had to combat the criticism of the members of the "Old Regime," consisting of Neal, Ketchum, and the Griswolds. In their efforts to gain the proxies of the British investors in order to oust Osborn from his position, they resorted to the newspapers and railroad journals, in which they published unfair statements about him and his work. He was accused of working for his own pocket, of borrowing money at exorbitant rates of interest, of being too lenient to the land purchasers, of extravagance in advertising the lands, and of wrongfully using proxies.[60] Osborn was not deterred from his course by these criticisms, and gradually won the confidence of the American and foreign shareholders.

Osborn inherited the policies which had been established by his predecessors and was forced to continue them for a time. He could not help seeing the mistake which had been made in issuing stock which was regarded as non-assessable, but on account of the opposition of the shareholders he could not immediately reverse this policy.

The Illinois Central, as we have seen, had practically promised in its financial prospectuses that few or no calls would be made on its stock.[61] This promise had been of much importance in inducing British capitalists to purchase Illinois Central bonds, with which there were stock subscription rights. The depressed market conditions of 1854 and 1855 and the inability of the Company to realize more than 70 per cent on the sale of its bonds had forced it to resort to calls on the stock or to short-term notes. Both means were employed. A call of $5 was made for August 10, 1854,[62] another for a similar amount on December 8,[63] and a third in the latter part of 1855.[64] In this year, however, market conditions for the bonds improved, owing in part to the extraordinary land sales, so this one small call was sufficient.[65] The same favorable condi-

---

[60] Osborn to Joseph Fisher, April 1, 1858, "Presidents Letters," No. 7, box 48, 63rd St.

[61] *New York Tribune*, June 26, 1852, April 5, 1853.

[62] *Ibid.*, July 12, 1854. The commercial editor of this paper strongly recommended this move in view of the depressed market conditions. See *ibid.*, July 12, 14, 1854.                                    [63] *Ibid.*, November 6, 1854.

[64] *Ibid.*, October 2, 1855.

[65] *Ibid.*, August 10, 1856.

tions continued throughout 1856 and the early part of 1857. During this period land sales were booming, the bonds were selling at a high of 97 to 100, and the stock at 120,[66] and the Company and its shareholders seemed to be on the high road to prosperity.

President Osborn, however, did not regard the Company's financial prospects with equanimity. Because the shareholders had so bitterly opposed the calls made upon their stock, the construction of the road had been financed almost entirely from the sale of bonds and short-term securities. Both the American and the British shareholders were responsible for this situation; the former had instituted the policy in the first years of the Company's existence and the latter had insisted on its continuance. Seeing the danger in the situation, Osborn advocated further calls on the outstanding stock. The British investors refused to accept his point of view, and as the future of the Illinois Central depended on their continued support the calls were withheld.[67] Then followed the depression of 1857, a tremendous reduction in land values and collections, a decline in traffic income, and the presentation of a large amount of short-term bills and notes amounting to nearly $4,000,000, which the New York office was unable to meet. These obligations could not be funded nor could they be extended.

A quick decision was necessary, and it was determined to assign the Company temporarily to a number of directors.[68] In consequence the Company's securities fell to a new low point of 50

[66] *Ibid.*, July 4, 13, 28, 1857.
[67] When the bonds of the Company again fell to a point at which it was not advisable to continue to sell them, Osborn found it necessary to raise short-term loans at rates as high as 1 or 2 per cent a month, according to Griswold. J. N. A. Griswold to Ackerman, December 20, 1890, Ackerman MSS., Newberry Library.
[68] The facts of this assignment are generally misunderstood. The Illinois Central did not go into bankruptcy nor was there any danger of it so doing. The decline in land sales and collections and traffic income together with the presentation of a large number of bills and short-term notes caught the Company at a time when it had little ready cash and when, because of the tight money situation which prevailed, none could be secured. The assignment was only a temporary measure to tide the situation over until calls could be made on the stock. Quick action by Osborn put the road back on its feet again shortly. Confidence in its future, however, was seriously impaired. For further material on this episode see circular of J. N. Perkins in *New York Tribune*, October 12, 1857, and another by Osborn in *ibid.*, October 24, 1857. See also *Chicago Democratic Press*, October 10, 12, 14, 1857.

for the bonds and 70 for the stock.[69] The situation was far worse in 1857 than it had been in 1853 and 1854, when the securities had fallen so low and heroic measures were required to remedy it. A call of $10 had already been made for September 25, 1857, but this proved inadequate and further calls were necessary.[70]

By this time the British investors were thoroughly aroused. Many of them had put large portions of their funds into the bonds of the Illinois Central on the understanding that the stock which went with the bonds would not be assessed. Even a small call of $5 or $10 would be severely felt by those who had taken a considerable block of the stock. Protective committees of the stockholders and bondholders were organized consisting of many of the most prominent Englishmen of the day. Among the members of Parliament who served on these committees were Richard Cobden, Charles Paget, Sir Joseph Paxton, William Moffatt, and William Gladstone.[71] The committees sent numerous representatives to America to investigate the management of the Company and its Land Department.[72] Among the investigators were Sir James Caird, Joseph Fisher, and a dozen other prominent Englishmen.[73] These investigators interviewed the officers of the Company, visited the Chicago and New York offices, where they went over the accounting systems, and travelled over the line of the Illinois Central to view its land grant and the agricultural possibilities of the region. They made many severe but frequently petty criticisms, which led to more rigorous measures of retrenchment. Many of their criticisms and complaints, as Osborn pointed out,[74] were frivolous and indicated a lack of understanding of the differences between railroad promotion in a near frontier community and in a well settled industrial area. A few of their suggestions were adopted by Osborn under protest, since with the majority of the stock now in British hands such action was necessary.

[69] Quotations from *New York Tribune* of October, 1857.

[70] Circular of Osborn, *ibid.*, October 24, 1857.

[71] *Railway Times*, July 31, 1858.

[72] Osborn to Geo. Moffatt, December 2, 1858, "Presidents Letters," No. 8, box 48, 63rd St.          [73] *Ibid.*

[74] Osborn commented on Captain Heyworth's extreme credulity, saying that he filled reams of paper with comments of a frivolous nature upon the management of the Illinois Central. To Moffatt, December 2, 1858, *ibid.*

One of the British investors in Illinois Central securities was Richard Cobden. He had received a gratuity of nearly $400,000 from the grateful British manufacturers who profited from his anti-corn law agitation.[75] Morley, Cobden's biographer, says that "Cobden was no speculator in the ordinary sense of the word," [76] but the facts do not seem to bear out this statement. Contrary to the better judgment of his friends, among whom was President Osborn, Cobden put a considerable portion of this gratuity into Illinois Central stock which was assessable and upon which there was little prospect of dividends for some years to come. Unquestionably this was a speculative investment, and only the desire for large profits could have induced Cobden to take the risk. When it was found necessary to make calls upon the stock, Cobden was caught in an extremely disagreeable situation. Practically his entire fortune was at stake, and he was unable to make the required payments. It was necessary for his business friends to come to his aid again by what Morley calls "an extraordinary example of grateful and considerate munificence." [77]

In 1859 Cobden determined to visit America to investigate for himself the affairs of the Company in which he had risked so much. He made a hurried trip to the United States and Canada, spending a little more than three months in his travels and in his investigation of the Illinois Central.[78] His contact with President Osborn, whose friendship he already enjoyed, and with the other officers of the Illinois Central, together with his trip over the line of the Illinois Central and his study of its affairs, gave him renewed confidence in it.[79] He wrote in glowing terms of the land grant and of the opportunities awaiting the settler in Illinois, and expressed his confidence in the present management of the Company. One of his letters was so enthusiastic about Illinois and the land grant that Osborn, realizing its publicity value, gave it to the press, where it was widely published.[80] He also paid to

---

[75] John Morley, *Life of Richard Cobden* (London, 1883), p. 265.

[76] *Ibid.*, p. 442.          [77] Morley, *op. cit.*, p. 442.

[78] Cobden's trip to America received a great deal of attention in the daily press, both in the United States and in Canada.

[79] Cobden to Walmsley, September 18, 1857, photographic copy, M. O.

[80] *American Railroad Journal* (September, 1859), p. 506; *Hillyer's American Railroad Magazine* (September, 1859), pp. 50–51. Cobden went so far as to say, "It is not

have it published in England. Cobden henceforth placed his complete confidence in Osborn and became one of his most loyal supporters. The proxies on Cobden's stock [81] and his influence with other investors did much to win for Osborn the confidence of the latter.

Some of the British investigators, as well as the more experienced shareholders, realized that further assessments on the stock were preferable to additional bond issues at the high interest rates and heavy discounts then prevailing.[82] Furthermore, men like Cobden, Caird, Moffatt, and others were coming to place great confidence in Osborn's management. Accordingly, with the consent of the British committee, it was decided to offer sufficient inducements to secure full payment on the shares.[83] Liberal terms were offered, and by 1861 87,169 shares were completely paid up and on 91,787 $80 was paid.[84] This was not accomplished without a great deal of protest and carping criticism on the part of many of the stockholders.

The payments by the stockholders enabled the Illinois Central to pay off the short-term loans and to reestablish its credit. The lean returns from traffic income, land sales, and collections, all of which were drastically reduced as the result of the Panic of 1857, prevented any further improvement in its financial position until business conditions improved in 1860. In that year the returns from these three items seemed to be increasing, but they soon declined as a result of the outbreak of the Civil War. In 1862, however, when large numbers of troops and quantities of supplies were transported over the line and when there were tremendous returns from land sales and collections, the tide turned permanently. Henceforth the credit of the Company was secure and additional loans for future expansion were easily secured.

as a *railroad* investment that I regard so favorably this undertaking, but its value, in my eyes depends on the landed estate, which is the noblest domain ever transferred in one conveyance." Cobden to Walmsley, September 18, 1857, photographic copy, M. O.

[81] Cobden held 441 shares of Illinois Central stock in 1864. List of stockholders, May, 1864, Ward's office.

[82] Osborn to Haven, July 1, 1858, Haven MSS.

[83] *Ibid.; New York Tribune*, May 27, 1859.

[84] MSS. dated December 1, 1861, Haven MSS.

The difficulties of raising capital for the construction of the Illinois Central did not prevent the completion of the line within the period of six years set by the charter. The financial problem was not the only one which retarded the progress of construction. Other factors intervened which make the story of construction an important and colorful chapter in the history of Illinois.

# CHAPTER V

## CONSTRUCTING A PRAIRIE RAILROAD

THE generation of 1830 to 1860 witnessed as new and as startling changes in transportation methods in the United States as has the generation of 1900 to 1930. The introduction of the steam locomotive and the development of the railroad network in this earlier period completely transformed the economic life of millions of Americans and vastly changed their social existence. Railroad construction first began in the more densely settled eastern states, but after 1840 the mid-western states caught up with them, and in their enthusiasm soon pushed railroad expansion far beyond their needs at the time.

Illinois in 1837 had mapped out for herself an over-ambitious program of railroad construction which had saddled her with a heavy burden of debt and had retarded her development. In the late 'forties, however, economic conditions improved, immigration increased, and eastern capital began to flow in again. New settlements were made and old ones added to their population, commerce and navigation developed, and the spirit of buoyancy and optimism characteristic of the frontier revived. In 1848 the Illinois and Michigan Canal was completed. The success of the canal in bringing new settlers to northern Illinois and in providing a market for their goods indicated to Illinoisians what improved methods of transportation could do.[1] Their desire for internal improvements, submerged since the debacle of 1837, was now revived, and on all sides was heard the demand for quicker methods of transportation.[2] It was to the railroad, however, and not to the canal that people turned.

Railroad construction in the potentially rich State of Illinois held out a constant invitation to capitalists and adventurers,

[1] Putnam, *The Illinois and Michigan Canal*, ch. iv, "Economic Influence," pp. 92–125.

[2] The frequent railroad conventions which were held throughout Illinois indicate the widespread interest in improved means of transportation.

particularly to local promoters, who were ready to commence railroads from anywhere to anywhere irrespective of the immediate needs for their construction. If the elaborate railroad network planned for Illinois by different groups and individuals during the 'fifties had been constructed, all parts of the State would have been brought within 2 to 5 miles of railroad lines.[3] The only obstacle which prevented the carrying out of these grand schemes was the lack of capital.

The readiness of promoters to undertake railroad construction in Illinois was stimulated by the action of towns, cities, and counties in giving direct assistance to those projects which promised immediate benefit to them. Fortunately the constitution of 1847, drawn up by men who had learned their lesson from bitter experience, prevented the State from loaning its credit to any "individual, association or corporation." [4] Except in the case of the Illinois Central there was no hope of railroads securing assistance from the State Government, but local governments in their competition with each other could easily be induced to subscribe for the bonds of projected railroads. In many cases this was the chief means of raising money for the lines. Another method used at this time was to induce farmers and land owners along the proposed routes to accept the bonds of the company in return for a mortgage upon their lands. The promoters would then sell the mortgages to eastern capitalists who would not buy the bonds.[5]

The first railroad of importance to be built in Illinois was, as would naturally be expected, one projected to connect the two chief cities, Galena and Chicago.[6] Promoted by an aggressive group of Chicago financiers, the Galena and Chicago Union Rail-

---

[3] Cole, *Era of the Civil War*, p. 47.

[4] *Journal of the Convention*, 1847, p. 549.

[5] For methods employed to secure financial support from the farmers see Frederick Merk, *Economic History of Wisconsin During the Civil War Decade* (*Publications*, Wisconsin Historical Society, "Studies," vol. I, Madison, 1916), ch. ix.

[6] For an account of the Jacksonville and Meredosia Railroad, the first road on which steam locomotives were actually operated in Illinois, see Ackerman, *Early Illinois Railroads*, pp. 99–107. This road was quickly abandoned and later sold to Robert Schuyler, who thus had some experience with Illinois railroads before he went into the Illinois Central. *Ibid.*, p. 106. In 1840, a tourist reported that the Jacksonville and Meredosia Railroad was then in operation for a distance of 23 miles. Steele, *A Summer Journey in the West*, p. 165.

road was rapidly pushed westward. It reached Elgin and Aurora in 1850, Rockford in 1852, and Freeport in 1853, where it joined the Illinois Central, which gave it connections with Galena in 1854 and with Dunleith on the Mississippi in 1855.[7] This road and the Rock Island Railroad, which was under construction at the same time, opened up for settlement many thousand acres of rich prairie land in the northern counties of Illinois.[8] In 1855 the Dixon Air Line, controlled by the same group as the Galena and Chicago Union Railroad, reached the Mississippi at Fulton. These roads tapped the rich hinterland of Chicago and prospered at once. The average dividend on the capital stock of the Galena and Chicago Union Railroad for the years 1850 to 1855 was 16 per cent,[9] and until the Panic of 1857 it was known as the most profitable line in the country. The phenomenal success of this company further stimulated railroad activity in Illinois and made the period from 1850 to 1857 one of feverish railroad expansion, as the following table shows:[10]

RAILROAD MILEAGE CONSTRUCTED ANNUALLY IN ILLINOIS

| Year | Miles | Year | Miles |
|------|-------|------|-------|
| 1848 | 10 | 1853 | 390 |
| 1849 | 5 | 1854 | 906 |
| 1850 | 47 | 1855 | 462 |
| 1851 | 45 | 1856 | 419 |
| 1852 | 140 | 1857 | 74 |

By the opening of the 'fifties eastern capitalists recognized the possibilities for profits in the railroads of Illinois and began to

[7] Frederic L. Paxson, "The Railroads of the 'Old Northwest' Before the Civil War," Wisconsin Academy of Sciences, Arts and Letters, *Transactions* (October, 1912), vol. XVII, part 1, maps, pp. 253–261.

[8] Report of S. F. Porter, *Home Missionary* (May, 1859), XXXII, 16.

[9] The dividends were as follows:

| Year | Dividend | Year | Dividend |
|------|----------|------|----------|
| 1850 | 10 % | 1853 | 20 % |
| 1851 | 15 | 1854 | 21 |
| 1852 | 15 | 1855 | 17 |

Its gross earnings jumped from $48,332 in 1850 to $1,506,710 in 1855. Bank circular issued by Edward F. Satterthwaite of London, August 9, 1855.

[10] Paxson, *loc. cit.*, pp. 268–273. Though substantially correct, there are some errors in these figures. The 10 miles from Chicago to Harlem on the Galena and Chicago are included for both 1848 and 1856. The mileage of the Michigan Central and the Michigan Southern from the Indiana-Illinois line to Chicago is not given, and the total mileage of the Illinois Central is slightly in error.

take over some of the local projects which as yet had not proceeded beyond the charter stage. As we have seen, the promoters of the Michigan Central Railroad were not content with building their road to Chicago but sought western connections. They built the Aurora Branch, which connected Aurora Junction with Chicago by way of the Galena and Chicago Union Railroad, and then bought into a number of local companies so that by 1856 they had secured control in and completed lines extending to Burlington and Quincy on the Mississippi. Beyond these points they were building the Hannibal and St. Joseph Railroad in Missouri and the Burlington and Missouri River Railroad in Iowa. What were to become known as the Joy lines were taking shape in this period under the direction of John Murray Forbes and his associates, and their construction in Illinois was helping to develop the western part of the State, particularly the Military Tract.[11]

More important in opening up new territory were the four cross-state railroads south of Chicago: the Peoria and Oquawka, the Great Western,[12] the Terre Haute and Alton, and the Ohio and Mississippi. The construction of these roads opened up eastern and central Illinois, which now for the first time were provided with transportation facilities. To be able to compete with other sections of the State eastern and central Illinois required direct connection with Chicago, where the grain trade, the lumber industry, and the railroads all centered. Transportation of grain to the East by rail was expensive, and it was found more economical to ship wheat and corn to Chicago, from which point they were transshipped by lake steamer to Buffalo and thence by the Erie Canal to the seaboard. The four cross-state railroads were feeders to the north-south lines which gave direct connections with Chicago to the eastern and central parts of the State. These north-south lines were the Chicago and Alton and the Illinois Central.

[11] Swift to Ward, December 9, 1850; Ward to Baring Brothers, November 19, December 28, 1852; Forbes to Ward (copy), December 27, 1852; Forbes to Baring Brothers, January 9, October 16, 1854, Baring MSS.

[12] The term Great Western was applied to a number of early American railroads and therefore its use is confusing. As here used it refers to the present line of the Wabash Railroad extending from Jacksonville to Danville.

The Alton railroad, completed from Bloomington to Alton in 1853, was the first line to reach the Mississippi and, through its connections with the Illinois Central and the Rock Island, to connect the Mississippi with Chicago. This line tapped a rich agricultural region hitherto tributary to St. Louis but which thenceforth sent its produce, for the most part, to Chicago. The reversal of the trade routes in Illinois previously described in connection with the Illinois and Michigan Canal was thus furthered by the completion of the Chicago and Alton and other railroads connecting the Mississippi with Chicago and the East. The Alton railroad cut through the prairie regions of Will, Grundy, Livingston, McLean, and Logan Counties, which had been developing slowly on account of inadequate transportation facilities.[13] Rapidly growing towns now sprang up along its line, and quickly became important shipping centers for agricultural products. This region, together with the section to the southeast which was being opened up by the Illinois Central, was destined to become one of the richest agricultural sections in the country.

The Illinois Central Railroad, with its longer mileage, tapped more undeveloped portions of the State than any other line, and was consequently more influential in opening up new land for settlement. That portion of the main line extending from Centralia to La Salle, with its branch to Dunleith, although destined to become merely a local carrier transshipping its freight for Chicago and the East over other railroads, nevertheless provided the only means of getting commodities to market from more than a million acres. The branch from Chicago to Centralia, together with that part of the old main line from Centralia to Cairo, now comprises the main line. It was this portion of the road which was most influential in the development of the State.

During the decade of the 'fifties, the number of miles of railroad in operation in Illinois increased from 110 to 2867. By 1860 Illinois possessed more railroad mileage than any other state in

---

[13] No study has been made of the Chicago and Alton. Scattered in the following books there is some material on this road and its effect upon the settlement of Illinois: Duis, *The Good Old Times in McLean County; History of McLean County;* Morehouse, *Life of Jesse W. Fell.*

the union except Ohio,[14] and Chicago, the terminus of eleven major lines, had become the railroad center of America.

The construction of so much mileage in a state so sparsely settled as was Illinois in the early 'fifties was a difficult task, owing to the lack of an adequate labor supply. The pioneer farmers showed little inclination to take part in the work and there was no mobile labor supply in the larger towns. Fortunately, during this period the immigration of Germans and Irish to the United States increased tremendously. These immigrants were looking for work and for land.[15] The Germans particularly, drawn as they were from the peasant class of their home country,[16] were attracted by the cheap lands of the West and went in large numbers to Illinois, Wisconsin, Iowa, and Missouri. Many of them were destitute and were only too glad of the opportunity offered them of working on the railroads. To them, however, such work was a means to an end. They only remained at it long enough to acquire sufficient capital to purchase land. The Irish, on the other hand, were drawn to the West by the promise of work and were not as anxious to take up farming. They generally worked as long as labor was required on a job and then moved on to the next sphere of operations. Of course some of the Irish laborers did settle on the land. This was especially true of the Irish workers on the Illinois and Michigan Canal. When funds for further construction gave out, the workers accepted scrip which rapidly depreciated in value. As the scrip was acceptable for canal lands at its face value, many of them purchased farms and settled on them.[17]

The Illinois Central did not begin construction until 1852, a

[14] *Eighth Census*, 1860, vol.: *Mortality and Miscellaneous Statistics*, p. 331.

[15] Kate Asaphine Everest, "How Wisconsin came by its large German Element," *Wisconsin Historical Society Collections* (1892), XII, 299–334.

[16] Marcus Lee Hansen, "Emigration from Continental Europe, 1815–1860, with Special Reference to the United States," 1924. This unpublished doctoral dissertation in Harvard College Library is not paged.

[17] Putnam, *op. cit.*, p. 71; W. J. Onahan, "Irish Settlements in Illinois," *Catholic World* (May, 1881), XXXIII, 157–162. The *Illinois State Register*, a paper friendly to the Irish, said that over three-fourths of those who had labored on the public works in the past twenty years had taken up homesteads. The statement that "A disposition to acquire land is notoriously peculiar to Irish character," appears to be somewhat exaggerated. *Register*, March 3, 1853.

year after its incorporation. By this time other roads were under way and had the advantage over it in the matter of possessing an adequate labor supply. Construction had been delayed by the fact that it was necessary for the Company not only to survey and establish its route but also to select its lands before construction could begin. Furthermore, the building of a line 700 miles in length by one corporation was an immense undertaking, unequalled in America at that time, and required a large capital investment. The hesitancy with which the Company's bonds were accepted in England and America likewise made for delay.[18] When construction was finally begun in earnest it was not on the main line but on that section of the branch from Chicago to Calumet that a start was made. The rivalry between the Michigan Central and the Michigan Southern, which has already been referred to, brought this about and hastened the construction of the Illinois Central.

The Michigan Central made its decision to build to Chicago in 1847, and thereafter the road was rapidly extended westward, reaching New Buffalo on Lake Michigan in 1849 and Michigan City in 1850.[19] The Michigan Southern was sold in 1846 to private promoters who were apparently possessed of less capital; [20] they started more slowly and did not reach La Porte, Indiana, until 1851.[21] Then began one of those great railroad struggles with which our western history has been so enlivened. Both roads were now straining every nerve to be the first to reach Chicago from the East, to tap its rich traffic and perhaps to prevent their rival from reaching that city at all. Both seemed to possess adequate capital, and neither was squeamish about the methods it employed. They fought each other in the courts, in the City Council of Chicago, in the local press, and in the Legislatures of Indiana and Illinois, and finally in actual physical combat.

By buying into local Indiana companies these roads secured the privilege of building to the Illinois line, where their progress was halted because they had no charters to enable them to proceed.

---

[18] Neal, Autobiography.
[19] Ibid.; Paxson, loc. cit., pp. 268–269.
[20] Journal of the Senate, Michigan, 1846, p. 465.
[21] Paxson, loc. cit., p. 256.

They succeeded in defeating each other's efforts to secure charters from the Illinois Legislature and to obtain from Chicago the right of entrance into that city. The next move of the two rivals was to attempt to make agreements with roads already building from Chicago by which they could secure trackage rights into the city. It was not surprising that the Michigan Central, some of the principal directors of which, as has been seen, were heavily interested in the Illinois Central, should turn to that company to secure entrance into Chicago. By the resulting secret agreement the Illinois Central undertook to deflect its line eastward to permit the Michigan Central to make connections with it and thereby reach Chicago.[22] The Michigan Southern, not to be outdone, made a somewhat similar agreement with the Rock Island Railroad by which the former was to use the latter's tracks into Chicago.

Chicago was at this time suffering from growing pains, and was extremely jealous of any attempt to advance the interests of any rival city at its expense. Chicago papers liked nothing better than to discuss the cholera epidemic in Detroit or St. Louis, the higher death rate of other towns or states, the unhealthy climate of Egypt, and the deep snow and rigorous winters of regions to the north. At the same time they were minimizing similar conditions in their own city. Residents of Chicago favored separate stations for every railroad in order that there might be more hack and inn business.[23] The city was particularly jealous of any attempt on the part of railroads to build around it from east to west in order to avoid entrance into it. Consequently, when it was rumored

[22] Brayman to Osborn, April 14, 1860, Brayman MSS. Brownson believed that the plan to extend the Illinois Central to the Indiana line was only a rumor, in spite of the fact that the "official" paper, the *Chicago Democrat*, had announced it. *History of the Illinois Central Railroad to 1870*, p. 49. As a matter of fact the Illinois Central had very definitely planned to deflect its line to the Indiana border and had made an agreement to this end with the Michigan Central. The fierce opposition of prominent citizens of Chicago forced it to change its plans. See the correspondence of R. B. Mason, the officials of the Michigan Central and of the Illinois Central and other documents in *Statements and Replies in Reference to the Compensation for the Use of the Road of the Illinois Central* (1860).

[23] Senator Morrison even went so far as to move an amendment to a bill to incorporate a road from the Indiana line to Chicago, to provide that every railroad which terminated in Chicago should occupy a distinct and separate depot. *Senate Journal*, 1851, p. 99. Cf. Pearson, *op. cit.*, pp. 48–49.

that the Illinois Central was planning to construct its line from Chicago to the Indiana line, where it would connect with the approaching Michigan Central, there was a great outcry. Chicago saw in this action a means by which the construction of one line and one station would be avoided. It was also feared that this connection and the proposed Joliet cut-off would cause it to lose a great deal of east-west traffic. Above all, Chicago was afraid that the point at which the Illinois Central proposed to effect a junction with the Michigan Central would develop into a rival city. Protest meetings were called, the City Council of Chicago appropriated $10,000 to fight the Illinois Central proposal, the services of Stephen A. Douglas — whose land interests would be adversely affected by the plan to deflect the route — were secured to bring pressure to bear upon the Company to change its plan, and an active press campaign was conducted.[24] The opposition to the plan became so bitter that it was abandoned, although the Illinois Central line was deflected eastward to a certain extent. The result of the whole affair was to enable the Michigan Southern to get to Chicago first. At the moment Chicago was kindly disposed towards the Rock Island Railroad and its ally the Michigan Southern. The city allowed the latter to build into its limits but refused entrance to the Michigan Central.[25]

The Illinois Central and its ally had not been dallying in the meantime. Though the former had definitely decided not to build to the Indiana line, it had retained its financial arrangements with the Michigan Central and was thus able to begin construction without waiting for its bond issue to be sold. The first contract for grading was made on March 15, 1852,[26] and a force of 700 men was placed upon this section of the line from Chicago to Calumet,[27] where the junction with the Michigan Central was to be effected. By May 21 the work was completed[28] and through connections between Chicago and the East were established.

[24] Brayman to Osborn, April 14, 1860, Brayman MSS.; *Chicago Journal*, March 17, 1852.

[25] Paxson, *loc. cit.*, p. 256. The Michigan Southern had train service to Chicago by February, 1852, but the first through train was in May of that year.

[26] *American Railway Times*, October 30, 1856.

[27] *Chicago Journal*, March 26, 1852.

[28] *American Railway Times*, October 30, 1856, says that the work was completed

As the charter of the Illinois Central provided that fifty miles of road should be completed within two years after the organization of the Company, the main line in four years, and the branch line in six years,[29] there was little time to be lost. As soon as the organization of the Company was completed,[30] surveying parties were sent out, and negotiations were commenced for securing the right-of-way where necessary.

A knotty question now presented itself in the location of the route. The considerations which would determine the route were the amount of government land available in the vicinity, the potential traffic which the various locations could be expected to provide, and the cost of constructing one route as compared with another. To choose a more populous route would diminish the amount of land which the Company would receive and increase the damages which would be required to secure the right-of-way. As the Company proposed to finance its construction wholly from the sale of bonds secured by a first mortgage on the lands, it was advisable to secure as large an allotment of lands as possible. Accordingly the route, as finally selected, was largely determined by the amount of government land in the vicinity, in so far as that was feasible.[31] Contrary to general expectations, it was decided that the branch line should diverge from the main line at a point 249 miles from Chicago instead of at some point between Decatur and Vandalia.[32] The grasping Shelbyville speculators found they had lost both the branch and the main line; Urbana advocates were unsuccessful in securing the road for their town; Freeport was substituted for Savannah, La Salle for Peru, and Kankakee for Bourbonnais. The branch line was to run almost entirely

on May 24 while the *American Railroad Journal*, August 3, 1861, and the *Chicago Democratic Press*, October 14, 1856, both state that this section was completed on May 15. R. B. Mason, engineer in charge of construction, gives some details on the work in a letter to C. C. P. Holden, October 12, 1883, in Andreas, *History of Chicago*, I, 253–255.     [29] *Charter*, pp. 22, 23.

[30] Ackerman, *Historical Sketch*, p. 20.

[31] Chapter on Illinois Central Railroad by C. C. P. Holden in Rufus Blanchard, *Discovery and Conquests of the Northwest with the History of Chicago*, II, 588. Holden, who was connected with the railroad almost from its beginning, was well able to write this brief chapter. He states that the shortness of the line was another important consideration.

[32] Mason to Holden, October 12, 1883, Andreas, *op. cit.*, I, 253.

through virgin territory, there being only a few settlements of no importance on it. The main line was to touch some towns of promise such as Jonesboro, Decatur, Bloomington, Dixon, Freeport, and Galena,[33] although for most of its distance it was to run through sparsely settled territory. After the route was selected, Neal, who was at this time in charge of affairs in Illinois, together with Roswell B. Mason, engineer in charge of construction, arranged with contractors for the construction of the entire line.

A large labor supply was needed to construct a railroad 700 miles in length, and it was planned to procure a force of 7000 to 12,000 men to work on the various sections.[34] This was not an easy task, as the available local supply of labor was already at work on other roads. Mason despairingly reported in April, 1853, that there were no men available in either St. Louis or Chicago, and although agents had been stationed at all points to secure men the force could not be much increased until additional help could be imported from the East.[35] Accordingly arrangements were made with immigration and labor agents in New York by which they were to secure and forward men to Illinois.[36] Special agents were likewise sent to New Orleans and New York to engage workers [37] and advertisements for laborers were inserted in the New York newspapers.[38] Furthermore, the contractors made arrangements with labor agents to furnish them with men. They were to receive $1 for every person furnished by them who remained a month.[39] These efforts were found to be inadequate to meet the demands.[40] The country was in the midst of one of its greatest periods of railroad expansion; thousands of miles were being built in the Northwest, and the cry for labor went up on all

[33] *Ibid.*, I, 253–254. See Jane Martin Johns, *Personal Recollections* (Decatur, 1912), p. 35, for the controversy over the route which was to be chosen in Macon County.

[34] *Illinois State Register*, April 29, 1851.

[35] Mason to Schuyler, April 22, 1853, M. O.

[36] Brayman to Schuyler, September 29, 1852, *ibid.*; Mason to Calhoun, December 29, 1852, green box, 63rd St.

[37] Mason to Holden, October 12, 1883, Andreas, *op. cit.*, I, 254.

[38] See advertisement for 500 to 1000 men to work on the Illinois Central at La Salle, in *New York Tribune*, June 2, 1852.

[39] Mason to Burrall, August 10, 1853, M. O.

[40] Same to same, May 8, 1853, *ibid.*

sides.[41] So acute became the labor shortage that some companies sent agents to Ireland to stimulate further immigration to Illinois.[42] One of the contractors on the Illinois Central sent directly to Ireland and there secured a large part of his crew of a thousand men.[43]

There were many counter attractions and many causes of friction which caused the laborers to give up their work for other things. For one thing, the western cities were growing rapidly and required large numbers of mechanics and artisans. Manual labor at $1.25 per day was far less remunerative than farming or the trades,[44] and could not long satisfy the frugal Scandinavian, the farm-loving Teuton, or the gregarious Celt. Epidemics were an important factor in increasing their discontent. In the years 1853, 1854, and 1855 cholera and the ague were prevalent in Illinois.[45] So dread was the former disease that when it appeared in a camp the force would immediately abandon work in a panic and flee.[46] So effectively did agents of other railroads and emigration agents of other states spread accounts of epidemics in Illinois that Mason reported it as a prevalent opinion in the East that a man could barely live more than six months in the State.[47] Difficulties over wages, kinds of specie, poor camp accommodations, improper food,[48] whiskey,[49] and Irish-German rivalry [50] were frequent, leading to riot, bloodshed, and murder. It was

[41] Paxson, *loc. cit.*, pp. 268 ff.; MacGill, *History of Transportation in the United States Before 1860*, plates 4 and 5 following p. 654.

[42] *Illinois State Register*, April 21, 1853.

[43] M. J. Mulvihill to the writer, March 16, 1927.

[44] The wages of common laborers on the Illinois Central ranged from $1 to $1.50 per day. There is much detail on the labor question in M. O. Such subjects as wages, strikes, competition between contractors for laborers, and sickness among the crews are treated in the material therein.

[45] B. F. Johnson to Perkins, September, 1855, and later, M. O.

[46] Burrall to Sturges, May 18, 1854, *ibid.* See also letters of Burrall to Sturges, June 22, 1854; Germain to Burrall, June 23, 1854; Mason to Sturges, August 8, 1854; *Galena Jeffersonian* quoted in *Chicago Democratic Press*, August 3, 1854. For a vivid picture of illness in railroad camps see Hans Mattson, *Reminiscences, The Story of an Emigrant*, pp. 29 ff.

[47] Mason to Burrall, May 8, 1853, M. O.

[48] *Illinois State Register*, December 22, 1853.

[49] Mason to Schuyler, April 19, 27, 1853, M. O.; *Illinois State Register*, December 22, 1853, January 5, 1854.

[50] Ashley to Schuyler, March 10, 1853, Mason to Burrall, August 6, 1854, M. O.; Johns, *op. cit.*, pp. 35–37.

stated, although with much exaggeration, that "a murder a mile" was committed on the Illinois Central.[51] Finally contractors stole men from each other by promises of higher wages or better living conditions.[52] The result was that there was a large labor turnover which necessitated recurring importations of new men. As the contractors on the Illinois Central required 10,000 or more men, it is easy to see how important labor importation by the railroad was in developing and settling Illinois.

David Neal had foreseen the importance of this factor, and in 1852 had stated in a prospectus that "One mode of increasing the population of the country will be the mass of laborers that must be introduced to build the road." [53] Neal pointed out that many laborers would bring their families to settle in the State and would in turn draw others who looked for profit from supplying the necessities of these laborers. Neal's error was on the side of moderation. He had estimated that a force of 4000 men would be sufficient to complete construction in the required time, but the contractors actually employed from 6000 to 10,000 men in the cooler months,[54] and would have engaged more had it been possible to obtain them.

When construction began most of the laborers were Irish, and they were important as a laboring force throughout. They were, however, a turbulent lot, fond of whiskey, prone to fight, and anything but docile. Their frequent outbreaks in riot and violence made them unpopular with the natives of Illinois,[55] and the high labor turnover among this racial group caused a great deal of annoyance and delay to the Illinois Central. The Company's agents therefore tried to secure men with families, as such men were more likely to be sober and industrious, to settle in the State,

[51] *Illinois Central Magazine* (August, 1926), xv, 60.

[52] Mason to Schuyler, April 19, 1853, M. O.

[53] *Documents Relating to the Organization of the Illinois Central Rail-Road Company* (New York, 1852), p. 83.

[54] Thus in the winter of 1852 and 1853 an average force of 6000 to 8000 men was maintained. *Annual Report*, Illinois Central, March 16, 1853. In July, 1853, over 10,000 were reported at work on the road. *St. Louis Intelligencer*, clipped in *Illinois State Register*, July 12, 1853. In 1854 the force was down to 7000 men and 2000 teams. *The Railroads, History, and Commerce of Chicago* (1854), p. 14.

[55] Johns, *op. cit.*, pp. 35-37.

# WANTED!
# 3,000 LABORERS
## On the 12th Division of the
## ILLINOIS CENTRAL RAILROAD

## Wages, $1.25 per Day.

## Fare, from New-York, only - - $4.75

By Railroad and Steamboat, to the work in the State of Illinois.

Constant employment for two years or more given. Good board can be obtained at two dollars per week.

This is a rare chance for persons to go West, being sure of permanent employment in a healthy climate, where land can be bought cheap, and for fertility is not surpassed in any part of the Union.

Men with families preferred.

For further information in regard to it, call at the Central Railroad Office,

# 173 BROADWAY,
## CORNER OF COURTLANDT ST.
## NEW-YORK.

## R. B. MASON, Chief Engineer.

H. PHELPS, Agent.

July, 1853.

ADVERTISEMENT FOR LABOR
(Reproduced from an original broadside in the archives of the Illinois Central Railroad)

and to take up lands from the Company.[56] Many of the Irish did, as a matter of fact, take up Illinois Central lands.[57] Even this policy did not enable the agents to maintain a constant supply of workers; they therefore turned to German immigrants, who were at this time landing on our shores in a more or less destitute condition. Although the Germans were less hardy and less suited to the rugged work required than the Irish, they were steadier and more docile,[58] and in the long run proved to be better adapted to the work. Realizing this, the agents worked strenuously in New York among the newly-arrived German immigrants to secure them for the Illinois Central. Arrangements were made with other railroads to transport them to Illinois for the sum of $4.75. High wages, constant employment, good board, a healthy climate, and cheap fertile land were promised them.[59] So attractive were these inducements that by 1853 the Illinois Central was able to secure large numbers of Germans for construction work.[60]

It is impossible to estimate accurately the number of immigrants who were brought to Illinois to work on the Illinois Central, but it does not seem an exaggeration to say that from 5000 to 10,000 men were sent to Illinois from 1852 to 1856 by the Company itself, by its labor agents, and by the agents of the contractors.[61] Many of these men simply added to the floating population

[56] Advertising bill of H. Phelps as in illustration. The bill is in M. O.

[57] Mulvihill to the writer, March 16, 1927. The tract books in the Land and Tax Commissioner's office, Central Station, indicate the purchase of many thousands of acres of land by Irishmen.

[58] Mason to Schuyler, April 3, 1853, M. O.; *Illinois State Register*, April 21, 1853. Cf. Johnson to Osborn, November 2, 1855, for expression by the owner of a large farm of a preference for Germans as farm laborers.

[59] Advertising bill of H. Phelps as in note 56, above.

[60] Mason reported to Schuyler on April 3, 1853, that 1200 Germans were being sent via New Orleans to Illinois and 250 more were on the way. Two weeks later Mason reported that he had an agreement with another agency to send a large number of Irish. Mason to Schuyler, April 18, 1853, M. O. Brownson says that the Illinois Central "was built almost entirely by Irish." Brownson, *op. cit.*, p. 60. His error was apparently caused by a too close dependence on the newspapers which, at this time, were attempting to curry favor with the Irish for political reasons. A subsequent writer has stated that mainly Germans were employed by the Illinois Central on construction work in the vicinity of Macon County. N. M. Baker, "The Pioneers of Macon County," Illinois State Historical Society, *Journal* (1921), XIV, 102.

[61] It is apparent that the Illinois Central had to draw most of its labor supply from the East. Mason to Schuyler, April 22, 1853, M. O. The New York agent had

and did not remain long in the State. On the other hand, there is much evidence to show that many of the laborers settled on the land and became successful farmers. This was particularly true of the Germans, who more frequently than the Irish brought their families with them with the idea of establishing permanent homes.[62]

The road itself was pushed as rapidly as circumstances would permit. It was divided into twelve sections, on all of which actual work was begun in 1852.[63] By 1855 the main line was completed and the Chicago branch was finished as far south as Mattoon.[64] The stretch from Mattoon to Sandoval was through a particularly unhealthy region, part of which was swampy and poorly drained. Here malignant fever and cholera were prevalent and only in the cooler months could work be carried on.[65] However, by the use of a large force in the proper season the work was rushed forward, and on September 21, 1856, the branch line was connected with the main road and the longest railroad yet projected in the United States was completed.[66]

sent out at least 600 men in 1852. Brayman to Schuyler, September 29, 1852, *ibid.* During the winter of 1852 and 1853 there was an average of 6000 to 8000 men at work on the railroad. *Annual Report,* 1853. So rapidly did the men leave that Mason was constantly seeking additional help. 1450 Germans were sent out by April 3, 1853, and in July 3000 additional men were advertised for in New York. Even these efforts proved insufficient. Constant complaints were made of the difficulties of securing an adequate labor supply. Thus Mason wrote to Schuyler on April 19, 1853, that there were not half enough men in McLean County to do the work then in progress. Cf. Mason to Schuyler, April 22, 1853; Lewis Broad to Mason, May 19, 1856; Mason to Osborn, May 22, 1856, M. O.; *Annual Reports,* 1853, 1854.

[62] Ashley to Schuyler, March 10, 1853; *Illinois State Register,* March 31, 1853.

[63] *Annual Report,* 1853.

[64] *Chicago Democratic Press,* October 14, 1856; *American Railroad Journal,* August 3, 1862, p. 562.

[65] *Railway Times,* XVII, 1260. In a neighboring town the cholera was so fatal that 200 out of a total population of 1600 died of it. B. F. Johnson to Osborn, August 15, 1855, M. O.

[66] *Chicago Democratic Press,* October 3, 1856.

# CHAPTER VI

## LAND SPECULATION

THE Illinois Central Railroad was only one of the large holders of land who were desirous of selling it on advantageous terms during the period from 1850 to 1870. There were many others, public and private, and the story of the disposal of the Illinois Central grant is profoundly influenced by their competition. In order to put the account of the sale of the Illinois Central lands in its proper setting it is necessary in this chapter to consider what those land-distributing agencies were doing and by what means large tracts of government land had passed into their hands.

Speculators were able to acquire extensive holdings in Illinois as a result of the military bounty land acts. These measures, passed in 1811 and 1812, granted to soldiers of the War of 1812 and of previous wars 3,500,000 acres in the Military Tract between the Illinois and Mississippi Rivers, most of which passed into the hands of members of Congress, high officials in the Army, and other large speculators.[1] The policy of rewarding soldiers by making them grants of land in the western states was resumed at the outbreak of the Mexican War on a much more generous scale than in the earlier period. On February 11, 1847, Congress enacted that all privates and non-commissioned officers who served in the Mexican War for a period of not less than twelve months should receive a warrant for 160 acres of government land, to be located anywhere in the surveyed areas of the public domain.[2] The Act of September 28, 1850, extended this provision to include all persons who had fought in the War of 1812 or in any Indian Wars since 1790 and all commissioned officers in the Mexican

---

[1] Acts of December 24, 1811; January 11 and February 6, 1812. 2 *U. S. Stat.* 669–670, 671–674, 676–677. Over 840,000 acres passed into the hands of congressmen. Holdings of 100,000 acres were not uncommon; twenty-five men together owned 558,000 acres. *House Executive Documents*, 26th Cong., 1st Sess., 1840, vol. VII, doc. 262.

[2] 9 *U. S. Stat.*, 123–126. Treasury scrip of $100 at 6 per cent interest could be chosen in place of the land warrant.

War.[3] A further extension of this liberal policy was made by the Act of March 22, 1852, according to which all officers of militia, volunteers, and others who had served in the pay of the Federal Government in connection with the recent wars were likewise to receive warrants.[4] The last of these bounty acts, approved on March 3, 1855, was the most extensive of all, but was passed after most of the Illinois land had been disposed of and so needs no discussion here.[5]

Although the land warrants issued under these acts were not made assignable until 1852, speculators were able to circumvent the intentions of Congress as easily as they had evaded the provisions of the similar military bounty acts of 1811 and 1812.[6] Perhaps this was the only practical thing to do, as many of the 551,193 ex-soldiers or heirs and their families would have found it inexpedient to go west to take up their lands.[7] At any rate the warrants soon appeared on the eastern markets, where they were quoted at prices ranging from 50 cents to $1.15 an acre.[8] They were purchased by speculators who used them to locate large blocks of land in Illinois and other public land states. More than one-fourth of the entire area of Illinois was taken up in this way, five to six million acres being located by warrants between 1847 and 1855.[9] After the passage of the land grant the lands along the line of the Illinois Central were not subject to location by these warrants, except for the payment of $1.25 an acre in addition to the land warrant.[10] Beyond the six-mile limit, however, there

[3] *Ibid.*, 520–521. By this act the amount of land receivable ranged from 40 to 160 acres according to the length of service of the recipient.

[4] 10 *U. S. Stat.*, 3–4.

[5] *Ibid.*, 701–702. Under this act of 1855 more than twice as much land was located as under the first three acts. Thomas Donaldson, *The Public Domain* (Washington, 1884), pp. 236–237.

[6] Benjamin Horace Hibbard, *History of the Public Land Policies* (New York, 1924), has a chapter on bounty lands.

[7] Donaldson, *op. cit.*, pp. 236–237.

[8] *New York Tribune*, February 5, 17, March 11, 29, 1852; *Freeport Journal*, May 23, 1856.

[9] A total of 8,745,930 acres was listed under "Grants for military services" to June 30, 1853. *Annual Report*, Commissioner of the General Land Office, 1853, p. 108.

[10] *Annual Report*, Commissioner of the General Land Office, 1851, p. 4, states that lands within 6 miles of the line of the Illinois Central were not subject to loca-

were no restrictions, and many large holdings were established by this means within close range of the Company's line.

The use of land warrants gave the large purchaser a distinct advantage over the small farmer seeking 80 or 160 acres. The large purchaser would be considered first by the registers and receivers of the land offices because the location of a large block of land could be accomplished more expeditiously than the location of many small lots and would involve fees commensurate with the size of the purchase. Furthermore, the land could be secured by warrants for 50 cents to $1 an acre, while the small purchaser, who had no means of securing a warrant, must perforce pay the Government $1.25 for his purchase. As a result of this situation, according to the constant complaint of Illinois politicians, newspapers, and residents, many prospective settlers were prevented from acquiring lands and were forced to go farther west, where they could be purchased more cheaply.[11]

From the beginning of the century the Federal Government had been turning over to Illinois lands within the State in a generous fashion. It had granted 500,000 acres for internal improvements, 46,000 acres for a seminary, 121,000 acres of salt spring and contiguous land, and 996,000 acres for the support of common schools.[12] In addition to the general grant of 500,000 acres for internal improvements, which included a specific grant of nearly 300,000 acres to aid in constructing the Illinois and Michigan Canal, the State received 2,595,000 acres for the central railroad.

The Swamp Land Act of September 28, 1850, which granted to the states the overflowed or swamp lands within their borders,[13] further hastened the final disposal of the government lands in Illinois. By this act a total of 1,457,399 acres was given to the

tion by land warrants. Apparently a modification was made later, as noted above, for which see *Annual Report*, Secretary of Interior, *House Executive Documents*, 33rd Cong., 2nd Sess., 1854–1855, vol. I, part 1, pp. 85–86.

[11] R. McClelland, Secretary of Interior, December 5, 1853, *Senate Executive Documents*, 33rd Cong., 1st Sess., 1853–1854, vol. I, p. 53; Richard Yates in *Congressional Globe*, 33rd Cong., 1st Sess., p. 505; *Chicago Democrat*, clipped in *Illinois State Register*, May 25, 1854; *Country Gentleman* (November 15, 1855), VI, 320; *Prairie Farmer*, June 11, 1857; James Caird, *Letter on the Lands of the Illinois Central Railway Company* (London, 1859), p. 5.

[12] *Annual Report*, Commissioner of the General Land Office, 1918, p. 88.

[13] 9 *U. S. Stat.*, 519–520.

State.[14] Illinois, in turn, granted these lands to the counties in which they were located "for the purpose of constructing the necessary levees and drains to reclaim the same, and the balance of said lands . . . shall be distributed in each county, equally, among the townships thereof, for the purposes of education, or the same may be applied to the construction of roads and bridges, or to such other purposes as may be deemed expedient. . . ." [15] The act required that the lands should be valued at not less than 10 cents per acre. The ostensible purpose of both the federal and State grants was to secure the drainage of the lands, but this was in no way carried out; it is more likely that the supporters of the bills were seeking only an additional method of liberalizing the federal land policy and of turning the lands over to the states and eventually to settlers and speculators at low prices. Many of these lands were actually sold for as little as 10 cents per acre,[16] and the proceeds were used for various purposes, though generally for schools.[17] Very little use was made of them to carry out the original purpose of the grant, to assist in draining low areas.[18]

The last act in this series of measures which hastened the transfer of government lands in Illinois into private hands was Thomas Hart Benton's pet measure, the Graduation Act of August 4, 1854.[19] This bill provided that government lands which had been on the market from 10 to 15 years should be sold for $1 an acre; lands on the market 15 to 20 years were to be sold for 75 cents an acre; lands on the market 20 to 25 years were to be sold for 50 cents an acre; lands on the market 25 to 30 years were to be sold for 25 cents an acre; and lands on the market over 30 years were to be sold for 12½ cents an acre. Although only a limited amount of graduation land could be legally acquired by any one person, it

[14] *Annual Report*, Commissioner of the General Land Office, 1925, p. 48.

[15] Act of June 22, 1852, *Laws of Illinois*, 1852, pp. 178–186.

[16] Gen. John Tillson, *History of the City of Quincy, Illinois* (Chicago), p. 100.

[17] Milo Erwin, *History of Williamson County, Illinois* . . . (Marion, Illinois, 1876), p. 247.

[18] There was also a great deal of shady work in connection with the selection of these lands, particularly in Illinois. See *Annual Report*, Commissioner of the General Land Office, 1886, p. 42.

[19] 10 *U. S. Stat.*, 574. Lands within the fifteen-mile indemnity area were not subject to this measure. *House Executive Documents*, 34th Cong., 1st Sess., 1855–1856, vol. v, doc. 13, p. 36.

was, as usual, fairly easy to avoid this restriction by the use of dummy purchasers.[20] Much of the land which was available under the Graduation Act was snapped up by local speculators who saw a chance to add to their holdings at a small cost.[21] The total graduation sales in Illinois, according to the price per acre, from the passage of the Act to June 30, 1856, were as follows:[22]

| Price per acre | No. of acres |
|---|---|
| $1.00 | 7,847 |
| .75 | 24,683 |
| .50 | 52,504 |
| .25 | 61,689 |
| .12½ | 736,107 |
| Total graduation sales | 882,830 |

As a result of this series of liberal land laws and of the extensive railroad mileage under construction in Illinois in the 'fifties, land sales and locations in the State assumed large proportions. A scramble for choice locations occurred, comparable only to the mad rush for lands in the 'thirties, and the land offices were so crowded that the officials were unable to handle the business. The entire State was in the grip of a speculative craze, and each of the land offices felt its effects, but the greatest enthusiasm was shown along the line of the Illinois Central.[23]

The Illinois Central Railroad was built through a less developed region than any of the other railroads, and consequently it did more than they to open up new regions to settlement, to develop the agriculture and industries of the State, and to hasten the sales of government land, especially in the region through which it ran. Even before the construction of the road was completed, it was reported that a large number of settlers were moving into its vicinity and that there was great activity in land sales on the part of the government agents and private speculators. The *St. Louis Times*

[20] By subsequent interpretation of the law the limitation upon the amount of land an individual could secure under its provisions was practically removed.

[21] Letters to Lyman Trumbull from D. P. Roberts, Kaskaskia, April 6; R. C. Mann, Randolph County, April 7; Amos C. Babcock, Canton, April 16, 1856, and W. H. Sweet to Wm. H. Seward, April 22, 1856, Trumbull MSS.

[22] Compiled from *Annual Reports*, Commissioner of the General Land Office, 1855, 1856.

[23] *Home Missionary* (December, 1852), xxv, 190; *Annual Report*, Commissioner of the General Land Office, 1852.

declared in 1851, "The emigration into Illinois is immense this season. There are some in every county of the state, but the middle and northern portions are overrun with men in search of new homes." [24] Governor Matteson, in his inaugural address of January 10, 1853, called the attention of the Legislature to the salutary effects of the construction of the Illinois Central, saying, "The line of the road is beginning to fill up with hardy and enterprising settlers." [25] An observer in Montgomery County wrote in the same year, "Emigration is constantly pouring in from every direction, filling up our town and county in a ratio never before equalled, since the settlement of the country." [26] From Stephenson County, in northern Illinois, it was reported in 1853,[27]

Immigrants of a new class are making their appearance on each side of the line of the road — men of character and influence, with means to pay well the original pioneers for their toils and hardships. Landed property has rapidly advanced within the past year, so that lots, which two years ago were eagerly seeking purchasers at almost any price, are now eagerly bought up at from five to ten dollars per acre.

Especially popular was the newly opened region south of Chicago on the Grand Prairie. In March, 1854, it was observed that immigration was pouring in, especially into Kankakee County.[28] Even the Commissioner of the General Land Office called attention to "the greatest anxiety which was manifested to obtain lands along the road, even at enhanced prices." [29]

In the Danville land district, where the largest body of government land in the State was situated, the effect of the construction of the road was particularly apparent. Of the 4,931,334 acres in this district only 918,365 had been sold by 1850.[30] When the railroad reached this region in 1853 and 1854, the sales of govern-

[24] Quoted in *Illinois State Register*, May 8, 1851.

[25] *Illinois Reports*, 1853, p. 6 (18).

[26] *Hillsboro Mirror*, quoted in *Illinois State Register*, March 31, 1853. Cf. *Home Missionary* (July, 1852), xxv, 69–70.

[27] *Ibid.* (December, 1853), xxvi, 190–191, report of J. N. Powell of Winslow. See also report of J. H. Russ of Effingham County, in *ibid.* (December, 1852), xxv, 190. Russ reported that a large number of Germans were coming into the vicinity.

[28] XYZ in *Chicago Weekly Democrat*, March 25, 1854.

[29] *Senate Executive Documents*, 32nd Cong., 2nd Sess., 1852–1853, vol. i, No. 1, p. 78.

[30] Biennial Report, Illinois Treasurer, *Illinois Documents*, 1851, p. 45.

ment land increased tremendously, so that they became larger than were the sales in any other district in the State. During the short space of five months nearly half a million acres were disposed of for cash or land warrants in this district,[31] and between 1852 and 1854 721,001 acres within fifteen miles of the Illinois Central were sold or located with land warrants.[32] Sales were also stimulated in the Edwardsville land district, which had been opened much longer than the Danville district. Between the passage of the land grant bill in September, 1850, and March, 1851, a total of 80,409 acres were sold or located with land warrants.[33]

Sales and locations in the two southernmost districts, Shawneetown and Kaskaskia, likewise increased greatly between 1850 and 1855. In these districts was located the largest amount of land available under the Graduation Act, and there was a great scramble to secure it. As many as 600 applicants were reported as standing in line at one time at the Shawneetown office to make their entries. Officers were unable to make out the papers, so great was the rush, and only applications and descriptions of the land could be taken. It was found that in the resulting confusion two or more persons had applied for the same land, and many such cases were later contested.[34]

It has frequently been said that the demand for government lands in the vicinity of the Illinois Central became so keen that the Government received greatly enhanced prices for its remaining sections. The story goes that prices were bid up as high as $5 to $10 an acre, and that the average price received was well over the double minimum for which the lands had been reserved. It has even been asserted that the prices received more than compensated the Government for the lands which it had granted to aid in the construction of the railroad. This, in fact, had been one of the chief arguments in favor of the land grant bill and the one which had been most plausibly offered by the strict constructionists to explain their *volte face* on the measure. Practically all writers on

---

[31] *Illinois State Register*, October 25, 1853.
[32] *Annual Report*, Commissioner of the General Land Office, 1854, pp. 85–86.
[33] *Alton Telegraph*, quoted in *Chicago Democrat*, April 15, 1851.
[34] *Chicago Journal*, April 24, 1854; *Chicago Weekly Democrat*, August 5, 1854; *Springfield Journal*, quoted in *Freeport Journal*, June 28, 1856.

the Illinois Central have maintained that this expectation was fulfilled. As early as 1852 a writer in the *Economist* declared that the Government stood to gain $9,000,000 by its grant in aid of the railroad, through the enhanced prices it was then receiving for its lands.[35] This error has been fostered by an ex-president of the Illinois Central, William K. Ackerman, in *An Historical Sketch of the Illinois Central Railroad* (1890), which he prepared and in which he states that a large proportion of the reserved sections were sold at prices ranging from $2.50 to $5 an acre.[36] The statement is certainly true with respect to the reserved sections within the six-mile limit; they were all to sell at a minimum price of $2.50 an acre, but as we shall see, few of them sold for much more than this. The story begun in this way has been repeated by subsequent writers without substantial verification.[37] A study of the records of the public land offices of Illinois leads to the conclusion that there is little truth in this statement, which has been so often repeated.

In the first place, as mentioned before, more land was being located with military land warrants after 1850 than was being sold for cash, and this, of course, tended to reduce the average payment in excess of the minimum price. At first warrants could not be used to locate lands within six miles of the route of the Illinois Central, but a later interpretation permitted location by warrants if an additional $1.25 was paid to provide for the double minimum price. Many thousand acres of land were located in this way within the six-mile limit as well as within the fifteen-mile indemnity area.[38] Secondly, there was much collusion between bidders for land, whose purpose was to keep the price down. The large buyers of land would get together before an auction took place, agree upon a division of the lands, and agree also to refrain

[35] *New York Tribune*, October 19, 1852, quoting the *Economist*.

[36] P. 75. Ackerman included this story in *Early Illinois Railroads* (*Fergus Historical Series*, No. 23), p. 37.

[37] Davidson and Stuvé actually claim that the average price which the Government received for the remaining sections was $5 an acre. See their *Complete History of Illinois from 1673 to 1873* (Springfield, 1874), p. 572. A more recent writer says that "the government lost nothing by giving half the land away." Brownson, *op. cit.*, p. 158.

[38] Separate books were kept in the land offices for warrant locations and are now in S. A. O.

from bidding against each other. A notorious example of this sort occurred in the Danville land office in 1854. According to an interested observer,[39]

All choice lands had long since been entered . . . and here the stragling (*sic*) speculators had all congregated, waiting for the office to open that they might seize upon the last acre worth taking. . . . When I arrived in Danville I was told by the Register that probably most of the lands that appeared from the plats to be vacant, had been applied for. . . . These strange applications had been made, it seems, by few individuals and were designed to cover all the unsold lands of any value and by mutual understanding between the operators were so arranged as not to conflict with each other. . . . With the sacred validity the officers attached to their papers, it was evident, that practically these few speculators had & could keep control of all the unsold lands in the district.

The *Chicago Journal* went so far as to accuse Dr. Moloney, who was in charge of the Danville office, of favoring speculators in preference to legitimate settlers.[40] Somewhat later it was reported that there was a large number of bidders for land in this district but that a combination of buyers had been successful in keeping the prices down.[41] Just how widespread such agreements were it is impossible to determine, but from a study of the records it seems safe to say that they were very common.

In the third place, there were only 1,223,921 acres left in the possession of the Government within the six-mile limit after the Illinois Central had selected its lands.[42] In order to secure a sum sufficient to compensate the Government for the grant of 2,595,-000 acres to the railroad, it would have been necessary to sell these remaining lands for approximately $4 per acre. No such price was obtained except in rare instances. The record books show sale after sale to large speculators of lands within the six-mile limit at the double minimum or two or three cents over. For example, Isaac Funk, a large holder of land in McLean County, purchased a considerable quantity of land within six miles of the Illinois Central, most of which was secured for the double minimum. For

[39] E. S. Prescott, Land Commissioner of the Illinois and Michigan Canal, to W. H. Swift, November 13, 1854, Swift MSS.

[40] *Chicago Journal*, May 10, 1854.

[41] *Chicago Daily Democratic Press*, January 7, 1857.

[42] *Annual Report*, Commissioner of the General Land Office, 1852, p. 109.

only a small amount was as much as $2.56 an acre paid.[43] Numerous examples of a like nature could be given, but perhaps the average price received for a considerable proportion of this land within the six-mile limit will show best how incorrect the story is. From July, 1852, when the lands in the vicinity of the Illinois Central Railroad were again offered for sale, to September 30, 1854, the Government sold 434,473 acres within the six-mile area for an average price of $2.54 an acre, while 341,216 acres were located with warrants together with additional payments of $430,075, representing a premium above the double minimum of slightly over 1 cent an acre.[44] These lands were among the best which the Government possessed in Illinois. It is thus evident that the double minimum was exceeded by only a few cents.

The joker in the bill was that the double minimum price applied only to the six-mile area. If it had likewise been applied to the large block of unsold government land between the six-mile and fifteen-mile limits, the Government might have profited to a considerable extent. On little of this land, however, did it receive anything more than the bare minimum price of $1.25 per acre.

From this study it seems clear that the alleged constitutional basis upon which the land grant bill rested was a rationalization to enable members of Congress to support a bill which their strict constructionist views made it difficult for them to countenance. It is likewise clear that writers upon the subject are in no way justified in their claim that the Government profited from the grant by the enhanced prices it received for its remaining lands. On the other hand, it is true that the construction of the Illinois Central did give a great impetus to the sale of the remaining government lands in Illinois, as has been shown, and led to their rapid disposal.

Of the 14,063,308 acres which the Government possessed in Illinois in 1849, there remained less than 100,000 at the opening of 1857.[45] Consequently the government land offices in the State were closed one by one. According to law, when a land district

---

[43] "Register of Receipts," 1841–1853, Danville land office, S. A. O.
[44] *Annual Report*, Commissioner of the General Land Office, 1854, pp. 85–86.
[45] *Chicago Daily Democratic Press*, January 7, 1857.

had less than 100,000 acres remaining, the office was to be closed and the books removed to another district which still contained a considerable amount of unsold land.[46] The first office to close in Illinois in accordance with this law was, it may be noted, the last one to open, namely the Chicago office. This was due in large measure to the influence which the Illinois and Michigan Canal and the railroads had exercised in this section. The closing of the Chicago office in July, 1855, was followed in the same year by the closing of the Dixon, Edwardsville, Palestine, and Quincy offices, and in the following year by the closing of the others with the exception of that at Springfield, which remained opened until 1877 [47] to take care of the small quantity of land still unsold, practically all of which was of little value.

It is now necessary to consider to whom the land was sold, how much of it went into the hands of speculators, and what efforts they made to resell the land they had obtained. Between 1849 and 1856, 12,000,000 of the 14,000,000 acres remaining of the public domain in Illinois were disposed of to two classes of purchasers, settlers and speculators. It seems fair to say that at least 6,000,-000 acres of this amount passed into the hands of speculators. This figure has been arrived at as follows: By 1856 the public domain in Illinois was practically extinguished. As the average annual amount of land going into farms in the decade of the 'fifties was 800,000 acres, it may be estimated that 5,600,000 acres were taken up by farmers between 1849 and 1856. This leaves at least 6,000,000 acres which must have gone into the hands of speculators. That the activity of speculators was on a sufficient scale to attract the attention of contemporaries is attested by the remarks of Richard Yates, who, speaking in the House of Representatives, declared that he believed over 2,500,000 of the 2,807,981 acres of land disposed of in Illinois in the year ending June 30, 1853, had gone to speculators.[48]

It is essential for a proper understanding of the role of the speculator in the history of Illinois to study in detail the activities

---

[46] *Annual Report*, Commissioner of the General Land Office, 1855, pp. 155–156.
[47] Donaldson, *op. cit.*, p. 174.
[48] *Congressional Globe*, 33rd Cong., 1st Sess., 1853–1854, p. 505.

of some of the important members of this class, which as a whole held in 1856 more than 15,000,000 acres of land in the State.[49]

Four distinct types of speculators may be distinguished. First and most numerous was the class of small farmers who purchased more land than they could reasonably hope to utilize for many years. Their purpose in buying this surplus land was partly to enlarge their farms, partly to reap the reward of enhanced prices, and partly in the hope, characteristic of the westerner, that a turn of good fortune would enable them to expand their activities and employ others. Second, there was a group of small businessmen, bankers, editors, judges, lawyers, politicians, and government officials who invested money in land on the side. In this group was to be found practically every prominent politician in Illinois with the exception of Lincoln. Altogether the holdings of politicians ran into many thousands of acres, and too frequently they were motivated by considerations touching the value of their lands. On the whole this class of speculators was less important than the third type, the professional speculator. This person, possessed of sufficient capital to operate on a large scale, purchased huge tracts of land at minimum prices or located them with land warrants secured for one-half or more of their presentation value at the land offices. The lands might be held by individuals or by corporations, which advertised extensively in the newspapers, maintained local agents, and perhaps owned land in several states. Finally, there was the eastern capitalist who wanted to take a flyer in western lands and purchased a few thousand acres which he planned to retain until a rise in their market value enabled him to make a good profit. Each of these types of speculators was represented in Illinois from 1848 to 1860, although frequently they shaded into one another so that it is not always easy to distinguish them.

The importance of the farmer-speculator is obvious from the fact that in 1850 approximately 7,000,000 acres of unimproved lands were entered in the census statistics as farm lands.[50] In 1860 the amount was 7,815,615.[51] A certain percentage of this

[49] Below, p. 111.     [50] *Seventh Census*, 1850, p. 729.
[51] *Eighth Census*, 1860, volume *Agriculture*, pp. 30-34.

land was used for pasturage or kept for timber, but most of it was held for speculative purposes. The farmer-speculator received much less criticism from contemporaries than did the men who were operating in the land business on a larger scale, and his excess holdings were not regarded with the disfavor that was shown the absentee speculator. Yet the farmer-speculator did not escape unnoticed. A correspondent of the *Prairie Farmer* deplored the "great error" made by most farmers who sacrificed almost everything to secure a large acreage but who thought little of improving the lands. He remarked that by overpurchasing they frequently became too deeply involved and found themselves unable to meet their payments, and that subsequently they had to give up all or a large part of their land.[52] It is not, however, the surplus lands held by the small farmers that interest us here, since their lands were gradually improved, subdivided among their families, or slowly sold off in small quantities. It is the holdings of the large speculators which merit our extended attention.

It seems safe to say that in 1856 9,000,000 acres of land in Illinois were in the hands of the other three classes of speculators. This figure has been computed as follows: If the 20,911,989 acres of improved and unimproved farm land in 1860 are subtracted from the total area of the State, 35,867,520 acres, there remain over 14,000,000 acres, of which at least 11,500,000 were suitable for agricultural purposes.[53] Since the public domain was practically extinguished in 1856, this 11,500,000 must have been held by speculators, or at least all but that portion owned by the Illinois Central and the State. As 2,500,000 acres will more than cover the amount of land still in the possession of the State and the railroad,[54] the remaining 9,000,000 acres seems a conservative estimate of the amount of land held by politicians and small businessmen, eastern capitalists, and professional speculators. We shall discuss the activities of each of these three classes in turn.

Representative of the second class of speculators was Stephen

[52] *Prairie Farmer*, January 13, 1860. See also correspondence from Dement, Illinois, in *New York Tribune*, August 24, 1858.

[53] *Thirteenth Census*, 1910, VI, 412.

[54] The Illinois Central had approximately 2,000,000 acres of land remaining unsold at the opening of 1856. *Annual Report*, Illinois Central Railroad, 1856.

A. Douglas. Though acting on a small scale, he was one of the most astute speculator-politicians in Illinois. His foresight is evident from his choice of locations — in and around Chicago. There he secured some fine lots on the lake front amounting to 100 acres.[55] Subsequently he purchased 2964 acres of land around Lake Calumet, paying $2.50 per acre.[56] In 1855 he added to his land investments by contracting with the Illinois Central at the price of $10 an acre for 4610 acres lying in the neighborhood of his previous holdings.[57] Large profits came to him from the sale of his Chicago lots, which greatly assisted him in financing the lavish expenses of his campaign in 1858.[58]

Douglas's colleague in Congress, John Wentworth, was likewise heavily interested in real estate in northern Illinois, especially in Chicago lots. He owned five parcels of valuable Chicago property, amounting to over 120 acres,[59] and several thousand acres along the Illinois and Michigan Canal.[60] Other prominent politicians who were interested in lands were Governor French, who secured 3840 acres in the Vandalia district with land warrants; David Davis, later Justice of the Supreme Court of the United States; Governor Bissell, who located 11,440 acres; Colonel "Don" Morrison, Stephen Logan, and Robert Smith.[61] This list could be greatly extended, but these persons seem to be fairly typical and indicate sufficiently how common the practice of land speculating was among politicians. For editors, one might mention John S. Wright, reaper-manufacturer, editor of the *Prairie Farmer*, Chicago booster, and real estate promoter.[62]

[55] "New Map of Chicago . . .," published by Hall & Co., October, 1855, Map Room, Harvard College Library. See also map in vol. 259, Land and Tax Commissioner's office, Central Station, Chicago. This map indicates that one lot extended from the present 22nd St. to 25th St., and the second lot from 33rd St. to 35th St.

[56] "Register of Receipts," Chicago district, No. 4, 1846–55; Tract Books, S. A. O.

[57] Vol. 262, Land and Tax Commissioner's office, Central Station; Osborn to Perkins, May 12, 1855, M. O.

[58] 100 acres were sold in 1856 for between $90,000 and $100,000. James W. Sheahan, *Life of Stephen A. Douglas* (New York, 1860), pp. 442–443; Johnson, *Stephen A. Douglas*, p. 309.     [59] Map as in note 55.

[60] E. S. Prescott to David Leavitt, September 26, 1853, Swift MSS.; "Register of Receipts," Chicago district, No. iv, 1846–1855; *Chicago Democrat*, May 12, 1851.

[61] Compiled from land office records.

[62] Wright's activities are discussed in his own book, *Chicago: Past, Present, Future* (Chicago, 1868).

The men employed in the government land offices had great advantages in securing land, for they knew better than anyone else the location, the kind of land, its accessibility, and thus its actual and potential value. Frequently they acquired large amounts of land, and there was some justification for the suspicion which rested on them of engaging in illegal practices or of collusion with speculators. Perhaps the most successful person in this group was John Dement, Receiver of the Dixon land office, who between the years 1849 and 1855 purchased, by cash or warrants, 90,670 acres in his district, while his brother located 53,200 acres.[63]

This large group of persons interested in speculation as a side issue comprised, perhaps, the most influential part of the population. Frequently, as in the case of Douglas, their land interests were subordinate to their political ambitions. This did not mean, however, that they did not seek special legislation for the benefit of their lands. It was they who sought to carry the Illinois Central and other railroads through out-of-the-way places. Moreover, they frequently made logrolling arrangements for their respective pet measures. As for their lands in general, they did little to improve them, nor were they able to advertise extensively or otherwise put their holdings before the public. Consequently the lands were on their hands for a longer period of time than were those owned by more active speculators. The taxes upon these holdings mounted rapidly and led to many forced sales. The Panic of 1857 obliged many members of this class to disgorge their holdings and thereby caused much financial suffering. On the whole, the interests of this group in land had a retarding effect upon the development of Illinois, except so far as they induced support of State and federal aid for various projects.

Turning to the third type, the professional speculator, we have a much more dynamic individual to consider. The man with capital secured large quantities of soldiers' land warrants at minimum prices, with which he located great tracts of land. He was not content to let immigration flow naturally into his territory, but expended his energies in arousing interest in the region in which his lands were located and in directing immigration toward it.

[63] Compiled from the record books of the Dixon land office.

His prices were too high for the poorer immigrants, but the more substantial foreigner or easterner with sufficient capital to pay a fair rate was induced to purchase. The result was that his lands were taken up by a better class of farmers. The promoter had no use for squatters or the shiftless pioneer farmers so common in southern Illinois, and made short work of them when public opinion permitted. As a result of his aggressive action, he frequently aroused the opposition of the natives as well as of his purchasers. They, in turn, had effective weapons to employ against him. His taxes and valuations were increased, his timber was stolen, and various kinds of unfavorable local regulations were directed against him.[64] This had the effect of causing him to close out his lands more rapidly or to transfer them to a local man. The activities of these speculators are interesting, and are important enough to warrant considerable attention — none more so than those of Solomon Sturges.

In 1836 or 1837 Sturges purchased Revolutionary bounty land warrants of the State of Virginia, for which Congress had authorized the issue of scrip receivable for any United States lands open for entry. With the scrip he was able to locate lands for much less than the minimum price of $1.25 per acre. In this way he acquired a large quantity of choice lands in Illinois and other western states, and continued to add to his holdings until they totalled over 100,000 acres. In the early 'fifties Sturges shrewdly selected 65,000 acres in the Danville district, most of which was rich prairie land that would be exceedingly valuable as soon as the Illinois Central was built.[65] He did not limit his activities to Illi-

---

[64] The Scully estate in Logan County has been the special object of unfavorable regulations and legislation. See N. S. B. Gras, *History of Agriculture in Europe and America* (New York, 1925), pp. 269–272.

[65] The material for this paragraph and the following quotation are taken from an advertisement inserted by Sturges in the *Prairie Farmer*, May 20, 1858, and from the books of the Danville land office. Sturges possessed in 1858 9300 acres in Iroquois County, 7200 in Vermilion, 36,000 in Livingston, 2900 in McLean, and 1280 in Woodford, besides a few thousand acres in Gallatin, Lawrence, Jasper, Moultrie, Logan, and Coles Counties. He also held 9000 acres in Missouri, 3000 in Michigan, 8000 in Ohio, and 33,000 in Indiana. Sturges and his partner built the first great grain elevator in Chicago, on land leased from the Illinois Central. It had a capacity of 700,000 bushels. Andreas, *op. cit.*, II, 374. His wealth in 1859 was estimated at $2,000,000, no inconsiderable sum for those days. Reuben Vose, *Wealth of the World Displayed* (New York, 1859), p. 79.

nois but also purchased large tracts in Ohio, Indiana, Michigan, Missouri, and Iowa. During the 'fifties when land prices skyrocketed he began selling slowly. He advertised extensively in agricultural papers, thereby contributing to the increased interest with which Illinois lands were coming to be regarded in the country.

Sturges's unique advertisement is quoted here in part:

> Now, as I hold in abhorence all speculators, none such need apply. I wish to sell to actual settlers — of course a great motive to enter the lands being to keep them from the Pro-Slavery "Lords" in Missouri and the "Sharks" in other states. I have preached that Congress should only sell lands to actual settlers. Congress never would do right, (everybody knows that) so I have tried to take care of the "dear People," as far as I could myself. Besides, as I hold that Congress should keep their lands as a sacred trust for this and succeeding generations, as it may be wanted for use and cultivation, and they won't, I want to take care of my part for my six sons, and I don't know how many grandsons. I hope, reader, you will think this right, and acquit me of all motives but those of the most benevolent character.

Unlike some of the land dealers, Sturges was able to give long-term credit to his purchasers, a fact which contributed largely to his success. His lands were in immediate juxtaposition to the Illinois Central lands along the branch line, and on account of his ability to give generous credit terms he was able to compete successfully with the Company. As in the case of all such dealers, he was handicapped by having to pay taxes on his lands. This the Illinois Central did not have to do. Furthermore, the purchaser of the Company's lands did not have to pay taxes until he had secured title to his land, which might be years after he had begun farming. The result was that, unless better lands or better terms were offered in other ways, the prospective settler preferred to purchase from the railroad company.

Equally important as a land operator was Andrew J. Galloway, one of the largest and most successful speculators in Illinois. He was the chief promoter of the Western Land Agency, a large organization with headquarters in Chicago and with local agents in numerous places in Illinois, Iowa, and Wisconsin.[66] This company possessed a large amount of land in the northwestern states; in

---

[66] Advertisement in *Chicago Democratic Press*, August 4, 1855.

Illinois alone it offered for sale 150,000 acres along the line of the Illinois Central and 50,000 acres along other railroads in the State.[67] It published a pamphlet describing the lands and distributed it widely for advertising purposes.[68] Like Sturges, the firm granted long-term credit and offered every possible inducement to prospective settlers. Galloway's activities included sales of farm lands, town sites, or lots, locating lands for other investors, dealing in land warrants, and a general real estate agency for the purchase or sale of land held by others.[69] He was enabled to operate on such a large scale as the result of financial arrangements with H. H. Hunnewell and other Boston capitalists, a fact which gave him an advantage over many of his competitors.[70] He was immensely successful in the sale and settlement of lands in the prairie region of eastern and central Illinois.

Perhaps the most extensive of all individual or corporate holdings were those of the Northwest Land Company, whose headquarters were in Chicago. This company claimed to have agents in every county in the western states and at every United States land office. It had for sale 450,000 acres of cultivated and uncultivated land, and also town sites, city lots, and mineral and timber lands. Its advertising by means of newspapers, pamphlets, and broadsides was extensive.[71]

Operating on a smaller scale, but equally interesting on account of its activities in the East, was the Illinois Land Company, whose headquarters were in Philadelphia. This company purchased 30,000 acres of land along the line of the Illinois Central in Champaign, Piatt, and Macon Counties. It published a typical land promoter's pamphlet,[72] advertised in the Philadelphia papers,[73] and maintained agencies in Chicago and Decatur.

---

[67] Advertisement of Western Land Agency in *Chicago Pictorial Advertiser*, 1858–1859, p. 354.     [68] A. Campbell, *A Glance at Illinois* (La Salle, 1856).

[69] *Chicago Democratic Press*, March 7, 1856.

[70] There are many letters relating to these financial arrangements in the Neal-Rantoul MSS. and in the Illinois Central archives.

[71] See broadside of this company in volume: "Chicago, 1847–1893," Harvard College Library. See also *Uebersicht der Geschichte und des Handels von Chicago*, published by the *Illinois Staats-Zeitung*, 1856.

[72] *The Illinois Land Company offers for sale 30,000 acres . . . at low prices* (1855).

[73] *Philadelphia Public Ledger*, August 27, 28, 1855; *Philadelphia Morning Times*, August 27, 1855.

The career of one other speculator is included because of the light which it throws on the methods of such men in working for their own ends. Jesse Fell arrived in Bloomington, Illinois, in 1832 and began to purchase large quantities of land in the vicinity. With the aid of eastern capital he gradually extended his activities.[74] He assisted in laying out the towns of Le Roy, El Paso, Pontiac, Lexington, Towanda, and Clinton, and made additions to Bloomington and Decatur.[75] He advertised his lands mostly in the local papers, and his activities were not instrumental to any great degree in bringing in new settlers, but rather in inducing persons to move from one section to another in the same general locality. For our purposes the main interest in Fell's career lies in the methods he employed to increase the value of his lands. Fell ardently supported all railroads which were to be constructed through territory adjacent to his lands. He induced the towns to offer large contributions to secure the lines and also persuaded many capitalists to invest in their securities. The routing of the Illinois Central through Clinton, Decatur, and Bloomington was due in no small part to Fell, and he was also influential in securing the Chicago and Alton Railroad for Bloomington. His efforts were rewarded by the sale of his town lots along these lines.[76]

One of Fell's most important achievements was the location of the normal school at Normal, near Bloomington. According to custom, the locality making the highest bid would secure the school. Bloomington, thanks to the aggressive Fell, who worked in conjunction with Asahel Gridley, David Davis, and other interested persons, outbid Peoria, Batavia, and other competitors and secured the school.[77] Again, when the location of a soldiers' orphans' home was being considered by the State, Fell organized a movement to bring it to Normal, starting it out by a donation of $10,000 in cash and lands. Ultimately over $50,000 was pledged for this purpose, and although this was not the highest sum offered by any locality, yet with the aid of sufficient wirepulling Fell was

---

[74] Morehouse, *Life of Jesse W. Fell*, p. 32. Fell acquired 14,560 acres in the Danville land district. Tract Books, Danville land district, S. A. O.
[75] Morehouse, *op. cit.*, p. 32.  [76] *Ibid.*, p. 86.
[77] J. H. Burnham, "How the Normal was located," McLean County Historical Society, *Transactions*, II, 170–175. Cf. Morehouse, *op. cit.*, pp. 39–40.

successful in bringing the institution to Normal.[78] However, when the location of the State University was being considered, Fell and his associates were not so successful in spite of the fact that they offered the highest bid. Political jobbery and bribery, employed by the Champaign delegation, defeated their efforts.[79] Fell's activities undoubtedly stimulated the growth of Bloomington and its vicinity, but his interests were too local to influence settlement to any great extent.[80]

The fourth type of speculator is the eastern capitalist who took a flyer in western lands. From the opening of the nineteenth century easterners had been interested in Illinois lands. The warrants of the bounty land acts of 1811 and 1812, as we have seen, had enabled them to pile up large holdings in the Military Tract of the Prairie State. Here Colonel Joseph Watson of New York owned 127,760 acres, while the Berrian brothers of the same state secured 140,000 acres. In 1819 practically every member of Congress owned lands in this section, the total amount so held being in excess of 640,000 acres.[81] In the 'thirties and 'forties easterners continued to purchase land in Illinois and numerous large holdings were built up. Romulus Riggs, a Philadelphia capitalist, built up an estate of over 42,000 acres in central Illinois by 1837. Another Philadelphian by the name of John Grigg procured 100,-000 acres in the Springfield district. Other easterners who invested in Illinois lands were Gurdon Hewitt, Jr., of Tioga, New York, who owned 12,000 acres; Robert Ives, of a well known Providence counting house, who held 80,000 acres; W. W. Corcoran, of Washington, who had nearly 20,000 acres; Ebenezer Lane of Oxford County, Ohio, who had 6220 acres; Daniel Webster; and many others.[82] Many of the directors and chief officials of the Illinois Central invested in Illinois lands. Ambrose Burnside, treasurer of the Company and later a general in the Civil War,

[78] Harvey C. DeMotte, "Illinois Soldiers' Orphans' Home," McLean County Historical Society, *Transactions*, II, 187–200.

[79] This affair is discussed in the following chapter.

[80] Fell's part in bringing the terminal shops of the Chicago and Alton Railroad to Bloomington should not be overlooked. Morehouse, *op. cit.*, p. 86.

[81] Compiled from *House Executive Documents*, 26th Cong., 1st Sess., vol. VII, doc. 262.

[82] Compiled from record books of public land offices, S. A. O.

purchased a quantity of land in Will County,[83] while Neal,[84] Haven,[85] Griswold,[86] Hunnewell,[87] and Osborn,[88] all directors of the Company, had considerable holdings.[89] Although these eastern capitalists possessed extensive holdings their influence was small in settling the State, for as a rule they took no active measures to induce immigration. Their lands were kept off the market until the demand for them had raised their value to a price at which the expected profit could be obtained.

The role of the speculator has been one of profound importance in the history of Illinois. He preceded the settler, selected the choice locations, purchased them with land warrants or cash, surveyed and located them, and then sought to turn immigration into his section. He was foremost in the advocacy of canals, railroads, plank roads, and river improvements; to secure these his influence was exerted on the Legislature, on county and city organizations, and on Congress. As a factor in politics his influence cannot be overestimated. His newspaper advertisements, his distribution of pamphlets, and the activities of his agents aroused in-

[83] W. M. Phillips to Osborn, September 10, 1861, "Secretarys Letters," 1861, box 48, 63rd St.; *History of Will County* (Chicago, 1878), p. 573.

[84] Neal's connection with the Associates, already referred to, is discussed in the following chapter.

[85] Franklin Haven owned 720 acres in Marion and Will Counties. See marginalia on pamphlet: *Sectional Maps*, 1857, Haven MSS., Harvard College Library. See also letter of Neal to Ward and Galloway in "Illinois Land Agency," No. 5, Neal-Rantoul MSS.

[86] Osborn to Capt. G. B. McClellan, November 13, 1858, "Presidents Letters," 1858, box 48. See also maps of Chicago in vol. 259 in Land and Tax Commissioner's office, Central Station.

[87] Neal and Hunnewell together bought 960 acres near Manteno. Recorded in "Journal, D. A. N.," December 30, 1852, Neal-Rantoul MSS. Hunnewell, as has been noted, was interested in Galloway's activities. See Theodore Neal to A. J. Galloway, April 22, 1862, "Illinois Land Agency," No. 3, Neal-Rantoul MSS.

[88] Osborn's interests were rather more extensive than most of the other directors except Neal and Hunnewell. See J. W. Foster to Osborn, May 5, 1856, M. O.; Walker to Ackerman, September 11, 1862, "Treasurers Letters," No. 19, box 48. The *Railway Times* (London), April 21, 1860, declared that Osborn owned 10,000 acres of land in Illinois.

[89] Peter Daggy later stated that no officer or employee of the Land Department was ever permitted to purchase lands of the Company. However, after working in the Department for some time, some of the employees resigned, went into the land business themselves and purchased tracts from the Company. C. C. P. Holden and Charles M. Dupuy later became prominent in real estate circles. See letters of Daggy to J. C. Clark, April 22, 1884, "Daggy Personal with officers I. C. R. R. Co.," 16th St.

terest in his particular locality. By means of his efforts thousands of people were induced to migrate to Illinois. Some of them later returned to the East, disillusioned, but the majority remained to become citizens.

The speculator's influence, however, was not always a favorable one. The truth of his advertising literature was often questionable, and frequently led to much suffering for the gullible. By holding the best lands for higher prices, he forced pioneer settlers with no capital to move farther west in their search for lands after the government holdings had been sold, and he thereby retarded the development of the State. His part in politics was not always above reproach; as a representative of a class he was frequently accused of bribery and collusion to secure legislation which would enhance the value of his lands. So far as he was able to do so, he subjected national interests to State interests and State interests to local interests. To the speculator belongs the responsibility of having brought upon Illinois the crushingly heavy debt which the internal improvement measure of 1837 left — a measure which perhaps more than anything else retarded the development of Illinois in the early 'forties. However one may regard the speculator's activities, there can be no doubt that he and the town-site promoter, with whom we must next deal, have wielded a powerful influence in Illinois.

# CHAPTER VII

## TOWN-SITE PROMOTION

Town-site promotion was one of the most popular forms of speculation in the early period of Illinois history. The number of persons engaged in it was so considerable as to impress almost every traveller who visited the State. As early as 1815, Fearon commented on the "medley of land jobbers . . . who traverse this immense continent, founding settlements and engaging in all kinds of speculation," and designated them as one of four types of persons to be distinguished in Illinois.[1] Buckingham, in the early 'forties, wrote, "In the mania for planting cities, and buying and selling house-lots, which then prevailed all over the United States, Chicago held a distinguished place; and perhaps in no spot throughout the Union were more absurd or more extravagant bargains made for land than here." [2]

Prior to the Panic of 1837 speculation in town sites was particularly active. Optimistic promoters laid out towns anywhere and everywhere, without regard to their location, drainage, or transportation facilities. Having duly registered the plat they would proceed to advertise it in the local papers, and in some cases would peddle the plat or the lots in the East, where gullible buyers could generally be secured. Lots were bought and immediately resold at increased prices, each sale having the effect of increasing the speculative fever. The Panic of 1837, which ruined thousands who believed fortune within their grasp, put a stop to this premature development of town sites. Many of the towns were abandoned and their sites reverted to their original state. Such forgotten or "ghost" towns as Montezuma, Gloster, Moscow, Caledonia, Adamsburg, Presque Isle, and New Bedford bear witness to vanished dreams.[3]

[1] Henry Bradshaw Fearon, *Sketches of America* . . . (London, 1818), pp. 263–264.

[2] J. S. Buckingham, *The Eastern and Western States of America* (London, 1842, 3 vols.), III, 260.

[3] Advertisements of lots in these towns appeared in Illinois newspapers in the 'thirties.

The tight credit conditions which followed the Panic, the decline in immigration, and the heavy debt incurred as a result of the internal improvement measure of 1837 placed a damper on speculation in the 'forties. Those towns which continued in existence were generally located along the streams, where transportation facilities of a sort were available. Most of them were small and straggling villages which seemed to have little future ahead of them.

With the coming of the railroads in the latter part of the decade the small towns of Illinois were galvanized into action. As the railroads were in many cases built with local capital, their financial needs frequently determined their choice of routes. By offering to subscribe large amounts to their bond issues, by donating rights-of-way and land for terminal facilities, and by promising other concessions, rival communities struggled to secure railroads. Every little town had hopes of becoming an important railroad center, and the business of speculating in town lots once more began to thrive.

Towns were certain to develop along the route of the Illinois Central wherever stations were established. With no artificial stimulus other than the construction of the road, such centers were likely to acquire considerable prominence as shipping and receiving points. Realizing this, the Company determined to establish stations approximately every ten miles along its line. The railroad itself was forbidden by an amendment to its charter of February 17, 1851, to lay out towns on or near its line,[4] but its promoters were resolved to secure for themselves a share of the benefits to be derived from the sale of town lots at the new station settlements. Four of the most influential directors, Neal, Griswold, Sturges, and Ketchum, together with R. B. Mason, the engineer in charge of construction, informally organized the "Associates" for the purpose of purchasing the Government's alternate sections of land in the vicinity of which they, as directors of the Illinois Central, planned to establish the new stations.[5] The Asso-

---

[4] *Charter*, pp. 37–38.

[5] The Neal-Rantoul MSS. contain the plat books and the letter books of the Associates Land Company and other material bearing on it.

ciates were certain of being able to sell part of their holdings for town lots. The remainder could be disposed of as agricultural land when settlement demanded it. From the sale of both kinds of land the Associates stood to gain a large return upon their investment.

An attempt to secure a monopoly of the alternate sections within the six-mile limit which the Government had reserved at the double minimum price had previously been planned by George W. Billings. As a reward for his services in securing the charter, Billings, as we have seen, had been given advance information concerning the route of the Illinois Central, and he planned to purchase the government sections before other speculators became aware of their value. Billings organized the Illinois Land Association with a capital of $600,000, which was to be used to purchase from the Government 250,000 acres of land within six miles of the road.[6] Cooperating with Billings in the project were Morris Ketchum, David Neal, Jonathon Sturges, and others interested in the Illinois Central. This group subscribed $100,000 and planned to raise the rest by selling stock in England. They were not successful, and consequently had to reduce the scope of their operations. Under the leadership of Neal the Associates or the Associates Land Company was then organized.

The Associates entrusted John C. Dodge with the task of attending the sales at the government land offices in order to purchase the land they desired.[7] The station sites were kept secret until Dodge's work was done in order that there might be no difficulty in securing the lands at reasonable rates. Dodge performed his task well. In the five land offices of Kaskaskia, Vandalia, Chicago, Danville, and Dixon he succeeded in purchasing 19,235 acres around the proposed sites for $52,965.[8] Although the Associates' lands were among the very choicest left in the possession of the Government after the railroad lands had

---

[6] Circular of the Illinois Land Association, Baring MSS.

[7] President Fillmore had instructed the registers of the land districts through which the central railroad was projected to suspend sales of all lands which were within 25 miles of the route.

[8] R. B. Mason to Morris Ketchum, August 14, 1852, Ward's office; Statement of account of R. B. Mason with Morris Ketchum, Treasurer of the Illinois Central, September 21, 1852, Ward's office; Journal, D. A. N., Neal-Rantoul MSS.

been selected, Dodge paid only an average of $2.75 per acre, or 25 cents over the government minimum, for them. On most of them the minimum only was paid, and as depreciated land warrants, acceptable for one-half the total purchase price, were used, the actual amount paid was even less than the above account shows. These lands, even if they had been resold for agricultural purposes, would have yielded a handsome profit, but as town sites they were far more valuable.

The station sites were located by the directors of the Illinois Central on the Associates' land or in their vicinity.[9] The Associates in turn deeded to the railroad sufficient land for its depots and yards in the new towns.[10] As soon as the station sites were announced and before construction was complete, there was a rush for locations at the incipient towns. As early as 1854 it was reported that applications had been received for 125 town lots at Urbana, 24 at Lena, 4 at Wenona, 10 at Nora, and 49 at Centralia.[11] The construction of freight and passenger stations at the selected locations was followed by an inrush of small tradesmen and mechanics who had been especially attracted by the land advertisements. Some enterprising individuals would then put up a "commodious" hotel. Next would follow the construction of small flour mills, sawmills if there was timber in the vicinity, packing houses, and grain elevators.[12] Churches and school buildings were soon required, and their construction frequently led to the development of brick-making, quarrying, and lumber yards. The retail business of the small tradesmen increased as the farming population increased, and thus towns in the center of the more rapidly developing agricultural communities grew swiftly.

This development of agricultural centers is best seen on the Chicago branch. Prior to 1850 there were but three settlements in the vicinity of this route, Bourbonnais, Urbana, and Spring

---

[9] Of the ninety-six stations established by 1857 thirty-three were so placed. *Sectional Maps*, outline map; plat books, Neal-Rantoul MSS.

[10] Theodore Neal to W. M. Phillips, December 2, 13, 1865, "Illinois Land Agency," No. 5, *ibid*.

[11] *Railway Times*, XVIII, 427; *Chicago Democratic Press*, March 10, 1855, quoting *New York Tribune*; *Illinois State Register*, November 6, 1854.

[12] *The Illinois Central Rail-Road Company offer for Sale over 2,500,000 acres*, pp. 11–12.

Creek, and they were only in the first stages of development.[13] Twenty years later there had grown up around the stations established by the Illinois Central on this line twenty-eight cities and towns of sufficient size to be listed in the census report, of which thirteen had been laid out by the Associates either in whole or in part. These towns ranged in population from 5189 for Kankakee, 4967 for Mattoon, and 4625 for Champaign to less than a thousand for the smaller settlements. Because these small communities owe their existence to the construction of the Illinois Central they deserve detailed consideration.

Manteno may be considered as representative of these new station settlements. Located 46 miles from Chicago on the Grand Prairie, in a region quite undeveloped but of rich potentialities, this town quickly became an important shipping center. It was located on Associates' land, but the railroad had laid out an addition to it on its own land, and consequently both groups competed in the sale of town lots.[14] In October, 1854, there was not a house in the village, but by June of the following year there were sixteen houses and a substantial freight and passenger traffic was in operation.[15] Manteno became the trading center for a considerable area;[16] grain elevators, gristmills, lumber yards, stores, and hotels sprang up, and large amounts of produce were imported to and exported from the community.[17] Being solely a trading center for an agricultural community, distant from rivers and lumber supplies, the town could not become a populous city. Nevertheless, by 1860 it had a population of 861 and a decade later one of 1681.

The Associates made every effort to promote the growth of the towns in which they were interested. They encouraged industries such as milling, lumbering,[18] mining, and manufacturing, and

---

[13] Only Urbana was mentioned in the census of 1850, it having at that time a population of 210. *Ninth Census*, I, 109; Report of R. B. Mason in *Annual Report* of the Illinois Central Railroad, 1855.

[14] Plat book of Associates' towns, Neal-Rantoul MSS., plate No. 24, *Sectional Maps*; vol. III, Illinois Central books, S. A. O.

[15] Satterthwaite circular, December 18, 1855.

[16] *Sectional Maps*, plate No. 24 and p. 64; *Guide to the Illinois Central Railroad Lands*, pp. 58–59.      [17] *Sectional Maps*, pp. 10–11.

[18] Neal gave land to saw- and grist-mill proprietors to assist them in getting started.

tried to secure public institutions and buildings for their towns. To secure the county seat for the village of Onarga they offered to donate a sum of money and a city block "provided said block shall be selected by us to benefit our property more than that of others."[19] Lots were likewise donated to religious organizations to secure the construction of churches in the vicinity of the Associates' land in order to increase its value. Strenuous efforts were made by the Associates to make the town of Kankakee the county seat of the county by the same name.[20] They offered a courthouse site and $5000 towards the cost of erecting a building. In this case they met with considerable opposition; three other towns, Momence, Aroma, and Bourbonnais, were likewise striving to secure the prize. At a special election held to decide the question none of the four towns was successful in securing the necessary majority of votes, and redoubled efforts were made by all four of them prior to the second election. But the bid of the Associates could not be approached by the local magnates of the rival towns, and in the later election Kankakee was selected.[21] The Associates carried on similar activities in other towns, and were rewarded in most cases by their rapid growth.

Until his death in 1860 David Neal managed the business of the Associates, spending much of his time in Illinois for this purpose.[22] After he resigned as vice-president of the Illinois Central in March, 1855, he was able to devote his full energies to their affairs. He was assisted by local agents, whom he appointed at different points, and who made sales on a commission basis.

Neal prepared a standard plat to be used in laying out the towns of the Associates. On this plat the streets running east and west were named after trees in the following order: Mulberry, Hickory, Walnut, Chestnut, Oak, Locust, Poplar, and Ash, while the streets

[19] Arthur Carroll for T. A. Neal to W. H. Musser, May 10, 1862, "Illinois Land Agency," No. 3, Neal-Rantoul MSS.

[20] The proprietors of Kankakee, Neal, Ketchum, Rogers & Bement, Griswold, Sturges and Mason, formed a separate organization from the Associates, although they were the same group. In this town they owned 960 acres which had been purchased from private holders. See pamphlet: Kankakee, Illinois. A Steady Growth, Not a Creation, 1913.

[21] Ibid.

[22] Autobiography of D. A. Neal for the year 1855 ff.

running north and south were numbered.[23] The towns were laid out in blocks and lots, the relative prices of which were determined on the basis of their distance from the center of the town and from the station. This plat was used for all the thirty-three towns of the Associates. Standardized town-site promotion on such a scale had never before occurred, but it was to be undertaken on a more extensive scale by trans-Mississippi railroads and land companies.

Under Neal's management the business of the Associates was exceedingly profitable, large dividends being paid on the shares during the 'fifties and 'sixties. Particularly profitable was the Kankakee investment. In less than two years this town acquired a population of 1200 people,[24] and this figure was reported to have increased to 3500 by 1858.[25] To May, 1855, $18,351, including interest, had been invested in this proposition. By the end of 1855 nearly $50,000 worth of town lots had been sold and the remaining property was valued at over $100,000.[26] For the next ten years large dividends were paid, and then the business was sold for $50,000.[27]

In 1860 Neal, while visiting Illinois, was taken ill, and in anticipation of his demise and in order to simplify the granting of deeds a more formal organization of the Associates was arranged. The "Associates Land Company" was incorporated under the laws of Connecticut, and to it all the remaining lands were conveyed.[28] After Neal's death the management devolved upon his son, Theodore, who carried it on until it was finally dissolved.

Another town-site company similar to the Associates was known as the Proprietors of Dunleith. It consisted of Neal,

[23] See plans and plats for the Associates' towns in volume of plats in Neal-Rantoul MSS. The Illinois Central was to run directly through the center of the towns between Chestnut and Oak Streets, according to the plan.

[24] *Annual Report*, 1854. But see Satterthwaite circular, December 18, 1855. See also Ferguson, *America by River and Rail*, p. 373.

[25] Caird, *Prairie Farming*, p. 42. Caird's estimate, however, seems too large because the census of 1860 reported only 2984 people at Kankakee. If the population of Bourbonnais, 2205, be added, this estimate would not be too large.

[26] "Journal, D. A. N.," Neal-Rantoul MSS.

[27] Account in "Illinois Land Agency," No. 1; T. A. Neal to E. Bement, August 8, 26, 1865, "Illinois Land Agency," No. 5, Neal-Rantoul MSS.

[28] Neal, Autobiography; letter of Francis Pallotti, Secretary of State of Connecticut, to the writer, August 28, 1928.

Sturges, Ketchum & Griswold, Senator Jones of Iowa, George Sanford, and Charles Gregoire, from whom the land was bought.[29] These men laid out the town of Dunleith and, under a resident agency, commenced sales in 1855. They organized or secured control of the Galena Packet Company, which operated a ferry across the Mississippi connecting Dunleith with Dubuque. The citizens of Dubuque protested to the Federal Government that the interlocking directorate of the Proprietors of Dunleith and the Illinois Central fixed the railroad and ferry schedules so as to favor Dunleith to the detriment of Dubuque. They pointed out that trains arrived at Dunleith so late at night as to make it practically impossible for travellers to get to Dubuque until the next day, thereby necessitating a stop in Dunleith over night.[30] Whether there was any truth in the accusation or not, the practice complained of was not unusual but, in fact, quite common. If the situation had been reversed Dubuque would have protested its innocence.

Throughout the 'fifties the town-lot business in Dunleith was prosperous,[31] but after the construction of the bridge across and the tunnel beneath the Mississippi business declined. The increasing taxes and the cost of maintaining an agent to manage collections and sales and keep off squatters, together with the decline in values and the practical stagnation of business, made the Proprietors anxious to sell out. When the low offer of $6000 was made for their remaining property they accepted it,[32] realizing that the town of Dunleith had seen its best days.[33]

Greatest of all town-site promoters was the Illinois Central

[29] "Journal, D. A. N."; *History of Jo Daviess County* (1878), p. 546.

[30] See memorial of Dubuque city authorities of January 17, 1856, in *House Executive Documents*, 34th Cong., 1st Sess., 1855–1856, vol. IX, doc. 88, and letter of George W. Jones to Franklin Pierce, December 14, 1855, *Senate Executive Documents*, 34th Cong., 1st Sess., 1855–1856, vol. X, doc. 39, pp. 2–3.

[31] Up to December 31, 1859, 128 lots had been deeded, 25 deeds were ready for issuing, and 128 other lots were contracted for. These sales amounted to $64,915. The ferry also was profitable. See "Private Journal from Jan. 1, 1849 to Sept. 6, 1851," Neal-Rantoul MSS.

[32] Theodore Neal to John H. Thompson, February 7, November 9, 1868; to G. E. Underhill, October 21, 1868, "Illinois Land Agency," No. 6, *ibid.*

[33] In 1890 the population of Dunleith was only 1069. It was then little more than a suburb of Dubuque, its name having been changed to East Dubuque. *Eleventh Census*, 1890, I, 107.

Railroad itself. Until 1855 its charter forbade it to lay out new towns on or near its line, but disregarding this restriction, on the ground that it was ambiguous, the Illinois Central ventured to lay out towns at four points on its line, Centralia, Tolono, Kinmundy, and Elmwood. The most important of these was Centralia.

The town of Centralia was most favorably located in the center of a small prairie, close to timber and to a branch of the Kaskaskia River and just south of the junction of the main line and the Chicago branch.[34] Because of the exorbitant demands of local speculators, the Company was forced to establish a town on its own land, a mile south of the site originally proposed.[35] The town was surveyed and platted in 1853, and in the following year the first house was erected. A branch office of the Land Department, the only subsidiary office in existence at this time, was established here for the sale of both town lots and farm lands.[36] The Company also established machine and car shops at Centralia and made it the central point for the division. This necessitated the employment of a considerable force of men, estimated in 1857 at 200.[37] As many of them brought in their families, following whom came tradesmen and other persons necessary to supply their needs, the town grew rapidly. In 1855 its population was estimated at nearly 2000,[38] and in 1870 at 3190.[39] The rapid growth of Centralia proved lucrative to the Illinois Central, which had practically a monopoly of the town lots. Up to 1879 the amount received from this source was well over $110,000,[40] making a handsome return to the Company. The road was not selfish in the sale of its Centralia lots; it gave to the town govern-

---

[34] See plate 6, *Sectional Maps.*

[35] J. H. Brinkerhoff, *History of Marion County, Illinois* (Indianapolis, 1909), pp. 141–142, 191–193.

[36] *Annual Report*, 1859.

[37] Letter of "Rural" in *Chicago Democratic Press*, July 10, 1857.

[38] *Home Missionary*, XXXI, 241.

[39] *Ninth Census*, I, 116.

[40] Daggy to Ackerman, January 25, 1879, "Daggy letter book," 16th St. The Chicago fire of 1871 had destroyed some of the town-lot records so Daggy was unable to give accurate figures of the amount received from this source but gives $111,455 as the minimum. This excludes the value of 93 lots which would have brought the total to about $120,000.

ment twelve lots, to churches eight lots, and to schools two lots.[41] The success at Centralia was not duplicated elsewhere. In most cases the Illinois Central only laid out additions to towns, and usually had to meet the competition of other speculators.

Fearing that its action in laying out new towns was illegal, the Illinois Central later resorted to the policy of selling sites for prospective towns to speculators at fancy prices,[42] with the understanding that stations would be established in the vicinity of their purchases. For example, the Company sold A. J. Galloway 240 acres in Effingham County for $36 an acre.[43] Galloway already owned a large amount of land in the neighborhood and made this purchase in order to secure a station, knowing that this would have the effect of increasing the value of his other lands. He laid out the town of Edgewood, which did some business for a while but did not prosper long and in 1889 was reported as "dead." [44] A handsome price was also received by the Company for the site of Tolono, at the junction of the Chicago branch with the Great Western Railroad: $25,000 was paid for 130 acres at this point.[45] It was then expected that the location, because of its railroad connections, would become a city of some size. These hopes were too sanguine; in 1870 the village numbered only 777 souls.[46]

In a number of instances the Illinois Central sold town sites to promoters at low prices to assist them in establishing colonies along its line. The promoters would purchase at a low rate a section or part of a section on which the railroad was to establish a

[41] Daggy to Ackerman, January 25, 1879, *ibid.*

[42] Osborn to Executive Committee, December 6, 1856; to Perkins, December 12, 1856, M. O.

[43] A sale of a similar sort was made by the Associates to a man by the name of Blackney. About 80 acres at Pera were sold to him for $50 per acre. The town was laid out on this plot and a station of the Illinois Central was located on it. Theodore Neal to Sturges, July 26, 1862, "Illinois Land Agency," No. 3, Neal-Rantoul MSS. The town was located too near Rantoul, a thriving city, to become important.

[44] Letters of Galloway of October 24, November 11; of Morehouse, November 14, 1889, with memo of Daggy on last, box of Galloway correspondence, 6th floor vault, Land and Tax Commissioner's office. Edgewood was reported to have a population of about 500 people in 1869. But for the past few years the grain crops had failed and the settlers had become dissatisfied with their location. *Prairie Farmer*, February 6, 1869.

[45] Osborn to Perkins, December 12, 1856, M. O.; Daggy to Ackerman, August 30, 1875, "Daggy Personal with officers I. C. R. R. Co.," 16th St.

[46] *Ninth Census*, I, 109.

station. The promoter would then lay out a town site upon his land. From the sale of town lots he was able to raise capital for the development of the colony more quickly than he could from the sale of his agricultural lands. Thus W. B. Burns, leader of the Vermont Emigrant Association, purchased that part of the section upon which the village of New Rutland or Rutland was established, paying for it the moderate price of $10.40 to $12.80 per acre.[47] Burns was an energetic Yankee, and was determined to make Rutland a town of importance. He succeeded in establishing there grain elevators and flour mills, but failed to build up an important city.[48] Owing to the nature of its location, Rutland could never be more than a business center for the surrounding agricultural community. Similarly, the Illinois Central sold to E. E. Malhiot land in the vicinity of Tacusah for town development. Changing its name to Assumption, Malhiot proceeded to develop the town by erecting stores, warehouses, packing houses, dwelling houses, and a hotel.[49] But the location was not as favorable for growth as that of Pana, its neighbor on the Illinois Central, and the town, like Rutland, failed to become more than a small agricultural center.[50] Likewise the Company sold town sites to the promoters of the German settlement at Sigel and the Polish colony at Radom, both of which will be discussed in other connections. The sites of Danforth, Thomasboro, and others were sold to and developed by private individuals, but they failed to grow to any extent.[51]

The promoters of the Illinois Central by organizing themselves as the Associates had sought to secure a share of the profits to be had from town-site promotion. This close connection between the Illinois Central and the Associates came to an end in 1855. By that time the new regime headed by Osborn was at war with the old leaders, Neal and Ketchum. Moreover, the railroad had succeeded in securing an amendment to its charter which permitted

[47] Vol. 79, plat books, Land and Tax Commissioner's office.
[48] *Sectional Maps*, p. 46.
[49] *Chicago Democratic Press*, March 7, 1857.
[50] *Ninth Census*, I, 109; *Sectional Maps*, p. 34.
[51] *Illinois Central Directory*, p. 45; vol. 265, Land and Tax Commissioner's office; Daggy to Ackerman, August 30, 1875, "Daggy Personal with officers I. C. R. R. Co.," 16th St.

it to lay out towns where depots had already been located but forbade the development of new towns at stations to be located in the future.[52] This qualifying provision was, of course, a safeguard against the removal of stations to new locations in order to reap the returns from the sale of town lots. This amendment made it possible for the Company to go into the town-lot business for itself, and it therefore determined to keep this profitable business in its own hands so far as possible. It even proposed to move eleven of the depots established on the Associates' lands to lands of the railroad, but apparently this was not done.[53] In numerous instances, however, the Company did lay out additions to the Associates' towns on its own land or, in regions where it possessed none, on land purchased from others for this purpose, for which it had to pay as high as $150 per acre.[54] Thus the Illinois Central came into direct competition with the Associates. After 1855 the former was able to develop a large town-lot business, its operations being carried on in twenty-nine cities and towns along its line.[55] The Company advertised its town lots in pamphlets and newspapers. Plats and maps of the locations were supplied to the station agents, whose duty it was to furnish all necessary information and assistance to prospective buyers.[56] Credit was granted on terms that were liberal though less extended than the terms for agricultural lands.

The Illinois Central made every possible effort to encourage the development of manufacturing in its towns by drawing the attention of capitalists to the opportunities which Illinois afforded and by making concessions to new industries in the way of reduced freights. In the southern part of the State lumbering especially was encouraged. In 1855, for $8 an acre, the railroad leased to a Bloomington concern the right to cut timber on its southern lands.

[52] Act of February 14, 1855, *Charter*, p. 43; *Chicago Democratic Press*, March 18, 1855, quoting *New York Tribune*.

[53] J. N. Perkins to Ketchum, Rogers & Bement, September 29, 1855, "J. N. Perkins, Treasurer," 1855, box 48, 63rd St.

[54] The Illinois Central and A. J. Galloway acting together were reported to have paid $150 an acre for 80 acres in the vicinity of West Urbana. *Chicago Democratic Press*, May 12, 1857, quoting *Urbana Union* of May 6.

[55] Report of Peter Daggy, Secretary of the Land Department, in vol. III, Illinois Central deed books, S. A. O.

[56] *Guide to the Illinois Central Railroad Lands*, p. 56.

The firm undertook to commence operations at once as there was a considerable demand for timber in the central part of the State.[57] So rapidly did this industry develop, not only on the Company's lands but also on the alternate sections, that in 1865 over 9,000,000 feet of lumber were shipped over the Illinois Central alone from the stations of Dongola, Wetaug, Ullin, Pulaski, and Villa Ridge.[58] The lumber industry became an important and profitable business for those engaged in it and also for the Illinois Central, which secured a large traffic in this commodity.

The Company likewise took steps to encourage the development of mining, both upon its own lands and in the vicinity of its stations. By 1858 it had already begun to convert its engines from wood burners to coal burners, thus increasing the demand for coal.[59] The services of John W. Foster, an eminent geologist, were secured to make an investigation of the mineral resources of the region through which the road extended. After a thorough investigation Foster published his findings in a pamphlet entitled *Report upon the Mineral Resources of the Illinois Central Railroad*,[60] which was widely distributed for the purpose of interesting capitalists. Even before this, arrangements had been made with a St. Louis concern for the mining of coal at Du Quoin, where it was known that there were large coal deposits. In this case the Company rented its lands on a royalty basis.[61] Foster observed in 1856 that forty miners were employed in getting out coal in this region.[62] Coal mining was likewise developing around La Salle, where one concern alone had a producing capacity of four hundred tons a day.[63] These two localities soon became important mining

---

[57] Robert Benson & Co. bank circular, November 13, 1855, Ward's office. Jesse Fell, who apparently was the leading promoter of this enterprise, plunged heavily into the lumbering business in this section. It failed to meet his expectations, however, and in 1856 he returned to the real estate business in Bloomington. Morehouse, *op. cit.*, p. 33.

[58] *Sectional Maps*, p. 11.

[59] *Guide to the Illinois Central Railroad Lands*, pp. 19–20. *Annual Reports* of the Illinois Central for these years contain considerable information on this change and its success.          [60] Published in March, 1856.

[61] Dupuy to Osborn, January 13, 1855, M. O.

[62] Foster, *op. cit.*, p. 12; *Prairie Farmer*, April 30, 1857.

[63] *Dubuque Herald* quoted in *American Railway Times*, January 18, 1862. For a discussion of coal mining around La Salle in 1856 see Gerhard, *Illinois As It Is*, pp. 382–385.

centers, which attracted large numbers of miners and thus helped to swell the population.[64]

The decades of the 'fifties and 'sixties saw the foundation of numerous institutions of higher learning in the states of the old Northwest. Every denomination desired its own colleges for the training of adherents to its faith; the coming of the New York-New England element to Illinois gave a stimulus to this movement. The Illinois Central, as the largest land owner in the State, was deluged with petitions from these incipient institutions for aid in one form or another, although generally land was desired.[65] The Company realized, as did the Associates, that the location of State or private institutions in the vicinity of its lands would enhance their value and bring added traffic to the road. With the help of local speculators five such institutions were secured for Illinois Central towns.

The first of these institutions was Normal College, which was located at Normal, just south of Bloomington on the Illinois Central. Jesse Fell, Asahel Gridley, and other speculators had interested themselves in securing the college for this community. The results obtained from the establishment of the institution were, however, disappointing. The town grew slowly, its population being only 1116 in 1870,[66] and consequently the real estate business did not flourish as had been anticipated.[67] Another semi-public institution of higher learning was established in 1861 at Irvington, just south of Centralia. For a brief period it flourished, but it was poorly managed and handicapped by insufficient funds, and before long was forced to close its doors.[68] Somewhat more

[64] D. L. Phillips to Brayman, November 8, 1854, Brayman MSS.; *Sectional Maps*, pp. 10–11, 22, 48. Ferguson, *op. cit.*, pp. 380–381, 392, discusses coal mining at Du Quoin and its possibilities.

[65] Blanchard to officials of the Illinois Central, March 11, 1853; letter of John Barger to same, March 7, 1854, M. O. Barger sought $100,000 for his institution.

[66] *Ninth Census*, I, 117.

[67] J. H. Burnham, "Early Days at Normal," McLean County Historical Society, *Transactions*, II, 153.

[68] Ezra M. Prince, "School Lands of McLean County and School Funds," McLean County Historical Society, *Transactions*, II, 43; *Sectional Maps*, p. 26; Burt E. Powell, *The Movement for Industrial Education and the Establishment of the University, 1840–1870 (Semi-Centennial History of the University of Illinois*, vol. I, Urbana, 1918), pp. 173–177.

successful was the seminary at Richview, just south of Irvington, to which the Illinois Central in 1867 gave seventy-five lots.[69] The college of the Swedish Lutherans, located at Paxton in 1862, also benefited from the generosity of the Illinois Central and of local speculators. The negotiations leading to its establishment at Paxton will be dealt with elsewhere.

Far more important a plum than the other institutions secured for the line of the Illinois Central was the State University. Under the provisions of the Morrill Act of 1862, this institution was to receive from the Federal Government an endowment of 480,000 acres of land, to be located by means of scrip anywhere on the public domain. The projected university, supported as it was by both the State and the Federal Governments, promised to become an important institution and a scramble ensued in which a number of communities fought to secure the prize. The jealousies of rival communities as well as of religious colleges delayed the location of the university for a time. Meanwhile the interested cities were building up support for their plans. Finally in January, 1867, the State Legislature, seeing no other way out of the controversy, and following its previous policy in the matter of selecting locations for institutions, passed an act which permitted all communities to submit bids for the location of the university.[70] This had the effect of narrowing down the number of serious contenders to Jacksonville, Bloomington, Lincoln, and Champaign. Each of these rival towns had its aggressive group of promoters who produced pledges in money, land, and other commodities, pulled wires, exchanged support with promoters of other measures, and used every possible means to advance their interests.

Champaign was best served by its representatives and advocates. Under the leadership of C. R. Griggs, an experienced lobbyist and a member of the State Legislature, a large sum of money was raised, not to increase the town's bids, but to disburse in lobbying. Griggs then set out on a tour of the State in the course of which he interviewed members of the Legislature, promised them support for other bills, and in turn secured pledges

[69] Ackerman, *Early Illinois Railroads*, p. 133; *Sectional Maps*, p. 26.
[70] *Laws of Illinois*, 1867, pp. 122–123.

of their support for his community.[71] He interviewed the bosses
of both parties, distributed money wisely, and exerted every effort
to build up a safe majority for Champaign. After the opening of
the Legislature in 1867 Griggs began lobbying on a lavish scale,
undeterred by the threat of legislative investigation of his
activities.

The Illinois Central was much interested in securing the State
University for Champaign. In this county it had received 216,000
acres of land from the Government, a larger amount than it had
received in any other county with the exception of Iroquois.[72] As
late as 1868, 80,000 acres were still unsold.[73] This land would
probably find a ready market if the university were brought to the
county. Furthermore, the Illinois Central owned town lots in
Champaign, the price of which would be much enhanced by the
location of the university there.[74] A final consideration, but perhaps the one which had most weight with the directors of the
Company, was the increased amount of freight and passenger
traffic which the institution would be the means of furnishing.
In view of all these circumstances, the Illinois Central determined to make a generous bid to aid in securing the university
for Champaign. It offered $50,000 in freight transportation for
this purpose.[75]

This pledge, with the other donations in land, money, and kind,
brought the Champaign offer to an estimated value of $285,000.
This bid was surpassed, however, by three others. Bloomington
and McLean County together offered a cash value of $470,000 to-
wards which the Chicago and Alton Railroad, in competition with
the Illinois Central, pledged $50,000 worth of freight; Logan
County offered $385,000; and Morgan County, with Jacksonville,
offered the largest bid, $491,000.[76] But here Griggs's clever ma-

[71] Griggs's part in this sordid affair is set forth in doc. 21 in Powell, *op. cit.*, pp.
515–522. This document is the result of an interview of Allan Nevins with Griggs.
[72] "Statement of Lands owned by I. C. R. R. Co. situated in Counties and Districts," by B. F. Ingraham, box 53, 63rd St.
[73] Advertisement in *Champaign Union*, December 3, 1868; *Sectional Maps*, p. 72.
[74] Vol. III, Illinois Central books, S. A. O.
[75] Ackerman, *op. cit.*, p. 126.
[76] "Report of the joint committee of the Industrial University," February 16,
1867, *Illinois Reports*, 1867, 1, 443–445.

nipulation of the Legislature and his lavish expenditures had a telling effect. After considerable skirmishing on the floor of the House, and much slander and recrimination, a bill designating Champaign as the location for the university was finally passed and signed by the Governor on February 28, 1867.[77]

The Illinois Central donation was well repaid. Champaign-Urbana became by 1870 the most populous community south of Chicago on the branch line,[78] and the Company reaped large returns from the sale of its town lots,[79] as well as from the speedy disposal of the remaining lands in the vicinity.

With the exception of Chicago, the most rapidly growing towns along the route of the Illinois Central were junction points at which the east-west roads crossed its line. Thus Freeport, Bloomington, Dixon, Mendota, La Salle, Decatur, and Mattoon were by 1870 among the leading towns in the State. The first three, however, had considerable development prior to the period of railroad construction. Indeed, when the route of the Illinois Central was selected there was very little government land remaining in the vicinity of any of these towns, much of it having passed into the hands of speculators and town-site promoters. In the townships in which Decatur and La Salle are located the Company received no sections at all,[80] and only a small quantity in the neighborhood of the other towns, excluding Mattoon. Except at Mendota and Mattoon the railroad had no town lots for sale at these rapidly growing junctions. The Associates likewise had been unable to purchase land near them. The benefit, therefore, which the Illinois Central brought to these towns redounded to the interests of individual speculators, who reaped large rewards for their foresight.

The most important of these junctions was Bloomington, a city located in the center of one of the richest prairie regions in the

---

[77] *Laws of Illinois*, 1867, pp. 123–129. Cf. Allan Nevins, *Illinois* (New York, 1917), pp. 29 ff.; Fred H. Turner, "Misconceptions concerning the Early History of the University of Illinois," Illinois State Historical Society, *Transactions*, 1932, pp. 82–85.

[78] *Ninth Census*, I, 109 ff.

[79] Vol. III, Illinois Central books, S. A. O.

[80] This is evident from a glance at the plats in *Sectional Maps*.

State and near adequate timber groves. The Funks had made this place the center of an important cattle and swine industry while Kersey and Jesse Fell, David Davis, Asahel Gridley and others had exerted themselves to bring railroads to Bloomington, to secure State institutions for the community, and to get local industries established. The location here of the Chicago and Alton Railroad shops gave a great boom to the city and brought in large numbers of mechanics and laborers. In the 'fifties no railroad crossed the Illinois Central for a distance of 43 miles south of Bloomington. Consequently this city was the transshipping place for a large amount of agricultural produce. These factors so stimulated Bloomington's growth that its population quadrupled in the 'fifties and doubled in the 'sixties, amounting to 14,590 in 1870.[81]

The construction of the Illinois and Michigan Canal had given an impetus to the growth of La Salle, which was located in a region already well settled by a farming population, and which was also to benefit from the development of coal mining in its vicinity. The decision of the Illinois Central to cross the Illinois River at this place rather than at Peru and thus to establish there its junction with the Rock Island Railroad further accelerated the growth of La Salle.

The city of Chicago,[82] during the decades of the 'fifties and 'sixties, experienced one of the most remarkable urban developments in American history. Its rapid growth has been attributed to the fact that by 1860 it had become the greatest railroad center in America, and this in turn has been credited to the energy and foresight of Stephen A. Douglas and other Chicago promoters. The importance of these two factors seems to have been generally exaggerated. Chicago was certain to enjoy rapid growth on account of its location on Lake Michigan, where water transporta-

[81] *Ninth Census*, I, 116.
[82] Few travellers came to America without visiting Chicago for a short period. For a few of their accounts see Ferguson, *op. cit.*, pp. 363 ff.; Anthony Trollope, *North America*, pp. 155–157; Edward Dicey, *Six Months in the Federal States* (London, 1863), pp. 151 ff.; J. G. Kohl, *Reisen im Nordwesten der Vereinigten Staaten* (New York, 1857), pp. 135–159. For a bibliography of such works see Solon Justus Buck, *Travel and Description, 1765–1865* (Illinois State Historical Library, *Collections*, vol. IX, Springfield, 1914).

tion through the lakes and the Erie Canal, or through the Illinois and Michigan Canal and the Illinois and Mississippi Rivers, was available. It early became the most important shipping point on the lake. On one day in September, 1857, the editor of the *Prairie Farmer* reported that there were 272 vessels loading or unloading in the port, including 1 steamer, 14 propellors, 31 barks, 47 brigs, and 179 schooners.[83] On account of its water transportation facilities alone, then, the city's future was assured. For the same reason, Chicago was certain to become a great railroad center and needed no artificial stimulus to bring this about. This is at once apparent from the fact that the city government spent not a cent to secure railroads by underwriting their bonds or by loaning its credit to them. Other Illinois cities such as Alton, Bloomington, Urbana, Peoria, and Rockford were subscribing to the stock and bonds of railroads to bring them to their locality, and so were most of the live western cities. Chicago could afford to maintain a conservative attitude in this matter.

Nevertheless, the railroads, although not essential to Chicago's development in this period, stimulated her growth tremendously. Practically all of the important lines converged at this point and none were through roads. The selfish efforts of the citizens to prevent any railroad from building through or around the city had been successful.[84] Chicago benefited more than any other city from the construction of railroads in the Old Northwest which in the 'fifties completely changed trade routes in that region. Produce which once had floated down the rivers to St. Louis and New Orleans was now carried by the iron horse to Chicago and eastern markets direct.[85] What was Chicago's gain was New Orleans's and St. Louis's loss. These cities, which had developed much

---

[83] *Prairie Farmer*, September 24, 1857.

[84] This was not entirely due to their efforts, since no eastern road extended beyond Chicago nor did any western road have any eastern connections under its own control. Some of the lines were under the same management but trains were operated independently. The same situation exists in effect today in spite of the combinations which have taken place. None of the eastern or western trunk lines extends through Chicago.

[85] Riley, *The Development of Chicago and Vicinity as a Manufacturing Center Prior to 1880*, has a chapter on this subject entitled "A Change in Commercial Routes," pp. 75-98.

earlier than Chicago, were now forced to watch the younger city on the lake rapidly forging to the front as the leading commercial center in the Mississippi Valley.

Probably no railroad contributed more to the development of Chicago than the Illinois Central. The main line of this road, from Sandoval to Dunleith, which was connected with Chicago by means of the Chicago and Alton, the Chicago, Burlington and Quincy, the Chicago and Rock Island, and the Chicago and Northwestern Railroads, furnished a great deal more traffic to the lake city than is generally credited to it. The branch line from Centralia to Chicago tapped a territory of immense agricultural potentialities which rapidly developed after it was connected with the lake port. Although some of the produce of this territory was shipped eastward by the Illinois Central's eastern connections, the Ohio and Mississippi, and the Terre Haute Railroads, the larger portion went directly to Chicago. Large quantities of cattle and hogs were carried there to be slaughtered and packed. The road likewise transported millions of bushels of grain to Chicago and thus aided in making it the greatest primary grain center in the world.[86] Shipments of flour and grain to the lake port necessitated the construction of great elevators and warehouses there, and in consequence the elevator capacity of the city was increased from 5,475,000 bushels in 1860 to 11,580,000 in 1870.[87] The meat packing business also became so large that a new union stockyard was established which extended over 345 acres of land and had yards and pens which could accommodate 10,000 cattle and 100,000 hogs.[88] In return for its receipts of grain, cattle, and hogs, Chicago shipped large amounts of farm implements and enormous quantities of lumber from Michigan and Wisconsin to the rapidly expanding prairie communities. The largest proportion of the lumber went over the Illinois Central to communities on its line.

---

[86] The statistics may be found in the *Annual Reports* of the Chicago Board of Trade, 1859 to date.

[87] Chicago Board of Trade, *Annual Report*, 1860, p. 9; *Annual Report*, 1870, p. 44.

[88] Illinois State Agricultural Society, *Transactions* (1865–1866), VI, 314–324; Chicago Board of Trade, *Annual Report*, 1866, p. 46.

The rapid growth of Chicago as a manufacturing center, railroad terminal, and port naturally attracted population. In the decade of the 'fifties its population increased from 29,963 to 112,172, and in the following decade it jumped to 298,977.[89] So rapid was the immigration into the city that, in spite of its one hundred and fifty hotels and the tremendous building development,—it was reported in September, 1855, that over 2700 buildings were in process of construction,[90] — newcomers found great difficulty in securing accommodations and it was practically impossible to rent a house.[91] As a result of this rapid increase of population the real estate business flourished, sites skyrocketed in value, and fortunes were made almost over night.[92] The assessed valuation of property increased with an acceleration hitherto unknown. From a total valuation in 1850 of $7,220,249 it increased to $36,335,281 in 1857 and to $275,986,550 in 1870.[93]

Neither the Illinois Central nor the Associates participated at first in the Chicago boom. The former had received but 16,368 acres in Cook County, all of which was over 6 miles from the city limits and unsuited for urban development. Much of it required draining before it could be put to any use.[94] With the extension of the city limits southward, however, the Illinois Central undertook a suburban development at Hyde Park, where in 1856 it laid out an addition and offered lots for sale.[95]

To some towns along its line the construction of the Illinois Central was anything but a blessing. This was particularly true

[89] *Ninth Census*, I, 110. See Chicago Board of Trade, *Annual Report*, 1866, p. 12, for official and estimated figures for briefer intervals.

[90] Johnson to Osborn, September 10, 1855, M. O.

[91] Neal to Burrall, July 25, 1854; Johnson to Perkins, September 19, December 20, 1855; Whitfield to Ackerman, June 13, 1856, M. O. See the comments of O. H. Browning made on his trip to Chicago in 1855 in Pease and Randall, editors, *The Diary of Orville Hickman Browning* (Illinois State Historical Library, *Collections*, vol. xx, Springfield, 1925), pp. 191–192.

[92] There is much information on the real estate business in Chicago in Wright, *Chicago: Past, Present, Future.*

[93] Andreas, *op. cit.*, I, 183; II, 52.

[94] MS. by B. F. Ingraham, "Statement of Lands Owned by I. C. R. R. Co. situated in Counties and Districts," box 53, 63rd St.; *Sectional Maps*, plates A and 23.

[95] *Ibid.*, p. 60. See an interesting article in *Illinois Central Magazine* (August, 1926), xv, 3–28, entitled "Suburban Service for Seventy Years."

of the city of Cairo, the promoters of which had expected that after the construction of the central railroad it would become the entrepôt for all of central and southern Illinois. Cairo seemed to have an excellent geographical location, being centrally situated at the confluence of the Ohio and Mississippi Rivers. Its site, however, was subject to frequent floods which, in the absence of adequate levee protection, were disastrous for the city. Poor drainage facilities caused much sickness, a fact which was constantly enlarged upon by newspapers of rival cities.[96] The original settlers of the southern tip of Illinois were largely southern uplanders who were ignorant, indolent, fond of strong drink, and opposed to public schools. They seemed to lack all the sturdy qualities necessary to develop a pioneer community successfully.

The town site of Cairo was owned by an avaricious corporation which at that time refused to sell lots and would lease them only for short periods.[97] To develop the location, large amounts of capital were needed to construct the levees, provide adequate drainage facilities, and establish industries. Capital had flowed into these undertakings for a time, but it had mostly been squandered by inefficient and unwise management and it was difficult to obtain more. In the end, the Cairo promoters pinned all their hopes for the city's future on its becoming the southern terminus of the central railroad.

As a result of the agreement entered into by the Cairo Company with the Illinois Central in 1851, some progress was made. By the terms of this and subsequent agreements, the Illinois Central was to construct embankments and levees to protect the city from inundation [98] and was to pay the Cairo Company $100,000 for the land required for station and trackage facilities.[99] The Cairo

[96] For an example of this fierce antagonism of rival southern Illinois cities see the biting comments on flood and sickness in Mound City in the *Cairo City Gazette*, July 2, 1858.

[97] Rev. E. B. Olmstead in *Home Missionary* (December, 1852), xxv, 188–189. See also chapter entitled "Cairo in Servitude to Land Companies," in Lansden, *History of the City of Cairo*, pp. 167–169.

[98] *Cairo, Illinois, 1856*, pp. 10–12. The agreements of June 11, 1851, and May 31, 1855, may be found in the pamphlet *The Past, Present, and Future of the City of Cairo, in North America*, pp. 85–95.

[99] See copy of deed dated August 12, 1853, Brayman MSS.

Company used its newly acquired capital to erect a large hotel, foundry, planing machine shop, sawmills, and other buildings for industrial purposes. The construction of the Illinois Central Railroad made for prosperity, as a large force of men was employed at this point,[100] and provisions, iron, and other materials were brought in by river to Cairo. As early as September, 1853, it was reported that the demand for city lots had become so keen that the Cairo Company felt warranted in beginning sales.[101] By 1854 over 600 lots had been sold to people who planned to locate on them shortly,[102] and in 1855 the number of lots sold increased to 1200, some having drawn fancy prices.[103] Meantime a building committee of the stockholders had been formed in New York to construct several entire blocks. So encouraging was the situation that one sanguine writer predicted that in a few years Cairo would become one of the most important commercial cities in the entire Mississippi Valley.[104] In 1856 there were said to be 453 houses actually erected in the city, in addition to 21 under construction, and contracts for many others had been signed. Industry was booming, especially the flour and sawmills, machine shops, and breweries.[105] Population continued to move in at a rapid rate and in 1860 the census reported 2188 residents in Cairo and a decade later 6267.[106]

Although the growth of Cairo was by no means inconsiderable, it entirely failed to meet the expectations of the city's promoters. The wonder is, however, that the settlement grew at all, given its unhealthy climate, its constant inundations, and the selfishness of its promoters. The very hand of Providence seemed directed

[100] *Home Missionary* (December, 1852), xxv, 189.

[101] Taylor to Brayman, September 21, 1853, Brayman MSS. The Illinois Central did not participate in the Cairo real estate boom until somewhat later. The *Annual Reports*, 1871, 1873, show sales to the extent of $7000 in Cairo city lots.

[102] *Chicago Weekly Democrat*, January 21, 1854.

[103] Clement Satterthwaite in Satterthwaite circular, June 27, 1855.

[104] *Chicago Weekly Democrat*, January 21, 1854. Advertisements for the sale of Cairo lots had been inserted as early as January 16, 1851, in the *Illinois State Register*, but apparently none were sold at that time. For comments on Cairo and its development see Ferguson, *op. cit.*, pp. 386–388. Ferguson visited Cairo in 1855 and was somewhat more favorably impressed with the city than were others of his countrymen.

[105] *Cairo, Illinois, 1857*, pp. 23–25.

[106] *Ninth Census*, I, 108. In 1850 the city had a population of 242.

against Cairo. In 1857 and 1858 it was visited by a series of misfortunes including an earthquake, fire, flood, and pestilence.[107] As in 1837, Cairo seemed to have fallen into decay after the first effects of the railroad boom began to lose their influence. Indeed, in 1862 travellers reported that the city had seen its best days and was then very noticeably on the down grade.[108] The Civil War, however, made it an important point for military and naval operations.[109] Gunboats and troops were stationed there and served to draw in that undesirable element which usually follows the Army. Large government expenditures and important developments in river transportation helped to revive the prosperity of this community,[110] and for the duration of the war the town was a busy center. But this was a temporary stimulus only and it did not produce a lasting effect upon Cairo.

In the 'fifties and 'sixties southern Illinois was largely neglected by incoming settlers; this prevented the building up of a productive hinterland to Cairo such as Chicago enjoyed. The decline of river navigation affected Cairo adversely, and thereafter much development was not to be expected. The Illinois Central had given a brief and temporary impetus to the growth of the city, but as we have seen the road actually reversed the trade routes and sent the agricultural produce of the State, particularly fruit, to Chicago. Cairo eventually became a mere way station on the line from Chicago to the Gulf, and today a cut-off is being constructed which will leave what was originally intended as the main terminus of the Illinois Central a small station on a branch line.

Galena, the lead-mine city, was similarly affected by the construction of the Illinois Central. This enterprising metropolis —

---

[107] There is much material on the misfortunes of the Cairo Company in 1857 and 1858 in *The Past, Present, and Future of the City of Cairo in North America.* See also the *New York Tribune,* July 1, 1858, quoting the *St. Louis Republican.*

[108] British travellers since the days of Charles Dickens have been hostile to Cairo. See the fulminations of Anthony Trollope in *North America,* 396 ff., and the criticism of Edward Dicey in *Six Months in the Federal States,* ii, 116 ff., and William Howard Russell, *My Diary North and South* (London, 1863), II, 53 *passim.*

[109] N. P. Banks to Osborn, April 16, 1861, "W. H. Osborn, President," 1860–1861, M. O.

[110] George S. Boutwell to Horatio Woodman, July 14, 1862, Woodman MSS.

the third city in size in Illinois in 1850 [111] — was to have been the northern terminus of the road, according to the original plan of Breese and other advocates of the central railroad. Political expediency and the city's distance from the Mississippi, however, had brought about modifications in the plan; Galena was made a way station and Dubuque was selected as the northern terminus.[112]

The residents of Galena were furious at this change in the original bill. Their representatives voted against the charter [113] and the city took steps to prevent the road from building west of it.[114] This antagonism was caused by fear that the future growth of Galena was doomed unless the railroad could be stopped there. There was good reason for this fear, as the lead-mining industry was already declining and was never again to be as important as it had been in the 'forties.[115] As mining in Jo Daviess County declined, agriculture became more attractive,[116] but this county, lying in the unglaciated region of northwestern Illinois, was less fertile than the prairie regions of eastern and central Illinois and farming never became really profitable. The Illinois Central lands in this county were taken up slowly during the 'fifties and 'sixties, and as late as 1865 over 15,000 acres remained unsold.[117] Furthermore, after the railroads were built the large wholesale trade which had developed in Galena prior to 1850 was rapidly lost to Dubuque and Chicago.[118] Finally, the operation of the ferry at Dunleith and later the construction of the railroad bridge across the Mississippi to Dubuque served to substitute the latter place for Galena as the commercial center of the old lead-mining

---

[111] *Ninth Census*, I, 108–121.

[112] See Chapter II of the present work for this change.

[113] *Journal of the Senate*, 1849–1851, p. 215.

[114] Ferguson, *op. cit.*, pp. 400–401.

[115] *New York Tribune*, July 9, 1852. For a graph of lead production from 1830 to 1880 in this district see B. H. Schockel, "Settlement and Development of the Lead and Zinc Mining Region of the Driftless Area with Special Emphasis upon Jo Daviess County, Illinois," *Mississippi Valley Historical Review*, IV, 180.

[116] Schockel, *loc. cit.*, p. 187 ff. For more detailed information see "History of Development of Jo Daviess County," by the same author in Illinois State Geological Survey, *Bulletin* (1916), No. 26, pp. 173–228.

[117] *Sectional Maps*, p. 58.

[118] Augustus L. Chetlain, *Recollections of Seventy Years* (Galena, 1899), pp. 46–48, 278–280.

region of northwestern Illinois and southwestern Wisconsin.[119] The development of Galena had reached its peak about the middle of the 'fifties, and since then it has been gradually declining.[120]

There were a number of less important communities which also suffered from the construction of the railroad. The Illinois Central, which was assured of sufficient income during its early years from the sale of its lands, did not have to establish its route in the most populous regions. It could even afford to avoid towns of considerable importance if there was a possibility of building up new centers which would rival the old ones. The provisions of the charter and political expediency prevented the Company from carrying this policy too far. It was impossible to avoid such important towns as Cairo, Decatur, Bloomington, Dixon, Freeport, and Galena, all of which were made stations on the main line. In some other cases, however, the route avoided existing settlements, and as a result new and rival towns were established not far from the older communities. Prominent examples of this substitution are Kankakee for Bourbonnais, West Urbana or Champaign for Urbana, Centralia for Central City, Anna for Jonesboro, and La Salle for Peru.

The considerations which induced these substitutions were various. Some of them have already been touched upon. In the case of Centralia the deciding factor was the inability of the Company to arrive at a satisfactory agreement with the local magnates of Central City. The chief reason for establishing the station at West Urbana was the saving which would result in the cost of constructing this route rather than that leading through Urbana.[121] This motive was of importance in other cases. A third factor was the desire on the part of the Company to secure the benefits of town-site promotion for itself or for the Associates.

In all the cases mentioned above the newer towns, having the advantage of railroad connections, quickly became more im-

[119] J. Ruggles to J. C. Fairchild, April 29, 1853, Fairchild MSS.; Chetlain, *op. cit.*, pp. 278–279.

[120] The population of Galena in 1850 was 6004; in 1860 it was 8196 and in 1870 7019. *Ninth Census*, I, 113. For a graph of the population changes in Galena from 1820 to 1900 see Schockel in *Mississippi Valley Historical Review*, IV, 177.

[121] Bateman and Selby, *Historical Encyclopedia of Illinois and History of Champaign County* (Chicago, 1905), II, 760–761.

portant than the older settlements. This was not caused entirely by new immigration to the locality but was partly due to the movement of population from the unsuccessful town to its growing rival. Thus West Urbana grew in a year from nothing to a community boasting 100 houses, 300 buildings under construction, 400 to 500 inhabitants, two large hotels, six stores, four or five lumber yards, and a Presbyterian church.[122] By 1860 this new town had displaced Urbana as the leading settlement in the county.[123] Urbana's growth was much slower till it received direct railroad connections of its own. The same results were apparent at Kankakee, which by 1860 surpassed Bourbonnais in population and a decade later was two and a half times as populous.[124] An even greater disparity was shown by Centralia, which in 1870 had a population of 3190, while its neighboring community, Central City, had but 833 people.[125] Similarly Anna and La Salle outdistanced Jonesboro and Peru, respectively.

Urban development along the line of the Illinois Central is strikingly shown by statistics. In the census of 1850 there were only ten towns listed in the immediate vicinity of its route; ten years later there were 47 towns listed and in 1870 81. The total population of these towns, excluding Chicago, was roughly speaking 12,000 in 1850, 70,000 in 1860, and 172,000 in 1870.[126]

The urban development of Illinois during the 'fifties and 'sixties was, to a considerable extent, the work of the Illinois Central. The road was a vital factor in Chicago's rapid expansion in this period; it was even more important to the development of the junction points such as Mattoon, Mendota, Freeport, La Salle, and Bloomington; it was of paramount importance in building up new towns in regions hitherto unsettled. Such lusty and growing towns as Kankakee, Champaign, Effingham, Onarga, Carbondale, Centralia, and Amboy were its creations, practically speaking.

---

[122] *Chicago Weekly Democrat*, May 5, 1855.

[123] *Ninth Census*, I, 109.

[124] *Ibid.*, I, 114.

[125] *Ibid.*, I, 116.

[126] Compiled from *ibid.* As it is not possible in many cases to separate the village and town population from that of the township in which they are located, these statistics include a considerable proportion of the rural population which it is difficult to estimate without an examination of the original records.

The town-lot business proved to be exceedingly profitable both to the Illinois Central and to private individuals. But the hopes of numerous sanguine town promoters, among them the Illinois Central and the Associates, in regard to the future growth of many of the towns discussed above, were to be sadly disappointed. Some towns which developed rapidly in the 'fifties and 'sixties began to decline in later decades as Galena had done earlier. Many of them are today little more than shipping and receiving centers for the surrounding communities. Brought into being by the need of their farming hinterland for a shopping and shipping center, they could expand only up to the limit of the needs of the community, a limit which was soon reached.

On the whole the Illinois Central as well as the Associates made an excellent thing out of the town-site business, the Company's income from this source amounting to over half a million dollars.[127] The towns helped to build up traffic for the line and their growth also served to increase the demand for agricultural lands. In the vicinity of flourishing towns such as Decatur and Bloomington, and in the hinterland of Chicago, the farming lands of the Illinois Central were quickly snapped up, while lands more remote remained unsold.[128] Town development and rural development acted and interacted upon each other, and their history cannot well be separated. It is now necessary to turn to these agricultural lands and see what policy the Company followed in disposing of them.

---

[127] By the close of 1871 the total income from the sale of town lots was $472,836. *Annual Report*, 1871. The sales from 1872 to 1897, the last year that figures for this item were given, amounted to $38,701. This does not include sales of $7000 of lots in Cairo, nor does it include lands sold to other promoters for town-site promotion. The figures are taken from the *Annual Reports*.
[128] *Sectional Maps, passim.*

# CHAPTER VIII

## THE LAND DEPARTMENT AND ITS POLICIES

THE Illinois Central Railroad, in the first decade of its existence, was primarily a land company and secondarily a railroad company.[1] Its construction was made possible by a mortgage secured upon its lands and the interest charges were paid and the bonds retired by the proceeds from land sales. Proper administration of the lands was, then, of the utmost importance.

Shortly after the organization of the Company David Neal was placed in charge of the lands.[2] Neal was a New Englander and had little acquaintance with the West except through his connection with the Michigan Central Railroad. He was not familiar with the land problems of the West, nor with the real estate business, as his energies had been largely devoted to commercial ventures and railroad promotion. He was not sufficiently tactful to avoid antagonizing certain powerful interests in Illinois, and in general he was poorly qualified for the direction of such a vast enterprise as the management and sale of the Illinois Central grant.

Neal sought assistance from E. S. Prescott, Land Commissioner of the Illinois and Michigan Canal. Prescott had been remarkably successful in selling the canal lands and was therefore called to New York to aid in establishing the land system of the Illinois Central.[3] He was offered the position of head of the newly created Land Department, but declined it because he was unable to share the optimistic views of Neal, Griswold, and Schuyler regarding the prices which the lands would fetch in the future. "I regard it as a hopeless effort to undertake to make the money out of their lands, that the program requires," wrote Prescott to Swift. "You and I know that the expectations of the Company on this part

---

[1] Richard Cobden had made this point in his letter to Walmsley of September 18, 1857, a photographic copy of which is in the 16th St. archives.
[2] Neal, Autobiography, Neal-Rantoul MSS.
[3] Prescott to Swift, October 23, 29, 1853, Swift MSS.

can never be realized in the 'field,' however pleasantly it may be
figured out on paper." [4] Prescott's strange lack of foresight — for
he was completely wrong in his predictions — is in strong contrast to the optimism of Neal and his associates.

Neal's first task was the selection of the lands. Under the
terms of the federal land grant, the Illinois Central was entitled
to the alternate even sections of land for a distance of 6 miles on
both sides of the road. Where any of these sections had already
been disposed of by the Government, the Company was entitled
to select indemnity lands from among the even sections in the area
from 6 to 15 miles from the road. On the day Congress passed the
land grant, the Commissioner of the General Land Office with-
drew the lands along the proposed route from sale in order to prevent speculators from anticipating the Company in choosing its
lands.[5] As the location of the route was not finally determined
until February, 1852,[6] Neal was delayed in selecting the lands.
Furthermore, the Swamp Land Act of September 28, 1850,[7]
greatly complicated his task because some of the Illinois counties
claimed lands which he claimed for the railroad. By March, 1852,
Neal succeeded in practically finishing the selection, location, and
transfer of titles and had 2,589,498 acres certified to the railroad.[8]
After a hurried trip to England to aid in negotiating a loan with
the British bankers Neal went to Illinois, where he organized the
Land Department as a separate and distinct branch of the Company and made preparations for the sale of its extensive holdings.[9]

A tremendous amount of work was involved in bringing the
lands on the market. After selection, they had to be located, sur-

[4] Prescott to Swift, April 16, 1854, *ibid*.
[5] *Chicago Democrat*, October 2, 1850. The Land Commissioner said that the
lands were withdrawn also for the purpose of preventing speculators from purchasing
the alternate sections which the Government would sell later for double the minimum price. *Annual Report*, Commissioner of the General Land Office, 1851, p 17.
[6] Letter of R. B. Mason, engineer in charge of construction, to C. C. P. Holden,
October 12, 1883, Andreas, *op. cit.*, I, 253.
[7] 9 *U. S. Stat.*, 519–520.
[8] Neal, Autobiography. It was reported at the annual meeting in March, 1853,
that all the lands had been selected with the exception of a small portion which had
still to be chosen to replace an equal amount of those first taken which, on subsequent examination, appeared to have been previously sold or entered by individuals.
*Annual Report*, 1853.                    [9] Neal, Autobiography.

veyed, and platted. Their relative value had to be ascertained, and this necessitated information as to their distance from the line of the road and from towns or cities, their proximity to timber, whether they were level, rolling or broken, dry or swampy, prairie or timber lands. Such information was obtained from the field notes, descriptions, and remarks of the government surveyors.[10] This proved to be a mistake, for inaccurate and incomplete descriptions of the land were thus obtained and, as will be seen later, the Company was forced to resurvey and re-plat practically the whole area of its lands.

The question of the terms on which the lands were to be sold aroused a great deal of controversy. Soon after the State granted the Illinois Central its charter, it was seen that the wishes of the people and of the newly formed company were in sharp opposition. The people of Illinois were insistent on three things: low prices to attract settlers, rapid sale to hasten the growth of the State, and immediate granting of title after sale in order that the lands, which were exempt from taxes as long as they were in the possession of the Company, might be taxed by the towns and counties. These desires had been met in part by the Legislature, which had included in the charter sections requiring that the lands be sold only for cash or bonds of the Company and that the lands remaining unsold after ten years from the date of the completion of the road be put up at auction and sold to the highest bidder.[11] By the former provision lands sold were made immediately taxable, and by the latter it was hoped that fairly quick sales were ensured.[12]

These safeguards did not satisfy the people of Illinois, who were afraid that the railroad, like the private speculators, would hold its lands for increased prices and thus retard the development of

[10] Neal in *Annual Report*, 1854. Neal's report is printed in the *Prairie Farmer* (June, 1854), XIV, 230–233.    [11] *Charter*, pp. 26–27.

[12] For purposes of comparison, it is interesting to note that the State Legislature, in regulating the sales of land granted for the construction of the Illinois and Michigan Canal, limited the amount of land which any person could purchase to 640 acres. Putnam, *op. cit.*, p. 82. Obviously this was to prevent speculators from monopolizing the lands. A similar provision in the Act of 1851 would have prevented the Company from committing one of its gravest errors in selling large tracts of land to speculators who were later forced to cancel.

the State.[13] Public sentiment on this point was expressed at a meeting at Bloomington on March 27, 1851, of "those opposed to Land Monopoly along the line of the Illinois Central Railroad." After pointing out that large speculative holdings had greatly increased of late, owing to completed and projected internal improvements, the meeting resolved that (1) Congress should restrict purchasers from entering large quantities of land along the proposed line, (2) the lands granted to the Illinois Central should be sold only to actual settlers, (3) sales of public land to wholesale purchasers were viewed by the people as a "source of great injury to the progress and improvement of the state. . . ." [14] The editors of the *Prairie Farmer* condemned any policy of withholding the lands from sale, and called upon the people to protest and to demand "a change which would allow the speediest sale and settlement of the lands. . . ." [15] In his annual message of 1851, Governor French, voicing the fear of the people, recommended that the lands be offered for sale at reasonable rates. He said, "Such a regulation is important to prevent a monopoly of a large and valuable body of lands from being held up for sale, and to induce their early settlement and cultivation." [16]

In determining its land policy the Illinois Central had to take into consideration a number of conflicting interests. Although large land companies had existed before, none had been faced with the problems which confronted this railroad in disposing of its holdings. Among these peculiar problems were the following: (1) the fact that the Illinois Central was a semi-public corporation and must avoid arousing public opposition which might endanger its charter or lead to forced sales of its lands at auction; (2) the need for early sales in order to satisfy hungry stockholders who

---

[13] Annual Message of Gov. Matteson to the Illinois Legislature, January 1, 1855, *Illinois Reports*, 1855, p. 3.

[14] *Prairie Farmer* (1852), XII, 244–245, quoting *Bloomington Intelligencer*.

[15] *Ibid.*, p. 245. Cf. *Prairie Farmer* (1850), X, 353. In February, 1854, the same paper demanded that the Legislature require annual sales of the lands. The charter only escaped being amended to this effect by a change of one vote. *Prairie Farmer* (1854), XIV, 230. The persistent criticisms of this paper did not cease until the Company inserted a large advertisement of its lands in the issue of February, 1855, when they finally ceased. *Ibid.*, XV, 42.

[16] Message of January 6, 1851, *Illinois Reports*, 1851, p. 20.

were expecting quick returns on their investment; (3) the fact that the Company was primarily a public carrier and needed to build up freight and passenger traffic more than it needed to receive high returns for its lands. This last consideration made it advisable that the lands be disposed of as rapidly as permanent settlers could be induced to take them up, not, however, without securing a good price for them.

President Schuyler at first determined to withhold the lands from sale until the increase in population and the construction of the road had enhanced their value.[17] Obviously, if the road were to be financed from the proceeds of land sales as planned, delay in bringing the lands on the market was necessary. They had been subject to sale for years at $1.25 per acre, had little present value, and until the road was constructed would yield but a small return. It was the construction of the road which would create their value. Schuyler could maintain that if the Government was to charge double the minimum price for its alternate sections the Illinois Central ought to be allowed to withhold its lands from sale until construction was complete and then charge what the market conditions warranted. The Legislature had inadvertently encouraged this plan by including in the charter a provision (intended to secure the completion of the entire road) to the effect that the lands along each division were not to be sold until that part of the road was completed.[18]

In the end, the directors determined to modify their original plan of withholding all the lands from sale, and instead to reserve 2,000,000 acres, called "Construction Lands," until their market price had reached a minimum valuation set upon them. These Construction Lands were sub-classified as follows: 50,000 acres were designated as of "special value" and were given a minimum price of $20 per acre; 350,000 acres were classed as "superior agricultural lands" and were valued at a minimum of $15 per acre;

---

[17] Pamphlet prepared by Schuyler: *To the Directors of the Illinois Central Railroad* (New York, April 23, 1851).

[18] *Charter*, pp. 25–26. There was an exception to this provision in that one-quarter of the lands, styled "Free Lands," could be sold after the entire road had been surveyed and located and the work actually commenced on the main line. *Ibid.*, p. 24.

1,300,000 acres were classed as of "high agricultural quality" and valued at $8 per acre; and 300,000 acres were priced at $5 per acre.[19] Upon the Construction Lands was placed the mortgage, the returns from which provided funds for the construction of the road. The remaining 595,000 acres were made available for early sale, as permitted by the charter.[20] Of these lands 345,000 acres, situated on the Chicago branch, were called "Free Lands." No price restrictions were placed on them and their proceeds were free to be used as the officials desired.[21] The remaining 250,000 acres were styled "Interest Lands." The returns from the sale of these lands were to be used to meet the interest charges on the construction bonds.

The Illinois Central was only one of many large land owners seeking immigrants to settle upon and purchase their lands. Michigan, Wisconsin, and Minnesota were actively bidding for settlers to take up the federal and state lands within their borders. In Illinois itself, the State, the counties, the Illinois and Michigan Canal, and the private speculators together held a much larger quantity of land than did the Illinois Central, and they were bringing their holdings on the market at the same time as the latter was preparing to offer its lands. In some respects the existence of these other land distributing agencies was beneficial to the railroad and in other respects detrimental.

It was fortunate for the Illinois Central that the competition of federal lands in Illinois had no longer to be faced. By 1855 the public domain in the State had been practically disposed of, having passed into the hands of settlers and the large holders mentioned above.[22] If the government lands had still been available for settlers at the minimum price of $1.25 an acre, or at the double minimum, the Company would have been unable to dispose of its

---

[19] *Annual Report*, 1856. Brownson accepts the classification of 1851 which was modified. Brownson, *op. cit.*, p. 118. The original plan was thus:

    100,000 acres at $25 per acre
    300,000    "    "  15   "    "
    1,200,000  "    "  10   "    "
    400,000    "    "   6   "    "

[20] *Charter*, p. 24.
[21] Report of Neal in *Annual Report* for 1854.
[22] See above, Chapter VI.

lands even at the minimum price of $5 required by its mortgage until a much later date. Such a situation would have been disastrous to the railroad, which, as we have seen, needed quick returns from land sales in order to meet its running expenses and the interest upon its construction bonds. Thus, by acquiring large tracts of government land, the private speculators had done the Illinois Central a great service.

There was another side to the speculators' activities which was less favorable to the interests of the Illinois Central. In the first place, although the speculators' lands were held for prices much higher than the old government minimum, they were not withdrawn from the market. The millions of acres held by this class were in the market in open competition with the lands of the railroad. The competition of these lands constantly hampered the Company in disposing of its grant at the prices which it hoped to receive.[23] Furthermore, by adopting the Company's own policy of holding its lands for higher prices, the speculators retarded the development of the State. Thus a correspondent in Coles County observed in 1857 that the great hindrance to the development of the county was the existence of large bodies of uncultivated land held by speculators.[24] Seven years later the same observation was made with respect to Shelby County.[25] The same situation existed in most of the prairie counties, although it was more noticeable in eastern Illinois. This situation not only slowed up the land sales of the Illinois Central but it also kept down its income from freight and passenger traffic. To some extent these unfavorable influences were offset by the efforts made by these speculators to induce immigration and settle colonies in Illinois. All such activities helped to settle the State and to develop traffic for the road.

In spite of the existence of numerous competitors, the Illinois Central seemed assured of success in rapidly disposing of its grant at substantial prices, as in the early 'fifties other large land owners in the State were able to sell their holdings profitably. The sale of 1000 acres near Kankakee for $15,000 was recorded; 400 acres

[23] See *Annual Reports*, 1857–1864; *Railway Times*, March 26, 1859.
[24] *Prairie Farmer*, June 11, 1857.
[25] *Country Gentleman* (March 10, 1864), XXIII, 164.

in Ogle County which had been purchased in 1850 for $2000 were now sold for $4800; 1800 acres in Lee County, held at $3 since 1843, brought $7 per acre; 300 acres in another location in Ogle County which had been purchased for $1000 now resold for $2200.[26] Even more reassuring were the high prices for which the lands of the Illinois and Michigan Canal sold. The total sales per year and the average price per acre for canal lands for the years 1848 to 1856 were as follows:[27]

| Year | Total acreage sold | Average price |
|---|---|---|
| 1848 | 45,809 | $4.63 |
| 1849 | 3,338 | 7.73 |
| 1850 | 6,443 | 6.24 |
| 1851 | 23,848 | 4.62 |
| 1852 | 32,871 | 8.82 |
| 1853 | 22,987 | 12.35 |
| 1854 | 42,559 | 7.88 |
| 1855 | 25,651 | 8.32 |
| 1856 | 10,922 | 11.96 |

These lands were no better for agricultural purposes than most of the lands included in the railroad grant.

The State of Illinois also was benefiting from the enhanced prices which the period of prosperity had brought, although to a less extent than the Canal Company or private speculators. The 80,000 acres of State land sold from December, 1852, to December, 1854, brought an average of $3.50 per acre,[28] and in the following two years the average price of the 42,000 acres sold was a little below $3.[29] With such prices prevailing, and with the government lands largely disposed of and the speculators' holdings reserved for further price increases, the time seemed ripe in 1854 for bringing on the market the lands of the Illinois Central.

Prior to 1854 the Illinois Central had begun to dispose of its lands to a favored class of purchasers, the preemption claimants. The people of Illinois had all the feelings of the frontiersmen in

---

[26] *Economist*, reprinted in *New York Tribune*, October 19, 1852.

[27] *Annual Reports* of the Illinois and Michigan Canal for 1848 to 1856. The town lots, which comprised by far the greater part of the land business, are not included here.

[28] Biennial Report of Auditor of Public Accounts, December 1, 1854, *Illinois Reports*, 1855, p. 36.

[29] Biennial Report of Auditor of Public Accounts, December, 1856, *Illinois Reports*, 1857, p. 97.

regard to the public lands. Their attitude led them to make frequent demands for federal grants, to connive at timber depredations, and above all to support the claims of squatters against absentee land owners and large speculators. The Legislature of Illinois, responsive to public sentiment, had thought it advisable to recognize the rights of the squatters by extending to them the principle of the federal preemption laws. Accordingly, it was provided in the Company's charter that persons who, on September 20, 1850, resided on any of the lands afterwards conveyed to the railroad should have the right of purchasing at $2.50 per acre that portion of the quarter section upon which they had made improvements.[30] Neal was well aware that the people of Illinois regarded the Illinois Central with suspicion. In an attempt to allay any ill-feeling he made sure that the Land Department, in its treatment of the preemption claimants, gave no cause for criticism. Extensions of time were granted to enable delinquents to take advantage of the preemption clause of the charter and every effort was made to assist them. So successful was Neal in dealing with the squatters that Governor Matteson, in his annual message of January 10, 1853, called attention to his wise policy.[31] By 1855, 106,591 acres had been deeded to approximately 1600 preemption claimants for the sum of $267,337.[32] As cash payment was required for these lands the Company received a quick return from them. Most of the preemption claims were in the southern counties, and often they comprised the best land in the district. Two or three years later they might have sold at prices ranging from $6 to $15 per acre. The preemption clause thus deprived the Company of nearly a million dollars. It had the further effect of reducing the subsequent demand for lands, as the needs of residents looking for land at the time were satisfied.

[30] *Charter*, p. 32.

[31] *Illinois State Register*, January 13, 1853.

[32] Report of John Wilson, Land Commissioner for 1855, *Annual Report* of the Illinois Central, March, 1856. This figure was not final for Peter Daggy, on October 4, 1882, reported 107,614 acres had been conveyed to preemption claimants. He admitted that this figure even was probably not complete because, owing to the loss of records in the Chicago Fire of 1871, it was impossible to ascertain it exactly. Daggy to Ackerman, October 4, 1882, "Daggy Personal with officers I. C. R. R. Co.," 16th St.

It was unfortunate that the Illinois Central was in such haste to bring its lands on the market. Neal, being imperfectly acquainted with the geographic conditions of the State and of the land grant itself, adopted an arbitrary method of pricing the lands which was to prove most unsatisfactory. In general, his plan was to base the price of the lands on the distance which separated them from the road.[33] Although their "agricultural capability" was likewise to be considered, the determining factor was to be the former. Under this plan there was to be added to the minimum prices already established for the various classes of Construction Lands the sum of $16 minus $1 for each mile they were distant from the road.[34] The Free and Interest Lands were not subject to this general method of valuation but were priced according to their individual circumstances. Neal's method of pricing the land was severely criticized by several of the directors of the Illinois Central, and was abandoned at the first opportunity.[35] It indicated Neal's ignorance of the fundamental factors governing land prices in the State which were known to all successful speculators. Among these factors might be mentioned: distance from and availability of timber for building and fencing purposes, proximity to water, and the competition of other speculators in the sale of land in the same district.

The credit plan which Neal devised to stimulate the sale of the lands was more favorably regarded by the public and by the other directors. Neal saw there was little chance of the lands being sold for cash at the prices placed upon them with the federal lands in other states, the swamp lands, the canal lands, and the speculators' holdings selling for lower prices. He therefore secured an amendment to the charter which permitted sales on credit.[36] He

[33] D. L. Phillips to Brayman, November (8 or 9), 1854, Brayman MSS.; J. N. A. Griswold to Ackerman, December 20, 1890, Ackerman MSS., Newberry Library.

[34] Sheet of instructions prepared to guide the land agents, M. O. Osborn is reported to have said later concerning this plan and its author, "that Mr. Neal's plan was regarded as perfectly Utopian. He spoke of Mr. Neal as a domineering old sea captain and extremely bigoted. He scouted a mathematical rule by which [land] could be sold along the line of the road, and said the whole thing would be overhauled soon." Phillips to Brayman, November 9, 1854, Brayman MSS.

[35] Letters of Phillips and Griswold as in note 33.

[36] Act of February 28, 1854, *Charter*, p. 43.

then recommended that extended credit and low interest rates be granted purchasers on condition that they make certain stipulated improvements on their land within a given time.[37] Although this recommendation later incurred some criticism, it was adopted and remained the basis of the Company's policy toward its grant until the lands were entirely sold. Any other policy would have been suicidal because it would have been impossible to sell the lands for cash except in small amounts. The pioneer farmer had little ready money at any time, and most immigrants would have found it difficult to invest a thousand dollars at once in a farm.

By the terms of Neal's credit plan, an advance payment of interest for two years at 2 per cent per annum was required on Construction Lands, with no payment upon the principal until the beginning of the third year. This advance payment entitled the purchaser to full use of the land. At the beginning of the third year, one-fifth of the principal was to be paid, together with the advance interest for a year upon the remainder. The four final payments, with advance interest, were similarly due upon the third, fourth, fifth, and sixth anniversaries of the signing of the contract. The free lands were to be sold for a cash payment of 25 per cent and the balance in one, two, and three years with interest at 6 per cent per annum. In view of the traditional attitude of the westerner towards timber lands, it was wisely decided not to apply these terms to them but to sell them on a cash basis only. The contracts stipulated that at least one-tenth of the land purchased under the credit terms should be fenced and cultivated the first year, and during each of the five following years an additional tenth should be fenced and cultivated, so that by the beginning of the sixth year one-half of the land would be under cultivation.[38] This provision and later modifications of it were constantly being pointed to by officials of the Company as an indication that speculation in its lands would not be permitted.

As a matter of fact, speculation in the lands was not prevented. In the first place, the very terms of the credit plan encouraged

---

[37] This part of the report is to be found in the *Prairie Farmer*, June, 1854.
[38] Sheet of instructions as in note 34.

large purchases by persons with very little capital but with a great deal of optimism. In the second place, the provision for fencing and cultivating one-half the land within five years was not enforced. To discourage speculators from purchasing the land, and to allay still further the feeling of the people, Neal did, indeed, recommend that persons purchasing for non-agricultural purposes should be required to pay cash. This recommendation, however, was little more than a gesture; it was not adopted, and in the same year Neal was suggesting to capitalists that no better investment could be found than the Illinois Central lands.[39] Further encouragement was given to speculation, though perhaps inadvertently, by the 20 per cent reduction permitted on cash sales. Bonds of the Company were acceptable in lieu of cash and, as the bonds were selling at 25 per cent discount in February, 1855, a total reduction for cash of 40 per cent was possible.[40] By this means persons with capital could secure the lands for practically one-half that which the small purchaser had to pay. This provision was not taken advantage of in the 'fifties, since very little land was purchased for cash, with the exception of town lots and timber lands.

Neal adopted the policy of dividing the lands of the Company into districts, over which agents were placed. The agents were to have charge of selling the lands at prices not below the minimum which had been established. They were chosen from residents of the district on the basis of their knowledge of the land as well as that of their ability as land agents.[41] By December, 1854, agents had been appointed at Urbana, Decatur, Vandalia, Clinton, Bloomington, La Salle, Dixon, Freeport, and Bourbonnais, while plans had been made for others at Jonesboro and Mt. Hawkins.[42] These towns were important focal points on the line of the road, in the vicinity of which the Company possessed much land. Sales offices were also established in Chicago and New York.

[39] Pamphlet prepared by Neal; *2,500,000 Acres of Land in Illinois belonging to the Illinois Central Rail-Road Company* (Salem, 1854), pp. 23–26.

[40] Sheet of instructions as in note 34. By July the bonds were quoted at around 86 to 87. *New York Times*, July 7, 1855.

[41] Neal, *2,500,000 Acres of Land in Illinois*, pp. 26–27.

[42] MS. draft of letter of D. A. Neal to Oscar Malmborg, December, 1854, M. O.

With local agents prepared to handle the lands at ten or a dozen places and officers in both New York and Chicago also authorized to sell them, there was certain to be confusion and difficulty.

Asahel Gridley was the agent appointed by Neal for McLean and Woodford Counties. His appointment was justified by his assistance in securing the charter and also by the success which he had obtained in his own land business. Gridley had foreseen the future value of land in McLean County and had purchased 15,530 acres at prices ranging from $1.25 to $3.75 per acre.[43] The construction of the Illinois Central and the Chicago and Alton Railroads had greatly increased the value of his property. Land values in the region jumped to $15 or more an acre, which made him a potentially wealthy man.[44] He had been successful in laying out towns, promoting their growth, securing public institutions for them, and inducing railroad companies to build through them. The development of McLean County in this period is practically a commentary upon the careers of Gridley, the Fells, David Davis, and Isaac Funk. The other agents appointed by Neal were less well known in the State than Gridley, and as their positions were soon abolished they do not seem to merit attention.

Neal's organization of the Land Department had progressed so well by May, 1854, that it was announced through the local press that persons "desirous of purchasing the lands of this company, in any part of the state for purposes of cultivation . . .," should make applications for them at once. Such applications were to constitute a prior claim to the tracts designated at prices to be fixed.[45] As there was now little government land remaining in Illinois there was a marked response to this announcement. By July about 200,000 acres had been applied for and registered, mostly in lots of 40 to 120 acres.[46] A month later this figure had jumped to 335,000 acres.[47] Neal was much gratified by the re-

---

[43] Tract Books, Danville District, S. A. O.

[44] The Illinois Central sold its prairie lands in McLean County for prices ranging from $13 to $20 per acre. Most of these lands were disposed of in the early days of railroad land sales. *Sectional Maps* (1867), plates 13 and 14.

[45] Advertisement in *Chicago Democratic Press*, May 31, 1854.

[46] *Chicago Weekly Democrat*, July 8, 1854.

[47] *Ibid.*, August 19, 1854. This was exclusive of the preemption sales.

sponse, and rightly so, for it vindicated his high prices as well as his plan for extended credit.[48]

Sale of the lands could now be proceeded with, and accordingly authority was sent to Asahel Gridley,[49] and shortly afterwards to the other agents, to begin sales.[50] These regional agents advertised the lands in the local papers,[51] appointed sub-agents,[52] sought out purchasers, and established the prices of the lands within the limits set by the Company.[53] Gridley commenced sales on September 27, 1854, and by October 31 he had sold 15,242 acres in his district for $151,972, or an average price of $9.97 per acre.[54] As long as the local agents were retained Gridley's sales were the largest. By the end of the year eight of the agents had reported sales which totalled 47,280 acres for the sum of $481,000.[55]

The sale of such a quantity of lands at an average price of $10.17 per acre within three months after the Land Department opened for business seems startling in view of the fact that less than four years before the lands had been available for a dollar or less per acre by means of land warrants. It should be remembered, however, that on the bulk of these sales only 4 per cent advance interest on the purchase price was paid,[56] and that purchasers could gain possession of railroad lands for a much smaller advance payment than was required for government lands. This fact was most important in enabling the Company to secure such prices. Furthermore, the more valuable lands were naturally being selected first. It appears that these early sales were made

[48] Pamphlet of Neal, *op. cit.*, p. 5.

[49] Neal to J. N. Perkins, August 25, 1854, M. O.

[50] *Annual Report*, 1854.

[51] Advertisement of John Campbell in *Urbana Union*, October 12, 1854, reproduced in Bateman & Selby, *op. cit.*, II, 767.

[52] *History of McLean County, Illinois* (1879), p. 552.

[53] Sketch of J. N. A. Griswold, Ackerman MSS., Newberry Library.

[54] A. Gridley to D. A. Neal in *Chicago Democratic Press*, November 21, 1854.

[55] The sales were divided as follows:

| | | |
|---|---|---|
| Free Lands | 8,358 acres for $ | 75,614 |
| Construction Lands | 38,921 acres for | 405,392 |

*Annual Report*, 1854.

[56] By this means lands could be purchased for an initial payment of from 20 cents to 80 cents per acre, thus necessitating less capital outlay than was required for the purchase of government lands for which the minimum price was $1.25, or about a dollar per acre by the use of land warrants.

partly to residents who desired to increase their holdings [57] and partly to farmers recently arrived from the eastern states.[58] The situation was promising, but already complaints were being made concerning Neal's administration of the lands.

Ever since the organization of the Land Department, its management and policies had been the subject of continued criticism. Both E. S. Prescott, Land Commissioner, and W. H. Swift, Trustee, of the Illinois and Michigan Canal, disagreed with the policies which were being worked out under the direction of Neal,[59] and, as we have seen, their criticisms had made it difficult for the Illinois Central to dispose of its bonds. After J. N. A. Griswold and W. H. Osborn became directors of the Company, the first internal dissension was heard. Neal's obstinacy and overbearing attitude antagonized these younger men and produced friction within the management. Osborn spoke of him as a "domineering old sea captain and extremely bigoted." [60] Neither Griswold nor Osborn doubted Neal's ability or impeached his honesty, but both felt that it had been a mistake to place in charge of the lands a man who was so unfamiliar with the West and who could not take advice from younger men. Neal stood by the land system which he had created, although both Osborn and Griswold felt that it needed many changes.

The most obvious mistake which Neal had made was to price the lands according to their distance from the Illinois Central Railroad "without reference to quality or distance from other settlements." [61] This policy won more ridicule and criticism for him than any other act of his administration. Neal himself had to make some modifications in it, and upon his withdrawal from the Company in 1855 it was immediately abandoned.

Neal's credit plan also came in for criticism which was, however, tempered by the realization that cash sales to newly arriving

[57] Neal to Sturges, May 6, 1854, M. O.
[58] Gridley reported that the sales were one-fifth to residents and four-fifths to immigrants from New York, Pennsylvania, Ohio, Virginia, Kentucky, and New England. Gridley to Neal, *Chicago Weekly Democrat*, November 25, 1854.
[59] See Chapter IV of the present work.
[60] D. L. Phillips to Brayman, November 9, 1854, Brayman MSS.
[61] *Ibid.*

immigrants at the established prices were impossible. Liberal credit had to be granted, but not to the extent that Neal provided. The requirement that only 4 per cent advance interest should be paid during the first two years of the contracts induced practically all purchasers to buy more land than they could use or reasonably hope to pay for within the six years the contracts had to run. Those who bought at the inflated values of the prosperity years 1854 to 1857 found it impossible to continue payments during the depression years 1858 to 1861. The result was that the Illinois Central failed to receive much income from its lands at a time when, in lieu of revenue from traffic, it was much needed to meet interest charges. It would have been better to have required a somewhat larger initial payment, which would have given the settler a greater stake in his land and at the same time would have prevented overpurchasing. Griswold and Osborn both retained the "no principal payment for the first two years" plan, but Neal's 2 per cent policy was abandoned within a year after he was displaced in the management of the lands. However, only 1 per cent additional interest for each of the first two years was charged and not until the end of the decade was the interest, rate made 6 per cent. Eventually further modifications in the credit terms were made with a view to shortening the life of the contracts.

The chief criticism which Griswold and Osborn made of Neal's administration of the lands was directed against the local agents. In the opinion of these directors, the local agents received a generous commission which, together with other outlays on their account, made their employment too expensive for the amount of work they were doing.[62] Moreover, these agents were not bonded and there was practically no check upon their work. As their compensation was in the form of a commission upon their sales, they naturally tried to make as many and as large sales as possible. They were accused of selling the best lands first, and the prices which they received for them suggest that they were not as

[62] Griswold to Perkins, December 21, 1854; same to (?), January 22, 1855, M. O.; Osborn to Wilson, December 7, 1857, "Presidents Letters," No. 7, box 48, 63rd St.; Osborn in *Annual Report*, 1863; MS. sketch of J. N. A. Griswold, Ackerman MSS., Newberry Library.

solicitious about getting the market value of the lands at the time as they were about making the sales. This was especially true of Gridley, the most active of the local agents. Gridley had been placed in charge of the lands in a region where there were certain to be many sales and in which the price of land was rapidly rising. Nevertheless, the prices he obtained were on the average lower than those for which the neighboring speculators, including himself, were holding their lands. Gridley was later accused of having sold large amounts of land under his charge to bogus purchasers who assigned their contracts over to him. He refused to pay the installments on these contracts and caused the Company much difficulty by arguing that it could not cancel them until the last note had matured.[63]

Griswold and Osborn not only objected to the appointment of sales agents in Illinois but also felt that it was unwise of Neal to give authority to travelling or resident agents elsewhere to sell the lands. Being distant from the State, these men could not be familiar with all the tracts which they might sell and the danger of misrepresentation was too great. Griswold especially disliked the easy way in which Neal had deputized agents to act at different points.[64]

The personnel of the Land Department under Neal also came in for much criticism. John C. Dodge, who had been placed in charge of this office, was, like Neal, poorly qualified for his position. According to his successor, he failed to institute a systematic organization, neglected to furnish the Chicago office with maps, plats, and information on the lands, and provided no means of inducing prospective settlers to purchase Illinois Central lands. He was rude to visitors at the office, and seemed to lack the necessary qualifications of the successful land agent.[65] His accounts were a "labarynth of mistification," the vouchers were not all delivered, and the books were so confusing that the Company was later put

---

[63] Foster to Walker, August 29, 1860, 63rd St.
[64] Griswold to Osborn, January 16, 1855, M. O.
[65] Charles M. Dupuy to Sturges, Osborn & Others, September 6, 1854, M. O. This is a long letter written by the man who was to replace Dodge as land agent. It contains a very critical analysis of the affairs of the Land Department and then proceeds to make recommendations for the future, most of which were put into effect.

to much difficulty in balancing them.[66] Dodge's accounts were even suspected; so far from balancing were they that this reflected upon Neal himself.[67] On two subsequent occasions, when changes were made in the Land Department, similar criticisms were directed by the newly appointed incumbents at the management of their predecessors, so perhaps this censure was partly caused by jealousy. In general, however, the entire management of the office was inefficient and complete changes were necessary.

A final factor which made Osborn anxious to remove Neal was that the latter's interest in the Associates frequently conflicted with his management of the Illinois Central lands. Having the interest of the railroad solely at heart, Osborn objected to the close relationship which existed between the "Old Regime" and the Associates. He felt that the members of this group were using their position as directors of the railroad to aid a land speculating venture. Osborn saw that the Associates were securing much of the profit from the construction of the railroad which should go to the Illinois Central, and that therefore Neal's removal was necessary in order that the railroad should not suffer.

Griswold and Osborn were able to put through the necessary reforms early in 1855, after the former had become president of the road. In January, 1855, the local agents were abolished, the New York office closed, and the business of the Land Department concentrated in Chicago, where in future all sales were to be made.[68] In the following month Charles M. Dupuy was appointed to replace Dodge in the Chicago office and Neal, who was persuaded to resign as vice-president, was "eased out" of his control of the Land Department.[69] For the remainder of the year Griswold, Osborn, and Dupuy cooperated closely in the management of the lands.

After Dupuy took office Neal's method of pricing the lands was

[66] Dupuy to Osborn, February 1, 1855; Ackerman to Osborn, April 28, 1855; Osborn to Perkins, January 1, 1856, M. O.

[67] Prescott to Swift, August 3, 1854, Swift MSS.; Ackerman to Osborn, April 28, 1855, M. O.

[68] Copy of letter of Griswold to the land agents notifying them of the change, January 22, 1855; Dupuy to Osborn, January 25, 1855; Griswold to Osborn, January 12, 1855, M. O.

[69] Prescott to Swift, March 20, 1855, Swift MSS.

abolished. It was seen that the Company possessed insufficient information in regard to its lands to enable it to determine their market value.[70] To remedy this defect, land examiners were appointed to make careful and complete surveys of all the land which the Company possessed. Among the points which the examiners were to consider were the following:[71]

(1) The quality of the land, whether it was rolling or flat, wet or dry; if wet land, whether there was grade enough to drain it by ditching to the nearest streams; if so, whether the land would be suitable for agriculture or grazing.

(2) Were there stock water, streams, or springs on the tract and, if so, how did dry weather affect them?

(3) What was the distance to the nearest farms, the character of the farm buildings, the valuation of the farms, the quantity and quality of the crops, the character of the soil, and the depth and quality of the wells?

(4) What was the distance to the nearest churches, schoolhouses, towns, and villages, and the population of all settlements in the vicinity?

(5) What was the distance to the nearest store, postoffice, gristmill, sawmill, to the nearest point on the Illinois Central, to the nearest station, to the nearest point on neighboring roads, and to their nearest station?

(6) What was the distance to county and township roads, did streams have to be crossed to get to the nearest station, and, if so, were such streams bridged or not?

(7) What was the distance to the nearest timber groves and what were the prices charged for cutting cord wood, posts, and rails?

(8) What was the distance to coal and other mineral deposits?

(9) What was the estimated valuation of tracts adjoining the Company's lands?

(10) What was the price of breaking prairie soil and the availability of persons to do it?

---

[70] Griswold to Osborn, January 23, 1855, M. O.

[71] Taken from "A Circular of Instructions to Examiners of Illinois Central Railroad Lands," issued by C. M. Dupuy, February 12, 1855, copy in Brayman MSS.

(11) What was the cost of fencing?

(12) What was the distance to the nearest stone quarries?

(13) What was the available stock for sale and the price of it?

From this summary it is evident that at last a thorough examination of the lands was undertaken. Elaborate plats were prepared from the notes of the examiners so that the prospective purchaser could see at a glance the nature of the land in each section.[72] On the basis of the information given in the examiners' reports, land prices were readjusted.

Having reorganized the Land Department, Dupuy next turned his attention to stimulating land sales. To accomplish this, he persuaded the Illinois Central to embark on an extensive campaign of immigration promotion. As the methods which the Illinois Central used to direct immigration to its lands were afterwards followed by other land grant railroads, they deserve to be considered in detail.

---

[72] These plats, reproduced on a smaller scale and with some material omitted, are available in the pamphlet, *Sectional Maps*, of which at least three editions were published. The edition of 1867, in addition to the plats, contains information in regard to the nationality of the settlers, the amount of land sold and the amount available, the progress of agriculture and the growth of population of each section.

# CHAPTER IX

## ADVERTISING THE "GARDEN STATE OF THE WEST"

"ILLINOIS presents the most wonderful example of great, continuous, and healthful increase . . .," observed the Superintendent of the Census in 1860. "The gain during the last decade was . . . 860,481, or 101.06 per cent. So large a population, more than doubling itself in ten years, by the regular course of settlement and natural increase, is without a parallel." [1] In this decade the population of Illinois increased more than that of any other state in the Union. The addition to its population was more than double the amount added in the 'forties and has since been surpassed only once.[2] The rapid growth of Illinois in the 'fifties was due in part to the high birth rate then prevailing, but was chiefly the result of the vast amount of immigration into the State. It may be conservatively estimated that over 600,000 native and foreign-born persons moved into the Prairie State in this decade. In the 'sixties the population of Illinois grew 50 per cent, the numerical increase being 827,940. In this decade, too, thousands of immigrants made Illinois their home. The migration of such large numbers of people and their settlement in new homes in Illinois is a subject which merits attention, particularly with reference to the part played by the Illinois Central.

For some years railroad contractors, land companies, and several of the western states had taken steps to direct immigration to particular localities. Michigan seems to have been the first state to foster immigration. In 1845 the Legislature of this state provided for the appointment of an immigration agent to be stationed at New York for the purpose of directing newly arriving immigrants to Michigan.[3] The purpose behind Michigan's activity

[1] *Eighth Census*, 1860, vol.: *Population*, p. vi.
[2] In the last decade of the nineteenth century Illinois's population increased almost a million. *Statistical Abstract* (1923), pp. 4–5.
[3] State of Michigan, *Senate Journal*, 1845, pp. 207, 234–235; *House Journal*, 1845, p. 461; Report of Governor Felch to the Senate, February 27, 1846, in G. N. Fuller, ed., *Messages of the Governors of Michigan* (Lansing, 1926), II, 51.

seems to have been the hope of securing customers for the state lands, the income from the sale of which was badly needed.[4] In 1849 more active measures were taken to secure immigration. Thousands of pamphlets were published and distributed in the East and in Germany, and from this advertising considerable results were obtained.[5]

Michigan's success quickly induced Wisconsin to follow her example.[6] In 1852 the latter made a much larger appropriation for immigration. An agency was established in New York; advertisements were inserted in the foreign language newspapers of that port, and in the papers of important German emigration centers; and advertising matter extolling the healthy climate, the fertile soil, and the general opportunities available in Wisconsin was widely distributed in New York and in Europe.[7] Later, most of the western states followed the examples of Michigan and Wisconsin, but Illinois took no part in such activities.

The Illinois Central was anxious to build up traffic for its line as quickly as possible. Dupuy realized that this could only be brought about by the rapid sale and settlement of the Company's grant. "The profit on the transportation of produce," he declared, "is of *more importance* than a protracted land speculation." [8] Dupuy came to the conclusion that the normal immigration to Illinois, if not stimulated by State or private action, would not be sufficient to take up the lands of the Company with the rapidity with which it hoped to dispose of them. He therefore recommended that the Illinois Central attempt to direct immigration to its lands by means of an extensive advertising campaign both in the eastern states and abroad.

[4] (Almy and Bostwick), *State of Michigan, 1845, To Emigrants*.

[5] Report of the Commissioner of Immigration for the State of Michigan, January 11, 1850, Senate Document, No. 8, pp. 9–23, *Senate Documents*, 1850. Cf. Document No. 12 in *ibid*. J. A. Russell, *The Germanic Influence in the Making of Michigan* (Detroit, 1927), pp. 55–60, discusses this activity.

[6] Theodore C. Blegen, "The Competition of the Northwestern States for Immigrants," *Wisconsin Magazine of History* (September, 1919), III, 4, says that Wisconsin took the lead in immigration activities.

[7] Report of G. Van Steenwyk, State Commissioner of Emigration, December 23, 1852, *Wisconsin Documents*, 1853. See also report of succeeding commissioner, Herman Haertal, for 1853, in *Wisconsin Documents*, 1854. The report of the commissioner for 1854 was not published. Blegen, *loc. cit.*, p. 9.

[8] Dupuy to Sturges, Osborn & Others, September 6, 1854, M. O.

Neal had previously made a similar recommendation. He had also suggested that agents be appointed in the eastern states and in the European countries.[9] Neal was not given sufficient time to work out his plans for stimulating immigration to Illinois, and it was left to Dupuy and Griswold to put into practice some of his ideas.

In September, 1854, Dupuy declared that in view of the unsettled state of Europe the time was ripe for an immigration campaign. He drew attention to the fact that the disturbed classes in Europe were largely agriculturists and mechanics who possessed little property and who, to avoid military service, would jump at the opportunity offered them of purchasing and settling on the fertile lands of Illinois. According to Dupuy, it was not so much a question of stimulating immigration as of directing it to the proper place — i. e. to the lands of the Illinois Central Railroad. He therefore advised the dissemination in suitable localities in Europe of clear and well defined information concerning the extended credit plans and small advance payments required by the Illinois Central for its lands.

Turning to the situation in the United States, Dupuy pointed out that owing to the financial stringency which had arisen that year large numbers of mechanics and skilled operatives had been thrown out of employment. These people, he believed, would be interested in the Illinois Central lands if the matter were properly presented to them. The farmers of the eastern and middle states, whose lands, valued at from $100 to $150 per acre, were no more fertile than the Company's, would likewise be interested.[10]

President Griswold, convinced of the soundness of Dupuy's ideas, and perhaps influenced by the activities of Michigan and Wisconsin and the apathy of the State of Illinois, determined to embark on the largest and most extensive advertising campaign ever entered upon by a land company up to that time.[11] As the

[9] See the two pamphlets by Neal; *The Illinois Central Railroad, Its Position and Prospects; Two Million Five Hundred Thousand Acres of Land in Illinois Belonging to the Illinois Central Rail Road Company.*
[10] Dupuy to Sturges, Osborn & Others, September 6, 1854, M. O.
[11] Dupuy was influenced by the activities of the Emigrant Aid Society, as witness the following: "In connection with this matter perhaps the course pursued by the

first step in this plan, it was proposed to collect through two thousand or more mercantile agencies in the eastern and southern states the names of farmers in their localities to whom advertising circulars could be sent. By this means, it was thought, the advertisements would reach a million farmers.[12] Accordingly, an attractive circular poster was prepared in which the lands were discussed in glowing terms, the prices and credit terms were given, testimonials by residents as to the richness of the soil of Illinois were included, and further information was promised to any persons who applied for it.[13] Copies of this circular were sent to each of the two thousand agencies, which were requested to send in the names of farmers. The lists began coming in at once, and 100,000 copies of the circular were printed and sent out.[14] The readers were urged to pass them on or to post them in some conspicuous place. In addition, they were sent to every post-office north of Tennessee and North Carolina and east of Indiana with the request that they be posted.[15] This circular distribution alone advertised the State more than anything in its previous history had done, but it was merely the beginning.

To bring the lands of the Company before the people who were not listed in these agencies and who might miss the circulars, it was determined to insert simple but attractive advertisements in the principal papers in the East.[16] Among those selected for this purpose were a few metropolitan dailies such as the *New York Times*, the *New York Tribune*, the *Pennsylvania Enquirer*, the *Philadelphia Post*, and the *Boston Traveler*.[17] These journals were chosen partly because they were located in important immigrant ports and would be read by English-speaking arrivals, and partly because land advertisements appearing in them would appeal to the mass of mechanics and laborers who were dissatisfied with their condition. Even more extensive was the advertising done in

'Kansas League' company in New York and Boston would be well worth following."
*Ibid.*                    [12] Dupuy to Osborn, January 10, 1855, M. O.
[13] A copy of this circular is in the Brayman MSS.
[14] Dupuy to Osborn, January 25, 1855, M. O.
[15] *Chicago Democratic Press*, February 12, 1855.
[16] Griswold to Osborn, February 17, 1855, M. O.
[17] List of newspapers in which the advertisement was inserted, February 23, 1855, M. O.

the papers of the smaller cities and towns. In February, 1855, brief advertisements were inserted for six months in one paper in Maine, three in New Hampshire, three in Vermont, one in Rhode Island, five in Massachusetts, three in Connecticut, five in New York, four in Pennsylvania, two in New Jersey, and one in Missouri.[18] As the Company expected to draw many of its purchasers from the discontented agricultural class of the East, large appropriations were expended for advertising in the more substantial agricultural journals such as the *Rural New Yorker*,[19] the *Country Gentleman*,[20] and the *Albany Cultivator*,[21] as well as the *Prairie Farmer*. Advertisements were likewise placed in emigrant gazettes such as the *Illinois Gazetteer & Emigrants Guide*,[22] and *Gerhard's Emigrant's Journal*.[23] In the newspapers of Chicago a great deal of advertising was placed, as that city was an important destination point for immigrants, particularly for those who had bought combination tickets in Europe from railroad and steamship company agents.[24] Advertising was also inserted in local Illinois papers to offset the competition which the Company encountered from other land owners.

The policy of the Illinois Central, when inserting an advertisement, was to request the editor to draw the attention of his read-

[18] The advertisements of the Land Department were not always inserted for the purpose of attracting customers. If that had been the case it would be difficult to explain why the *Chicago Democrat*, whose circulation was smaller than that of the *Press* and the *Tribune*, received the most advertising. It has already been seen how effectively a generous advertisement in the *Prairie Farmer* quieted the carping criticism of John S. Wright. Another example of what appears to have been either poor judgment or an attempt to retain good will for the Company was a large expenditure for advertising in the *American Railway Times* and in the *American Railroad Journal*. In 1855, one of the largest appropriations was made for the former paper which was not widely read by the agricultural and emigrating classes. Wilson to John Haven, December 27, 1856, M. O. It may be accounted for by the fact that in those days railroad journals were more important in railroad financing than today and it was necessary, consequently, for companies to retain their good will. The practice was continued throughout the 'fifties and 'sixties.

[19] $165 was paid for advertising six months in this paper. Correspondence of Moore and Dupuy, September 10, 1855, M. O.

[20] Advertisement in *Country Gentleman* (August 9, 1855), VI, 102.

[21] List of newspapers as in note 17.        [22] Published in June, 1855.

[23] Dupuy to Osborn, October 25, 1855, M. O. See also Wilson to Osborn, May 19, 1856, *ibid*.

[24] *Chicago Democratic Press*, June 21, 1855, and following issues; *Chicago Weekly Democrat*, March 17, 1855.

ers to it by an editorial on the lands and their possibilities.[25] Copy was supplied from the *Annual Reports* or the land pamphlets; the monthly and even the weekly statistics of land sales were also freely furnished. This policy gave the Illinois Central a great deal of publicity at a time when it was much needed.

There were a number of circumstances which brought to the railroad considerable publicity, most of which was favorable. The project for a great central railroad which, when completed, would run the entire length of the State and would be the longest railroad in the country, appealed to the imagination of the people and aroused widespread interest. That clause of its charter which provided that 7 per cent of the gross revenue should be paid into the State treasury made the corporation a semi-public institution whose progress was watched closely. The directors, who were all influential people in the eastern states, were constantly inserting news items concerning their Company and its business in local papers.[26] So widespread was the interest in the Illinois Central Railroad that nearly every mercantile newspaper in the country published periodically the amount of land sold by it.[27] Probably no railroad before the construction of the Union Pacific received as much publicity as the Illinois Central.[28]

The publication and distribution of advertising pamphlets on a vast scale proved to be an equally effective way of making known Illinois and the Illinois Central lands. The evolution of these land pamphlets is interesting and seems worth considering briefly. The first one of the series was prepared by David Neal in 1854.[29] Lack-

[25] Dupuy to Osborn, January 25, 1855, M. O. Dupuy wrote, "Please request the publisher [of the *New York Staats Zeitung*] to give an article on the Subject and under the plea of advantage to German Emigration request him to induce other papers to reprint it or notice it at length, which I think they will do without charge to the Company." Cf. Griswold to Osborn, February 17, 1855, M. O. See also James R. Quinn, advertising agent of the Illinois Central, to Osborn, n. d., but marked received October 20, 1857, *ibid.* See the *Chicago Democratic Press*, July 25, 1857, for one of the advertisements and a brief editorial item calling attention to it.

[26] See *Boston Advertiser* for article inserted by Franklin Haven, Haven to Perkins, November 14, 1855, M. O.

[27] *Central Illinois Farm, Coal and Lumber Co.*, p. 4.

[28] The financial columns of the New York dailies contain much information on the road.

[29] *Two Million Five Hundred Thousand Acres of Land in Illinois Belonging to the Illinois Central Rail Road Company.* This was the first land pamphlet properly so

ing cuts or other embellishments, its appearance was very sombre and unattractive. In this pamphlet the terms of payment were discussed and the agricultural opportunities of the different sections were pointed out. Fifteen hundred of these pamphlets were published and distributed partly to stockholders in England [30] and America and the remainder to prospective purchasers of the lands. They were quickly exhausted and a demand was voiced for more.[31] With the substitution of the Griswold-Dupuy administration of the Land Department for the Neal and Dodge regime, a new pamphlet was prepared, but again without cuts or pictures.[32] A lithographed map was included, however, which greatly added to its value. After discussing the title of the lands, their location, terms, and agricultural value, the cost of moving to Chicago from the East, and the price of town lots, the pamphlet presented a number of testimonial letters from farmers and others in regard to the fertile soil of Illinois. From reading these letters an uncritical person would gather that Illinois lands were not only among the richest and most productive in the world, admirably adapted to the growth of wheat, corn, barley, flax, castor beans, sweet potatoes, and every kind of garden vegetable raised in New England,[33] but were also extremely healthy, easy to plow, and possessed of inexhaustible fertility. In 1856 a more pretentious pamphlet, double the size of the former, was issued; [34] it included additional

called. Three pamphlets, written to secure financial support for the Company, had previously been published, among them Robert Rantoul, Jr., *Letter on the Value of the Public Lands of Illinois* (Boston, 1851). Extracts from this pamphlet were widely reproduced in Illinois newspapers. The *Illinois State Register* (October 23, 1851) said of it, "Its publication and circulation throughout the union would contribute more to increase immigration than anything ever before published." The other two pamphlets were Neal's *The Illinois Central Railroad, Its Position and Prospects* and Robert J. Walker, *Examination of the Value of the Bonds of the Illinois Central Railroad Company* (London, 1851).

[30] Neal to Perkins, August 28, 1854; Devaux & Co. to M. B. Edgar, November 3, December (?), 1854, M. O.

[31] Neal to Perkins, October 11, 1854, *ibid.*

[32] *The Illinois Central Rail Road Company offer for Sale over 2,500,000 Acres . . .* (1855), 32 pp. At least two editions were published in this year, one by Scott and Fulton of Chicago and the other by J. W. Ammerman of New York. Buck, *Travel and Description,* lists only the former. [33] Pamphlet, p. 17.

[34] *The Illinois Central Rail Road Company offers for Sale over 2,000,000 acres . . .* (1856). At least two editions of this were published by Ammerman and one by Oliver of New York.

letters, extracts from newspapers, and statistics on the great profits to be made in farming Illinois lands.

One of the chief criticisms of the pamphlets issued prior to 1857 was that they were too dry and barren and needed some enticing cuts. Joseph Austin, Registrar of the Land Department, suggested the inclusion of "a fancy sketch of an *ideal prairie farm*, with a neat house, an adjacent grove, distant view of the *much dreaded rolling prairie* covered with waving grain, some good-looking stock in the foreground, a living stream of water, handsome Maclura hedges, etc." He added:

> Pictures go a great way in correcting one's ideas, and one of Church's compositions might be so introduced as to create a furor in favor of the rolling prairie. This handsomely engraved or lithographed . . . and placed on the back of every pamphlet, would be, in itself, a capital advertisement, by the effect it would have of giving a pleasant idea of the prairies to the Eastern reader.[35]

In accordance with Austin's advice important changes were made in the pamphlet for 1857.[36] For the first time elaborate cuts were introduced showing most attractive prairie scenes. The frontispiece depicted a cozy one-and-a-half story house on the prairie, fields of wheat and corn carefully fenced, sleek fat cattle feeding in the foreground, a timber grove in the background together with a gently flowing stream and a train passing in the distance. Everything necessary for successful prairie farming was thereby included. Other cuts showed the methods employed in breaking the prairie, and a reaper cutting the rich yield of wheat. In each of the five scenes presented growing timber was pictured, a feature which would apply to only a small part of the Illinois Central lands in central and northern Illinois. By this time the Company was feeling keenly the competition of Iowa lands, and so the pamphlet carefully pointed out the advantages which Illinois possessed over the trans-Mississippi states.[37] To supplement this generous discussion of the attractions of Illinois, a twelve-page extract was reprinted from an advertising circular of a private

[35] Austin to Osborn, April 21, 1856, M. O.
[36] *The Illinois Central Railroad Company offers for Sale over 1,500,000 Acres . . .* (Boston, 1857).
[37] *Ibid.*, pp. 13–17.

PRAIRIE SCENE IN ILLINOIS

(From *A Guide to the Illinois Central Railroad Lands*, Chicago, 1859)

Illinois speculator; two maps showing the line of the road and its lands were also included. Subsequent editions of these pamphlets added no further change of importance.

In common with most real estate literature, the pamphlets exaggerated conditions by magnifying the good qualities and minimizing the less favorable factors such as the difficulty of breaking the prairie, the lack of timber and drinking-water, poor drainage, and the prevalence of epidemics. A later writer, discussing Dupuy's pamphlets, said,[38]

> Some of the pamphlets he got out . . . would do credit to the most accomplished General Passenger Agent of today. If an Eastern or European immigrant could doubt that the Garden of Eden of Palestine was a myth, and that the real scene of Adam and Eve's interview with the apple lay anywhere else than down about Kankakee, he must indeed have been wedded to his biblical gods. In the vernacular of today, Mr. Dupuy "piled it on thick."

President Osborn later admitted that the Land Department had "possibly exaggerated statements of the profits of Illinois farming . . .," [39] but he failed to remedy the situation to any great extent by making corrections in subsequent issues.[40]

It was originally intended to send these pamphlets to persons who, after seeing the circulars or advertisements, desired further information before applying in person at the office of the Land Department.[41] This policy was followed in 1855, but it did not lead to wide-scale distribution. The following year, when Osborn had succeeded Griswold as President, and John Wilson, who had recently retired as federal land commissioner, had replaced Dupuy as head of the Land Department, a more vigorous policy was instituted. Where Griswold and Dupuy were moderate and conservative in their expenditures, Osborn and Wilson were rash and

[38] *Chicago Tribune*, March 6, 1887.
[39] Osborn to Geo. Moffatt, M.P., November 16, 1858, "Presidents Letters," 1858, box 48, 63rd St.
[40] For a bitter criticism of the pamphlet of 1856 by one who felt that he had been misled by it see letter of Malhiot to Daggy, November 29, 1873, box: "Land Dept., Misc. Corr., 1871–1895," 16th St.
[41] Dupuy to Osborn, January 13, 1855, M. O. At least one exception to this was noted. 33,000 copies of the pamphlet were ordered published in sundry papers for $460. Perkins to W. M. Meyer, May 26, 1855, 'J. N. Perkins, Treasurer," No. 6, box 48, 63rd St.

extravagant. For a brief time, they carried out the plans of their predecessors on a grand scale.

Pamphlet distribution of an immense scope began at once. Quantities were sent to presidents and secretaries of agricultural societies for distribution among their members.[42] Dupuy's plan for securing the names of agriculturists was again followed; agents were sent out to secure such names; others were secured from publishing houses, magazine subscription lists, and advertising firms.[43] Copies of the pamphlet were sent to each person whose name was thus secured. An arrangement was made with the publishers of the *New York Day Book* by which the latter contracted to publish the entire pamphlet in a supplement to their paper, guaranteeing that over 20,000 copies would be so issued.[44] Another agreement was made with the editors of the *Maine Farmer* according to which pamphlets were to be sent to their subscribers.[45] One agency alone, it was estimated, distributed 300,000 copies of the pamphlet by placing them in the folds of newspapers in Ohio, Kentucky, Virginia, and western Pennsylvania.[46]

Travelling agents were employed to visit the rural sections of the eastern and southern states to distribute the pamphlets, placards, handbills, and other advertising literature to interested persons. At times there were reported to be between twenty and thirty travelling agents on the road. These agents attended the country fairs, markets, and public meetings and canvassed broad areas giving addresses and distributing literature on Illinois and the Illinois Central lands.

These travelling agents were under the charge of John Corning, who was employed jointly by the Operating and the Land Departments. Corning made his headquarters at Niagara Falls, where he could influence immigrants coming from the East and

[42] Austin to Perkins, April 4, 1856, M. O.

[43] Letters of Austin to Perkins, April 4, September 20, 1856; to Osborn, April 7, 9, 1856, M. O.

[44] Memorandum dated April 29, 1856, Ward's office.

[45] J. N. Perkins to Editors of *Maine Farmer*, May 1, 7, 1856, "Perkins Treasurer," No. 9, 63rd St.; Russell Eaton of Augusta to J. N. Perkins, June 13, 1856, M. O.

[46] *Report of Joseph Fisher to British Shareholders*, p. 58. Cf. Osborn to J. N. Perkins, June 13, 1856, M. O.

from Canada. His task was to secure freight and passenger traffic for the Illinois Central and at the same time to advertise the lands of the Company and supervise the agents who were performing the same work elsewhere; [47] he had two agents assisting him in Niagara Falls and Buffalo. They were also sent into other parts of New York and New England. One of them, Richard Brower, made a tour of eastern New York and New England in August, 1856, and distributed nearly 30,000 pamphlets. He spent considerable time around Troy, Boston, and New Haven, each of which was made a sort of headquarters for his activities.[48] There were also two agents for the central and southern states; one spent his time chiefly in Virginia and North and South Carolina, and the other worked in Maryland and Pennsylvania. In 1856 these two agents distributed between 10,000 and 15,000 copies of the land pamphlet, beside the other material with which they were supplied.[49] In addition to Corning and his subordinates, there were a number of resident agents in New England who were active in promoting the interests of the Illinois Central and in advertising its lands.

Altogether many hundreds of thousands of pamphlets were distributed by the travelling agents or were sent through the mails to interested persons in the regions from which population was moving westward. This method of advertising was most extensively used in the years 1856 and 1857. In the following year the appropriation for advertising was reduced, but many thousands of pamphlets were sent out.[50] The distribution of pamphlets was not entirely given up until the Land Department had passed out of

[47] *Report of Joseph Fisher to British Shareholders*, p. 58; Osborn to Corning, December 8, 1857, "Presidents Letters," No. 7, box 48, 63rd St.

[48] Ackerman to Brower, August 27, September 8, 13, 19, 22, 23, 29, October 2, 1856; Ackerman to Osborn, October 2, 1856, "W. K. Ackerman Letters," 1856, *ibid.*

[49] Austin to Ackerman, October 29, 1856, M. O.; Ackerman to Ammerman, October 16, 28, 1856; Ackerman to Gray, October 28, 31, 1856, "Ackerman Secretary," 1856–1858, box 48; Perkins to Osborn, November 28, 1856, "J. N. Perkins, Treasurer," *ibid.*

[50] Osborn to Wilson, June 28, 1858, "Osborn Letter Book," No. 8, box 48, 63rd St. These pamphlets have been gradually drifting into the larger libraries of the country until today they may be found in practically every important collection of Americana in larger or smaller numbers. The Harvard libraries possess over a score of them, and other libraries have smaller numbers.

existence, but never again was as elaborate a scheme followed for their distribution as in 1856 and 1857.

It should be noted that these pamphlets widely affected the writing of travel accounts, emigrant guides, and other such ephemeral literature concerning Illinois. They furnished in brief compass material on various aspects of Illinois life which has been extensively utilized by travellers in preparing their accounts. Many of the more superficial travellers took large parts of their accounts directly from this advertising literature, and most writers seem to have made use of the material in one way or another.[51]

A more modern method of advertising the lands, arranged by President Osborn, was that of inserting placards in the panels of the Second, Third, and Sixth Avenue cars in New York City. For this purpose the sum of $375 was expended in 1855, in return for which one of the placards was placed in each car on those lines.[52] In 1856 the arrangement was extended for another year with the Second and Sixth Avenue Companies.[53]

Thinking it important to concentrate immigration activities in

[51] Innumerable examples could be given but only a few of the more obvious ones which have come to the attention of the writer will be included. Fred. Gerhard, *Illinois As It Is* . . . (Chicago, 1857), draws large extracts from the 1856 pamphlet. Gerhard, in a letter to Osborn, June 4, 1856, M. O., says he intends to use material in the Illinois Central pamphlet and asks for further information on that part of the line, Urbana to Centralia, which was not finished when the pamphlet was compiled. The pamphlet: *Central Illinois Farm, Coal and Lumber Co.* (Philadelphia, 1856), re-publishes some of the letters first printed in the 1855 pamphlet. Anon., *How to get a Farm and Where to find one* (New York, 1864), quotes part of Barger's letter, and its chapter on the Illinois Central lands is largely taken from these pamphlets. See pp. 176–177, 253–269. James Shaw, *Twelve Years in America: Being Observations on the Country, the People, Institutions, and Religion; with notices of slavery, and the late war and facts and incidents illustrative of ministerial life and labor in Illinois* . . . (Dublin, 1867), quotes extensively from James Caird, *Prairie Farming in America with notes by the way on Canada and the United States* (New York and London, 1859). So also does the reviewer of Caird's pamphlet in *London Spectator*, March 19, 1859. See also Thomas Spence, *The Settlers Guide in the United States and British North American Provinces*, pp. 183–187; William Hancock, *An Emigrant's Five Years in the Free States of America* (London, 1860). The *Prairie Farmer* (1855), xv, 204–206, gives two and a half pages to a quotation from the pamphlet dealing with southern Illinois.

[52] Ackerman to Austin, October 27, November 8, 1856, "W. K. Ackerman, Secretary," 1856–1858, box 48. Austin to Ackerman, October 30, 1856, M. O.

[53] Ackerman to Austin, November 8, 1856, "W. K. Ackerman, Secretary," 1856–1858.

New York, the great immigration port, Osborn determined, in the latter part of 1857, to establish an "intelligence office" there which would be the central office for all immigration work in the eastern part of the United States. Parke Godwin was placed in charge of this office, and the force which had been working from the Buffalo office under the direction of Corning was transferred thither and placed under Godwin's charge.[54] Brief advertisements were inserted in twelve city papers announcing the opening of the office, and many articles written or supplied by Godwin were published in these journals. Three runners, of whom one was a German, were employed to work among the arriving immigrants.[55] The horde of agents of one kind or another who were endeavoring to influence the new arrivals at Castle Garden was thus increased. The runners distributed to the immigrants handbills which invited them to visit Godwin's office, where information on Illinois lands and the means of getting there could be secured free of cost.[56] Although satisfied with the work which the New York office was accomplishing, Osborn decided to discontinue it on July 1, 1858, because of the financial stringency.[57]

The Illinois Central spent substantial sums on its advertising campaigns, especially during the years 1856 and 1857. In 1856 $16,922 was expended for newspaper and periodical advertising, $11,769 for printing and circulars, and $14,408 for agents' salaries.[58] In 1857 newspaper and periodical advertising cost $15,416, printing and circulars $11,811, and agents' salaries $7094.[59] To the investigators sent over by the London shareholders, after the assignment in 1857, these large expenditures seemed unwise.[60] Joseph Fisher censured the officials for their liberality in this respect, and his report to the London shareholders led the latter to exert pressure on President Osborn to reduce the expenditures for immigration promotion to a minimum. Osborn consented to

[54] Osborn to Wilson, December 29, 1857, "Presidents Letters," No. 7, box 48.
[55] Osborn to Wilson, April 1, 1857, *ibid*. Perkins to Silas Bent, May 1, 1858, "J. N. Perkins, Treasurer," No. 13, box 48.
[56] *Ibid*.
[57] Osborn to Wilson, June 22, 1858, "Osborn Letter Book," No. 8, box 48.
[58] *Annual Report*, 1856.
[59] *Annual Report*, 1857.
[60] *Report of Joseph Fisher to the British Shareholders*, *passim*.

the reduced appropriation against his better judgment, and with great reluctance — for he was firmly convinced of the value of advertising.  On this point he wrote in 1859: [61]

> I differ entirely from the view of the London committee and many of the shareholders, who have censured the administration of the Land Department as unnecessarily extravagant.  Under this imputation the expenses are reduced to one half of those of 1856 and 1857 — we are not advertising — have no outside agents & distribute very few pamphlets and sell very little land.  I would prefer to spend 50 even $100,000 per annum in advertising & believe the effect would soon appear in large sales.  Emigration is being diverted to other localities and we are lost sight of.

The immigration promotion work of the Illinois Central was brought to a halt by the Panic of 1857 and by the interference of the London shareholders.  After July, 1858, very little advertising was done until the opening of the next decade.  In 1858 only $463 was spent on printing and circulars and $4505 on advertising.  In 1859 these items totalled $2258 and $3257 respectively.[62]

Towards the close of the year 1860 domestic conditions changed for the better, and the financial condition of the Illinois Central itself improved to such an extent that President Osborn felt he could safely resume, on an even greater scale than before, the advertising which he had abandoned in 1857.  He was a firm believer in printer's ink to get the Illinois Central lands before the public, and always advocated large expenditures for this purpose.  During the latter part of 1860 he was especially eager to resume advertising because he felt that the time was propitious for so doing.  In the first place, the political strife was threatening the economic well-being of the non-planter class in the South to whom, therefore, Illinois might prove attractive.  In the second place, the prosperity of western states, land companies, and railroads depended on continued success in attracting settlers to their vacant lands, and consequently the rivalry between them was keen and even bitter at times.  The competition of the various land companies for immigration had led to constantly increasing appropriations for advertising until the Panic of 1857 put a stop to all

[61] Osborn to Robt. Benson & Co., July 2, 1859, "Osborn President"; same to same, June 1, 1858, "Osborn Letter Book," No. 8, box 48.
[62] *Annual Reports* for 1858 and 1859.

such activities; but President Osborn realized that as soon as conditions had improved a little the old struggle would commence anew, and was naturally anxious to get the lead on his rivals.[63] Consequently, in the latter part of 1860, a new advertising campaign was begun.

Before dealing with the advertising activities of the Illinois Central in the 'sixties, it may be well to consider the situation which faced the Company at the opening of the decade. At this time Iowa, in particular, was attracting large numbers of immigrants by means of its cheap lands, which the railroads had made accessible. As early as 1856, the officials of the Illinois Central had attributed their small land sales to the popularity of Iowa.[64] Naturally, in their advertising matter they sought to discredit their chief rival, pointing out that Iowa lands were more remote from markets, poorly supplied with transportation facilities, and held by speculators for higher prices than Illinois lands.[65] When government lands in Iowa were withdrawn from the market to allow selections of alternate sections by land grant railroads, they were much relieved.[66] They were likewise pleased when they detected any dissatisfaction among the settlers in Iowa. Constant mention is made in the correspondence, *Annual Reports*, and public statements of the Land Department of the return of settlers from Iowa, Minnesota, or Wisconsin who had become discontented with the severe climate and long winters.[67]

More serious rivals with which the Illinois Central had to contend were the land companies and other land grant railroads. The Illinois Central had a great advantage over the latter in that it had placed its lands on the market first, but shortly before the

---

[63] Osborn to Foster, January 21, 1861, "Presidents & Chairmans Letters," No. 16, box 48.

[64] Letter of John Wilson, marked "Private," May 2, 1856, M. O. See also the *Prairie Farmer*, January 31, February 7, 1856.

[65] *The Illinois Central Railroad Company offers for Sale over 1,500,000 Acres* (1857), pp. 12–17, 28 *passim*. The *Emigrant Aid Journal of Minnesota* replied by saying that the State of Illinois would welcome the immigrant with the fever and the ague. See note in *Minnesota History* (September, 1927), VIII, 299.

[66] Wilson to Osborn, May 26, 1856, M. O.

[67] *Annual Report*, 1856; *Railway Times*, April 18, 1857; *Freeport Weekly Journal*, August 27, 1857; Nathaniel Banks to . . ., March 30, 1861, green box, 63rd St.; J. F. Tucker to Osborn, June 19, 1862, "Osborn Letter Book," M. O.

outbreak of the Civil War it began to feel the effects of their com-petition. In 1856 the Fort Des Moines Navigation Company, having received a land grant from Congress, began an extensive advertising campaign which rivalled that of the Illinois Central.[68] Soon afterwards the Mobile and Ohio,[69] the Galena and Fond du Lac,[70] and the Hannibal and St. Joseph Railroads began selling lands and participating in immigration promotion. In 1859 two other railroads brought a portion of their lands on the market, the Pacific Railroad, another Missouri concern, and the Dubuque and Pacific Railroad, which possessed over a million acres in Iowa.[71] Of these roads, the Hannibal and St. Joseph was the most active. This company had received a grant of 600,000 acres in northern Missouri, which it brought on the market in 1858. In that year it began an active advertising campaign in eastern and northwestern and even in Illinois papers.[72]  It prepared a pamphlet in many respects identical with that of the Illinois Central and quite ob-viously patterned after it, and circulated it in the same generous way.[73]  In 1861 the Hannibal and St. Joseph established an agency of its Land Department in Boston and began an intensive adver-tising program in New England.[74]  The bonds of this road were accepted in payment for lands, and as they were selling in 1861 at 47 its lands could thus be purchased very cheaply. This gave the Hannibal and St. Joseph an advantage over its Illinois rival.[75]

The new advertising campaign which President Osborn planned

   [68] Wilson to Osborn, April 5, 1858; Corning to Osborn, June 27, 1856, *ibid*.
   [69] *American Railway Times*, March 3, 1860.
   [70] Foster to Walker, June 10, 1861, green box, 63rd St.
   [71] Sales book of Dubuque & Pacific Railroad Company, vol. 244, Land and Tax Commissioner's office, Central Station.
   [72] Paul W. Gates, "The Railroads of Missouri, 1850–1870," *Missouri Historical Review* (January, 1932), XXVI, 130 ff. See advertisement of Josiah Hunt, Land Com-missioner of the Hannibal and St. Joseph Railroad, in *Illinois State Journal*, August 10, 1859, and in *Prairie Farmer*, January 12, 1860.
   [73] *The Hannibal and St. Joseph Railroad Company, Farming & Wood Lands* (Hannibal, 1859). Entire sentences and paragraphs are copied from the Illinois Cen-tral pamphlet of 1857.
   [74] Advertisement on back cover of *New England Farmer*, April, 1861. During the brief period in 1859 when its lands were on sale, the Hannibal & St. Joseph sold 14,031 acres of land for an average of $10.24 per acre. *American Railway Times*, March 3, 1860. This price was little below that received by the Illinois Central in spite of the fact that the lands of the Hannibal & St. Joseph were more remote.
   [75] Foster to Walker, April 4, 1861, green box, 63rd St.

for 1860 was entrusted to G. F. Thomas, advertising agent of D. Appleton & Co., and an appropriation of $35,000 was provided.[76] Thomas was instructed to travel through New England, New York, Pennsylvania, Ohio, Indiana, and as far south as the Carolinas, as well as through the Canadian provinces, making advertising contracts with publishers, editors, and managers of news dailies and weeklies, literary, religious, rural, and fashion journals, and in fact with practically every publication of note in the country. Fancy advertisements with cuts under the caption "Homes for the Industrious in the Garden State of the West," were furnished him as well as copy in the form of brief notes to accompany the advertisements in the news and editorial columns.[77]

Thomas went at his task with great thoroughness. Through his knowledge of the advertising business he was able to make combinations and secure such reductions that the appropriation covered much more than it would have done in the hands of a novice. He inserted long and attractive advertisements in conspicuous places in practically every New York and Boston newspaper and in many papers in the smaller cities of New England and New York. Philadelphia, Baltimore, Washington, and Richmond papers,[78] and journals which circulated in the lower South, such as the *Southern Planter*, were likewise employed. Thomas also made favorable contracts with all the prominent agricultural papers such as the *New England Farmer*, the *American Agriculturist*, and the *Valley Farmer*; with the then popular magazines such as *Godey's Lady's Book*, *Phrenological Journal*, *Water Cure Magazine*, *Fisk's Family Journal*, *Knickerbocker*, and *Baloon's Dollar Monthly*; with many religious and foreign language newspapers and journals; and with such outstanding literary magazines as the *Atlantic Monthly* and *Putnam's Monthly*.[79] So rapidly

[76] Thomas to Osborn, May 6, 1861, *ibid.*; J. M. Redmond in *Annual Report*, 1861.

[77] Osborn to Foster, December 31, 1860, January 5, 10, 12, 21, 1861, "Presidents & Chairmans Letters," No. 16, box 48.

[78] Osborn was anxious to get advertisements in southern papers, particularly the *Charleston Mercury*, but Thomas dared not go into South Carolina. Osborn to Foster, January 5, 12, 1861, "Presidents & Chairmans Letters," No. 16, box 48.

[79] Osborn to Foster, January 31, 1861, *ibid.*; W. M. Phillips to Osborn, March 5, 1861, "Ackerman Letters," 1858–1861, box 48. Obviously Allan Nevins is incorrect

did Thomas push his work that in a few weeks nearly a hundred papers and journals of different descriptions were carrying large advertisements of the Land Department.

To supplement the work of Thomas, the services of Nathaniel P. Banks of Massachusetts were secured. Banks was appointed resident director and vice-president, and was instructed to pay particular attention to the affairs of the Land Department and to act as a sort of publicity agent for the Illinois Central. After acquainting himself with the business of the department, Banks proceeded to write numerous articles on Illinois and the railroad lands which were given wide publicity in newspapers and journals. He attempted to arouse interest in Illinois particularly in his own state, where his popularity served him well for this purpose.[80] Prior to the outbreak of the war, he had plans well under way with a group of Massachusetts capitalists who were to purchase from 40,000 to 100,000 acres of the Illinois Central for the purpose of settling mechanics and laborers on them.[81]

Some of the methods of the advertising campaign of the 'fifties were again employed. Interested persons were invited to write to the Land Department for further information and received the land pamphlet in reply. The pamphlet was not, however, distributed as lavishly as it had been in 1856 and 1857. Travelling agents were also employed again to visit regions from which there was a strong movement to the West for the purpose of arousing interest in Illinois. The most capable of these agents was Ovid Miner; he visited the rural communities of northern New York, talked with mechanics in the shops and farmers in their homes, and boosted emigration, Illinois, and Illinois Central lands. Frequently he presented himself to local pastors, who permitted

in saying that not until 1870 did any American monthly print advertisements other than those of the books which its publishers issued. *The Emergence of Modern America* (Schlesinger and Fox, editors, *A History of American Life*, vol. VIII, New York, 1927), p. 245. See *Atlantic Monthly*, January, April, May, and June, 1861, and *De Bow's Review*, August, 1861.

[80] An article on General Banks in the *Illinois Central Magazine* (July, 1913), II, 13–22, gives numerous extracts from letters of Banks which have considerable interest. There is a wealth of material in these letters, impression copies of which are in "Osborn Letter Book," 1860–1861, M. O.

[81] Banks to Osborn, February 9, 1861, *ibid.*

## IN THE GARDEN STATE OF THE WEST.

### THE ILLINOIS CENTRAL RAILROAD CO., HAVE FOR SALE

# 1,200,000 ACRES OF RICH FARMING LANDS,

### In Tracts of Forty Acres and upward on Long Credit and at Low Prices.

THE attention of the enterprising and industrious portion of the community is directed to the following statements and liberal inducements offered them by the

#### ILLINOIS CENTRAL RAILROAD COMPANY.

which, as they will perceive, will enable them, by proper energy, perseverance and industry, to provide comfortable homes for themselves and families, with, comparatively speaking, very little capital.

#### LANDS OF ILLINOIS.

No State in the Valley of the Mississippi offers so great an inducement to the settler as the State of Illinois, There is no portion of the world where all the conditions of climate and soil so admirably combine to produce those two great staples, CORN and WHEAT, as the Prairies of Illinois.

#### EASTERN AND SOUTHERN MARKETS.

These lands are contiguous to a railroad 700 miles in length, which connects with other roads and navigable lakes and rivers, thus affording an unbroken communication with the Eastern and Southern markets.

#### RAILROAD SYSTEM OF ILLINOIS.

Over $100,000,000 of private capital have been expended on the railroad system of Illinois. Inasmuch as part of the income from several of these works, with a valuable public fund in lands, go to diminish the State expenses; the TAXES ARE LIGHT, and must consequently every day decrease.

#### THE STATE DEBT.

*The State debt is only $10,106,398 14, and within the last three years has been reduced $2,959,746 80, and we may reasonably expect that in ten years it will become extinct.*

#### PRESENT POPULATION.

The State is rapidly filling up with population; 868,025 persons having been added since 1850, making the present population 1,723,663, a ratio of 102 per cent. in ten years.

#### AGRICULTURAL PRODUCTS.

The Agricultural Products of Illinois are greater than those of any other State. The products sent out during the past year exceeded 1,500,000 tons. The wheat crop of 1860 approaches

35,000,000 bushels, while the corn crop yields not less than 140,000,000 bushels.

#### FERTILITY OF THE SOIL.

Nowhere can the industrious farmer secure such immediate results for his labor as upon these prairie soils, they being composed of a deep rich loam, the fertility of which is unsurpassed by any on the globe.

#### TO ACTUAL CULTIVATORS.

*Since 1854 the Company have sold 1,300,000 acres. They sell only to actual cultivators, and every contract contains an agreement to cultivate. The road has been constructed through these lands at an expense of $30,000,000. In 1850 the population of forty-nine counties, through which it passes, was only 335,598 since which 479,293 have been added; making the whole population 814,891, a gain of 143 per cent.*

#### EVIDENCES OF PROSPERITY.

As an evidence of the thrift of the people, it may be stated that 600,000 tons of freight, including 8,600,000 bushels of grain, and 250,000 barrels of flour were forwarded over the line last year.

#### PRICES AND TERMS OF PAYMENT.

The prices of these lands vary from $6 to $25 per acre, according to location, quality, &c. First class farming lands sell for about $10 to $12 per acre; and the relative expense of subduing prairie land as compared with wood land is in the ratio of 1 to 10 in favor of the former. The terms of sale for the bulk of these lands will be

#### ONE YEAR'S INTEREST IN ADVANCE,

at six per cent per annum, and six interest notes at six per cent., payable respectively in one, two, three, four, five and six years from date of sale; and four notes for principal, payable in four, five, six and seven years from date of sale; the contract stipulating that one-tenth of the tract purchased shall be fenced and cultivated, each and every year, for five years from date of sale, so that at the end of five years one-half shall be fenced and under cultivation.

#### TWENTY PER CENT. WILL BE DEDUCTED

from the valuation for cash, except the same should be at six dollars per acre, when the cash price will be five dollars

Pamphlets descriptive of the lands, soil, climate, productions, prices, and terms of payment, can be had on application to

### J. W. FOSTER, Land Commissioner,
#### CHICAGO, ILLINOIS

For the name of the Towns, Villages and Cities situated upon the Illinois Central Railroad, see pages 188, 189 and 190 Appleton's Railway Guide.

## HOMES FOR THE INDUSTRIOUS
#### (Advertising cut widely used by the Illinois Central Railroad in 1860 and 1861)

him to make public addresses in their churches. Miner worked through religious organizations with the idea of interesting groups in settling in colonies on the lands of the Illinois Central.[82]

Throughout the 'sixties the Illinois Central continued to advertise its lands extensively, expending on an average $11,000 annually for this purpose. During this decade the Land Department paid considerable attention to promoting immigration from European countries and was assisted in this task by leading foreigners already domiciled in the United States. To this phase of the Company's activities we must now turn.

[82] Miner discusses his methods in a letter to J. B. Austin, March 29, 1861, M. O.

# CHAPTER X

## COMPETITION FOR FOREIGN IMMIGRANTS

THE outward movement of Europe's surplus population in the mid-nineteenth century surpassed in size if not in significance any previous emigration of peoples. Keen competition for the business of transporting these emigrants led the shipping companies to station agents throughout the districts from which emigration was flowing for the purpose of securing passenger traffic for their lines. At the same time, many of the land companies, some of the American states, the British colonies, and a number of Latin-American countries which were seeking to colonize their undeveloped areas appointed agents in Europe to direct emigration to their localities. There was thus being created a hierarchy of emigration agents in Europe whose numbers were steadily increasing.[1] In the 'fifties the American land grant railroads which were seeking settlers for their lands began to supplement the work of the government agencies and the land companies. The first railroad to attempt to stimulate and direct immigration was the Illinois Central. The foreign immigration work of this railroad was sporadic and poorly integrated in the 'fifties, but in the next decade it was greatly expanded along the lines already laid down. The methods which the Illinois Central worked out during these years were to be followed on a more extensive scale by the later land grant railroads.

David Neal had early seen that the natural flow of immigration into Illinois would not settle the Company's lands nor build up traffic for the road as rapidly as was desired. He believed the European countries to be as promising a source of immigrants as the eastern states, and he planned to direct this immigration to Illinois by stationing agents throughout Norway, Sweden, and

---

[1] Marcus Lee Hansen, "Emigration from Continental Europe, 1815–1860, with special reference to the United States," unpublished manuscript, Harvard College Library.

Germany.[2] In 1854 Neal made a beginning in the work of immigration promotion by sending Oscar Malmborg as immigration agent to Norway and Sweden.

Malmborg was an educated Swede who had come to America in the 'forties.[3] After serving in the Mexican War he had taken a position under R. B. Mason, engineer in charge of construction, and had later been transferred to the Land Department of the Illinois Central where he had won the confidence of Neal and had become familiar with the lands.[4] Neal commissioned Malmborg to visit the rural communities of Norway and Sweden, to talk with people who might be interested in coming to America, and to persuade them to settle upon Illinois Central land. He was encouraged to assemble a colony to return with him to Illinois where a special tract was to be reserved for them.

Malmborg began his work in Sweden by translating and publishing, in the newspapers of the various provinces, material which was furnished him by the Land Department. He travelled through the country, distributing pamphlets and other literature and visiting people interested in emigrating. There were a large number of them, he reported, in both Norway and Sweden.[5]

Neal had planned to make Malmborg's work the beginning of a large campaign of immigration promotion, but the appointment of the latter failed of confirmation by the Executive Committee and Neal himself lost control of the Land Department. As a result, Malmborg was forced to discontinue his activities and to return to America where he resumed his former position in the Land Department.

Charles M. Dupuy, who replaced Neal and his agent Dodge as head of the Land Department, was as anxious to promote immigration to Illinois, but he was inclined to stress the work abroad much less than similar activities in the United States. Throughout the 'fifties the Illinois Central made few efforts to stimulate immigration from the Scandinavian countries. The agents of

---

[2] *Prairie Farmer*, XIV, 232.

[3] There is a brief sketch of Malmborg in Ernst Olson, *History of the Swedes of Illinois* (Chicago, 1908) part 1, pp. 643–655.

[4] Malmborg to Neal, May 28, 1854; Neal to Perkins, October 30, 1854, M. O.

[5] Malmborg to Neal, May 28, 1854, M. O.

other interests, however, particularly of Wisconsin, Minnesota, and Iowa, continued with marked success their campaigns to gain Scandinavian immigrants. President Osborn realized that the Illinois Central could not afford to let its competitors for immigrants make the Scandinavian field their own. He therefore decided in 1860 to send Malmborg back to Norway and Sweden to resume the work left off in 1854.[6]

President Osborn was well aware of the frauds that had in the past been perpetrated upon immigrants by land and emigration agents, and specifically warned Malmborg against making exaggerated statements in regard to the Illinois Central lands.[7] It was left to Malmborg's discretion to determine the means and methods of making known as widely as possible the character of the lands, the inducements the Company offered to prospective purchasers, the rapid growth of the State, the immense crops, and other pertinent facts. Malmborg was instructed to inform the New York office regularly of his movements and progress. His letters, which have been published in part, indicate his faithfulness in carrying out his instructions.[8]

As Malmborg was authorized to spend only four months in the two countries of Norway and Sweden he had to devote most of his time to the larger emigration centers, and was forced to neglect the smaller rural communities from which people were leaving for America. Thus, during the first forty days, he visited Gothenburg, went from there to Christiania and to Bergen, and then back to Stavanger, Christiansand, Christiania, Fredrikshald, Stromstad, and Gothenburg. During this time he published 2500 circulars and maps in Swedish and 1000 in Norwegian; he inserted advertisements in the newspapers in Gothenburg, Christiania, and

---

[6] Osborn to Malmborg, May 16, 1860, "Presidents Letters," No. 14, box 48.

[7] Osborn to Foster, April 24, 1860, "Presidents Letters," No. 13; Osborn to Malmborg, May 16, 1860, "Presidents Letters," No. 14, box 48.

[8] Malmborg's letters, originally scattered in the various archives of the Illinois Central, were gathered by the writer into one collection in the Magazine Office, where they now remain. The Illinois Central officials kindly gave photostatic copies of these letters to Gustavus Adolphus College, Augustana College, the Swedish American Historical Society and the present writer. A. A. Stomberg has published these letters in part in the *Swedish-American Historical Bulletin* (June, 1930), vol. III, No. 2, pp. 9–52.

Stavanger, and in twelve rural papers in the two countries; he prepared editorials for publication and conducted a heavy correspondence with people who expressed their interest in emigrating to America. So far Malmborg's work had been more or less that of a publicity director, and except in the large cities he had come into little direct contact with the emigrating class. Moreover, many of the emigrants from rural sections had chosen their destination before they arrived at the ports. Malmborg soon realized that in the time allotted he could accomplish little, and asked the officials of the Illinois Central for a longer period of time in order that he might visit the rural districts and make direct contacts with prospective emigrants before they had decided on their future location. His request was granted, and he was instructed to remain throughout the winter and to follow out the itinerary he had proposed.[9]

In the extended period granted to him Malmborg worked largely among the peasant-farmers and the lower middle-class land owners. The former, he reported, were slowly being squeezed out of their possessions in Sweden by the large land owners and were easily induced to leave for America. The difficulty was that they had little money, and Malmborg found it advisable to work more with the class of farmers who had some resources with which they could pay their passage to their new homes and also make first payments upon their land.

Malmborg employed various methods for establishing contacts with the farmers of Norway and Sweden. He travelled through the rural sections of both countries, arranging meetings in parish houses and other public buildings. Previous notices of the meetings were sent to sextons or parsons of the churches, who read them to the congregations; advertisements announcing the meetings were inserted in the local papers; personal letters were sent to many people who were reported to be interested in emigrating; circulars were distributed by sextons among the parishoners; and special messengers were sometimes employed. Many of these meetings were well attended.[10] After a short talk by Malmborg

[9] Walker to Malmborg, August 24, 1860, "Presidents and Chairmans Letters," No. 15, box 48. Malmborg to Burnside, February 6, 17, 20, 1861.

[10] Same to same, February 6, 17, 20, 1861.

on Illinois and Illinois Central lands, maps and circulars would be distributed among the people, following which opportunities for personal interviews were given. Malmborg also went to the fairs at Kalmar, Wexjø, Jønkøping, and other centers, his attendance being announced by advertisements.[11] At these fairs he met people who had come long distances, and would discuss with them the subject of emigration.

Malmborg prepared a pamphlet in Swedish and Norwegian, of which four editions were published, and distributed it by the thousands;[12] he made arrangements with port and shipping officials to assist him in distributing this literature among the emigrants. The railroad and shipping concerns agreed to sell emigrants through tickets from Swedish and Norwegian ports to Chicago. Malmborg continued to advertise extensively in the papers. This policy not only called attention to his meetings and gave him an opportunity to praise America, but also established helpful contacts with editors of some of the more important papers. These editors frequently published free articles on emigration and America that he had prepared.[13] The advertising also helped to keep the editors neutral when controversy sprang up between Malmborg and the group who were opposed to emigration.

It was inevitable that Malmborg's activities should arouse opposition among the anti-emigration groups in the two countries. Perhaps the first attack was one that appeared in *Barometern* of October 31, 1860, in answer to Malmborg's writing and advertising. It fulminated strongly against the "swindlers which so often beset the emigrant on his first arrival" in the new country. The runners who were employed by the railroads, land companies, hotels, and lodging-houses in the immigration ports were guilty of practicing deception and knavery upon the innocent immigrant, and the author of this article was striking at one of the worst evils. Malmborg replied in *Barometern* of February 6, 1861, "in as moderate terms as possible in order not to excite opposition."

[11] Same to same, February 15, 1861.
[12] Statement of expenses in letter of Malmborg to Burnside, May 2, 1861.
[13] Malmborg to Walker, March 9, 1861.

He pointed out that he had promised that the Illinois Central Railroad should have its own agents at Quebec and New York to meet all immigrants who were planning to go to the Company's lands in order to safeguard them against the runners. To give as wide publicity as possible to his reply, he had it republished in the *Wexjö Bladet*; special editions of both papers were printed for distribution in the rural sections.[14] A second attack, which was likewise published in *Barometern*, was answered in a different way. Malmborg arranged for a Swede who had spent many years in America to prepare a reply, to which he himself added further material; he then had it published in the same paper over the signature of the Swede.[15] It seems that on the whole Malmborg, who was a good publicist, did not emerge second-best from the controversies.

The chief opponents of emigration in the Scandinavian countries seem to have been the large farmers, who were loath to lose their laborers. Malmborg reported that they circulated stories to the effect that emigrants shipping to New York were taken to Siberia or to the southern states, where they were sold as slaves. In contrast to the attitude of some of the German princes, who exerted themselves to prevent the emigration of their subjects, the public authorities of the Scandinavian countries remained neutral in the controversy.[16]

Malmborg also came into competition with the Canadian immigration agents. The Province of Canada had two agents in the Scandinavian countries, and one of them, Christopher O. Closter, a Norwegian, had made such "gross misrepresentations" in his work that a clergyman who had resided in Canada, Wisconsin, and Minnesota publicly denounced him and his mission "in the hardest terms" before a crowd of four thousand in the Stavanger Cathedral. The two Canadian immigration agents were attempting to combat in Norway and Sweden the prejudice that the people of those countries had against Canada in favor of Illinois and Wisconsin. They used the same methods that Malmborg

14 Malmborg to Burnside, February 6, 1861.
15 Same to same, March 30, 1861.
16 Malmborg to Walker, March 9, 1861.

employed, with somewhat more immediate success. Malmborg warned his employers to beware of the runners maintained by the Canadian Government at Quebec, "who spare no pains or expense in inducing the arriving to settle in the Canadas." [17]

Early in 1861 it was apparent that a large emigration was preparing to leave Norway and Sweden for America. The Norwegian press estimated that 10,000 Norwegians would leave, although Malmborg set the figure at 7000. This, he said, was 30 per cent more than had left in any previous year.[18] He was equally optimistic in regard to the number of Swedish emigrants. With the coming of spring, Malmborg visited the various ports: Bergen, Stavanger, Drammen, Christiania, Gothenburg, Kalmar, and Stockholm, where he met emigrants who were about to leave for America. He aided them in securing their tickets, furnished them with additional information on Illinois, promised to have an agent of the Land Department meet them, and employed every possible means to prejudice them in favor of Illinois. He prepared lists of those who had given him reason to think they were going to that state, and sent them to the Land Commissioner of the Illinois Central with the request that agents be sent to meet the immigrants.[19]

Rumors of conflict in America led many prospective emigrants to change their plans. Those who had already sold their farms were committed to leaving, but others who had been delaying now decided to wait for more propitious circumstances before they left the homeland. Malmborg wrote that the prospective emigrants were becoming panicky over the stories of piracy by southern privateers, and in June he reported that trade with the United States was practically at a standstill.[20] Thus it was almost impossible to secure transportation from Norway and Sweden to the

[17] A. C. Buchanan, report, February 12, 1862, paper No. 355, *Imperial Blue Books, Canada*, vol. 34, *passim*; Buchanan, report, January 19, 1863, *Sessional Papers*, 7th Parl., 2nd Sess., III, 4; Malmborg to Burnside, April 14, 1861. For a more detailed discussion of Closter's activities in Norway, see Theodore C. Blegen, "An Early Norwegian Settlement in Canada," Canadian Historical Association, *Annual Report* (1930), pp. 84 ff.

[18] Malmborg to Burnside, May 2, 1861.

[19] Same to same, May 2, 22, 1861.

[20] Same to same, June 10, 20, 1861.

United States. Some who had pushed their arrangements too far to retreat went to Hamburg, from which port they were able to secure passage to New York, and others took ship for Quebec, whence they left for the western states.[21] Malmborg closed out his business in Norway and Sweden in July and accompanied a group of sixty Swedes to Hamburg and thence to New York.[22]

In accordance with Malmborg's advice, the Land Department sent agents to Quebec to meet the immigrants, lists of whom had been supplied.[23] This precaution seemed essential, because the Canadian Government had its most able agents stationed there to induce the new arrivals to settle in Upper or Lower Canada. The Illinois Central instructed its men to employ every facility for the comfort of the immigrants. J. W. Whitcher, one of the agents stationed at Quebec, reported in the early part of June that three hundred Norwegians had left for Chicago and that three or four hundred more would leave in two or three days. To make certain that they would arrive there safe from the blandishments of other immigration agents, he was advised to send a man to accompany them to that city.[24] Fearful that even these precautions would not properly safeguard the immigrants, Land Commissioner Foster sent two additional agents, one to Detroit and the other to Quebec, to meet the Norwegians. Through the exertions of these men and with the expenditure of a few hundred dollars to counteract (as Foster put it) the exertions of the Galena road, it was hoped that some results would be obtained. Ill success drove Foster to desperation, for on June 12 he suggested that the Company secure

[21] It is apparent that the statistics of Swedish and Norwegian immigration to the United States in 1860 and the following years, given in the *Report* of the Immigration Commission (1911), I, *passim*, are inaccurate. They do not include the large number of Scandinavians who came to the United States by way of Quebec and Montreal. In 1861, the Canadian Emigration Agent, A. C. Buchanan, reported that a total of 8668 Norwegian and Swedish immigrants had arrived in Quebec, of which less than 800 remained in the province. A. C. Buchanan, Chief Emigration Agent, report, February 12, 1862, paper 355, *Imperial Blue Books*, vol. 34, pp. 4–6. In the *Report* of the Immigration Commission it is stated that only 616 Norwegians came to the United States in 1861.

[22] Malmborg to Burnside, July 5, 1861; Foster to Walker, June 12, 13, 19, 24, 1861, M. O.; Walker to Redmond, July 31, 1861, "Treasurers Letters," No. 18, box 48.

[23] Foster to Walker, June 5, 12, 13, 1861, M. O.

[24] Same to same, May 18, June 5, 1861, green box, 63rd St.

some of the immigrant runners at Quebec by paying more than the other roads paid for their services. On June 19 Foster reported that there was a considerable movement of Norwegians through Chicago but that they had little money; he still hoped to secure a portion of them, although as yet he had met with little success. Most of them, he remarked, apparently had heard nothing of Malmborg or of his work in Norway. On June 24 Foster wrote from Chicago, "Some of Malmborg's Swedes begin to arrive. I trust we shall have better luck than with the Norwegians, most of whom are destitute of means, & are headed to Minnesota and Wisconsin." [25]

What were the results achieved by Malmborg? Redmond, Land Commissioner of the Illinois Central after August, 1861, said that there were no results from the work of the Scandinavian and Canadian agents; that large numbers of Scandinavian immigrants passed through Chicago but that none of them purchased land from the Illinois Central.[26] President Osborn also declared that Malmborg's trip had been a failure.[27] Despite the statements of Redmond and Osborn, there were some early results from Malmborg's work. In February, 1861, Foster reported that the Norwegians were beginning to come in. In May Foster located four Swedes on Illinois Central land, and during June he was kept busy dealing with Swedes and Norwegians. Thus on June 6 he piloted six Swedes down the line on a tour of inspection; on June 26 he wrote that quite a party of Swedes had gone down the line and another was to go that night; and on July 13 it was reported that "a very intelligent lot of Swedes" were sent down to Neoga in charge of an agent who was positive he could sell to them.[28] However, relatively few of the Scandinavian immigrants coming to the United States in 1860 and the early part of 1861 settled upon Illinois Central lands.

[25] Same to same, June 12, 13, 19, 24, 1861; Malmborg to Burnside, July 5, 1861, M. O.

[26] Redmond to Walker, August 16, 1861, M. O.

[27] Osborn to directors of the Illinois Central Railroad, May 8, 1862, "Osborn Letter Book," 1861–1862, M. O.

[28] Letter of J. W. Foster, February 15, 1861, and Foster to Walker, May 31, June 6, 26, 1861, M. O.; J. M. Douglas to Osborn, July 13, 1861, 63rd St.

With the outbreak of the Civil War, the movement of population to Illinois from the East virtually ceased, but the Swedish and Norwegian immigration that had been looked for in the first part of 1861 now began, and this was in part the result of Malmborg's work. Most pleasing to the officials of the Illinois Central was the fact that most of these new immigrants were going to eastern Illinois. Through the efforts of one of the Swedish agents, P. G. Peterson, a considerable colony of Swedes had settled 180 miles south of Chicago at Big Spring, which under the encouragement of the railroad became a prosperous agricultural center. The Company donated a lot for the church, and shipped quantities of lumber at reduced rates. Within a short time thirty families had taken up land there.[29] In 1862 a larger number of Scandinavians moved into the vicinity of Big Spring and Neoga. At the same time both Swedes and Norwegians were beginning to settle around Pera and Paxton, about 100 miles south of Chicago.[30]

In May, 1862, Osborn resumed his efforts to secure Scandinavian immigrants by engaging a Norwegian clergyman, Abraham Jacobson, to work at Quebec for four months during the immigration season. He was supplied with 5000 circulars printed in Swedish on one side and in Norwegian on the other. Jacobson plunged into the work among his fellow-countrymen who were landing at Quebec, devoting as much of his time to relief work as to directing immigration. Indeed, so valuable did his relief work become that the Canadian Government made him a grant of money to show its gratitude, unaware that he was at the same time acting as immigration agent of the Illinois Central.[31] In the same year Osborn requested Erland Carlson to engage for him another Swedish or Norwegian clergyman to carry on the same sort of work in New York.[32] To prevent ticket agents from selling the

[29] Osborn to P. Peterson, May 13, 1862, "Osborn Letter Book," 1861–1862, M. O. See an article on this colony by J. Peterson in *Hemlandet*, January 21, 1864.

[30] *Minnesalbum Sv. Ev. Luth. Forsamlingen Paxton, Illinois, 1863–1903* (Paxton, 1903), p. 8.

[31] Memorandum signed by F. Evanturel, September, 1862, in MS. vol., "Emigration Letters Sent 1862–1864," and letter of A. C. Buchanan, September 23, MS. vol., "Agriculture letters Received 1862–18  ," Dominion Archives. See also J. N. Jacobson, "A Pioneer Pastor's Journey to Dakota in 1861," Norwegian American Historical Society, *Studies and Records* (1931), VI, 53 ff.

[32] Osborn to Walker, May 24, 1862, "Osborn Letter Book," 1861–1862, M. O.

immigrants passage to Wisconsin or Minnesota, the Illinois Central men were instructed to caution them against buying tickets beyond Chicago.[33]

Chicago, on account of its railroad facilities, had become the great *entrepôt* for western settlers, practically all of whom had to stop there. In this city gathered runners and agents of the western states, railroads, and land companies which were making efforts to attract immigrants. These agents met incoming trains, distributed advertising matter among the immigrants, and sought to induce them to go to the regions for which they were working. The Illinois Central, because the main office of its Land Department was at Chicago and because its lands were not far distant and were easy of access by direct rail communication on its own line, had a great advantage in this respect over competing interests.

At the same time that the Illinois Central was promoting immigration from Norway and Sweden, it was also attempting to interest German immigrants in its lands. This work was begun in 1854, when the Company published a circular which called attention to the large number of Germans already residing in Illinois and gave the terms of purchase of its lands and other relevant information.[34] Pamphlets and maps in German were prepared for distribution in immigrant ports of the United States and embarkation ports of Europe;[35] advertisements were inserted in the German language newspapers in New York; and arrangements were made with a German house to sell the lands on a commission basis.[36] Further arrangements were made with the publishers of two leading newspapers in Germany[37] and with the *New Yorker Handels Zeitung*, pursuant to which a great deal of material on the Illinois Central was published in these three papers. The editor of the latter journal also prepared a pamphlet for the Company based on a two or three weeks tour at the expense of the railroad;

[33] Osborn to Carlson, May 24, 1862, *ibid*.
[34] Copy of this paper is in the Brayman MSS.
[35] Neal to Perkins, May 29, 1855, M. O.; Perkins to Wilson, March 6, 1856, "Perkins Letter Book," 1855–1856, box 48.
[36] Griswold to Osborn, February 17, 1855, M. O.
[37] MS. bill of Herman Meyer, July 9, 1855, M. O.

at least 2000 copies of this pamphlet were published.[38] The services of captains of emigrant ships and of agents and runners at Havre and other embarkation ports in Europe were secured to distribute the German pamphlets among the emigrants. These agents were encouraged to use all possible means to induce the emigrants to go to Illinois.

Probably the most pretentious effort made by the Illinois Central in the 'fifties to attract Germans was the publication of a book on the Old Northwest by Dr. J. G. Kohl, an eminent German cartographer and traveller. An agreement was entered into between Dr. Kohl, D. Appleton and Company, and the Illinois Central according to which D. Appleton and Company were to publish Kohl's book in the United States, arrange for its publication in Europe, and secure its extensive circulation there; the Illinois Central was to assume sole responsibility for it and to receive any royalties after the first $4000 had been paid to Kohl.[39] The latter proceeded to Illinois, where he was given every opportunity to satisfy himself concerning the lands, the crops, and the prosperity of the settlers. He was piloted around the State by B. F. Johnson, taken to interview many of the successful cattle-raisers and farmers, and in general made thoroughly acquainted with those parts of the State through which the Illinois Central ran.[40] Much impressed by his observations,[41] Kohl wrote his account, entitled *Reisen im Nordwesten der Vereinigten Staaten*, which was published in 1857. This work contains reports of con-

---

[38] *Ibid.*; Wilson to Perkins, March 29, 1856, M. O. Meyer calls this a book but very likely it was only a pamphlet. I have been unable to locate a single one of these German pamphlets of either kind, although Marcus Lee Hansen assures me that he has seen copies abroad.

[39] D. Appleton & Co. to Osborn, February 12, 1855, M. O. Apparently the terms of this agreement were later modified for see Osborn to Perkins, December 10, 1856, M. O.

[40] Kohl's tour through Illinois is described in great detail in the letters of B. F. Johnson to Osborn, October and November, 1855, M. O. Kohl's personal views may be seen in his book. Another companion on this tour through Illinois was William Ferguson, a British stockholder of the Illinois Central, who was investigating the affairs of the Land Department. He wrote his account of the journey in *America by River and Rail; Or Notes by the Way on the New World and its People*. He makes some interesting observations on the growth of the towns along the line of the road.

[41] Johnson to Osborn, November 2, 3, 5, 6, etc., 1855, M. O.

versations with German immigrants and a great deal of information on the State and the Illinois Central Railroad Company, presented in a very favorable light. Apparently three editions were published [42] and an English translation was planned.[43]

Somewhat later Osborn endeavored to secure some capable Germans to go to Europe to work among their fellow-countrymen in the important emigration centers.[44] He sought out Louis H. Mayer, an influential German merchant, to induce him to undertake this work.[45] He also made arrangements with the Reverend N. E. Childs, pastor of a German Reformed Church in Pennsylvania, to promote emigration among his people. Childs was to make a trip over the Illinois Central line and to publish an account of his observations in German newspapers.[46] Obsorn made a similar agreement with Josiah Marshall of Albany, who was planning to make a trip to Europe. Marshall's expenses and fair wages were to be paid him while he was occupied in examining the lands. Although he was not to receive a stated salary, if his efforts were at all successful a generous commission was to be allowed him.[47]

The results which the Land Department obtained from working among the northern European immigrants, especially during the years 1858 to 1862, were indeed encouraging, but in the absence of any large immigration from the eastern states gross sales were not large, and they were far from satisfying the officials of the Company. Osborn estimated that at the rate at which sales were being made it would take over twenty years to dispose of the remaining lands, and he well knew that the people of Illinois would

[42] Joseph Sabin, *Dictionary of Books relating to America, From its Discovery to the Present Time* (New York, 1868–1891), IX, 36, lists the above edition and "Zweite Auflage, St. Louis, Witter, Map, 11 plates, 1859, 8vo, pp. vi, 534." The British Museum catalogue lists a Zweite Auflage for 1857, New York, and Buck, *Travel and Description*, p. 219, does likewise. Copies of the first edition are in Harvard College Library, the Chicago Historical Society's Library, and in the Library of Congress. Copies of the second New York edition are in the University of Illinois Library and the British Museum.

[43] Perkins to D. Appleton & Co., June 3, 1856, "Perkins Letters," No. 9, box 48.

[44] Osborn to Foster, June 25, 1860, "Presidents Letters," No. 14, *ibid.*

[45] Same to same, June 26, 1860; Osborn to McClellan, June 26, 1860, *ibid.*

[46] Osborn to Rev'd N. E. Childs, n. d., "Osborn Official Letter Book," 1862–1865, *ibid.*

[47] Osborn to Josiah Marshall, April 23, 1862, "Osborn Letter Book," 1861–1862, M. O.

never consent to such slow disposition of lands untaxable until deeded.[48] He considered attempting to secure from the Legislature a repeal of that portion of the charter which provided for forced sales of the Company's unsold lands ten years after the road was completed, but the time did not seem propitious for such an attempt.[49] The Company exerted itself, however, to retain the good will both of its own settlers and of farmers in general in the State.[50] In addition to the fear of forced sales, there was the necessity of retiring the construction bonds, the interest on which was eating up both the operating income of the road and a portion of the returns from collections on the land contracts. Finally, the Company was anxious to continue the policy, already well developed, of building up the region through which its route lay in order to ensure larger traffic for the future.

With these considerations in mind, Osborn determined to make more direct appeal to the foreign immigrants, particularly the Germans and Scandinavians. But this time, instead of sending agents abroad to stimulate immigration to Illinois he planned to establish subsidiary agents in Illinois to whom would be given a commission on all lands sold through their efforts, a plan similar to that followed with Andrew J. Galloway in the 'fifties. It was obvious to Osborn that an agent of the same nationality as the people with whom he worked would have a great advantage over others, and accordingly he looked around for some prominent Scandinavians and Germans for this purpose.

The most outstanding German in Illinois at this time was Lieutenent-Governor Francis Hoffman; he had come to America in 1839 and had settled in Du Page County, just west of Chicago. He readily acquired an excellent command of the English language, which was to serve him well on the political platform. At a later date he moved to Chicago and became a powerful figure in its local politics. In common with most educated Germans he was greatly aroused by the passage of the Kansas-Nebraska Act and became an ardent leader in the Republican Party. While acting

[48] Osborn to Walker, May 18, 1862, *ibid.*
[49] Osborn to William Tracy, October 10, 1862, "Osborn Official Letter Book," 1862–1865, box 48.
[50] Osborn to Col. E. D. Taylor, December 30, 1862, *ibid.*

as consul for a number of German states [51] he was elected a member of the city council of Chicago, and in 1860 was rewarded for his efforts in behalf of the Republican Party by being nominated and subsequently elected Lieutenant-Governor.[52] In the meantime he had established a bank in Chicago and opened a land agency. He published pamphlets on the commerce and industry of Chicago which were widely distributed in Germany, helping thereby to establish his reputation in his native country and also to popularize Illinois in the minds of Germans planning to emigrate.[53] He was reported to have sold through his land agency a large amount of Illinois Central land, and consequently was familiar with the business of the Land Department.[54] He was well fitted for Osborn's purpose, and the latter opened negotiations with him in May, 1862.[55]

Osborn proposed to make Hoffman German Land Agent and to allow him an initial appropriation of $8000 to be used for the employment of agents, advertising, and printing and distributing pamphlets in Germany and the United States. Hoffman was to receive a commission of $1 on each of the first 20,000 acres sold and 50 cents on all remaining sales,[56] but amounts advanced for his expenses and all later expenditures were to be deducted from his commissions.[57] His sales were to be limited to the region south of Mattoon, and even in this restricted locality he was not to be given an exclusive agency. The Company planned to keep down its own expenses for advertising and agents' salaries and to leave most of the active work to Hoffman, reserving the right, however, to sell lands on any part of its line.[58] His contract was to run for a term of four years. The Board of Directors and the Executive

[51] *Chicago Weekly Democrat*, December 30, 1854. See also advertisements of Hoffman in *Illinois Staats-Zeitung*, issues of 1862.

[52] Hoffman had received the Republican nomination for the same office in 1856 but was found to be ineligible for it.

[53] Gustav Körner, *Das Deutsche Element in den Vereinigten Staaten von Nordamerika* (Cincinnati, 1880), pp. 279–280.

[54] Emil Mannhardt, "Franz Arnold Hoffman," *Deutsch-Amerikanische Geschichtsblätter* (1903), vol. III, No. 3, pp. 56–62.

[55] Osborn to Walker, May 6, 1862, "Osborn Letter Book," 1861–1862, M. O.

[56] Same to same, May 8, 1862, *ibid.*

[57] Same to same, May 27, 1862, *ibid.*

[58] Same to same, May 12, 13, 1862, *ibid.*

Committee, which had to pass on this proposal, regarded the appropriation and the commission as too generous. They refused to agree to the contract, much to the disgust of Osborn, who was greatly impressed with Hoffman [59] and convinced of his influence with the German immigrants and his ability to sell to them. He strongly urged the Executive Committee to reverse its action, and finally made a hurried trip to New York to interview the members personally.[60] This time he was successful, the contract, with certain minor changes, being authorized on May 29, 1862.[61] Among the changes, additions, and added privileges were the following: the Illinois Central reserved the right to raise or lower the price of lands at any time; a commission of 5 cents was to be given Hoffman for any sales made through his efforts north of Mattoon; [62] conductors and other officials on all trains were instructed to give all possible assistance to Hoffman in his work, and passes on freight trains were to be given to all prospective purchasers going down the line.[63]

Hoffman's first step in carrying out his contract was to acquaint himself with the lands which he was to handle. He made a detailed survey of the region from Mattoon to Centralia, and was reported to be "pleased with the looks of the land, and thinks he can do wonders in selling them." [64] He delayed no longer, but set out to turn the tide of German immigration into eastern Illinois. Hoffman employed the usual methods to attract the attention of his fellow-countrymen to the lands under his care. He advertised in the German newspapers and journals in the United States,[65] employed a dozen agents and runners to work among the Germans

[59] Same to same, May 29, 1862, *ibid.*

[60] Same to same, May 14, 18, 1862, *ibid.*; Walker to Osborn, May 31, 1862, "Treasurers Letters," No. 19, box 48.

[61] Osborn to Hoffman, May 29, 1862, "Osborn Letter Book," 1861–1862. A copy of the contract is in box marked "1854–1855, Special," M. O. This copy was at one time misplaced and as Hoffman lost all his papers in the Chicago fire there was considerable difficulty in settling up the business at a later date. L. V. F. Randolph to Peter Daggy, May 18, 1874, box: "Land Dept., Misc. Corr., 1871–1895," 16th St.

[62] Copy of contract as in previous note.

[63] Copy of order by Osborn, May 29, 1862, " Osborn Letter Book," 1861–1862.

[64] J. F. Tucker to Osborn, June 19, 1862, M. O.

[65] See advertisements in *Illinois Staats-Zeitung*, June 30, 1862, and *Gerhard's Illustrirten Familier-Kalendar fur 1864.*

in immigration ports and other cities,[66] and printed and distributed large quantities of advertising pamphlets and circulars. Germans going through Chicago from the East were accosted and urged to go into Hoffman's district. In Germany itself Hoffman employed the same means to stimulate migration to and interest in Illinois, doing a more thorough job than the Company had attempted to do in that country. His wide popularity was a great asset in all these undertakings.[67]

Hoffman's activities brought results at once. The western movement of Germans through Chicago was in part deflected from its previous path and turned into eastern Illinois. At the same time a movement was started from Missouri, where, because of the turmoil and civil strife, the Germans were ready to listen to agents discourse on the advantages of peaceful and prosperous Illinois.[68] The Illinois Central had previously attempted to interest the Missouri Germans in its lands. Hearing that there was much discontent and dissatisfaction with that state among these people, Osborn had sent two men to St. Louis in December, 1861, with instructions to post bills and circulars, work through the papers, and by personal intercourse call the attention of the dissatisfied Germans to the Illinois Central lands. Free passes were offered them from Odin northward for 150 miles.[69] These activities, now continued by Hoffman, led to important results. In November, 1862, Hoffman sold 2300 acres, chiefly to St. Louis Germans, and for some time thereafter the immigration of this group into Illinois continued.[70] By 1863, when Hoffman was advertising on a large scale, Germans were pouring in from all sides, from Missouri, Wisconsin, Indiana, states farther east, and direct from Germany. In 1862 he sold 8910 acres, and in 1863 his sales, which were mostly

[66] Osborn to Walker, July 19, 1862, green box, 63rd St.
[67] Osborn to J. M. Redmond, June 17, 1862, "Presidents and Chairmans Letters," No. 18, box 48; *Illinois Staats-Zeitung*, May 29, 1862. For an example of Hoffman's activities in Germany see the long article entitled "Für jeden Heimathlosen eine Heimstätte!" in a "Beilage" to the *Allgemeine Auswanderungs Zeitung*, December 12, 1862. This reference was kindly furnished the writer by Dr. M. L. Hansen. See the *Chicago Tribune*, May 29, 1862, for favorable comment on Hoffman's work.
[68] Osborn to Walker, October 20, 1862, green box, 63rd St.
[69] Osborn to N. Stevens, December 4, 1861, "Osborn Letter Book," 1861–1862.
[70] Osborn to Walker, December 1, 1862, green box, 63rd St.

40-acre tracts, amounted to 29,813 acres.[71] The following year the total was about the same as the average for the two preceding years, but sales fell off considerably in 1865 and 1866, when the contract ran out. In these four years Hoffman was instrumental in selling and settling over 80,000 acres.[72]

The success of this venture cannot be measured in mere sales statistics. The figures mean more than may be thought, because they represent small sales to actual settlers. Most of the purchasers bought only 40-acre tracts, and it is therefore evident that between one and two thousand families settled in the region between Centralia and Mattoon, hitherto largely untouched. These figures would safely represent an addition of from five to eight thousand people to the State. Hoffman founded the town of Sigel, where, to assist him, a station and a siding were established by the railroad; [73] it soon became a flourishing little German center.[74] Through Hoffman's efforts many Germans were colonized in south central Illinois who otherwise would very likely have gone to Wisconsin and northern Illinois. The counties of Washington, Marion, Effingham, Shelby, and Cumberland owe their large German population to him.[75]

After completing his arrangements for a German agent, Osborn then looked for some well known person to interest the Scandinavians in Illinois. At this time the Lutherans in the Northwest had withdrawn their support from Illinois State University at Springfield and had determined to establish a college of their own.[76] Various communities offered land to secure the location of the proposed college, and a site was finally selected in Iowa. The outbreak of the Civil War, however, prevented these plans from

---

[71] Osborn to Phillips, February 18, 1863; to Walker, February 27, 1863, "Osborn Letter Book," 1863–1865, M. O.; ledger "A1, A to F," 16th St.

[72] *Ibid.*

[73] See article "Die Gründung von Sigel, Ill.," in *Deutsch-Amerikanische Geschichtsblätter* (1910), X, 209. Cf. Osborn to W. R. Arthur, December 26, 1862, January 10, 1863, "Osborn Official Letter Book," 1862–1865, box 48.

[74] *Sectional Maps* (1867), p. 80.

[75] Mannhardt, *loc. cit.*, p. 60.

[76] *Chicago Tribune*, June 13, 1862. There is considerable information on the founding and history of Augustana College in George M. Stephenson, *The Religious Aspects of Swedish Immigration* (Minneapolis, 1932), *passim*. The institution at Springfield must not be confused with the university later established at Urbana.

being carried out and the location was abandoned.[77] Osborn, learning of this, got in touch with Erland Carlson and T. N. Hasselquist, two of the leaders of Augustana Synod, and urged them to locate the proposed college at some point on the Chicago branch of the Illinois Central. He offered to give the college a commission of 50 cents on each acre of land sold through its efforts and also the privilege of purchasing 1000 acres as a location at reduced prices.[78] The directors of the Illinois Central were more favorably impressed with this plan of Osborn's than with the offer he had made to Hoffman, and ratified his action at once.[79]

By May 14 Osborn had sufficiently interested the Scandinavians in his proposal so that they agreed to go on a tour of inspection over the line of the road to view prospective sites for the college. Accompanied by President Osborn and officials of the Land Department, two Swedish and two Norwegian clergymen set out over the line on a special train and travelled as far south as Jonesboro. Hasselquist was especially struck by three places: Neoga, Pera, and Paxton. At the first place, as we have seen, there was already a considerable settlement of Swedes and Norwegians, there was a good deal of vacant land, and the soil and agricultural possibilities seemed favorable. Neoga's chief drawback was its distance from Chicago — 180 miles. It was feared that the location was too distant from the main body of Scandinavians, who were much farther north. Pera was more favorably situated and already had a small settlement of Swedes. The proprietors of this town, who had purchased the site from the Associates at $50 per acre,[80] regarded the proposed college as a means of making good their investment and left no stone unturned to secure the institution.[81] The Associates, who still owned land in the same section in

---

[77] Olson, *op. cit.*, part 1, pp. 508–513; G. M. Stephenson, "The Founding of Augustana Synod: Illustrative Documents," Swedish American Historical *Bulletin* (March, 1928), I, 1 *passim.*

[78] Osborn to Directors of Illinois Central, May 8, 1862, "Osborn Letter Book," 1861–1862, M. O.; Walker to Haven, May 13, 1862, "Treasurers Letters," No. 19, box 48; Carlson to Hasselquist, January 30, 1863, Hasselquist MSS.

[79] Walker to Osborn, May 17, 1862, "Treasurers Letters," No. 19.

[80] Theodore Neal to C. B. Phillips, November 7, 1865, "Illinois Land Agency," No. 5, Neal-Rantoul MSS.

[81] Theodore Neal to Jonathon Sturges, July 26, 1862, "Illinois Land Agency," No. 3, *ibid.*

which Pera was laid out, were importuned by the Illinois Central to offer a land donation to secure the location of the college, but refused to do so. The proprietors of Pera by themselves were unable to compete with the more powerful speculators of Paxton, and so the former place was dropped from further consideration. Despite the fact that the site of Paxton was owned by two speculators, Pells and Mix,[82] this town appealed particularly to Hasselquist, who was struck by the richness of the surrounding soil, the large amount of land available, and the relative proximity of the location to Chicago.[83] Mix was inclined to demand of the Lutheran leaders a high price for a site at Paxton, but Pells was more generous, and by offering a donation of 20 acres [84] made possible the establishment of the college there.

Henceforth Hasselquist urged the Lutheran group to accept President Osborn's offer, but he was opposed by most of the other leaders, among them Engberg, Esbjorn, Carl Carlson, and Norelius. These men were of the opinion that to locate the college so far south as Paxton would be to place it in a region far distant from the main body of Lutherans, who would thus be prevented from enjoying its benefits. Many thought it should be located in Minnesota, where large numbers of Swedes and Norwegians were settling.[85] On the other hand, Osborn's offer had the advantage of providing a source of income for the college in its early days. Erland Carlson supported Hasselquist, and together they convinced the Synod that Paxton was the ideal location for Augustana College.

The negotiations between Carlson and Hasselquist on the one hand and Osborn on the other were long and involved. The two

[82] Carlson to Hasselquist, August 21, October 30, 1862; Hasselquist to Estrem, April 15, 1865, "Hasselquist Letter Book," No. 1; advertising letter-head of letter of Mrs. Mix to Hasselquist, May 22, 1869, Hasselquist MSS. It appears from this letter-head that Mix owned 30,000 acres in Kankakee, Ford, Iroquois, Champaign, and Vermillion Counties, and 300 town lots in Paxton.

[83] Osborn to Walker, May 14, 1862, "Osborn Letter Book," 1861–1862; report of Hasselquist in Augustana Synodens Protokoll, *Minutes* (1862), pp. 16–18.

[84] Related to the writer by J. Hasselquist of Rock Island, a son of T. N. Hasselquist. Cf. Hasselquist to Estrem, April 15, 1865, "Hasselquist Letter Book," No. 1, Hasselquist MSS.; *Minnesalbum Sv. Ev. Luth. Forsamlingen, Paxton, Illinois,* p. 20.

[85] J. Enberg to Norelius, February 13, 1863, Norelius MSS.; Carl Carlson to Hasselquist, February 27, 1863, Hasselquist MSS.; Olson, *op. cit.,* part 1, pp. 508–513.

Lutheran leaders were suspicious of the President, and investigated every aspect of the proposition before accepting it. They succeeded in getting Osborn to make a more generous offer, which included the following terms: the Company was to sell the college 1000 acres of choice land in the neighborhood of Paxton for $6 an acre, and was to reserve 5000 more in the same region, the price of which was not to exceed $10 per acre. A commission of $1 an acre was to be given to the college on all sales made through the influence of its leaders up to 30,000 acres and 50 cents on the next 30,000. This offer finally won the Synod, and was accepted on February 12, 1863.[86]

Both Hasselquist and Carlson were situated favorably for carrying on immigration work among their countrymen. Hasselquist, as editor of *Hemlandet*, an influential Swedish newspaper, was able to give much free publicity to the proposed colony; he was also able to give a favorable start to the new settlement by bringing to Paxton a group of eighty-three Lutherans who had been members of his congregation at Galesburg.[87] Carlson, being in Chicago where thousands of Norwegians and Swedes were arriving, was in touch with the newcomers and thus was able to induce many to go to Paxton who otherwise might have gone to Minnesota or Wisconsin.[88] These two men gave much publicity to the colony through their extensive correspondence with prominent Lutherans in Norway and Sweden; the visits that the leaders of the Synod made to their home countries were likewise valuable. Finally *Hemlandet*, which was sent to friends in Sweden by its editors and by American subscribers, carried abroad the articles and advertisements on Paxton and the new college.[89] Indeed, the connection between Augustana Synod and Augustana College

[86] Carlson to Hasselquist, January 30, 1863, Hasselquist MSS.; J. Engberg to Norelius, February 13, 1863, Norelius MSS.; Osborn to Walker, February 12, 1863, M. O. This agreement was ratified at the meeting of Augustana Synod in June, 1863. Olson, *op. cit.*, part 1, pp. 513–515.

[87] Oscar F. Ander, *T. N. Hasselquist* (Augustana Library *Publications*, No. 14, 1931), p. 57.

[88] Carlson, writing to Hasselquist, September 15, 1865, said he was attending to the large Swedish immigration which was going through Chicago and was sending as many as possible to the new colony at Paxton.

[89] Hasselquist sent twenty copies of *Hemlandet* abroad. Ander, *op. cit.*, pp. 32–33.

and the publicity that the leaders of the latter gave to their colony became so prominent that a writer in Sweden reported, "It has come to the point that in some quarters in Sweden the Augustana Synod is suspected of being a kind of emigration bureau and that ministers who visit Sweden are emigration agents to get recruits for their congregations." [90]

Although both Hasselquist and Carlson spent considerable time in promoting the movement of immigration to Paxton, they were not able to care adequately for the work, and therefore decided to appoint P. L. Hawkinson as land agent for Augustana College. Hawkinson visited Paxton and its neighborhood in order to acquaint himself with the region before he began his work.

An early advertisement placed in *Hemlandet* by Hawkinson is interesting as showing the broad appeal he made to his countrymen.[91] It is directed to all who were interested in the college that was being established, to all interested in Paxton, to persons wishing to settle in a community where good instruction by Lutheran pastors was available in both English and Swedish, and to those anxious to secure good farming lands. Hawkinson points out that some of the land in the vicinity surpasses in richness all other land in northern and central Illinois and that much of it is suitable for wheat, although corn, which produces from 50 to 90 bushels per acre, is more profitable. In spite of the fact that Paxton was situated in the midst of a large prairie miles distant from timber, the advertisement declares that woodland is within four or five miles of the town and wood may be procured at much lower prices than in Galesburg or Aurora. The climate is suitable; in fact, the region is the healthiest place in America, according to the residents of Paxton.

Hawkinson then gives the particular advantages of buying land of the Illinois Central. In the first place, the prospective purchaser is given a free trip to Paxton by the railroad, and if he purchases from the Company his family will likewise be given free passage to the community. In the second place, he will be allowed

[90] Norelius, writing from Goteborg, May 12, 1868, to the editor of *Hemlandet*. The translation of the letter appears in Swedish Historical Society of America, *Yearbook* (1922–1923), VIII, 143–144.

[91] *Hemlandet*, February 25, May 6, 1863.

seven years to pay for his land at 6 per cent interest. One of the biggest advantages is that his land will be exempt from all taxes until the purchaser has made his last payment on it and received title. Finally, the Illinois Central will accept the products of his land as payment and will give the highest prices for them, in addition to allowing 33⅓ per cent discount on the freight charges. With such an advertisement appearing in a semi-religious weekly, backed by the prestige of Hasselquist and Carlson, it is no wonder that many Scandinavian Lutherans were encouraged to settle in Paxton.

With the group that Hasselquist brought with him from Galesburg as a nucleus, and the constant additions that were brought to Paxton by Hawkinson, the colony at Paxton developed rapidly during its first few years. Within a year *Hemlandet* reported that over 6000 acres had been sold and that there was a Swedish Lutheran congregation of over fifty members which would represent a group of two hundred people.[92] The following year Hasselquist wrote that Paxton had a population of 1000; unlike most town site promoters, he added frankly that the place would probably not be a large city.[93] Strangely enough, immigration fell off markedly in 1865 and 1866, in spite of the fact that both Swedes and Norwegians were coming to the United States during this period in much larger numbers than ever before. In 1867 and 1868 the colony experienced its most active growth; in these two years, between 20,000 and 30,000 acres were sold by agents of the college. This brought to a virtual close the land operations of the group.

The total land sales that the officials of Augustana College made for the Illinois Central Railroad were over 36,000 acres.[94] As the average number of acres per sale in this period was about seventy, this would represent approximately 500 individual sales to perhaps as many families.[95] This figure, however, does not include all the land sales that were made directly or indirectly through the influence of Hawkinson, Hasselquist, and Carlson.

[92] *Hemlandet*, February 2, 1864.

[93] Hasselquist to Ahlenius, March 3, 1865, "Hasselquist Letter Book," No. 1, Hasselquist MSS.

[94] Compiled from Ledger "A1, A to F," 16th St.

[95] The average size of land per sale is given in the *Annual Reports*.

Many Swedes who were induced to come to the region by these men subsequently purchased land from other agents of the Company. Captain Stevens, station-agent for the Illinois Central at Paxton, was authorized to make sales, and, as the Swedes maintained no resident agent at Paxton, but instead had an agent go there from Chicago two or three times a week, they lost many sales to him. Stevens received a commission ranging from 15 to 25 cents per acre. To October, 1867, his total commissions reached $1000, which would represent land sales of from 4000 to 6000 acres.[96] As the incoming Swedes did not settle only in Paxton and its immediate neighborhood, it is probable that other agents north and south of Paxton benefited from the work of the Lutheran leaders.

Another factor which diminished the sales of the college was the large quantity of land in the vicinity of Paxton which was held by local speculators such as Pells and James Mix. Their holdings were now purchased by incoming Swedes. Moreover, those newcomers who possessed sufficient capital preferred to buy improved land, and in 1865 Hasselquist gave this as the principal cause for his small success in making sales that year.[97] Furthermore, not all who came to Paxton purchased land for farming; some engaged in business in the town. Thus it is impossible to measure fully the results of the immigration work of the Augustana leaders.

It is interesting to note the localities from which the Paxton settlers came. Mention has already been made of the original group that came with Hasselquist from Galesburg. At the first meeting of the congregation in 1863, members joined the church who had come from Knoxville, Moline, Galesburg, and Berlin, Illinois, from Chandlers Valley, Pennsylvania, and from points in Minnesota. In 1865 and 1866 a group came from Attica, Indiana, and small numbers came from other Swedish centers in America. After 1866 the largest influx of settlers came directly from Sweden.[98]

[96] Hasselquist to Carlson, November 10, 1865, "Hasselquist Letter Book," No. 2; Hasselquist to Captain Stevens, September 3, 1867, "Hasselquist Letter Book," No. 3; Carlson to Hasselquist, October 24, 1867, Hasselquist MSS.

[97] Hasselquist to Chrisman, March 20, 1865, "Hasselquist Letter Book," No. 1, ibid.     [98] *Minnesalbum*, pp. 12 ff.

Hasselquist was unsuccessful in drawing any important number of Norwegians to his colony. Few of the immigrant groups coming to America during the first three-quarters of the nineteenth century settled so largely in one section as did the Norwegians. Wisconsin, Minnesota, Iowa, and northern Illinois contained in 1870 90 per cent of the Norwegian population of the country, while the same area contained less than 66 per cent of the Swedish population.[99] It seemed to be much more difficult to induce the Norwegians to settle outside this area than it was to induce the Swedes.

Although Hasselquist, Carlson, Hawkinson, and others were successful in bringing many of their countrymen to Paxton, they were not able to overcome the prejudice of the Scandinavians against settling in a region so far south. Wisconsin, Minnesota, and even northern Illinois had much more attraction for them, and in spite of all the work that was done by these men, they were able to persuade only a small portion of the Scandinavian immigrants to go to Paxton. *Hemlandet* gave much attention in its columns to the Swedes and Norwegians who were passing through Chicago, and frequently observed that relatively large groups went to Wisconsin and Minnesota, many went to Galesburg and Andover, some stayed in Chicago, and a few went to Paxton.[100]

As early as 1865 Hasselquist became convinced that Paxton was not going to become a large colony, and in the following year he wrote that the settlement had not grown as rapidly as he had expected. Nor had the college developed as had been anticipated; in 1866 its total enrollment was but 40, of whom 7 were Americans, 6 were Norwegians, and the remainder were Swedes.[101] It was apparent by now that its location at a point so far south was unfortunate, and already a movement was on foot to transfer the institution to some more central location. As early as 1868 Has-

[99] Computed from *Ninth Census*, I, 340–342.

[100] *Hemlandet*, July 6, August 24, 1864.

[101] Hasselquist to Ahlenius, March 3, 1865, "Hasselquist Letter Book," No. 1, and Hasselquist to Harkey, March 12, 1866, "Hasselquist Letter Book," No. 3, Hasselquist MSS. There is some material on the history of Augustana College in Augustana College and Theological Seminary, *Catalogue* (1924–1925), pp. 115–117.

selquist was corresponding with the Land Department of the Union Pacific Railroad in regard to moving the colony of Swedes from Paxton to Kansas.[102] No change was made until the 'seventies, when Augustana College was moved to Rock Island, but such a move had seemed inevitable much earlier.

Despite the success of Hoffman and the leaders of Augustana College in selling and settling the lands of the Illinois Central, the contracts with them were not renewed. The reasons were various. Osborn's original plan had been to make these agencies perform the activities previously undertaken by the Land Department. They were to advertise, employ agents and runners, publish and distribute circulars and pamphlets, and make the sales. In consequence the expenses of the Land Department were greatly reduced, its sales agents were mostly discharged, and its energies were largely devoted to the collection of payments due on old contracts.[103] There still remained unsold, however, several hundred thousand acres on the main line above Centralia and on the Chicago branch above Paxton,[104] in regions where neither the Swedes nor Hoffman were working. After a short period of inertia, the road's officials realized that definite efforts must be made to sell these lands. Consequently in 1863 and 1864 they gradually resumed their previous activities, being stimulated in so doing by the favorable economic conditions of those years, and their efforts gradually came to duplicate those of the subsidiary agents. Thus by 1867 the Land Department was distributing circulars among the Swedes and advertising in half a dozen German and Scandinavian newspapers.[105] Such duplication was wasteful and unnecessary, and must have been a factor in inducing the Company not to renew the agreements with the Swedes and Hoffman.

Another consideration was the feeling aroused in the Land Department and among other agents against granting to these organizations commissions so much more generous than those

[102] W. F. Downs, Land Commissioner of the Union Pacific Railroad, to Hasselquist, July 24, 1868, Hasselquist MSS.
[103] Walker to Osborn, June 2, 1862, "Treasurers Letters," No. 19, box 48; Carlson to Hasselquist, October 25, 1862, Hasselquist MSS.
[104] See plates 9 to 27, *Sectional Maps* (1865).
[105] Journal No. 7, Land Department, 16th St.

ordinarily given.[106] Moreover, there developed a certain amount of friction between the Swedes and the officials of the Illinois Central. Osborn's action in 1863 in raising the price of lands around Paxton $3 an acre seemed to the Swedes to be contrary to the spirit of their contract, and made Carlson lose "all confidence in Osborn's sincerity." [107] Finally, it was obvious that the immigration of Germans and Swedes into southeastern Illinois had gained sufficient momentum to carry on by itself. Thus the special efforts which had been necessary to begin the movement were no longer warranted.

Turning to the activities of the Illinois Central in England, we find an equally interesting story. In that country there were two factors which directly or indirectly aroused interest in Illinois and its lands among all classes. The first was the activities of the Land Department itself; the second was the work carried on by British investors in the Company, who constantly sought to stimulate emigration to Illinois.

With each succeeding assessment upon the stock of the Illinois Central Railroad, the British investors took an increased interest in its affairs until the assignment of the Company during the Panic of 1857, when they became most pressing in their suggestions and advice. The reports of the investigating committees sent over by them were carefully read, and those parts referring to the Land Department and its policies were republished widely. The investigators were unanimous in their high opinion of the value of the lands, and their descriptions were frequently as colored as were the advertising pamphlets of the Land Department itself. After 1857 the British investors were not content to continue their passive role as far as the Illinois Central was concerned. Instead, they actively worked to direct emigration to Illinois and to the Illinois Central lands. They aided in distributing the advertising material of the Land Department and published many items upon the lands in the British papers; and two of their investigators, Richard Cobden and James Caird, wrote

[106] Osborn to Walker, July 9, 1862, "Osborn Official Letter Book," 1862–1865, box 48. The commission allowed to station agents was only fifteen cents per acre. See Cash Book, No. 14, Land Department, 16th St.

[107] Carlson to Hasselquist, March 3, 1863, Hasselquist MSS.

most effective bits of propaganda for the road. The publication of Cobden's letter on the lands of the Illinois Central proved to be a most valuable advertisement, but the works of Caird surpassed this in scope and in influence. Caird was a prominent authority on British agriculture, a contributor to the *London Times*, and a Member of Parliament. Because of his familiarity with agricultural problems he was selected in 1858 by the British investors to go to America to make a thorough investigation of the Illinois Central Land Department.[108] Caird's selection was most judicious, since his prestige, his ability as a writer, and his flair for publicity ensured a favorable reception for anything he wrote. Though not at the time an investor in the railroad, Caird soon took a keen interest in it and in its president, with whom he formed a deep and lasting friendship.[109]

Caird left England in September, 1858, for the United States. After landing at New York on the twelfth, he proceeded by way of the Hudson River to Albany, thence to Troy and Ticonderoga by rail, took the steamer on Lake Champlain to Burlington, and then the train to Montreal. From Montreal he went to Ottawa by river and rail transportation, and from there he proceeded through Upper Canada to Detroit, and then to Chicago. By this leisurely and roundabout route, Caird was enabled to view a considerable part of Upper Canada, which at that time was vying with the American states in attracting British immigration. His observations on this region, as will be seen, aroused a veritable storm of criticism when published.

After arriving in Illinois, Caird proceeded to make as thorough an examination of the Company's lands and their prospects as was possible in a limited time. He traversed almost the entire line on three different occasions, and at several points spent many days in driving about the country.[110] He interviewed many of the

[108] Professor Edwin F. Gay assures the writer that Caird's writings on English agriculture are still recognized as standard works.

[109] Caird was accused of being an owner of some shares in the Illinois Central at the time he made his trip to the United States, an accusation which he denied. *Caird's Slanders on Canada Answered and Refuted* (Toronto, 1859), p. 2, note.

[110] Caird to George Moffatt, published as *Letter on the Lands of the Illinois Central Railway Company* (1859), p. 3. Also in *Chicago Press and Tribune*, March 2, 1859.

farmers and tradesmen along the road, visited Springfield and there talked with some of the leading politicians of the State, gathering information on the nature and character of the settlers, the crops and the causes for their recent failure, and the development of the Illinois Central towns.[111] Caird was immensely impressed with Illinois as a result of his survey, and reached "the most settled conviction that the Illinois lands are superior to any other in the West." [112] Indeed, so optimistic was he of the future of the State that he decided to take an active part in its advancement.

Caird wrote for publication a number of long letters, descriptive of Illinois lands and the Company's terms for them, the scenery, the types of farming, the towns, the people, and the railroads. So highly colored and optimistic were they that such an ardent booster's paper as the *Chicago Press and Tribune* felt it necessary to correct certain of the exaggerations by editorial criticism.[113] These letters were widely printed in England and America in newspapers and journals of various descriptions,[114] and gave a tremendous amount of publicity to the Illinois Central.[115] One of them was published as a separate pamphlet in at least two editions and distributed broadcast in England.[116]

A more pretentious literary effort by Caird for the purpose of advertising the lands was the booklet entitled *Prairie Farming in America, with Notes by The Way on Canada and the United States.* This booklet includes much of the material contained in the above-mentioned letters, with supplementary detail and discussion. The author begins by pointing out the unfavorable economic situation then existing in England by which the small farmer was being ruined. The remedy, in Caird's opinion, was

[111] This account is largely taken from Caird's booklet *Prairie Farming in America, with Notes By the Way on Canada And the United States.*

[112] Osborn to Lane, November 15, 1858, "Presidents Letters," 1858, box 48.

[113] *Chicago Press and Tribune,* April 1, 1859.

[114] *Chicago Press and Tribune,* March 2, 31, April 1, 2, 4, 8, 9, 1859; *American Railroad Journal* (1859), pp. 114–115. The letters were published in the *Toronto Globe* for which the sum of $200 was expended. Perkins to A. E. Burnside, April 19, 1859, "Perkins Treasurer," No. 14, box 48.

[115] Editorial in *Chicago Press and Tribune,* May 17, 1859.

[116] Caird, *Letter on the Lands of the Illinois Central. . . .*

emigration to Illinois.[117] The first and second letters or chapters are devoted to a narrative of the voyage and a discussion of the territory through which Caird passed on his trip from New York to Chicago by way of Upper Canada. Although his stops had been brief, and limited to the more populous terminals, Caird had managed to pick up information, such as it was, on farming and agriculture, which he here presents. And what a disconsolate picture of Canadian farming he draws! A few extracts may prove interesting. Concerning Lower Canada, Caird wrote:[118] "The land is cold and poor, held in strips by French Canadians, whose listless gait and lean cattle betoken a poor business. . . ." He travelled

through a wooded country, which, where partially cleared, is nearly covered with huge boulders of granite, a poor country, supporting a poor French population. . . . The summers are very hot, and the mosquitoes abound in the woods to such an extent as to render it impossible almost to live in them at that season; and the winters are long and severe, costly in fodder for cattle over such an extended period. . . .

Caird points out that in Upper Canada the land, although more fertile, is wooded, its price is extremely high, a great deal of labor is required to farm it, and that is costly; the grain crops are small, and sickness is prevalent.[119] In short, his opinion of the land and agriculture of that portion of Canada through which he passed is extremely unfavorable.

Caird's tone changes, however, when Illinois is discussed. These lands, he declares, are part of "the greatest tract of fertile land on the surface of the globe." [120] They do not have to be cleared, but there is plenty of timber in their vicinity; their prices are relatively low and exceedingly easy credit terms are granted; so fertile are they that they will stand constant cropping without manuring; they produce enormous crops per acre and labor is extraordinarily cheap in their vicinity. Caird does mention the disastrous wheat failure in the State, but lays it to an unfavorable combination of climatic conditions which hitherto had been quite

[117] *Prairie Farming*, pp. 7–12.
[118] *Ibid.*, pp. 16–20.
[119] *Ibid.*, pp. 20–22.
[120] *Ibid.*, p. 37.

uncommon. He likewise deprecates the prevailing opinion that the climate of Illinois is particularly unhealthy.

Concerning the lands of Wisconsin, Iowa, and Minnesota, which were then attracting large numbers of immigrants, the reader is informed that they are either higher in price, less fertile, less profitable, more distant from the railroad, or subject to the grasshopper plague.[121] The only possible conclusion to be drawn from a perusal of the booklet is that Illinois lands far surpassed for agricultural purposes all other lands in North America.

It is not strange that the officials of the Illinois Central saw in Caird's booklet an excellent bit of propaganda which would aid the sale of their lands. It was published simultaneously in England and America. D. Appleton and Company, who were the American publishers, advertised it to retail for 25 cents.[122] A large number of copies were used by the Illinois Central in stimulating immigration.[123] According to report, it was distributed by the tens of thousands in Great Britain and Canada.[124] Two years later the Company was retailing it, with an attached map, in Canada for the sum of 15 cents.[125] It was also translated into French for distribution among the French Canadians of Quebec, who were already emigrating in considerable numbers to Illinois.[126]

Canadian emigration to Illinois, both French and English, was looked upon by the Illinois Central as very desirable. Two important settlements of French Canadians had already been made along the road, Assumption on the main line, and Kankakee on the Chicago branch, both of which will be discussed later. It was determined to foster this movement as much as possible. The publication of Caird's letters and the distribution of his pamphlet were the first step in this direction. Agents were sent to Kingston to flood the provincial exhibition with the Company's advertise-

---

[121] *Ibid.*, pp. 99–113.

[122] Advertisement in *New York Tribune*, May 26, 1859.

[123] W. M. Phillips to Osborn, May 12, 1859, "W. H. Osborn, President," No. 11, box 48. A generous extract was reprinted in the land pamphlet of 1859: *Guide to the Illinois Central Railroad Lands.*

[124] *Caird's Slanders on Canada Answered and Refuted*, p. 1.

[125] Osborn to Foster, January 23, 1861, "Presidents & Chairmans Letters," No. 16, box 48.

[126] *Letters from Canada* (London, 1863), p. 55, note.

ments and pamphlets.[127]  Other agents were stationed at Toronto, Quebec, and London to work among the incoming immigrants as well as among the residents of these localities.[128]

As a final step in the campaign to induce Canadian immigration, an excursion over the line of the Illinois Central was arranged for the mayors and principal officers of all the cities on the line of the Grand Trunk and Great Western Railroads between Detroit and Quebec, as well as for Canadian editors, publishers, prominent farmers, officials of agricultural societies, and members of the Provincial Parliament. The purpose of this excursion was to interest Canadians in Illinois and to counteract the storm of criticism which rained upon the State as the result of the publication of Caird's pamphlet.[129]  A party of sixty persons accepted the invitation, and under the guidance of Joseph Austin, the chief lecturer in the Land Department, set out over the line. Between Chicago and Cairo brief stops were made at Loda, Rantoul, Champaign, Mattoon, and Cobden, where the participants were fêted by the residents and addressed by Austin and other speakers.[130]  On the northward trip over the main line a stop was made at Decatur in order that a visit might be paid to the farm of Dr. Johns, an eminent agricultural authority, and at Clinton the guests were addressed by Senator Lyman Trumbull. Stops were also made at Mendota, Amboy, where a visit was made to the car shops of the Company, and Dixon, where a dance and an elaborate entertainment were provided by the citizens.[131]  At Galena they were given a cordial welcome by the Mayor, and were then shown the mines and smelting works in the vicinity. Throughout the journey Austin was solicitous for the welfare of the guests, and nothing was neglected to secure their comfort. Before leaving Chicago the visitors gave Austin a dinner at which they expressed their warm regard for his kindness and to the Illinois Central their thanks for its generosity.[132]  As a result of the excursion the Com-

---

[127] *Caird's Slanders on Canada Answered and Refuted*, p. 7.

[128] J. W. Whitcher, Toronto, May 1, 1861, to Osborn, green box, 63rd St.; Foster to Walker, April 2, June 5, 12, 1861, *ibid.*

[129] Osborn to Robt. Benson & Co., June 26, 1860, "Presidents Letters," No. 14, box 48; *Prairie Farmer*, July 26, 1860.

[130] *Ibid.*, August 2, 1860.                [131] *Ibid.*, August 9, 1860.

[132] *Ibid.*, August 16, 1860.

pany received a large amount of publicity in the *Canadian Agriculturist*, the *Prairie Farmer*, the Chicago dailies, and other papers.[133]

The Canadian immigration officials, land agents, and certain newspaper editors were furious at this activity within their borders. Spending, as they were, thousands of dollars to attract immigration from abroad, they could not view with equanimity similar efforts to draw immigrants from their country. They were particularly incensed by Caird's unjust criticisms of Canadian agriculture, and in retaliation they commenced a literary attack upon Illinois. This attack soon assumed the proportions of a barrage and quite drowned out the weak protests of Caird. It was begun in the *Toronto Leader*, the *Hamilton Spectator*, and the *Old Countryman*. In the latter paper William Hutton, Secretary of the Bureau of Agriculture of Upper Canada, commented in a long article on the prevalence of sickness in Illinois, accused Caird of making his observations on an altogether too superficial investigation of farming in Canada, denied that labor costs were higher in Canada than in Illinois, pointed out that the quality of Illinois wheat was notably inferior to that of Canada and the yield per acre less, and maintained that farming in Canada was a great deal more profitable than in Illinois.[134] A contributor to the *Hamilton Spectator*, who preferred to remain anonymous, charged Caird with "underrating and slandering Canada." He maintained [135] that Illinois was "not a fitting field for European enterprise and colonization, that its geographical position renders it unfit for the production of European cereals, and that its climate is highly injurious and very often fatal to European constitutions." He further characterized Illinois as the land of "disease, disappointment and ruin," [136] as a "wretched" district, a "tree-less, water-less" unhealthy place.[137]

Probably the most effective bit of all this controversial writing

---

[133] *Canadian Agriculturist* (1860), XII, 427–429; *Chicago Press and Tribune*, August 1, 1860; *Prairie Farmer*, August 2, 9, 16, 1860.
[134] This letter is reprinted in (1) *Caird's Slanders on Canada Answered and Refuted*, pp. 15–26; (2) *The Canadian Settlers Guide* (London, 1860), pp. 141–154; (3) *Letters from Canada*, pp. 55–66, and (4) *Canadian Agriculturist* (1859), XI, 172–179.
[135] *Caird's Slanders on Canada Answered and Refuted*, p. 3.
[136] *Ibid.*, p. 7.                    [137] *Ibid.*, p. 1.

was Charles Lindsey's account of his journey through the middle western states in the summer of 1859, originally published in the *Toronto Leader*. Lindsey followed Caird's methods, visited the states of the enemy, interviewed various persons, gathered all the unfavorable reports available, and wrote them up in an exaggerated manner. After discoursing on the "indifferent" and inferior soils of Wisconsin and Minnesota, the disastrous effects of over-speculation and of the Panic of 1857 on the West, the unfortunate crop failures of 1859, and the general unhealthiness of the warmer regions of Iowa and Illinois, the writer came to his main topic, Illinois and the Illinois Central lands. He observed that here the winters were frigidly cold and the summers torridly hot, the mosquitoes unbearable, and malaria, ague, and bilious diseases unavoidable. Furthermore, Illinois had an extremely high death rate, its prairies lacked wood and water, and the lands of the Illinois Central — the flat and sickly prairies [138] — were held for extravagantly high prices and were "the least desirable lands in America for a settler to purchase." [139] This material was widely published in Canadian and English newspapers, and in pamphlet form was given broad circulation by the immigration agents of the Canadian provinces. The agents were distributing these pamphlets gratuitously in England as late as three years after the original publication of Caird's booklet.[140] The latter complained of the tone of "acerbity" in which they were written,[141] but seems to have been no match for such polemical journalists and refrained from carrying on the controversy.

Before the controversy had broken out, Caird had determined to carry further his efforts to promote British and Irish emigration to Illinois. To give him a personal interest in the matter, the Executive Committee of the Illinois Central made him a liberal offer by which he was either to purchase a large block of land for

[138] Charles Lindsey, *The Prairies of the Western States; Their Advantages and their Drawbacks* (Toronto, 1860), p. 100. These remarks are partly reprinted in *Caird's Slanders on Canada*, pp. 27–36, and in Agricultural Report of Province of New Brunswick, *Journal* of Legislative Council, New Brunswick, 1861, pp. 16–18.

[139] Lindsey, *op. cit.*, p. 66.

[140] *The Canadian Settlers Guide*, p. 213; *Emigration to Canada; Canada; A Brief Outline of her Geographical Position* . . . (Quebec, 1861), advertisement on back cover. [141] *Caird's Slanders*, p. 1.

resale or was to receive the exclusive agency for the Illinois Central lands in Great Britain and Ireland for a term of three years with a commission on sales made through his efforts.[142] Caird set about the task of organizing a company to take over a part of the lands. He succeeded in interesting Richard Cobden, Sir Joseph Paxton, and other prominent Englishmen.[143] They planned to organize a land company with a capital of £500,000, which was to be invested in the bonds of the Illinois Central, then selling on the New York exchange for 84;[144] the bonds in turn were to be used to purchase 250,000 acres of Illinois Central lands.[145] The scheme seemed well along toward completion but, owing to various circumstances, was abandoned for a less awkward arrangement.

The second plan provided that Caird should open a London agency for the Land Department, not so much to sell the lands as to be a central headquarters in England from which immigration activities could be carried on.[146] Before receiving definite confirmation from the Executive Committee, Caird proceeded to carry out this plan. He opened an office where the land pamphlets and other advertising literature could be secured by interested persons,[147] published another and briefer pamphlet of his own composition which would appeal more to British farmers and artisans,[148] and employed the usual means to interest the emigrating class in Illinois.[149] Although he did a great deal of work and spent a considerable sum of money, Caird's efforts were not very successful and the plan was dropped. Caird was, of course, com-

[142] Osborn to James Caird, November 12, 1858, enclosing copy of resolution of Executive Committee of November 12, "Presidents Letters," 1858, box 48; Caird to Osborn, November 12, 1858, ibid.; Osborn to Walker, May 6, 1862, "Osborn Letter Book," 1861–1862, M. O.

[143] Osborn to Moffatt, August 10, 1859, "Osborn President," No. 11, box 48.

[144] New York Tribune, August 8, 1859.

[145] Osborn to Caird, August 12, 1859, "Osborn President," No. 11, box 48; Chicago Press and Tribune, August 5, 1859.

[146] Osborn to Caird, April 3, 1860, "Presidents Letters," No. 13, box 48.

[147] Osborn to Robt. Benson & Co., September 7, 1859, "Osborn President," No. 11, ibid.

[148] A Brief Description of the Prairies of Illinois. 1,300,000 acres of the nearest and best of these are for sale in tracts of 40 acres and upwards, to suit purchasers, either for cash or on long terms of credit (London, 1859).

[149] Osborn to Foster, January 23, 26, 1861, "Presidents & Chairmans Letters," No. 16, says 500 maps were sent to the English agents for the purpose of assisting in their activities.

pensated for his work, and the Company did not feel that the expenditure was a bad investment even though immediate returns in land sales were not forthcoming. Osborn reasoned that the seed had been sown and that the Company would reap the benefit later when circumstances were more propitious than they were in 1860 and 1861.

At the same time that Caird was endeavoring to direct British emigration to Illinois, it was reported that the officials of the Grand Trunk Railroad of Canada had made an agreement with the British investors in the Illinois Central by which immigrants were to be sent to Illinois over the line of the former railroad. Small groups consisting of a dozen to twenty families were to be sent out under the leadership of some wealthy farmer and to be assisted in purchasing and settling on Illinois Central lands.[150]

President Osborn felt that one of the most effective ways of advertising Illinois in England was to exhibit there the products of the State. Accordingly he made plans to ship thither fifty Durham cattle which had been raised along the line of the Illinois Central; only cattle weighing over 2000 pounds were to be shipped. Osborn hoped that the exhibition of these fine cattle would not only interest prospective immigrants in Illinois but also would lead to the development of an export business in cattle from Illinois to England.[151]

In March, 1861, the Illinois Central proposed to send one of its most promising agents, Joseph Austin, to England, to carry on the work which Caird had begun.[152] The Civil War broke out, however, before anything could be done, and largely put a stop to emigration to America. As a result the Company discontinued most of its foreign activities. Yet Osborn did make an agreement with Peter Sinclair to distribute and post 5000 advertising cards or posters in strategic places in England, Scotland, and Ireland.[153] These posters were drawn in an excellent style and were colored in

[150] *Chicago Press and Tribune*, May 17, 1859.

[151] Osborn to Foster, July 16; to Arthur, July 17; to Borthwick, July 31, 1860, "Presidents Letters," No. 14, box 49.

[152] Copy of agreement with Austin in "Osborn Letter Book," 1861–1862, M. O.; letter of J. W. Foster, April 28, 1861, green box, 63rd St.

[153] Sinclair to Osborn, May 10, 1861, *ibid.*; Walker to Sinclair, July 2, 1861, "Treasurers Letters," No. 17, box 48.

order to make them more attractive.[154] Sinclair was instructed to use much care in posting them in order that they might receive as much attention as possible, and his compensation was generous enough so that he could spend six or eight months in the task.[155]

Save for a few isolated and unimportant incidents this concluded the organized efforts on the part of the Illinois Central to promote emigration from Great Britain, but British financiers, who until nearly the end of the century had large investments in the Company, continued the work of the Land Department.[156] By publishing articles and excerpts from the *Annual Reports* of the Illinois Central in the railroad periodicals, newspapers, and journals they sought to promote emigration to Illinois. So successful were their efforts that in 1859 a prominent Canadian paper complained of their action.[157] The *Toronto Leader* sorrowfully remarked that European immigration to Canada in that year had declined, although the movement from Europe was increasing, and gave as the cause that English stock- and bondholders in American railroads, motivated by selfish reasons, were advising British and Irish emigrants to go to the United States.[158] The *Leader* also stated that certain members of the House of Commons in particular were guilty in this respect, meaning probably Caird, Cobden, Paxton, Moffatt, and other prominent English stockholders in the Illinois Central.

[154] N. P. Banks to Osborn, April 15, 1861, reprinted in *Illinois Central Magazine* (July, 1913), pp. 18–19. The 5000 posters cost the Company $750. Phillips to Osborn, June 25, 1861, "Secretarys Letters," 1861, box 48.

[155] Bills of Robt. Benson & Co., of October 5, December 7, 1861, January 31, April 4, June 4, 1862, green box, 63rd St.

[156] Robt. Benson & Co. to L. A. Catlin, June 27, 1863, Ward's office. It is interesting to note that Robert Benson, whose bank had replaced Devaux & Co. as the financial agent of the Illinois Central in England, later became president of the N. A. T. & A. Co., in which capacity he made an arrangement similar to the one which Caird had made to promote the sale of the lands. Daggy to Benson, December 5, 1872, box: "Land Dept., Misc. Corr.," 16th St. It is doubtful whether much came from this negotiation, although a quantity of pamphlets were shipped to the firm in London. Rand, Avery & Co. to Peter Daggy, March 27, 1873, *ibid.*

[157] The circulars, daily and weekly, of the Satterthwaite bank and Robert Benson & Co., many of which are in the archives of the Illinois Central, contain much information on the Illinois Central Railroad. The *New York Tribune* in the 'fifties frequently reprinted in its commercial column large extracts from the Satterthwaite circulars.

[158] *Toronto Leader*, May 25, 1859; *Chicago Press and Tribune*, June 1, 1859.

# CHAPTER XI

## COLONIZING THE PRAIRIES OF ILLINOIS

THE influx of settlers into Illinois during the years 1850 to 1870 was only part of the larger movement of population into the West, which assumed tremendous proportions. The discovery of gold in California increased the amount of money in circulation, made credit easier, and brought about rapid expansion, particularly in railroad construction, which, as we have seen, was already making great progress in the Mississippi Valley. A period of inflation and speculation resulted which swept over the entire West and did not leave Illinois untouched. In the early 'fifties this state enjoyed a series of excellent grain crops which brought unbounded prosperity to the farmer.[1] Not only were crops large but the prices received for them were high. This was particularly true of wheat, the price of which skyrocketed in the years 1853, 1854, 1855, and 1856, reaching in 1855 the almost unprecedented price of $1.55 per bushel in the Chicago Market.[2] These prices were the result of short wheat crops in England and the blockade of the Black Sea during the Crimean War, which shut out the Russian wheat.[3] The corn crop also yielded abundant harvests in the West.[4] The prosperity of Illinois, emblazoned throughout the country by the Illinois Central, by the agricultural journals, and by letters published in the eastern papers, aroused the western fever among eastern farmers and mechanics.

It will be remembered that from 1854 to 1860 the Illinois Central concentrated its attention upon stimulating immigration

---

[1] James Caird stated that the Illinois wheat crop of 1855 was larger by 10 per cent than that of any previous year. *Chicago Press and Tribune*, March 2, 1859.

[2] John G. Thompson, *The Rise and Decline of the Wheat Growing Industry in Wisconsin* (*Bulletin*, University of Wisconsin, No. 292, Madison, 1909), p. 203. See Ferguson, *America by River and Rail*, p. 268.

[3] Caird, *Prairie Farming*, p. 39; *Country Gentleman* (November 15, 1855), VI, 316.

[4] Dupuy to Osborn, September 15, 1855, M. O.; *Wisconsin Farmer* (1856), VIII, 106. See also the letters published in *The Illinois Central Rail Road Company offer for Sale over 2,500,000 Acres . . .* (1855), pp. 13–32.

from the eastern and middle states, and, to a lesser degree, from Canada and northern Europe. The advertising of the Land Department produced the greatest effect in New England. Most of the sales made between 1855 and 1858 were to American citizens from New England, New York, and Ohio. Indeed, an official of the Land Department stated in 1855, although not quite accurately, that not one in five hundred of the purchasers was of foreign birth and scarcely any were from states south of New York.[5]

Emigration from New England had been under way since the beginning of the century, but it was much accentuated by the declining returns from agriculture which were caused by the competition of the new and more fertile lands of the West. In the middle of the century the tragic decay of rural New England was becoming a phenomenon of major social significance. John Wilson, Land Commissioner of the Illinois Central, observed, "The whole of New England, with New York, Pennsylvania & Virginia seem alive to the expediency of moving west . . . .," [6] and the *New York Herald* estimated that 300,000 people would emigrate to the West from New England alone during the season of 1857.[7]

So pronounced became the emigration from this section that property values in many districts declined alarmingly. In Rutland County, Vermont, from which many people had gone to Illinois, it was stated in 1858 that farm property was selling at prices from 25 to 40 per cent less than at any time during the past ten years.[8] The *State of Maine* in 1857 looked upon the departure of young farmers for the West "with no small degree of discouragement, as taking from us one of the most vital elements of progress and our future good condition." [9] The *Albany Argus* declared in the same year that land values had dropped in New York in the past four years, and laid the decline to the emigration of population and capital.[10]

---

[5] This was told to Perkins who quotes it in letter to Robt. Benson & Co., January 2, 1857, "J. N. Perkins, Treasurer," box 48, 63rd St.

[6] Wilson to Osborn, April 18, 1856, M. O.

[7] Quoted in *Chicago Democratic Press*, June 3, 1857.

[8] *New England Farmer* (April, 1858), X, 181.

[9] Quoted in *Chicago Democratic Press*, October 12, 1857.

[10] Quoted in *ibid.*, May 19, 1857.

The constantly increasing emigration to the West and especially to Illinois was not to go unhindered from the East; the newspapers there, alarmed at the movement, inveighed against it with much feeling. Eastern employers, according to report, aroused by the fear that their labor supply would be drained off, attempted to discredit the title which the Illinois Central was giving the purchasers of its lands. This attempt was carried out on a large scale, and many immigrants going through Chicago indicated their distrust of the Company's titles to other travellers.[11] Indeed the rumors became so widespread that the Illinois Central was forced to combat them. It therefore published an abstract of its titles in all its advertising matter and threatened to prosecute any persons caught spreading such false and slanderous stories.[12]

The colonial practice of migrating in groups was followed by New Englanders until well into the nineteenth century. A number of people who resided in the same community, and who were interested in moving to the West, would form an organization and send out agents to investigate different locations and to report on the best and most suitable regions for settlement.[13]

One of the most successful of these colonies, and also one of the most outstanding results obtained from the advertising campaign of 1855, was the location of a large number of Vermont farmers on the main line of the Illinois Central, 25 miles south of the Canal. It will be recalled that in February, 1855, advertisements of Illinois Central lands had been inserted in newspapers in every New England state.[14] In Vermont, papers in Burlington, Mont-

---

[11] There is considerable material on this attempt to discredit the title in the following letters, Wilson to New York office, May 2, 1856; Austin to Perkins, May 9, 1856; Wilson to Osborn, April 22, 1858, M. O.

[12] There was another group which was fighting the Illinois Central and its plans to colonize its lands. This group consisted of a number of Wall Street operators who were apparently selling Illinois Central stock short and were endeavoring to force down its price. The so-called "Ingersoll pamphlet," a copy of which I have not been able to locate, was written and distributed for this purpose. The commercial editor of the *New York Tribune*, a "Bull" on Illinois Central securities in the years 1855 to 1859, frequently mentions the efforts of the "Bears" to depress the stock quotations.

[13] For accounts of many of these New England colonies, see Lois Kimball Mathews, *The Expansion of New England* (Boston, 1909), and Pooley, *The Settlement of Illinois from 1830 to 1850.*

[14] MS. list of newspapers advertised in, dated February 8, 1855, M. O.

pelier, and Rutland had carried the advertisement.[15] Whether the association was formed prior to this time the records do not show, but by July the "Vermont Emigrant Association," consisting of 200 families, was organized. The leader of this group, William Burns, went to Illinois, where he met Dupuy and Osborn. He was taken over the line of the road, shown various locations, and informed of the extended credit terms which the Company granted. Burns became enthusiastic over the railroad lands and returned to Rutland to lay the matter before the Association. To assist him, 500 land pamphlets were provided for distribution to members of the Association and any other prospective emigrants.[16] The Association adopted Burns's recommendation by voting unanimously to accept a special offer of a block of lands near Wenona.[17] In the same year the group purchased between 20,000 and 25,000 acres from the railroad at prices ranging from $11.20 to $17 per acre and secured an option on an additional 25,000 acres.[18] The leaders of the Association preceded the others to Illinois to make the necessary arrangements for settlement. Plans were made for the construction of a flour mill and a plant to manufacture agricultural tools.[19] The erection of a number of houses was also begun. Then followed the exodus of about 200 families, who settled in the neighborhood of "New Rutland."[20] This region, although located in the heart of one of the richest prairie sections in the entire country, had been almost entirely neglected because

[15] See the *Green Mountain Freeman*, March 8, 1855, for copy of this advertisement. Apparently encouraged by its success in working through the Vermont papers the Illinois Central increased the size of its advertisement from two inches to eight inches in the December 20, 1855, issue of the same.

[16] Dupuy to Ackerman, August 22, 1855; Ackerman to Dupuy, August 25, 1855, "Burrall & Ackerman," 1854–1855, box 48.

[17] Wm. Burns to Dupuy, July 7, 1855 (copy); Dupuy to Osborn, July 16, 1855, M. O. James Caird says the investigating committee spent four months in Illinois and other states farther west studying possible locations before finally determining to accept the offer of the Illinois Central. See his letter in *Chicago Press and Tribune*, March 31, 1859.

[18] Vol. 79 of plat books in Land and Tax Commissioner's office; *Chicago Democratic Press*, December 6, 1855; letter of James Caird in *Chicago Press and Tribune*, March 31, 1859.

[19] *New York Tribune*, December 15, 1855; *Chicago Democratic Press*, December 6, 1855.

[20] Caird, *op. cit.*, p. 45; *Illinois Central Directory*, p. 282; *Sectional Maps* (1867), p. 46.

it lacked wood and transportation facilities.[21] Under the leadership of Burns, who himself purchased 1460 acres,[22] the settlement quickly became a thriving agricultural community.[23]

Another "Yankee colony" at Hoyleton, 6 miles from Irvington on the Illinois Central, is of peculiar interest because of its location in southern Illinois. It has been seen that Yankees were not liked by the residents of Egypt, and in general they avoided that part of the State. It was even alleged in 1858 that the old settlers in southern Illinois were driving off the newcomers and threatening to kill them if they returned.[24] In spite of this hostile feeling, there was established in this region in 1857, under the leadership of the Rev. J. A. Bent, one of the most interesting colonies of immigrants from New England. An excellent location was chosen on a rich prairie, lacking in timber, to be sure, but close to tributaries of the Kaskaskia where plenty could easily be secured.[25] Practically all the Illinois Central lands in the township were quickly taken up and placed under cultivation. Bent himself purchased 2640 acres for prices ranging from $8 to $11, much of which was probably bought for his followers, and large amounts were also purchased by his associates directly from the road.[26] Primarily an agricultural settlement, the colony did not attain large proportions; nevertheless the population of the township amounted in 1860 to 1231.[27] A seminary was established at an early date, and the settlement at Hoyleton became noted for its educational facilities and its propensities for Congregationalism, Temperance, and the Republican Party.[28]

The Yankee colony at Hoyleton was not the only bit of transplanted New England to be found in Egypt. At Rosemond, three miles from Pana in Christian County, there settled in 1856 a

---

[21] *Ibid.*

[22] Vol. 79 of plat books in Land and Tax Commissioner's office.

[23] Osborn quoted in letter of Burnside to Robt. Benson & Co., June 9, 1860, "Treasurers Letters," No. 16; Osborn to Foster, August 14, 1860, "Presidents Letters," No. 14; Osborn to Walker, October 5, 1860, green box, 63rd St.

[24] Wilson to Osborn, April 30, 1858, M. O. .

[25] See plate 6 in *Sectional Maps.*

[26] Taken from the plat books in Land and Tax Commissioner's office.

[27] *Ninth Census*, I, 120.

[28] Vol. IV, Illinois Central books, S. A. O.; Cole, *Era of the Civil War*, p. 13; *Sectional Maps*, p. 26.

colony of Massachusetts farmers consisting of fourteen families. The leader, B. R. Hawley, had visited Illinois in the early 'fifties and had become enthusiastic over the possibilities of establishing a settlement on Illinois Central land. Armed with a quantity of land pamphlets and advertising literature, he returned to Franklin and Berkshire Counties of his native state and sought to interest the farmers in his project. His efforts were successful. With a nucleus of fourteen families, the number grew until in December, 1857, there were forty-one farmers settled at Rosemond; 9000 acres were purchased, mostly at $8 per acre, and in 1857 2771 acres were under cultivation. A Congregational church with twenty-three members was organized in September, 1856, and a Sabbath School with fifty members was begun. Plans were made for the construction of church and school buildings, a post-office was opened in the village, and the community attained a prosperous and thriving position.[29]

Another emigration society, the "Working Man's Settlement Association," was organized in New London, Connecticut, in the winter of 1855–56. This group sent three agents to the West to select a location. These men proceeded to Chicago, whence they were taken over the line of the Illinois Central and shown its lands. They decided to locate in Lyman township, near Paxton on the Chicago branch. Arrangements were quickly completed, and in September, 1856, the first contingent of settlers arrived in Chicago on their way to their new homes. Their settlement was important in opening up and developing a region heretofore neglected.[30]

An Ohio colony, organized on lines similar to those of the Yankee colonies, was settled at Rantoul on the Chicago branch. In 1855 a number of people in Summit County, Ohio, sent John W. Dodge to Illinois to select lands for a settlement. Dodge made arrangements with a speculating group headed by

[29] Wm. Bross, editor of the *Chicago Democratic Press*, visited Rosemond in April, 1857, and was much impressed by the rapid development of the community. His communication in the *Prairie Farmer* of April 9, 1857, contains some interesting details concerning the colony. See also *ibid.*, December 24, 1857, and letter of B. R. Hawley to the Illinois Central, August 21, 1855, M. O.

[30] Letter of John Wilson, marked "Private," May 2, 1856, M. O.; *Historical Atlas of Ford County* (1884), pp. 12–13, 75.

Galloway and Campbell by which they were to purchase lands for him at the government land sale. Why he did not do this himself does not appear; at any rate, he secured a quantity of land at prices much lower than the Illinois Central was charging. Dodge then set about providing homes for the incoming settlers, and by November he had erected eighteen houses or shanties on as many quarter sections. Shortly afterward, the Ohio colony came in and established a substantial farming settlement.[31] The region about Rantoul, however, was poorly drained, and agriculture could not flourish until this obstacle had been removed. This was not accomplished until much later. It may be noted that on this account the Illinois Central had 90,000 acres of rich prairie land still on its hands in this locality as late as 1867.[32]

The American Emigration Association, which was organized in Louisville, Kentucky, in 1855, was also influential in settling a large number of colonists on Illinois Central land. At the first meeting of the Association two hundred people, many of whom were Germans, met together to make plans for settling in Illinois. Shortly afterwards the members of the Association began moving to Illinois, and their purchases of land substantially increased the sales of the railroad in 1855.[33]

Individual or family migration was, in our period, more important than collective and organized movements. The former method frequently led to similar results, however; an individual would leave an eastern community, go to the West, select a homestead, and begin farming. If successful, he would write his eastern friends of his results and they would in turn catch the western fever and perchance move to the same locality. This practice was common among foreigners, but was also followed by Americans.

Individual New York-New England immigration led to the establishment of numerous settlements in eastern and northern Illinois, of which Onarga is a good illustration. Individual immigrants from the northeastern states began to settle here in 1855,

---

[31] *History of Champaign Co., Illinois* (1878), pp. 147–158; *Annual Report*, 1858; *Sectional Maps*, p. 72.

[32] *Ibid.*, p. 72, and plate 28.

[33] Ingraham to Osborn, September 2, 1855, M. O.; *Chicago Weekly Democrat*, September 15, 1855; *Chicago Democratic Press*, March 2, 1857.

and in two years a hundred dwellings had been constructed on as many farms. The usual Congregational church was established, as was the case in most of the New England colonies.[34] The churches of this denomination founded at Monee, Kankakee, Clifton, Bulkley, Loda, Paxton, and Champaign on the branch, and El Paso, Rutland, La Salle, Tonica, Nora, Galena, and Dunleith on the main line, together with growing organizations at Amboy, Mendota, Bloomington, Hoyleton, Rosemond, and Sandoval, indicate other New England settlements.[35]

The haphazard efforts made by the Illinois Central in the 'fifties to attract German immigrants to Illinois were not without effect. The movement of Germans into northern Illinois, which was under way before the railroad was constructed, was accelerated, and this section became one of the great German centers in the United States. In 1856 it was reported that a party of seventy German farmers from Hanover had arrived in Chicago on their way to settle in Stephenson County, where there was already a growing German population.[36] Will and Effingham Counties in eastern Illinois had likewise, for a decade before the construction of the Illinois Central, been receiving considerable numbers of Germans. This movement was greatly stimulated by the advertising of the Land Department. Teutopolis and New Minden, which, as their names suggest, were German settlements, had been receiving these people for some years before the railroad reached them. The construction of the road served to continue the movement of Germans into Marion and Effingham Counties, in which these towns were located.

In general during the 'fifties the German immigration was by individuals, and consequently its importance was overlooked by the officials of the Company. Yet during this decade the immigration was sufficient to lead to the establishment or growth of German churches at Lena, Bloomington (2), Freeport (2), Eleroy, Kankakee, Galena (2), Champaign, Anna (2), Centralia, Dixon,

---

[34] *Prairie Farmer*, July 23, 1857; *Sectional Maps*, p. 68.

[35] There were also seven strong Congregational churches in Chicago. *Minutes of the General Congregational Association of Illinois* (Quincy, 1860); *Sectional Maps, passim.*

[36] *Chicago Democratic Press*, June 27, 1856.

Mendota (2), Monee (3), Decatur, Kappa, Assumption, Wapella, and Effingham, all on the line of the Illinois Central.[37] By the close of 1860, the Illinois Central was selling more land to Germans than to any other group of purchasers. The Germans were generally better supplied with money than most of the other foreign immigrants; they were sturdy, honest, industrious, and well adapted to the hard labor involved in breaking up new farms on the prairie.[38]

In 1860 and 1861 three German colonies were established on the branch line in Will and Effingham Counties, near other German settlements. The first of these, a group of Germans from Niagara Falls who were discontented with their location and environment, sent representatives to Illinois in 1860 to investigate possible sites for their removal. They met John W. Foster, Land Commissioner of the Illinois Central, who showed them various desirable locations. They determined to settle in Effingham County, a region where land sales were exceedingly slow, and their selection was thus doubly welcome to President Osborn and Land Commissioner Foster;[39] sixty-nine men purchased 3000 acres and prepared to move to the new location.[40] In February they arrived in Illinois and began farming operations. Their number was presently increased to eighty families.[41] President Osborn was delighted with the sale, and gave it much publicity in the hope of bringing further business to the Land Department. The Germans were treated royally and furnished with special cars free, and notices of the successful colonization of this large group were sent to all the important papers in the country for publication.[42] The second German colony was begun in 1861, west of Neoga; begin-

[37] "Lutherische Gemeinden-Chronik," *Deutsch-Amerikanische Geschichtsblätter* (1903), vol. III, No. 4, pp. 16–21.

[38] Foster to Osborn, January 18, 1861; Foster to Walker, January 18, 1861, green box, 63rd St.

[39] Osborn to Foster, November 21, 1860, "Presidents & Chairmans Letters," No. 16, box 48; *Annual Report* for 1860.

[40] Osborn to Foster, November 21, 22, 1860 "Presidents & Chairmans Letters," No. 16, box 48.

[41] Foster to Walker, February 14, 18, 1861, green box.

[42] Osborn to Foster, November 22, 1860; to Arthur, December 1, 1860, "Presidents & Chairmans Letters," No. 16. See notice of the colony in *American Agriculturist* (January, 1861), XX, 6; *Prairie Farmer*, November 22, 1860.

ning with a nucleus of eight families in April, it had increased to nineteen families in June.[43] At the same time the Illinois Central was colonizing a third group of Germans in Will County, southeast of Monee. By February, 1861, Foster reported that he had located in this region ninety-three men of German descent — "the best kind of settlers." [44]

There were also a good many Irish who purchased land and settled along the line of the road. There was a tendency for the Irish laborers, who predominated among those employed on the construction of the Illinois Central, to leave work and to take up land. The Irish settled particularly in Will County, south of Chicago, and in La Salle, in the vicinity of the Canal.[45]

English and Canadian immigrants had first become interested in Illinois by reading Caird's pamphlets. In May, 1859, it was reported that substantial English and Scotch farmers were arriving in Chicago on their way to settle on the Illinois Central lands.[46] This immigration had soon assumed considerable proportions. Slightly later a similar movement set in from Canada; a colony from London, Upper Canada, settled at Farina on the Chicago branch and took up a large amount of the Company's lands.[47] This movement continued throughout the decade, the Canadians settling for the most part in the great prairie region south of Chicago. In 1870 there were reported to be more than 7000 Canadians in the counties south of Cook.[48]

French Canadians were settling on the railroad lands in large numbers, and two of their colonies were as important as the German colonies. Before the Illinois Central was begun a considerable number of these people had settled at Bourbonnais, about 56

[43] Foster to Walker, April 20, 1861; letter of Foster, June 19, 1861, green box.

[44] Foster to Walker, January 10, 16, February 12, 1861, green box.

[45] See vol. 262, Land and Tax Commissioner's office, for names of many Irish who purchased land around Monee.

[46] *Chicago Press and Tribune*, May 17, 1859; Osborn to Foster, May 24, 1859, "W. H. Osborn, Pres.," No. 11, box 48; Foster to Directors, July 7, 1860, in *Railway Times* (July 28, 1860), XXIII, 839.

[47] Osborn to Robt. Benson & Co., May 18, 1860, "Presidents Letters," No. 14; *Railway Times* (June 9, 1860), XXIII, 656.

[48] "E. H." of Champaign, Illinois, in *Country Gentleman* (March 16, 1865), XXV, 173; *Ninth Census*, I, 351–352; *Sectional Maps*, p. 30.

miles south of Chicago.[49] In the following years there appeared in this quiet village Father Chiniquy, the stormy petrel of Illinois Catholicism, who was to cause much trouble to the leaders of his church. Chiniquy was much impressed with the attractions of the region around Bourbonnais. To stimulate the immigration of French Canadians to this garden spot, he wrote a long article on the advantages of the locality and published it in the Canadian press. According to its ardent author the effects were immediate. "In a few days after its appearance, their farms fell to half their value. Everyone, in some parishes, wanted to sell their lands and emigrate to the West. It was only for want of purchasers that we did not see an emigration which would have surely ruined Canada." [50] Chiniquy's statement is obviously exaggerated, but he did succeed in drawing large numbers of French Canadians to the vicinity of Bourbonnais, Kankakee, and St. Anne. It was in this latter community that Chiniquy set up his church, where he hurled his defiance at the Pope and the Catholic hierarchy. Chiniquy's bold utterances and his exaggerated account of Illinois drew so many of his countrymen to the State that the Canadian government was forced to take cognizance of the movement. It appointed a "Special Committee on Emigration" to study the causes of the emigration of such large numbers of Canadians to the United States. The Committee reported that most of the emigrants were going to Illinois and to the Bourbonnais colony.[51] The immigration of the French Canadians was welcomed by the Illinois Central, as these people purchased a large quantity of its lands in the vicinity of St. Anne, Momence, Kankakee, Manteno, and Bourbonnais.[52]

[49] Vandeveld to Chiniquy, December 1, 1850, in Father (Charles) Chiniquy, *Fifty Years in the Church of Rome* (Chicago, 1888), p. 498. A strong polemic against the Catholic church, this book has some value to the person interested in Chiniquy's activities at Bourbonnais. There is some material on the settlement in Joseph Tassé, *Les Canadiens de L'Ouest* (Montreal, 1878), II, 110 ff.

[50] Chiniquy, *op. cit.*, p. 512.

[51] Report of Special Committee on Emigration, *Sessional Papers*, 5th Parl., 3rd Sess., 1857, Appendix 47, Province of Canada.

[52] Chiniquy to Schuyler, January 9, 1853, with comments on same by R. B. Mason, M. O.; Walker to Foster, October 23, 26, 1860, "Presidents & Chairmans Letters," No. 16, box 48. See also Chiniquy, *op. cit.*, pp. 536 ff., and *Sectional Maps*, pp. 64–66. Cf. Cole, *op. cit.*, p. 17.

Another French Canadian colony of note was commenced at Tacusah, near Pana, on the main line. The promoter of this colony, E. E. Malhiot, a wealthy sugar planter of Louisiana, conceived the idea of establishing a colony in Illinois for the benefit of his fellow-countrymen, the French Canadians of Lower Canada.[53] He also wanted to make the proposed colony a distributing center for the products of his Louisiana plantation. Malhiot's original plan was to purchase about 7000 acres in the neighborhood of Tacusah, but against his better judgement he was induced in December, 1856, by John Wilson, Land Commissioner, and Andrew J. Galloway, a land agent, to contract for over 22,000 acres at $11 per acre.[54] This land was part of a high rolling prairie, not far from timber or water, but itself entirely free from any hindrance to cultivation except the tough prairie sod.[55] Malhiot offered liberal inducements to French Canadians in the region where he had formerly lived in Lower Canada, and by March, 1857, arrangements had been completed according to which fifty families from Canada were to move to his lands. Malhiot, in anticipation of their arrival, took a number of his associates in Louisiana with him to Tacusah, where they began preparations for the housing and feeding of this group which was to come. The town was laid out and plans were made for the construction of a hotel, flour mill, packing house, and grain warehouses. The farms were surveyed, building materials prepared, and stock purchased.[56] Teams and agricultural implements were forwarded as

---

[53] *Chicago Democratic Press*, March 7, 1857.

[54] Osborn to Perkins, December 28, 1856, M. O.; Malhiot to Daggy, November 29, 1873, box: "Land Dept., Misc. Corr., 1871–1895," 16th St. See vols. 268 and 269, Land and Tax Commissioner's office, for location of a portion of this sale. Properly speaking Malhiot purchased about 13,000 acres directly from the railroad and the remainder from Galloway, who was selling the Company's lands on a special contract. Daggy to Newell, November 28, 1872, "Daggy Personal with officers I. C. R. R. Co.," 16th St.         [55] *Sectional Maps*, plate 10 and p. 34.

[56] H. H., H. Hickley, or H. Hinckley, as he variously signed himself, was a Yankee who had been associated with Malhiot in Louisiana and had accompanied the latter to Assumption. He became enthusiastic about the possibilities of the region selected by Malhiot and purchased a half section from the railroad in 1855. He hauled lumber from Chicago, bought mules, horses, and oxen, hired help, built a substantial house, and placed 70 acres under cultivation the first year and soon increased this to 200. He wrote frequent letters which were published in the *Country Gentleman* and the *American Agriculturist*, in which he described the activities of the

rapidly as possible,[57] and a month later plowing, planting, and construction work were begun on a large scale.[58] By July a dozen houses had been erected, in addition to a large store and other buildings.[59] Shortly afterwards appeared the vanguard of the new colony, which soon grew to considerable proportions. In April, 1858, it was reported that a hundred French Canadian families had settled in the locality,[60] and James Caird noted in the latter part of the same year that approximately eight hundred of these people were living in the neighborhood of Assumption, as the town was now called.[61] So rapidly did the community develop that in 1861 the amount of corn to be shipped from it was estimated at 500,000 bushels.[62]

Like many other purchasers of the 'fifties, Malhiot had gone in too deeply and was unable to meet the payments on his land when they came due; in addition he owed other sums which he had previously borrowed amounting to $40,000. These debts finally led to the forced sale of his sugar plantation in Louisiana.[63] Liberal extensions were granted him by the railroad from time to time,[64] and his estate was not settled until the 'nineties. The Malhiot sale provided further difficulty for the Illinois Central, because Malhiot had failed to give deeds to his tenants when they had paid in full for their farms, and after his death the Company was put to much bother in trying to straighten out the titles.[65] Mal-

---

settlement, prairie farming, and his personal experiences. Three successive crop failures, however, with two deaths in the family and other discouragements, made life so miserable for him that he gave up and returned to the practice of medicine in Louisiana. See communications in *Country Gentleman*, IX, 195, 240 (March 19, 1857); X, 17–18 (July 2, 1857); XI, 68 (January 28, 1858). See also the *Prairie Farmer* and the *American Agriculturist* for the years 1857–1860.

[57] *Chicago Democratic Press*, March 7, 1857.

[58] *Country Gentleman* (April 9, 1857), IX, 240.

[59] *Ibid.* (July 2, 1857), X, 18.

[60] Wilson to Osborn, April 6, 1858, M. O. Cf. *Illinois Farmer* (February, 1863), VIII, 44–45.

[61] *Chicago Press and Tribune*, April 2, 1859. Cf. his *Prairie Farming*, p. 68.

[62] H. Hinckley in *American Agriculturist* (February, 1861), XX, 43.

[63] Malhiot to Daggy, November 26, 1873, box, "Land Dept., Misc. Corr., 1871–1895," 16th St.

[64] Osborn to Wilson, April 10, 1858, "Presidents Letters," No. 7, box 48; Osborn to J. M. Douglas, October 23, 1863, "Presidents and Chairmans Letters," No. 18, box 48.

[65] J. E. Trottier to Daggy, April 4, 1876; note of Daggy on letter of Malhiot to

hiot's case was the worst one on the books of the Land Department in regard to payments, and bore witness throughout the century to its unfortunate policy of selling large tracts of land to speculators or persons with insufficient capital.[66]

The construction of the Illinois Central Railroad through the great prairie regions of eastern and central Illinois was a most important factor in reversing the relative popularity of prairie and timber lands. Prairie lands, which had once been largely avoided by settlers, were in greater demand during the 'fifties, and the southern part of the State, where timber land predominated, ceased to attract purchasers. This is at once apparent from the fact that prior to April, 1857,[67] the Illinois Central sold only 50,000 acres in the region from Centralia to Cairo, a large part of which went to preemption claimants.[68] The relatively small increase of population in the counties south of Centralia likewise bears out this assertion.

The fact that southern Illinois was largely timbered land does not entirely explain its failure to increase in population during these years. Marion County, for example, which contained many fair-sized prairies, advanced little, agriculturally, from 1850 to 1860.[69] The same situation prevailed in other counties in that locality. This state of affairs is to be explained partly by the fact that Chicago and other northern Illinois newspapers fostered the opinion that in Egypt cholera and malaria were prevalent and a constant danger to newcomers; the hostility of the old southern uplanders to Yankees and foreigners and the lack of educational facilities must also be taken into account. Moreover, the continued decline of the Kentucky-Tennessee-Virginia immigration to Illinois was not compensated for in this region by other elements, as those immigrants who were coming to Illinois between 1850 and 1870 were largely from northern regions, and naturally sought lands with a more moderate summer temperature than

Daggy, June 17, 1874; H. C. Abbott to Daggy, May 29, 1874, box, "Land Dept., Misc. Corr., 1871-1895."

[66] The case is reviewed in letter of Daggy to Newell, November 28, 1871, "Daggy Personal with officers I. C. R. R. Co.," 16th St.

[67] *Sectional Maps* (1857), computed from plates 1-6.

[68] Vol. 262, Land and Tax Commissioner's office.

[69] *Home Missionary* (December, 1859), XXXII, 197.

GRAND PRAIRIE

Prairie

Woodland

PRAIRIE MAP OF ILLINOIS

(Reproduced by permission of Professor Harlan H. Barrows from his
*Geography of the Middle Illinois Valley*)

that of southern Illinois. Another consideration was the inferior soil of Egypt and the unsuitability of the land for wheat, the cash crop of the State. The final factor in the declining importance of southern Illinois was the small attention paid to that section by the Illinois Central. Although the Company had received over 500,000 acres south of Centralia, it directed its efforts largely to settling its lands in the central and eastern part of the State. Its advertisements dealt principally with wheat and corn and the cattle and hog business. Not until the following decade did the Illinois Central make any particular efforts to sell its lands south of Centralia.

The prairie counties of eastern and central Illinois — Will, Kankakee, Livingston, Ford, Champaign, Iroquois, McLean, De Witt, Macon, and Piatt — also suffered under a number of handicaps which retarded their development. In the first place, these counties were inadequately supplied with transportation facilities. For many parts of them the Illinois Central was the only railroad which connected them with their natural market, Chicago, and for a distance of 250 miles this road was crossed by only five east-west railroads. A great deal of land in these counties lay between 10 and 25 miles from railroads, and as there were practically no navigable rivers to supplement the railroads, the situation for development was not the best. Moreover, on account of poor drainage in this section the dirt roads were impassable for considerable periods of time.[70] The cost of purchasing and transporting sufficient lumber for building, fencing, and fuel purposes over the necessary distances was greater than most settlers could bear. Another most important factor which retarded the development of parts of eastern and central Illinois after the railroad was constructed was poor drainage. The low relief, the sluggish streams, and the flat prairies of Champaign, Iroquois, and Kankakee Counties combined to make large areas of rich land of little use until they could be artificially drained.[71] To effect this object the expenditure of large amounts of capital was required. Finally,

---

[70] Jonathon Sturges to Franklin Haven, May 26, 1856, Haven MSS.
[71] For a topographic map of Illinois, see Frank Leverett, *The Illinois Glacial Lobe* (Washington, 1899), pp. 6, 498, 506 ff.; Pickels and Leonard, *Engineering and Legal Aspects of Land Drainage in Illinois* (Urbana, 1921), *passim*.

the settlers who were coming to Illinois in the 'fifties, unlike the earlier pioneers, were more gregarious and wanted to be near friends, churches, schools, and, in the case of foreigners, fellow-countrymen. Such advantages were best offered in northern Illinois, and in this respect eastern Illinois and parts of central Illinois were handicapped.

Since the Illinois Central possessed large holdings in central and eastern Illinois, it put forth every effort to offset these handicaps and to encourage the settlement of the prairie counties. Prior to 1850, these counties were among the least populated in Illinois, and because they had been so generally neglected it was more difficult to guide immigration to them than to the northern part of the State. In 1856 the Illinois Central therefore raised the price of its remaining lands in northern Illinois to such a degree that immigration was turned into the less settled sections, where the prices remained constant.[72] Special inducements in the way of longer credit terms were also offered purchasers of land in these districts, in some cases eleven years being allowed for the payment of contracts.[73] In the advertising literature attention was particularly drawn to the less settled sections of central and eastern Illinois, far more space being devoted to them than to the northern or southern sections of the State.

As a result of these efforts population began to flow into the region along the branch line. German immigrants, as we have noted, were developing Will and Effingham Counties; the Irish also settled in Will County; and the French Canadians were locating in Kankakee County. New York-New England immigrants also began to make their homes in this prairie region. By the end of 1857 a total of 1321 houses had been built on Illinois Central land between Richton and Mattoon, on the branch, and over 100,000 acres of virgin land had been plowed for the first time.[74] It was estimated that a total capital of over $3,000,000 had been expended on improvements in this section alone.[75] At

---

[72] Ackerman to Courvoissiert, June 30, 1857, "Ackerman Secretary," 1856-1858, box 48.  [73] Satterthwaite circular, October 31, 1855.

[74] MS. volume: "Records & Minutes of Directors in N. Y.," South Water St. archives. See also report of John Wilson in *Annual Report*, 1857.

[75] Osborn to Schuchard & Gebhard, April 23, 1858, "Osborn Letter Book," No. 8, box 48.

the same time an equal if not larger amount had been invested in improvements on the alternate sections not owned by the rail-road. Champaign and Vermillion Counties particularly under-went rapid development in these years, in spite of the fact that, in the case of the former, there was much wet and flat land un-suitable for agriculture till artificially drained.[76]

Population statistics attest the growth of these central and eastern counties; they were indeed growing more rapidly than the State as a whole. Champaign County, whose population increased by 1174 in the 'forties, added 11,980 to its total in the 'fifties. Livingston's population jumped from 1552 in 1850 to 11,637; McLean's from 10,163 to 28,772; Piatt's from 1606 to 6127; Iroquois's from 4149 to 12,325; Macon's from 3988 to 13,738; and Christian's from 3203 to 10,492.[77] The census of 1860 showed no counties with a population of less than 11 to the square mile, and by 1870 there was only a small area, comprising parts of Kanka-kee and Iroquois Counties, which did not have a density of 18 or more to the square mile.[78] The increase in population during the 'sixties was due in no small measure to the work of the two agents of the Illinois Central in eastern Illinois, Francis Hoffman and Augustana College, whose activities in securing German and Scandinavian settlers for the lands have already been discussed.

The increase of population in the more northern counties in which the Illinois Central lands were located was of deep eco-nomic, social, and political significance for the State and for the country as a whole. Between 1850 and 1860 the growth of popu-lation in Jo Daviess, Stephenson, Ogle, Lee, La Salle, Bureau, Woodford, and Marshall Counties was well over 100,000. This increased population was largely composed of natives of New England, New York, Pennsylvania, and Ohio, with a considera-ble element of Germans and Scandinavians and smaller numbers of Irish and French Canadians. With the exception of the Irish, these elements were in a large degree drawn into the newly or-ganized Republican Party. The Democratic Party, which had

---

[76] Dupuy to Osborn, October 25, 1855, M. O.

[77] *Ninth Census*, I, 23.

[78] For density of population by counties see Cole, *op. cit.*, opposite p. 330; for density maps in general, see *Tenth Census*, 1880, *Population*.

dominated the State for so many years, was receiving much smaller additions to its numbers by reason of the fact that the Virginia, Kentucky, and Tennessee immigration, which had hitherto poured into Egypt, was now seeking other localities for settlement. The Germans who previously had contributed to the success of that party were alienated by the passage of the Kansas-Nebraska Act and transferred their support to the Republican Party.

The presidential election of 1856 first revealed the political changes which were taking place in Illinois. In this election Buchanan carried the State over Fremont by a majority of only 9159, a decline of more than 6000 from the majority which Pierce had over Scott in 1852. More startling, however, was the fact that Buchanan received but 43 per cent of the total vote, Fremont and Fillmore together having polled 133,633 votes to 105,348 for Buchanan.[79] The Democrats succeeded in retaining control of the upper branch of the State Legislature, but in the House the Republicans and Americans had a majority of one. Most outstanding among the results of this election was the success of the entire State ticket of the Republican Party, William H. Bissell, previously met with as lobbyist and solicitor for the Illinois Central, being chosen Governor over Colonel William A. Richardson, the Democratic candidate, by a plurality of nearly 5000.[80]   The triumph of the Republican State ticket seems to have been in a large degree the result of the personal popularity of Bissell, who drew support from all parties.[81]  President Osborn of the Illinois Central was aware of the changes which were taking place in the political situation in the State in these years. Immediately following the election of 1856 he wrote: [82]

The election returns show the preponderance of Northern feeling in the part of the State that has acquired increased population the last five years — this is important to the interests of the Company as incurring constructive and sound legislation upon other than political questions.

---

[79] *Tribune Almanac*, 1857, p. 60.
[80] *Ibid.*, p. 61.
[81] Cole, *op. cit.*, pp. 151–152.
[82] Osborn to Perkins, November 8, 1856, M. O.

The election results of 1856 boded ill for Stephen A. Douglas and the Democratic Party in Illinois. Douglas was aware that his position as Senator was in danger, and apparently realized that some concessions would have to be made to the newer elements which were coming into the State. His break with Buchanan over Kansas affairs and the Lecompton Constitution may have been partly the result of this realization, as was commonly charged,[83] although political expediency was probably not the only motive. Popular sovereignty as a political principle he firmly adhered to. Nevertheless there is no gainsaying the fact that his break with the administration was effective in winning much support for him in the senatorial election of 1858.[84]

Douglas recognized that he had a hard fight ahead of him in his campaign against Lincoln for reelection to the Senate. Lincoln was a consummate politician.[85] He had powerful political backing, the support of the more important newspapers, and the advantage of a united party behind him, whereas Douglas was meeting the vindictive opposition of the Buchanan administration as well as that of the Republicans. Douglas realized that northern Illinois was lost to him and consequently made little effort in that section to secure votes. Similarly Lincoln saw that he could do little in Egypt to break Douglas's power there, but hoped that the factional strife within the party would seriously reduce his rival's vote in that section. Both candidates were aware that the ultimate decision would be made in central Illinois, the region which the Illinois Central had been so effectively colonizing.

The political significance of the colonization activities of the Illinois Central even as far south as Jonesboro was recognized at the time. A correspondent of the *New York Evening Post* made this clear in the following dispatch to his paper: [86]

---

[83] Correspondence of "Philo," July 20, 1858, in *New York Tribune*, July 26, 1858.
[84] Cole, *op. cit.*, p. 158; Johnson, *op. cit.*, pp. 334 ff.
[85] This is nowhere shown as well as in Albert J. Beveridge, *Abraham Lincoln, 1809-1859*. For a comparison of the two candidates in 1858 see *ibid.*, II, 636-640.
[86] *New York Evening Post*, September 22, 1858, quoted in Edwin Erle Sparks, ed., *The Lincoln-Douglas Debates of 1858* (Illinois State Historical Library, *Collections*, vol. VIII, Springfield, 1908), p. 261.

Jonesboro' is a mile and a half from the railroad. The station is called "Anna," and is as large as the town itself. The Station is Republican; the town is democratic. The land sales of the Illinois Central Railroad, by opening the country to the advent of settlers, have introduced the men of the East, who bring certain uncomfortable and antagonistical political maxims, and thus the time-honored darkness of Egypt is made to fade away before the approach of middle state and New England ideas. Let these land sales go on, and a change will take place in the political physiognomy of Southern Illinois. All things suffer a "sea change," and already the alterative influence of these new ideas is sensibly felt in this section.

It was in the doubtful area of central Illinois that the efforts of Lincoln and Douglas were mostly concentrated during the campaign of 1858.[87]

The so-called "Lincoln-Douglas Debates" were but a small part of the campaign between these two leaders. The seven joint debates, given in as many congressional districts, received more attention at the hands of journalists and newspapers than the other political meetings, but perhaps the latter were as important in influencing opinion for the approaching election. During the campaign Douglas made one hundred and thirteen speeches in fifty-seven counties, mostly in central Illinois, and Lincoln probably made an equal number.[88] Four of the joint debates were given in Illinois Central towns or in neighboring towns,[89] and Lincoln and Douglas visited many of the other communities in the vicinity of the road such as Bloomington, Clinton, Mattoon, and Urbana.[90] Lincoln recognized the sectional differences between northern, central, and southern Illinois, and attempted to meet them by varying his emphasis upon salient arguments in conformity with the views of the section.[91] For this he was accused, with some justification, of having one set of principles for northern Illinois and another for southern Illinois.[92]

[87] Beveridge, *op. cit.*, II, 557; Johnson, *op. cit.*, p. 363; Cole, *op. cit.*, pp. 169–170. Perhaps no senatorial campaign has received so much careful attention as has the Lincoln-Douglas conflict.

[88] Cole, *op. cit.*, p. 170.

[89] These were Freeport, Ottawa, near La Salle, Jonesboro, and Charleston, Coles County.

[90] *Illinois State Journal*, August 18, 25, 1858.

[91] Johnson observes concerning Lincoln's arguments in these diverse sections: "There was a marked difference in point of emphasis between his utterances in Northern and in Southern Illinois." Johnson, *op. cit.*, p. 385. Cf. Beveridge, *op. cit.*, II, 680.          [92] Sparkes, *op. cit.*, p. 365.

The relations of Lincoln and Douglas with the Illinois Central furnished material for political vilification during the campaign. Douglas was reported to have accused Lincoln of being employed by the Illinois Central at a salary of $5000 to cheat the State of its 7 per cent of the gross earnings of the road.[93] In retaliation the Lincoln papers pointed to Douglas's use of a private car furnished by the Illinois Central as proof that he was subservient to corporation interests. They also accused him of having made a corrupt bargain with the railroad, according to which it was to colonize Irish Democrats in doubtful counties in order to carry them for the Douglas ticket; in return Douglas was to use his influence to secure for the Company a release from all its obligations to the State. In October, one newspaper reported:[94]

Day after day during the past three weeks the trains leaving Chicago on the Central Company's road have been loaded with Irishmen, many of them sent on from Wisconsin and Indiana, and the others picked up by the hired agents in the alleys and by-ways of the great prairie metropolis. They are dropped in droves of from twenty to forty at Pana, Urbana, and other stations . . . where they are quartered . . . until after the election.

Such accusations and recriminations were the mere effervescence of political controversies, and seem to have had no substantial foundation. Both men had intimate connections with the Illinois Central in the past, Lincoln as attorney, and Douglas as original promoter, stockholder, and unofficial mentor.

The election returns show strikingly the great changes which had taken place in central Illinois in the brief period since 1856. The Republican State ticket was carried to victory by a plurality of 3921 over the Democratic ticket,[95] while the Lincoln candidates for the House received a majority of 16,000 votes over the Democratic candidates.[96] Nevertheless the Democrats secured control of both branches of the State Legislature owing to the under-

---

[93] *Galesburg Democrat*, October 13, 1858, *Chicago Journal*, October 5, 1858, reproduced in Sparkes, *op. cit.*, pp. 83, 553.

[94] *Peoria Transcript*, quoted in *Illinois State Journal*, October 27, 1858. Beveridge presents evidence to show that in 1857 high Republican officials sought to ensure victory for their party in the following year by employing the very tactics which their journals ascribed to the Democrats. See II, 555.

[95] *Illinois State Journal*, December 1, 1858.

[96] Johnson, *op. cit.*, p. 392.

representation of the Republican strongholds and to the fact that the districts had been so gerrymandered that Democratic victory was practically certain.[97] This of course ensured the reelection of Douglas as senator. An examination of the election returns, however, proved most encouraging to the defeated Republicans. They had lost not one county which they had carried in 1856, but instead had carried seven which had previously been Democratic.[98] These seven counties were all in south central Illinois; five of them contained large amounts of land which the railroad had been actively colonizing, and Edgar, a neighboring county, received direct benefit from its proximity to this road. While the Republican vote in northern Illinois fell off heavily as compared with 1856, perhaps because Lincoln had given more time to central Illinois than to that section, the party vote in the central counties was much larger.[99] Thus the Republican vote increased over the 1856 returns by 574 in Champaign County, 786 in McLean, 651 in Logan, 1040 in Coles, 455 in Piatt, and 416 in Livingston.[100] Much smaller gains were made by the Democratic Party. A complicating factor in this connection is the American vote, which probably went largely to the Republicans after the disintegration of the Fillmore party. Such additions, however, fail to account for all the Republican increases in these doubtful counties.

Lincoln, in spite of defeat, came out of the election with increased prestige, and in the following year was openly mentioned as a likely candidate for the presidential nomination. Backed by such local capitalists as Jesse Fell and David Davis, supported by a powerful press under the leadership of Scripps, Bross, Ray, and Medill of the *Chicago Press and Tribune*, Baker and Bailhache of the *Illinois State Journal*, and George Schneider of the *Illinois Staats Zeitung*, and aided by a host of minor papers, Lincoln had an excellent chance of winning the Republican nomination.

[97] *Illinois State Journal*, November 10, 1858; *Tribune Almanac*, 1859, pp. 60–61; Johnson, *op. cit.*, p. 392.

[98] *Chicago Press and Tribune* clipped in *Illinois State Journal*, November 24, 1858.

[99] In the first district, comprising the most northern counties, Washburn's vote fell off 2000 from his total in 1856. The same situation prevailed in the counties in the second district.

[100] *Tribune Almanac*, 1859, p. 60.

Astute leadership and clever manipulation at the Chicago convention brought the prize; Lincoln was nominated. A factor of importance in bringing about his nomination was the realization that Douglas would probably be the Democratic nominee and that no Republican would be a better match for him in the fight for the eleven electoral votes of Illinois than Lincoln.

The resulting campaign in Illinois was not as spectacular nor as interesting as that of 1858. Lincoln refused to make any speeches, and Douglas devoted most of his time to other sections of the country. Nevertheless there was no apathy shown, for the enormous vote rolled up by all parties indicated an intense interest on the part of the masses of people, old residents and new settlers alike. The vote was larger by 100,000 than the number cast in the previous presidential election — an unprecedented increase.[101] Lincoln carried the State by a plurality of 4629 over all the candidates and with a lead of 11,946 over Douglas. The entire Republican State ticket was elected, and for the first time this party gained control of the Legislature.

In this election also the Republican vote increased by a much larger amount than the Democratic vote. The prairie counties — Champaign, Iroquois, Vermillion, Ford, Coles, Piatt, Douglas, De Witt, Logan, McLean, Livingston, and Kankakee — were all carried by Lincoln. The Republican increase over the Fremont vote of 1856 in these counties was 3212 more than the Democratic increase over the Buchanan vote of 1856. Even in Egypt, in such Democratic strongholds as Washington, Shelby, Montgomery, Marion, Effingham, Cumberland, Clay, and Christian Counties, the Republican vote increased more than the Democratic vote. It will be remembered that in these counties had settled the Yankee colony near Irvington, the Canadians at Farina, and the Germans and Swedes at Neoga and Effingham. In the more northern counties in which the Illinois Central was successfully selling its lands the same trend was apparent; the increased population was predominantly Republican.

A recent writer has endeavored to show that the election of Lincoln in 1860 was due to the German element which had been

---

[101] *Tribune Almanac*, 1861, p. 56.

coming into the five states of the Old Northwest in such large numbers since 1830.[102] His main argument seems to be that if the Germans had not voted for Lincoln the loss of their vote would have been sufficient to give the election to Douglas, or to throw it into the House. By the same token, it might be maintained that had the transplanted New Englanders or New Yorkers in the Old Northwest failed to vote for Lincoln he would have been defeated. It is true that the Germans helped to win the election for Lincoln, but so also did the New York-New Englanders who came to eastern, central and northern Illinois in large numbers in this period and who overthrew the old balance of power which had existed in Illinois and in the Old Northwest.

From this brief study it seems clear that the activities of the Illinois Central in colonizing its land grant were an important factor in changing the political situation in the State and in bringing about the Republican victory of 1860.

The outbreak of the Civil War gave the Illinois Central an opportunity of disposing of some of its lands in Egypt. Even in 1860 and 1861 fear of impending trouble caused many southerners to migrate to the northwestern states.[103] The advertisements which Foster and Osborn inserted in southern papers during 1860 brought to the Land Department a marked increase in inquiries from states south of the Mason and Dixon line. Residents of the border states in particular evinced an interest in Illinois.[104] After the outbreak of hostilities, many southerners sought refuge in Illinois, arriving there in a destitute condition.[105] Although these refugees were not the best and most substantial type of settler, Osborn felt it advisable to make efforts to retain them in southern Illinois rather than to let them pass on to Iowa and states farther north. Accordingly he made plans to distribute circulars

---

[102] Donnal V. Smith, "The Influence of the Foreign-Born of the Northwest in the Election of 1860," *Mississippi Valley Historical Review* (September, 1932), XIX, 192–204. Cf. William E. Dodd, "The Fight for the Northwest, 1860," *American Historical Review* (July, 1911), XVI, 774–788.

[103] Foster to Walker, February 25, 1861, green box, 63rd St.; Banks to Osborn, March 14, April 8, 9, 1861, "Osborn Letter Book," 1860–1861, M. O.

[104] Osborn to Robt. Benson & Co., January 29, 1861, *ibid.*

[105] Osborn in *Annual Report*, 1862.

and pamphlets in Tennessee and possibly Kentucky, the states from which the largest proportion of refugees were fleeing.[106] In 1862 a branch of the Land Department was established at Cairo,[107] largely to attract the refugees, and the Illinois Central tried to induce them to settle along the branch line as far north as Rantoul,[108] or on the main line from Cairo to Centralia. These immigrants sought cheap lands, which could now be secured, so far as Illinois was concerned, only in the prairie regions of the central and eastern counties or in the more rugged and timbered portions of Egypt. Many of the refugees, however, were too destitute to make even the small initial payment required for the lands, and turned to localities where homestead or cheap lands were still available. Others of this class did settle in southern Illinois and purchased lands from the railroad; indeed, in 1863 they composed one-third of the purchasers of the Company's lands.[109]

Southern Illinois was at this time suffering under a new handicap in addition to those of climate, soil, and topography. Its population, being composed to a very considerable extent of southern upland stock, was inclined to look with favor upon the efforts of the slave states to establish an independent government, and the region was honeycombed with copperheadism. On account of the strategic importance of Cairo and the Illinois Central Railroad, continued efforts were made to destroy the line and its rolling stock.[110] Such activities were not conducive to making southern Illinois more popular with incoming settlers.

As the Illinois Central owned large tracts of land in Egypt, it constantly sought to diminish the disfavor with which this section was regarded. Realizing that Egypt could never compete with central and northern Illinois as a grain-growing area, the Land

---

[106] Osborn to Walker, March 7, 1861, "Osborn Letter Book," 1863–1865, M. O.; Osborn to Douglas, May 1, 1863, "Presidents and Chairmans Letters," No. 18, box 48.

[107] Walker to Osborn, March 25, 1862, "Treasurers Letters," No. 19, *ibid.*

[108] Osborn to N. Stevens, December 4, 1861, "Osborn Letter Book," 1861–1862, M. O.    [109] *Annual Report,* 1863.

[110] Osborn to Alfred Pell and Henry Grinnel, May 30, 1861; to Gen. Banks, August 9, 1861, "Osborn Letter Book," 1860–1861, M. O.

Department encouraged the purchasers of its southern lands to raise other crops, particularly fruit and cotton. Its efforts in this direction will be dealt with more fully elsewhere. Suffice it to say that during the 'sixties the six southernmost counties in which Illinois Central land was located — Washington, Perry, Jackson, Union, Marion, and Alexander — increased 57 per cent in population, while the increase of the entire State was only 48 per cent. The steady development of southern Illinois during the decade was partly due to the advertising which the Company gave it, and is partly to be accounted for by the fact that the best lands in other sections of the State had been sold.

The Illinois Central Railroad, its agents, and the large purchasers of its lands were remarkably successful in bringing into the State settlers from other parts of the country and, to a lesser extent, from abroad. Between 1854 and 1870 the Company and its agents made 34,000 sales, all but a small percentage of which were to actual settlers. It is incorrect to maintain that each of these sales represents a new family coming into the State, because a considerable quantity of land was purchased by old residents along the line, while others sold their farms in less favored parts of the State and purchased from the railroad.[111] Furthermore, these figures include a certain amount of duplication, cancellation, and repurchasing. It seems probable that at least 25,000 of the sales were made to new and permanent families. This must have added over 100,000 people to the population of Illinois.

The importance of the colonization work of the Illinois Central Railroad cannot be measured only by the number of sales made by its Land Department, since many people were induced to come to the State by its publicity who afterwards purchased land from others. It will be remembered that many million acres were held by speculators, and these holdings were in direct competition with the railroad lands. Their owners benefited both by the enhanced value which the railroad gave to their lands and by the increased immigration which resulted from the advertising work of the

---

[111] *Boston Traveler* clipped in *Mining Register & Pottsville Emporium*, October 27, 1855.

Land Department. It is impossible to make accurate estimates of the amount of land which was sold by speculators during this period, but it is evident that the quantity was large.

The Illinois Central constantly felt the competition of speculators' lands, but did not entirely regret it because its officials realized that all efforts to settle the State would increase the traffic of the railroad. Nevertheless, this competition was an important factor in keeping down the Company's land sales.[112] In one important case, at least, an agent of two British capitalists, sent to Illinois to investigate the opportunities for a considerable investment in Illinois Central lands, was persuaded by one of the private land companies to buy 2240 acres at $18 an acre from it instead of from the railroad.[113] Another important purchase of competitors' lands was made by a colony of French Waldenses. It is not clear how this group first became interested in Illinois, but in 1857 their pastor, M. Lorraix, negotiated the purchase of 1800 acres at Odell on the Chicago and Alton Railroad, a few miles southeast of La Salle. These lands were purchased from Bronson Murray, who earlier in the decade had secured from the Government 6250 acres in Livingston County at the minimum price.[114] From two hundred to three hundred families from Vaudois, France, planned to settle in this region.[115]

[112] Wilson to Osborn, September 1, 1856, M. O.

[113] Devaux & Co. to Directors of the Illinois Central, April 11, 1855, Ward's office; Johnson to Perkins, September 19, 1855, M. O.; MS. in Brayman collection: "Geo. Willson Reed, 2,240 acres at $18.00 per acre $40,320." These lands were bought from the Associates. T. A. Neal to Jonathon Sturges, July 26, 1862, "Illinois Land Agency," No. 3, Neal-Rantoul MSS.

[114] Compiled from records of Danville land office, S. A. O.

[115] *Chicago Democratic Press*, August 20, 1856; March 26, 1858, quoting *Peoria Transcript*. Cole, *op. cit.*, p. 18, apparently is in error in thinking there were two colonies of this racial group established in this general locality. His references are to the same group.

The evidence does not seem to warrant Professor Cole's statement (p. 341) that a colony of three hundred English families settled in Alexander and Pulaski Counties about 1867 and that a colony of six hundred Italian families located at the same time a few miles from Pana. Professor Cole cites but one reference for each colony and both are local newspapers which, unless otherwise verified, are in such cases doubtful sources. The local papers of this period were constantly mentioning proposed colonies many of which never materialized, and these two seem to be in this category. If there had been any such large movement into the vicinity of its lands

The prosperity of the war period greatly stimulated immigration into Illinois. Germans, Scandinavians, easterners, and southern refugees poured into the State from all sides in constantly increasing numbers. During this period Illinois became the destination point of more immigrants from Europe than any other western state. This position had been held by Wisconsin in 1855 and 1856, thanks to the activities of its immigration agents in Germany, but by 1857 Illinois had displaced Wisconsin [116] and during the 'sixties far outdistanced all rivals. In 1865, 17,914 immigrants at the port of New York gave Illinois as their destination, 12,098 named Kentucky, 11,240 named Ohio, only 5219 named Wisconsin, and still smaller groups named Iowa and Minnesota.[117] The largest foreign elements coming into Illinois in the 'sixties continued to be the Germans and Scandinavians, with the Irish running a close third. Over 70,000 Germans, 33,000 Scandinavians, and 32,000 Irish settled in Illinois during these years.[118] Immigrants from Canada and Great Britain added approximately 30,000 more. Of the American-born who migrated to Illinois in this decade, Ohio came first, furnishing 32,000; Indiana followed with 24,000; then came Missouri with 18,000, Pennsylvania with 15,000, and New York

the officials of the Illinois Central would have been aware of it and would have mentioned it in their reports and correspondence. The writer has seen no reference to these colonies in the Illinois Central material, in the local histories, or in any other source. Furthermore, the census returns for 1870 leave no possible doubt that such colonies were not established. In 1870 Alexander and Pulaski Counties together had but 116 persons of English and Welsh birth while Christian County, in which Pana is located, had but 1919 foreigners of which 1901 were non-Italians (*Ninth Census*, I, 351–352). Another doubtful story to the effect that a large colony of wealthy Germans, among them several barons, had purchased 20,000 acres of land in Illinois and Wisconsin and planned to settle on them, was widely published in the press. *Chicago Tribune*, May 9, 1862; *Missouri Republican* clipped in *Wochentlicher Anzeiger des Westens*, May 14, 1862; *Alton Telegraph* quoted in *Illinois Staats Zeitung*, June 3, 1862.

[116] Commissioners of Emigration of the State of New York, *Annual Reports*, 1847–1860 (New York, 1861), p. 340.

[117] *Commercial and Financial Chronicle* (1866), II, 39.

[118] These statistics do not include the total immigration. They represent the increase during the decade of the various peoples residing in Illinois. They do not include those who moved in and died before the census of 1870 was taken, nor do they include those who moved into Illinois, resided there temporarily, and moved on again before 1870. The figures are taken from the *Census Reports* of 1860 and 1870.

with 12,000. The southern upland element from Virginia, Kentucky, and Tennessee steadily declined in importance, although about 18,000 of them were added to Illinois's population. The direct immigration from New England was also smaller. Altogether, the population of the State increased 48 per cent during the decade in spite of the casualties in the Civil War and the migration of 150,000 people from Illinois to states farther west.[119]

[119] *Ibid.*

# CHAPTER XII

## LAND SALES AND COLLECTIONS

IN DISPOSING of its land grant of 2,595,000 acres, the Illinois Central found itself face to face with many of the problems with which the Government had contended: squatters, preemption claimants, timber thieves, overpurchasing by small farmers and speculating by capitalists, slow collections, and the cancellations of contracts. The sale of its lands was further hindered by the Panic of 1857 and the outbreak of the Civil War. Statistics of land sales, collections, and cancellations for the years 1854 to 1870 closely reflect economic conditions throughout the country at the time. Despite certain unfavorable circumstances the prices which the Illinois Central succeeded in obtaining for its lands fulfilled the expectations of its most optimistic promoters and testified to the poor judgment of many critics who prophesied that the lands could not be sold for sufficient money to meet the cost of constructing the central railroad.

The land sales of the Illinois Central may be most conveniently treated in three periods: 1854 to 1857, 1858 to 1862, and 1863 to 1870.

Apart from the preemption sales, which have already been discussed, it was not until the latter part of August, 1854, that the Illinois Central was able to begin actual sales, which even then were restricted to certain localities as construction was not yet complete. Nevertheless, from October 1 to December 31, 1854, 47,280 acres were sold for $481,006,[1] exclusive of preemption sales. These early sales seem to have been made largely to farmers who wished to add to their holdings or to persons desiring town lots for business sites in the newly developing towns.[2] There were 2211 sales made prior to 1855, of which 1253 were for 40 acres, 673 were for 80 acres, 97 were for 120 acres, 155 were for 160 acres, and the

---

[1] *Annual Report*, 1854.
[2] Neal to Sturges, May 6, 1854, M. O. This statement does not apply to the preemption lands sold to squatters.

rest were for larger tracts up to 640 acres. No tract larger than a section was sold, and consequently it seems safe to assume that most of this land was purchased for actual settlement, although many of the purchasers bought tracts so large that they were unable to complete their payments in the required time.[3]

After January, 1855, the great campaign to advertise the lands was begun, and the Land Department was flooded with letters asking for further information, following which came the land buyers.[4] In May it was reported that the land office was crowded and that there were not sufficient clerks to handle the business.[5] The rush for lands exceeded all expectations, and so completely swamped the Chicago office that by December it was found necessary to discontinue sales long enough to permit the clerks to catch up with the bookkeeping.[6] Before the office was closed it was announced that the rate of interest on the purchase money of sales made after January 1, 1856, would be increased to 3 per cent.[7] This had the effect of further stimulating land sales, so that the totals for November and December were the largest monthly totals yet reached.[8] After the reopening of the office in the early part of 1856 sales were resumed at the same rate.[9]

The period of large sales continued through 1856 to September, 1857, when the financial depression commenced which soon developed into the great Panic of October, 1857.[10] At once sales were practically suspended, and not until the following decade did the operations of the Land Department again assume large proportions.

In these years, 1854 to 1857, nearly one-half of the lands of the Illinois Central were sold at prices only anticipated by the Com-

---

[3] MS. vol.: "Land Sales," 16th St.; *Annual Report*, 1858; *American Railroad Journal*, August 3, 1861.

[4] Dupuy to Osborn, January 10, 13, February 24, 1855, M. O.

[5] Osborn to Perkins, May 14, 1855, *ibid*.

[6] Dupuy to Osborn, September 15, 1855, *ibid*. *Railway Times*, December 15, 1855; Satterthwaite bank circular, July 11, 1855, Ward's office.

[7] Satterthwaite circular, December 18, 1855.

[8] *Ibid.*; Dupuy to Osborn, November 17, 1855, M. O.

[9] Johnson to Osborn, April 14, 1856, *ibid*. Cf. the account of the activities of the Land Department by an observer in Fred. Gerhard, *Illinois as it is* (Chicago, 1857), p. 408. See also letter of C. C. P. Holden in Andreas, *History of Chicago*, I, 256.

[10] *New York Tribune*, October 10, 11, 13, 14, 1857.

pany's most sanguine promoters. By the end of December, 1855, 528,863 acres had been sold for a total sum, principal and interest on notes, of $5,598,577.[11] In 1856, 336,347 acres were sold for $4,548,561 principal and $526,930 advance interest. In 1857, in spite of the fact that the panic occurred in October, 335,722 acres were sold for $4,064,717 principal and $533,494 advance interest.[12] The total sales then amounted to 1,200,932 acres for the sum of $15,311,440, including principal and interest.[13] Such large returns from land sales were unprecedented in the history of the State. It is doubtful if any such large amount of land ever appreciated in value as rapidly as the lands of the Illinois Central, which five to seven years earlier had gone begging at prices of 50 cents to $1.25 an acre.

Periods of inflation and overexpansion are inevitably followed in the economic cycle by lean years characterized by contraction, tightened credit, industrial inactivity, and low commodity prices. This was the situation from 1857 to 1860. The panic put a stop to further inflation, while normal crops abroad and the opening of the Black Sea lessened the demand for American grain, which as a result declined sharply in price.[14] With the markets glutted and prices down, the Illinois Central found itself in a position very different from that of the preceding years. One despairing farmer wrote from Will County late in 1857:[15]

The financial panic of the East has cast its dark shadow over Illinois. There is little money in circulation, compared with three months ago. Every thing down to the lowest figure. We are overflowing with grain of all kinds, and it is worth little or nothing. Wheat down to 50 cts., oats 17 cts., and still going down, down, down; cows that could not be bought for $30, three months ago, are now down to $18. Every thing is coming down but land — that is still up.

The distress of the settlers in Illinois was further aggravated by a series of total or partial crop failures caused by unseasonable rains and early frosts. The wheat crop of 1857 was fair, but the

---

[11] *Annual Report*, 1855.       [12] *Annual Reports*, 1856, 1857.

[13] *Ibid.* This latter figure includes a small amount received from the sale of town lots. It is not always possible to separate the town lot statistics from the agricultural land statistics.

[14] Bidwell and Falconer, *History of Agriculture*, p. 500; Thompson, *The Rise and Decline of the Wheat Growing Industry in Wisconsin*, p. 203.

[15] *New England Farmer* (1858), x, 23.

corn was of distinctly inferior quality and both grains brought low prices.[16] In 1858 the incessant rains so saturated the ground in the spring that the crops could not be sown until late;[17] as a result both the corn and wheat crops were below normal.[18] This year was regarded by Land Commissioner Foster as the "gloomiest that ever settled upon Illinois."[19] The following year a severe frost struck the State in June and greatly retarded the corn; in September another unseasonable frost completed the destruction of this crop. During the same year the ravages of the chinch bug proved so disastrous to the wheat crop that Foster estimated the yield would be less than 10 bushels per acre.[20]

The effect of this series of disasters was to reduce immigration to Illinois to a minimum, and the land sales of the railroad fell off markedly. In the first year after the panic only 52,387 acres were sold, and for the two succeeding years sales were 28,063 and 71,287 acres respectively.[21] Most of these purchases were nothing but cancellations and resales. After subtracting the cancellations it will be found that the net sales for 1858, 1859, and 1860 were 28,901, 7425, and 23,013 acres respectively.[22] Some of this land went to residents who desired to increase their holdings,[23] and a small portion was sold to new settlers.[24] This was a period of practical stagnation on the part of the Land Department, both as regards its advertising and its sales. Collections at the same time declined alarmingly. The assignment of the Illinois Central in 1857 was partly due to its inability to collect from its purchasers and thus to meet its own obligations when they came due in the panic of that fall. President Osborn found collections so low in November, 1859, that he wrote despairingly of them:[25]

[16] Chicago Board of Trade, *Annual Report*, 1859, pp. 18–19.

[17] The heavy rains made the prairies impassable and thus prevented the transportation of lumber and grain to and from the farms. Sturges to Haven, May 26, 1859, Haven MSS.

[18] Chicago Board of Trade, *Annual Report*, 1860, pp. 38, 43; Illinois Central Railroad, *Annual Report*, 1859, statement of J. W. Foster.

[19] *Ibid.*

[20] *Ibid.* See also Chicago Board of Trade, *Annual Reports*, 1859, 1860.

[21] Illinois Central Railroad, *Annual Reports*, 1858, 1859, 1860.

[22] *Ibid.*

[23] Report of James Wheeler in *Railway Times* (November 27, 1858), XXI, 1389.

[24] Wilson to Perkins, March 6, 1858, M. O.

[25] Osborn to Richard Cobden, December 1, 1859, "Osborn No. 12," box 48.

There is no getting away from the fact; it is a sad disappointment to every one, and I confess to coming out completely heart sick, and at fault how to meet this great blow to our hopes. . . . Foster and Burnside are both dismayed and discouraged for they have worked hard and in earnest without effect.

Conditions indeed seemed gloomy for the success of the Land Department and for the economic future of the State.

The situation was not as bad as it appeared, however. As a result of the panic, many large speculators had been forced to allow the banks and other creditors to take over their holdings. In the years 1858 to 1861 these lands were dumped on the market at greatly reduced prices. They were snapped up by incoming settlers or old residents, and were being put under cultivation. This affected the sales of the Illinois Central adversely for a time,[26] but it prepared the way for larger traffic for its line and less competition for its lands when prosperity returned.

Eventually, in the latter part of 1860, an improvement was apparent. Sales, which previously had averaged from 2000 to 4000 acres monthly, now jumped to 8495 in September, 17,192 in October, approximately 11,000 in November, and 11,070 in December.[27] Along with the increased land sales went larger collections on the outstanding contracts. In September, 1860, the returns from crops enabled the settlers to make payments on their lands, which for two years had been alarmingly behind.[28] In that month collections totalled $80,000, jumped to $140,000 in October, but fell to $100,000 in November and $84,000 in December.[29] These figures compared very favorably with the collections of the two preceding years, which had averaged about $50,000 monthly. The total collections for 1860 ran well above the figures for 1858 and 1859, in spite of the poor start at the opening of the year.[30] This improvement in collections was only a beginning, however,

[26] J. W. Foster in *Annual Report*, 1859.

[27] *Railway Times* (1860), XXXIII, 1209, 1369.

[28] Large shipments of wheat, corn, and hogs over the line of the Illinois Central to Chicago in the latter part of 1860 are shown in the Chicago Board of Trade, *Annual Report*, 1861, p. 74.

[29] *American Railway Times*, January 19, 1861.

[30] MS. vol.: "Ill. Cent. R. R. Office, N. Y.," prepared by W. M. Phillips, South Water St. archives, Illinois Central Railroad.

representing as it did little more than interest on the outstanding contracts, which totalled at the end of 1860 $12,598,083.[31]

These encouraging conditions continued until well into 1861, in spite of the troubled state of affairs. The January sales and collections were regarded as extraordinary for mid-winter,[32] and for the first three months the land sales were reported, though erroneously, to exceed the amounts sold for the same period in any previous year.[33] So encouraged was President Osborn, who was now giving his full time to the business of the Land Department,[34] that in his annual report to the stockholders in February, 1861, he suggested that the prices of the remaining lands, which then amounted to 1,334,727 acres, be gradually advanced to prices ranging between $13 and $50 per acre.[35]

With the outbreak of hostilities between the North and the South, Osborn's optimism suffered a rude shock. European immigration had already ceased, and the movement from the eastern states now came to a halt. The demand for lands fell off at once,[36] declining in June to 6408 acres, in July to 5941 acres, and in August to 3472 acres.[37] At the same time collections, which had started out well at the beginning of the year, fell off so rapidly that the total for the year amounted to only $521,334,[38] the lowest point being reached in July, when only $34,786 was collected.[39] In consequence the advertising campaign was discontinued and the force of the Land Department materially reduced.[40] Conditions were back to what they had been in 1858 and 1859.

It was only for a short time after the outbreak of the Civil War

---

[31] This amount included principal and interest on notes. *Annual Report*, 1860.

[32] Osborn to Banks, February 2, 1861, "Presidents & Chairmans Letters," No. 16, box 48.

[33] *American Railroad Journal*, April 6, 1861.

[34] Osborn to Walker, February 25, 1861, green box, 63rd St.

[35] Osborn estimated the value of the unsold lands to be $27,788,953 according to his plan of increasing their prices, in spite of the fact that the best lands had already been sold. *Annual Report*, 1860; *New York Times*, February 18, 1861.

[36] Foster to Walker, April 20, 25, 26, 1861, green box.

[37] *American Railway Times*, July 13, August 24, September 14, 1861.

[38] MS. vol.: "Ill. Cent. R. R. Office, N. Y.," prepared by W. M. Phillips, South Water St.

[39] *New York Tribune*, August 8, 1861.

[40] W. M. Phillips to G. F. Thomas, April 22, 1861, "Ackerman Letters," 1858–1861, box 48; Foster to Walker, April 26, 1861, green box.

that business in Illinois remained poor. War-time demands, especially for wheat, sent agricultural prices upward, and higher prices helped to bring about another period of expansion and inflation, which was to prove more lasting than the false start of 1860. Immigration from Europe, which set in again once confi-

TABLE I

STATISTICS RELATING TO THE LAND SALES OF THE ILLINOIS CENTRAL[a]

| Year | Number | Sales Acres | Value[b] | Cancellations Acres | Value[b] | Collections Value |
|------|--------|-------|--------|------|--------|------------|
| 1854 ..... | 2,211[c] | 47,280[d] | $481,886 | | | |
| | | 107,614[e] | 268,035[f] | | | |
| 1855 ..... | 2,119 | 373,969[d] | 4,848,655 | | | $591,386[g] |
| 1856 ..... | 2,429 | 336,347 | 4,548,561 | | | 393,793 |
| 1857 ..... | 3,419 | 335,722 | 4,064,717 | | | — [h] |
| 1858 ..... | 822 | 52,387 | 610,969 | 23,486 | $375,447 | 626,628 |
| 1859 ..... | 403 | 28,063 | 336,861 | 20,638 | — [h] | 590,430 |
| 1860 ..... | 1,050 | 71,287 | 878,677 | 48,274 | 725,400 | 780,097 |
| 1861 ..... | 1,402 | 102,109 | 1,405,932 | 125,932 | 1,523,643 | 521,334 |
| 1862 ..... | 1,168[d] | 87,599 | 914,428 | 125,723 | 1,845,596 | 546,377 |
| 1863 ..... | 2,954[d] | 221,578 | 2,269,294 | 107,530 | — [h] | 1,403,145 |
| 1864 ..... | 3,501 | 265,520[i] | 2,745,320 | 92,349 | 1,287,351 | 2,575,928 |
| 1865 ..... | 2,364 | 154,252 | 1,791,917 | 41,768 | 587,659 | 2,191,630 |
| 1866 ..... | 2,218 | 157,861 | 1,586,885 | 28,633 | — [h] | 2,056,205 |
| 1867 ..... | 2,633 | 203,532 | 2,080,154 | 45,144 | 597,294 | 3,166,264 |
| 1868 ..... | 2,776 | 207,351 | 2,130,525 | 23,245 | 302,696 | 3,200,289 |
| 1869 ..... | 1,521 | 85,860 | 857,753 | 16,748 | 215,378 | 2,551,717 |
| 1870 ..... | 1,127 | 60,858 | 595,269 | 18,489 | 201,628 | 2,111,865 |

(a) Compiled from *Annual Reports* of the Illinois Central and unpublished documents.
(b) Principal and interest.
(c) Total number of sales through 1854 including preemption sales.
(d) Computed.
(e) Total acreage of preemption sales.
(f) Total value of preemption sales.
(g) Total collections to December 31, 1855, including receipts from preemption sales.
(h) Unavailable.
(i) Includes a small quantity of purchased lands.

dence in the North had been restored, created a demand for land which had been a drug on the market since the Panic of 1857 and led to the rapid sale of speculators' holdings in central and northern Illinois; 4,000,000 acres of land held by this group were sold to settlers at high prices during this decade.[41]

[41] The land not in farms in 1860 was almost entirely owned by the Illinois Central and private speculators. As the amount of land included in farms increased in the 'sixties 4,970,872 acres, it seems fair to assume that 4,000,000 acres of this amount were sold by speculators. The statistics are from the *Fourteenth Census* (1910), vol. VI, part I, p. 367.

This heavy demand for land naturally affected the Land Department of the Illinois Central and justified the expensive advertising campaign it had carried on both at home and abroad. In December, 1862, sales showed a remarkable increase.[42] For the months of January to May, 1863, they were 14,586, 18,310,

TABLE II

NUMBER OF SALES AND CANCELLATIONS PER UNIT, 1855 TO 1860[a]

| Date | 40 | 80 | 120 | 160 | 200 | 240 | 280 | 320 |
|---|---|---|---|---|---|---|---|---|
| 1854 ............... | 1,253 | 673 | 97 | 155 | 6 | 2 | 1 | 8 |
| 1855 ............... | 646 | 642 | 97 | 356 | 29 | 48 | 16 | 141 |
| 1856 ............... | 814 | 804 | 108 | 376 | 32 | 36 | 5 | 128 |
| 1857 ............... | 1,538 | 1,018 | 144 | 422 | 33 | 55 | 15 | 97 |
| 1858 ............... | 519 | 216 | 15 | 45 | 3 | 5 | 1 | 6 |
| 1859 ............... | 286 | 83 | 4 | 15 | 0 | 0 | 1 | 7 |
| 1860 ............... | 611 | 318 | 27 | 66 | 8 | 5 | 1 | 9 |
| Gross Totals .... | 5,667 | 3,754 | 492 | 1,435 | 111 | 151 | 40 | 396 |
| Cancellations ... | 57 | 88 | 19 | 68 | 5 | 9 | 2 | 33 |
| Net Totals ..... | 5,610 | 3,666 | 473 | 1,367 | 106 | 142 | 38 | 363 |

| Date | 360 | 400 | 440 | 480 | 520 | 560 | 600 | 640 | over 640 | Total |
|---|---|---|---|---|---|---|---|---|---|---|
| 1854 ............... | 1 | 1 | 2 | 2 | 0 | 0 | 0 | 10 | 0 | 2,211 |
| 1855 ............... | 6 | 7 | 6 | 11 | 3 | 10 | 7 | 66 | 28 | 2,119 |
| 1856 ............... | 11 | 10 | 4 | 9 | 3 | 4 | 3 | 69 | 13 | 2,429 |
| 1857 ............... | 9 | 12 | 2 | 13 | 9 | 10 | 5 | 29 | 8 | 3,419 |
| 1858 ............... | 0 | 3 | 1 | 2 | 0 | 0 | 0 | 5 | 1 | 822 |
| 1859 ............... | 1 | 1 | 0 | 0 | 1 | 0 | 0 | 2 | 2 | 403 |
| 1860 ............... | 2 | 1 | 0 | 0 | 0 | 0 | 0 | 2 | 0 | 1,050 |
| Gross Totals .... | 30 | 35 | 15 | 37 | 16 | 24 | 15 | 183 | 52 | 12,453 |
| Cancellations ... | 5 | 4 | 1 | 6 | 2 | 1 | 1 | 22 | 8 | 331 |
| Net Totals ...... | 25 | 31 | 14 | 31 | 14 | 23 | 14 | 161 | 44 | 12,122 |

(a) Compiled from various sources. The statistics for later years are not available in this detailed form.

15,885, 14,518, and 20,831 acres respectively,[43] or more than double the amounts for the same months of the preceding year. During the remainder of 1863 sales averaged nearly 20,000 acres monthly, the total for the year being 221,578 acres.[44] For the next five years, owing to the prosperity which the West was enjoying,

[42] *Annual Report*, 1862.
[43] *New York Tribune*, February 9, March 9, April 7, June 6, 1863.
[44] *Annual Report*, 1863.

the Illinois Central achieved great success in selling its lands and in making collections upon the contracts. With the year 1868 the large land sales came to an end. By the close of the decade the Illinois Central had disposed of well over 2,000,000 acres of its grant.

The prices for which the Illinois Central lands sold at first surpassed the most optimistic expectations. The average price received during the years 1854 to 1861, exclusive of the preemption lands, was $12.75 an acre. This was an advance of $11.50 an acre over the old government minimum of $1.25. Much to its disappointment, the Illinois Central was to find that this high price level could not be maintained. From 1862 to 1868, the average price obtained was less than $11 an acre and thereafter it declined sharply.

The officials of the Land Department fully expected to be able to maintain the old prices for the lands; indeed they even thought that as the lands became scarcer their price would rise. In 1861, as we have seen, Osborn considered raising the price on all grades of land to a minimum of $13 an acre,[45] but the outbreak of the Civil War prevented any change being made. In 1863, however, with increased immigration, improved sales, and high prices for farm products it was felt that such a step could safely be taken. There was justification for such a move, since greenback currency was already declining in value. In order to avoid arousing public sentiment, no arbitrary increase was made but from time to time the minimum price on certain grades of land was raised.

In January, 1863, Osborn ordered the minimum price of the lands being sold by Hoffman to be raised from $6 to $7 per acre.[46] Slightly later he ordered a general increase of $1, and for some tracts where sales were most frequent, increases as high as $3 were made.[47] These increases did not bring the level of prices up to those demanded by local speculators,[48] and Osborn determined

---

[45] *Supra*, note 35.

[46] Osborn to W. M. Phillips, January 21, 1863, "Presidents and Chairmans Letters," No. 18, box 48.

[47] Carlson to Hasselquist, March 3, 1863, Hasselquist MSS. Carlson was much disturbed because he felt that the lands around Paxton had been raised proportionately more than elsewhere, contrary to the contract between the railroad and the college.     [48] *Country Gentleman* (March 10, 1864), XXIII, 164.

to impose another. In March, 1864, the last general increase was made when the minimum price on all grades of land was established at $8 per acre.[49]

These price increases were wise so far as they applied to the dry prairie lands of central and northern Illinois, where the demand for land was sending its price up rapidly. They were unwise in their application to southern Illinois, where the Company still had a great deal of unsold land, and to the wet lands of eastern Illinois, where drainage was such an expensive proposition, and they proved a further hindrance to sales. Within a few years the officials saw to their dismay that prices instead of being raised must be lowered if the remaining lands were to be sold. As early as 1867 the minimum price on some tracts was lowered to the former level of $6 an acre, and in the 'seventies it was found necessary to accept as low as $4.40 an acre in order to dispose of the wet lands.[50]

The decline in the price of Illinois Central land, which began as early as 1863 and became more and more marked in succeeding years, may be explained in two ways; by 1863 the choicest lands were gone, and by that date the Company was beginning to feel the competition of the trans-Mississippi land grant railroads, whose lands had come on the market after those of the Illinois Central and who still had choice lands to offer. In the correspondence of the officials of the Illinois Central Railroad constant mention is made during the 'sixties and 'seventies of the land sales of rival land companies and railroads.

The Illinois Central would have found it impossible to sell over 2,000,000 acres of its grant within twelve years, and for the prices which it received, had it not granted liberal credit terms to the purchasers. These liberal terms led many speculators to buy large tracts at prices considerably higher than those paid for government land in the same neighborhood. Most writers on the history of Illinois during the 'fifties assume that the million acres of Illinois Central land sold during the years 1855 to 1857

---

[49] Osborn to J. M. Douglas, March 21, 1864, "Presidents Letters," 1864, box 48.
[50] Daggy to J. M. Douglas, January 26, 1874, "Daggy Personal with officers I. C. R. R. Co.," 16th St.

were purchased by actual settlers.[51] One writer even states that the million acres were sold to foreign immigrants.[52] This was by no means the case. We have already seen that in the 'fifties the majority of newcomers to Illinois who purchased from the railroad were from the eastern states — not from abroad. Furthermore, as the officials noted, many of the purchases of the 'fifties, in contrast to those of the 'sixties, were made for speculative purposes.

Error on this point has arisen from the fact that the Company constantly stressed in its advertisements, *Annual Reports*, and statements given to the press that it would not sell land except to actual settlers under contract to place a portion of their holdings under cultivation at once.[53] This clause of the contracts was not strictly enforced, however, and exceptions were made in certain sales to large purchasers. The purpose behind these exceptions was partly to encourage promoters of colonies to bring in settlers upon the land, and partly to make the statistics of land sales appear as promising as possible. There was also a personal motive on the part of those officials who felt that their success depended on large sales. Dupuy and Wilson, heads of the Land Department successively from 1855 to 1857, were in a large degree responsible for this situation, but not entirely so. The more important contracts were not made without the consent either of the President (Griswold or Osborn) or of the Executive Committee.[54]

[51] In "The Fight for the Northwest," *American Historical Review*, XVI, 774–788, Professor Dodd presents a map which purports to show the Illinois Central lands sold in 1855–1859. On this map he indicates Illinois Central lands in the vicinity of the Canal where the Company owned only a few scattered tracts; he shows a heavy sale of land on the Chicago branch south of Iroquois County where actually very little land was sold prior to the Civil War; he fails to show any sales on the main line from Centralia to Christian County where considerable sales were really made. Dodd states that "About one million acres of land was disposed of to settlers during the years 1856 to 1857 . . ." (p. 787). He probably means 1855 to 1857, during which time this amount was sold, but by no means entirely to settlers, as the cancellations discussed below indicate. See also Brownson, *op. cit.*, p. 136, and Cole, *op. cit.*, pp. 87–88.     [52] Smith, *loc. cit.*, pp. 192–202.

[53] Report of D. A. Neal in *Annual Report* for 1853; *ibid.*, for 1855; *The Illinois Central Rail Road Company offer for sale over 2,500,000 acres* (1855), p. 6, and later land pamphlets; *Chicago Democratic Press*, May 31, 1854, advertisement and editorial item; letter of John Wilson to the President of the Illinois Central, July 1, 1857, *American Railroad Journal* (1857), p. 467.

[54] Dupuy to Osborn, October 25, 1855, M. O.

Although it was difficult to collect on these contracts, and although in certain places they served to keep large tracts of land out of cultivation or resale, yet the Company's policy in this respect is not wholly to be condemned. From the day of its incorporation, the Illinois Central constantly feared that the Legislature would enact a law which would provide for forced sales of its land at auction. Such a measure as an amendment to another bill was actually introduced in the Illinois Legislature, and was defeated in the House only by the casting vote of the Speaker after a long and bitter fight in which the Company's representatives played a prominent part.[55] This defeat did not settle the matter, because the charter of the road provided that all lands remaining unsold ten years after its completion should be offered annually at public sales until all were sold.[56] According to this provision the lands would be subject to public sale in 1866. This was an important factor in inducing the officials to make these large land sales to non-settlers.

The modifications which were made in the policy of requiring improvements upon the lands seemed justified at the time because many of the large purchasers had definite plans for bringing colonies from the East to settle in Illinois. Some of these colony promoters were partially successful, although it must be admitted that most of them failed. The Panic of 1857 put a quietus upon their plans, and the ensuing tight money situation prevented them from meeting their payments.

One of these large purchasers who was unable to meet his payments was Andrew J. Galloway, one of the largest and most successful real estate agents in Illinois. Galloway had first been employed by the Illinois Central as chief of a corps of engineers running the route of the main line; he had then been transferred to the Land Department, where he aided in the selection of the lands.[57] This gave him an excellent knowledge of the region through which the route of the Illinois Central ran. In November, 1855, in connection with two other parties, Galloway purchased

---

[55] *Journal of the House*, 1854, pp. 181–182; telegrams of Joy to Burrall and Johnson to Mason, February 27, 1854; letter of Joy to Burrall, February 28, 1854, M. O.

[56] *Charter*, p. 27.

[57] *Illinois State Register*, September 30, 1851.

from the railroad 60,000 acres of land on long-term credits.[58] This purchase was particularly welcomed by the railroad because the bulk of the lands so sold were located below Rantoul on the branch line and Decatur on the main line, in regions where very little land was being sold.[59] The Illinois Central could not feel that Galloway's subsequent efforts to resell these lands were rivalling their own, since most of their purchasers wanted to locate in the central or northern part of the State and only by special inducements could they be persuaded to locate in the region where Galloway was operating. The latter began an active campaign to sell his lands; he advertised in the newspapers,[60] and published a land pamphlet somewhat similar to that of the Illinois Central.[61] So successful was he that by February, 1856, he reported to the officials of the road that within three months he would have every acre of his land — where the road was completed — in the hands of actual settlers.[62]

At this time the officials of the Land Department, having noted that the southern lands were not attracting settlers, made a special contract with Galloway to promote their sale.[63] Galloway was not given an exclusive agency for the southern lands, but a certain amount of them were listed to him upon the sale of which he was to receive a commission.[64] Needing more financial backing to carry out such a large undertaking, Galloway obtained the assistance of several eastern capitalists, among whom was H. H. Hunnewell, a director of the Illinois Central.[65] He also made

[58] Galloway to Skeene, January 28, 1899, box of Galloway correspondence, 6th floor vault, Land and Tax Commissioner's office; plat books, *ibid.*

[59] Plat books; Ackerman to Courvoissiert Co., June 30, 1857, "Ackerman Secretary," 1856–1858, box 48; letter of December 20, 1856 by "Rural" in *Chicago Democratic Press*, December 30, 1856; *Home Missionary* (December, 1859), XXXII, 197.

[60] See advertisements in *Chicago Democratic Press*, August 4, December 28, 1855, October 18, 1856, and July 25, 1857; *Chicago Pictorial Advertiser*, 1858–1859, p. 354; *Chicago Directory* (1859–1860), p. 372.

[61] A. Campbell, *A Glance at Illinois* (1856). Campbell was a partner of Galloway.

[62] Galloway to Osborn, January 19, 1856, M. O.

[63] Advertisement of Western Land Agency in *Chicago Democratic Press*, July 25, 1857. By this time Mason Brayman was associated with Galloway in the sale of these lands. Cf. copy of letter of Galloway to Osborn, June 18, 1860, "Presidents Letters," No. 14, and copy of letter of Foster to Osborn, May 23, 1860, *ibid.*; Hunnewell to Osborn, January 1, 19, 1861, M. O.

[64] Osborn to Walker, February 1, 1861, green box, 63rd St.

[65] *Ibid.*

arrangements with a prominent New York land agency by which the latter was to sell the lands listed to Galloway.[66] With the aid of his New York and Chicago associates, Galloway was successful in selling large quantities of the lands in the boom period. Like the railroad itself, Galloway granted liberal credit terms, and after the crash of 1857 found great difficulty in making collections. Because his sub-purchasers were unable to meet their payments, Galloway could not meet his. The Company disliked to cancel his contracts because of the large amount of work involved in readjusting them with his sub-purchasers; consequently continued extensions had to be granted him. Much difficulty was encountered in settling up his contracts, and at times ill feeling was displayed by the officials of the Company. Throughout the 'sixties there was constant bickering over these contracts between Galloway and his eastern associates, Hunnewell, Neal, and Pratt of Boston on one side, and Osborn and the officials of the Land Department on the other. The latter, while recognizing the fact that most of the Company's own purchasers needed extensions and while granting them freely, failed to accord the same treatment to Galloway and his sub-purchasers, or at best begrudged him any extension.[67] This attitude was probably justified because of Galloway's inertia in the 'sixties.

Another sale of a similar sort was made to Charles M. Dupuy after he retired as Land Agent of the Illinois Central in 1856.[68] Dupuy apparently thought he could capitalize the experience he had acquired in the service of the Land Department. In company with another agent Dupuy purchased 10,250 acres near Ashkum at $10 per acre on long-term credits.[69] These lands were in a low, poorly drained region where, as late as 1867, the Company still possessed a large block of land.[70] Somewhat later Dupuy tried to

---

[66] Wilson to Galloway, November 12, 1856 (copy); Wilson to Perkins, November 12, 1856, with note by Osborn on same, M. O.

[67] There is a mass of correspondence between Theodore Neal, son of David Neal, and Galloway concerning collections in the impression letter books in the Neal-Rantoul MSS. There is also a great deal of correspondence between Osborn and Pratt and Hunnewell in the archives of the Illinois Central.

[68] Dupuy to Osborn, November 24, 1855; Osborn to Perkins, January 17, 1856, M. O.; vols. 265 and 266, Land and Tax Commissioner's office.

[69] Osborn to Perkins, January 17, 1856, M. O.

[70] *Sectional Maps*, plate 26 and p. 68; Dupuy to Osborn, October 25, 1855, M. O.

purchase 20,000 acres more, promising, if the sale went through, to settle them with farmers from Pennsylvania.[71] But Wilson was not as anxious to sell to speculators as Dupuy had been when in charge of the land office, and he frowned upon the proposition. Dupuy opened a land office in Chicago, "put up a conspicuous sign," [72] and advertised in New York, Chicago, and Springfield papers.[73] He had extensive plans for promoting land sales in the East. His partner was stationed in New York, where he was to answer enquiries from people seeing the advertisements. Dupuy's success was immediate, and a large part of his land was quickly sold. But his purchasers were no better able to meet their payments after 1857 than were the sub-purchasers of Galloway. Dupuy was unable to carry his contracts, and they were taken over by David Neal and H. H. Hunnewell, for whom Galloway acted as agent. From this time until the contracts were either paid up or cancelled Neal and Hunnewell experienced the same difficulties in collecting from the sub-purchasers, meeting their own payments or securing extensions, and pacifying the officials of the Land Department.

On a comparatively small scale, but more bitterly criticized, was the sale in 1855 of 4619 acres at $10 per acre to Stephen A. Douglas.[74] Douglas's purpose in buying the land, which was in the vicinity of Lake Calumet, was reported to be that of establishing a stock farm similar to that of John Wentworth in the same county. The land, however, was totally unsuited to such a purpose, and it appears that nothing was done to improve it. It is more likely that it was purchased as a pure speculation. The *Chicago Democratic Press*, a rabid Republican organ, fulminated against the Illinois Central for its action in selling a large body of land to a "notorious politician," in violation of its principle of making sales only to actual settlers.[75] The sale was not at the time

---

[71] Wilson to Executive Committee, January 19, 1856, *ibid.* Dupuy already had considerable land in the Dixon district which he had purchased from the Government. See "Register of Receipts," Springfield district, 1849–1856, S. A. O.

[72] Johnson to Perkins, January 15, 1856, M. O.

[73] See advertisements in *New York Tribune*, April 7, 1856, *Chicago Democratic Press*, October 18, 1856, and *Illinois State Register*, January 24, 1856.

[74] Osborn to Perkins, May 12, 1855, M. O.; vol. 262, Land and Tax Commissioner's office; *Chicago Weekly Democrat*, May 26, 1855.

[75] *Chicago Democratic Press*, July 2, 1855.

unfavorable to the interests of the Company, but as only the advance interest payments were ever made upon it and as the Company feared to cancel it,[76] the sale was kept on the books without further payments until 1867, when it was finally cancelled and the land resold at double the price which Douglas had agreed to pay.[77]

The Illinois Central never completely gave up sales to speculators, notwithstanding the oft-repeated assertion of the officials of the Land Department and despite its ill-success in collecting on such contracts. On April 17, 1857, the Company sold to Joseph Paine 9920 acres at prices ranging from $8 to $9.25 per acre, but was forced to cancel the sale in 1861.[78] In 1859 and 1860 it proposed to sell 250,000 acres for prices ranging from $8 to $25 to James Caird for resale in England, and even offered to leave out the clause requiring cultivation upon each separate tract each year upon their resale.[79] Another large tract of from 100,000 to 150,000 acres was offered to a European firm in 1860, to be paid for in cash at one-third discount from the credit price.[80]

The liberal credit terms granted by the Illinois Central tempted the ordinary settler, as well as the professional speculator, to overpurchase. New immigrants as well as old settlers had the land fever and overpurchased railroad lands precisely as, prior to 1855, earlier immigrants had bought more government land than they were able to farm successfully. People with little or no means would buy from 160 to 640 acres, making the initial payment and trusting in fortune to bring good crops and high prices to enable them to meet subsequent payments. Not only did settlers pur-

---

[76] Douglas was a stockholder in the Illinois Central in 1855 and aided considerably in the sale of the Company's lands. He attended an excursion to Urbana in May, 1855, and made a speech which Osborn thought would aid considerably in the sale of the lands. Wilson to Osborn, July 24, 1855; Osborn to Perkins, May 14, 1855, M. O. See also letter of Sturges to Burrall, June 9, 1854, in regard to Douglas's willingness to aid the Company.

[77] Vol. 262, Land and Tax Commissioner's office.

[78] Vol. 266, *ibid.*

[79] Osborn to Caird, August 12, 1859, "W. H. Osborn, Pres.," No. 11, box 48; same to same, November 12, 1858, "Presidents Letters," 1858, *ibid.*

[80] Walker to Schuchard & Gebhard, September 10, 1860, "Presidents and Chairmans Letters," No. 15, *ibid.* A rule was later established according to which no large tracts were to be sold on long credit. For anything over 160 acres a substantial cash payment was required. See memorandum in "Osborn Letter Book," 1863–1865, M. O.

chase beyond their ability to pay, but they also acquired more land than they were able to use. A considerable amount of capital was necessary to break the tough prairie sod, fence the lands, purchase farm implements and stock, and plant the crops. The ordinary farmer found himself unable to use much more than 160 acres, and even that amount was too large for many of the settlers. When the time arrived for them to make payments upon the principal they were hard pressed, and besought the Company for extensions. The officials were not anxious to press the farmers too severely, and treated them with the utmost consideration. It was found necessary, however, to adopt a general policy toward the delinquents, whose delayed payments began to assume alarming proportions.

The problem of collections did not become acute until 1857 and 1858, when the first payments upon the principal of the early contracts fell due, but thenceforth it was one of the most difficult questions confronting the Company. By that time both the large speculators and the small farmers were finding difficulty in making payments and were appealing for extensions. The large purchasers who had been unsuccessful in settling their lands were, in general, forced to cancel their holdings. In 1858 the first of these cancellations took place when two contracts for 20,000 acres were voided.[81] From then on until well into the 'sixties these large contracts were gradually cancelled and the lands offered again for sale.

It was not the larger contracts, however, which were the source of worry to the officials of the road, but rather the small sales which had been made to actual settlers. In 1860 there was a body of more than 11,000 settlers holding land of the Illinois Central, and their political influence in the State was not to be ignored. Drastic action in cancelling their contracts might lead to an anti-rent war, as one of the officials feared,[82] and the Illinois Central was not anxious to stir up trouble for itself at this time — nor for that matter at any time in its history. The Company, on account of its peculiar relationship to the State, and because of its large

[81] *Annual Report*, 1859.
[82] Lane to Osborn, November 30, 1858, M. O.

landed possessions, was especially vulnerable, and political trouble was the last thing it desired. Furthermore, in order to build up freight and passenger traffic it was to its own interest to keep the settlers upon the lands and assist them in developing their holdings. The officials did not forget that the Company was primarily a railroad company and secondarily a land company. Consequently they determined to grant extensions to settlers who had conformed to the requirement of their contracts calling for actual cultivation.[83] On such extensions 10 per cent interest was charged, which was not an extortionate rate as rates went in the 'fifties.[84]

The policy of granting extensions to delinquents was later modified, and farmers in default were urged to cancel their contracts and repurchase that portion of their land which they had improved. Where this was done the owner was given credit on the new purchase for the amount he had paid on the original. The inflation of the currency and the increase in land prices made it desirable that contracts for land which was not being improved and upon which payments were not being made should be cancelled. The Company could thereby partly avoid the loss which currency inflation brought it by reselling such lands at the enhanced prices. Accordingly, great pressure was brought to bear upon small farmers who had bought from 160 to 640 acres of land — if they were not meeting their payments — to persuade them to make such an arrangement. Many settlers were unwilling to give up any of their land, but continued pressure forced them to acquiesce and several thousand contracts were cancelled and new ones made for smaller amounts of land.[85]

[83] For the treatment of delinquents by the Illinois Central see *Country Gentleman* (January 28, 1858), XI, 68, and *Historical Atlas of Ford County*, p. 12.

[84] The London shareholders resented the Company's lenient attitude towards the delinquents. They severely criticized Osborn and the other directors for their laxity in enforcing payments and demanded that the rate of interest be increased, that more thorough investigation be made of each case before extensions were granted, that the extensions be for shorter periods, and finally, when partial cancellations were made, that the best and most improved land be returned to the Company. The editors of the *Railway Times* were most severe in their indictment of the officials. See especially *ibid.* (November 27, 1858), XXI, 1388. See also the letters of George Moffatt, Chairman of the London Committee, to Osborn, November 18, December 18, 1858, and others in Ward's office.

[85] *Annual Reports*, 1865, 1866. See plat books in Land and Tax Commissioner's office.

One type of delinquent who gave the Land Department much trouble was the person who had secured control of original contracts as assignee and who refused either to complete the payments or to cancel the contracts. Many cases of this sort were reported on the main line, where respected and wealthy persons living in Bloomington and Peoria had secured possession of contracts originally issued to irresponsible persons and were renting the lands to others for $2 per acre or one-third of the crop. These lands were being worn out and the Company was receiving no return from them.[86]

The Land Department found it had a vast amount of work to do in supervising and enforcing or extending collections. To take charge of this matter, R. B. Mason was appointed in August, 1861, to the newly created position of Comptroller of the Land Department. Previous to 1861 a system of careful examination of the progress of all persons owing for lands had been worked out. The lands were divided into six districts, over each of which was placed an examiner who made detailed reports on delinquents for consideration by the higher officials.[87] Mason was now placed in charge of the land examinations with the duties of recommending or rejecting proposals for further extensions of credit, of bringing pressure to bear upon settlers to hasten their payments,[88] and of prosecuting the timber thieves who were operating on the railroad lands in southern Illinois.[89] After Mason's appointment, although purchasers were shown continued leniency stricter supervision was employed, and settlers who had overpurchased were urged to surrender their old contracts and to accept new ones for smaller areas, and to make as large payments as possible. Yet by December, 1862, only a small portion of the Illinois Central lands — 271,890 acres — had been deeded, and contracts for

[86] Osborn to J. M. Douglas, June 3, 1862, "Osborn Letter Book," 1861–1862, M. O. The case of Asahel Gridley, already referred to, was the most flagrant. Gridley's action encouraged many other purchasers likewise to refuse payment, and drastic action had to be taken against him in the courts. See above, Chapter VIII. See also Foster to Walker, August 29, 1860, green box, 63rd St.

[87] J. W. Foster in Annual Report, 1859.

[88] Osborn to Redmond, August 9, 1861, "Osborn Letter Book," 1860–1861, M. O.; Ackerman, Historical Sketch, p. 88.

[89] Osborn to John Barnard, January 28, 1862, "Osborn Letter Book," 1861–1862, M. O.

nearly 900,000 acres, amounting to $12,000,000, were still outstanding.[90]

Between 1858 and 1870 the Illinois Central found it necessary to cancel sales contracts for 717,959 acres of land.[91] In 1858 23,486 acres were returned to the Company, and the figures for 1859 and 1860 were 20,638 and 48,274 acres respectively. In 1861, the year that Mason began weeding out the worst cases of contract violation, cancellations reached their highest point, 125,932 acres, but in 1862 the value of the cancelled contracts was greater. In both these years cancellations considerably exceeded sales. In the four years from 1861 to 1864 contracts for 450,000 acres were revoked. Subsequently the amount of cancellations declined sharply, but nevertheless they continued to annoy the officials for years to come. In 1865 and 1866 most of the cancellations were caused by the need of revising contracts on current terms or of issuing the titles to new owners to whom the original purchasers had assigned them.[92] A glance at the sales books of the Land Department reveals that a great many tracts were sold and resold three, four, and even five times before the title was finally given.

Most of the cancelled contracts had been made during the years 1855, 1856, and 1857, when active encouragement rather than opposition was given to overpurchasing. In these years 49 sales of over 640 acres were made, some of them running as high as 20,000 to 60,000 acres. By 1857 the officials had begun to doubt the wisdom of selling large tracts of land to speculators without some certainty of their being able to fulfill the contracts, and were more ready to enforce the avowed policy of requiring cultivation of the soil by all purchasers. Experience also showed that few of the settlers who purchased 160 acres or more were able to meet their payments when they came due. The officials of the Land Department therefore gradually came to advise settlers to make smaller and smaller purchases. This policy led to a constantly diminishing number of acres per sale; the average fell from 176 acres in 1855 to 67 in 1860, and to 55 in 1870. After 1860 the Land Commissioners were constantly alluding to the smaller average sales and observ-

---

[90] *Annual Report*, 1862.  
[91] See Table I, p. 260.  
[92] *Annual Reports*, 1865, 1866.

ing that a more permanent body of settlers was buying the lands for homes rather than for speculation.

The Illinois Central's difficulties with slow collections were not entirely caused by overpurchasing on the part of speculators and settlers; after 1860 they were in part the result of war conditions. The severing of trade routes between North and South upon the outbreak of the Civil War was disastrous to the Illinois farmers and the Illinois Central Railroad. Corn, wheat, and flour had come to be important commodities in the trade between the Northwest and the South, the latter section taking a considerable portion of the agricultural products of Illinois. Corn frequently brought $1.50 per bushel from the southern planter, and its sale was immensely profitable to the farmers, dealers, and shippers.[93] In the previous year, contracts to furnish over 1,000,000 bushels of Illinois corn for the New Orleans market were made.[94] When this trade was cut off, prices immediately declined. Corn fell from 30 cents to 23 cents per bushel at Chicago from January 5 to December 28;[95] No. 1 spring wheat fell from 80 cents to 69 cents;[96] flour fell proportionately;[97] and the Chicago quotations on hogs were practically halved during this period.[98] Such prices, with the freight charges to Chicago subtracted, left little or no profit to the farmer. Within a hundred miles of Chicago, on the Chicago, Burlington and Quincy and the Illinois Central Railroads, corn is said to have brought as low as 6 cents per bushel,[99] while at Bloomington it could be bought for 8 to 10 cents per bushel. At these prices there was no profit for the farmer, and corn was consequently burned for fuel.[100] It was impossible for the settlers to continue payments on their contracts with such small returns from their crops. Unlike the situation in 1858 and 1859, it was not poor crops — for the crops of 1860 and 1861 were normal — but low prices which brought distress to the settlers and to the Land Department.

[93] H. Hinckley in *American Agriculturist* (February, 1861), xx, 43.
[94] *Prairie Farmer*, December 27, 1860.
[95] Chicago Board of Trade, *Annual Report*, 1862, p. 24.
[96] *Ibid.*, p. 21.          [97] *Ibid.*, p. 18.          [98] *Ibid.*, p. 32.
[99] Letter of Henry Hamlin Turner, January 22, 1929, *Boston Herald*, January 26, 1929.
[100] Anthony Trollope, *North America*, p. 152.

The freight traffic of the Illinois Central also suffered by the cutting of trade connections with the South. In the latter part of the 'fifties the railroad, with its shipping connections at Cairo, had to a very considerable extent replaced the upper Mississippi River system as the means of transporting commodities to the South. True, one of the original purposes of the land grant of 1850, to build up the communities of Cairo and Mobile, had not been effected, but a large trade by this line had developed between the Northwest and the South. The shipping of foodstuffs was particularly important both to the Illinois Central and to the farmers from whom the produce was bought. Even in such an unfavorable year as 1859, over 350,000 bushels of grain, 27,000 barrels of flour, and large quantities of beef, pork, whiskey, and other commodities were shipped to Cairo on their way to the South.[101] So extensive was the southern business that the Company made arrangements in 1860 for a regular line of steamboats from Cairo to New Orleans.[102] There was not only a large movement of grain and foodstuffs southward over the Illinois Central, but also a relatively large amount of shipping from the South to Illinois by way of Cairo.[103] Thus the Illinois Central received at Cairo for shipment north in 1859 15,152 hogsheads and 2269 barrels of sugar, 6902 barrels of molasses, and 6,686,560 pounds of wool and cotton. Indeed, Cairo became so important as a shipping and receiving center that by 1859 it ranked next to Chicago among the Company's stations in the amount of commodities received and third in the amount shipped. As for passenger traffic, Cairo was little behind Chicago in the amount of receipts from this business.[104] The closing of this freight and passenger traffic, although partially compensated for by subsequent returns from the transportation of men and supplies for the Army, was a great blow to the railroad.[105] Retrenchments were necessary all along the line, and expenditures in all departments were cut to the barest minimum.

---

[101] Chicago Board of Trade, *Annual Report*, 1861, p. 18; *Annual Report*, Illinois Central Railroad, 1859.     [102] *Prairie Farmer*, December 27, 1860.
[103] *New York Times*, January 25, February 4, 1861.
[104] *Annual Report*, 1859.
[105] Osborn to H. H. Hunnewell, November 12, 1862, "Osborn Official Letter

The Company was at this time in an extremely bad situation, and quick action was necessary to save it from going on the rocks. With its southern traffic cut off, its collections reduced alarmingly, and its land sales diminishing to a negligible quantity, there seemed little likelihood of its being able to meet its obligations when due. To add to this tense situation, most of the Illinois banks, which held large amounts of southern state bonds, were forced to the wall with the outbreak of the war and the holders of their securities suffered large losses.[106]

To meet this situation, and to enable the stricken farmers to move their crops to market, the Illinois Central reduced transportation rates on corn.[107] This action failing to relieve the situation, a more radical step was taken. It was determined to accept the farmers' corn at Chicago prices, minus transportation charges, for payments on their contracts.[108] Such a move was a great help to the farmers, whose bins were overflowing with corn, owing to the abundant crops of 1860 and 1861, but who had no money to ship the grain to market; it also ensured them better prices since it avoided the middleman. Circulars were sent to each person owing the Illinois Central for land,[109] and advertisements were inserted in the local papers calling attention to this means of making payments.[110]

Corn began coming in at once, eight carloads being received on July 8, three on July 10, ten on July 12, four on the 13th, and

Book," box 48; *New York Tribune*, August 19, 1861. So disastrous were the results of the suspension of commerce with the South that the Illinois Central was forced to make a call of $5 on its scrip stock in December, 1861. See *New York Tribune*, November 4, December 7, 1861.

[106] *Ibid.*, July 16, 1861. There is a discussion of the disastrous bank failures in Illinois in 1861 in George William Dowrie, *The Development of Banking in Illinois, 1817–1863* (University of Illinois, *Studies in the Social Sciences*, vol. II, No. 4, Urbana, 1913), pp. 155 ff.

[107] *New York Tribune*, June 26, 1861,

[108] Osborn to Lockwood and Moore, July 1, 1861, "Osborn Letter Book," 1860–1861, M. O. In this letter Osborn states that the Illinois Central offered to purchase the corn at five to eight cents above the current rate. Cf. *New York Tribune*, July 16, 1861.

[109] J. M. Douglas to Osborn, July 6, 1861, Ward's office. A copy of the wheat circular, dated August 8, 1861, is in M. O.

[110] Osborn to Walker, December 4, 1861, "Osborn Letter Book," 1861–1862, M. O. See advertisement of J. M. Redmond, acting Land Commissioner, in *Illinois Staats-Zeitung*, June 30, 1862.

twelve on the 20th, and this continued throughout the year.[111] Within a month over 50,000 bushels had been received and sold by the officials without the loss, as Osborn reported, of a cent.[112] So vast became the business that extensive preparations were made to store the corn, miles of cribs being constructed at Burnside for this purpose,[113] and 500 additional grain cars were ordered to be built.[114] The grain, after reaching Chicago, was temporarily stored or transshipped by lake steamers to Buffalo and Oswego, where some was disposed of and the remainder sent by canal and rail to New York, whence part was sent to Liverpool.[115] More than 3,000,000 bushels of corn were accepted by the Company from its debtors in 1861 and 1862.

The Illinois Central suffered considerable losses in disposing of this grain. On one cargo alone, of 100,000 bushels, there was a loss of $45,000.[116] During the first year the plan was in operation the total losses amounted to $73,987 and in 1862 to $32,302.[117] The causes of such losses were the generous prices allowed to the settlers, shrinkage, spoiling, unfamiliarity with market conditions, and inability to compete with experienced grain dealers. Recognizing these handicaps, the Company determined to withdraw from the business of grain collection and sale and instead to give to parties owing for land a drawback of 30 per cent on the regular freight charges. According to this plan, the Company would carry the grain to Chicago at these reduced rates and there sell it at market prices, crediting the settler with the receipts less transportation charges.[118] The Company assumed all responsibility after the produce was shipped, and guaranteed the shipper the highest market price and prompt returns.[119]

---

[111] The letters of J. M. Douglas, resident director, to Osborn, of July 8, 10, 12, 30, 1861, and of later dates in Ward's office give more details on the grain business.

[112] Osborn to Walker, August 7, 1861, green box, 63rd St.

[113] *New York Tribune*, November 26, 1861; Ackerman, *Early Illinois Railroads*, p. 115.

[114] *New York Tribune*, September 23, 1861; *Annual Report*, 1862.

[115] Douglas to Osborn, October 29, 1861, Ward's office; Osborn to Walker, June 3, 1862, "Osborn Letter Book," 1861–1862, M. O.

[116] Osborn to Walker, May 12, 1862, *ibid*.

[117] *Annual Report*, 1862. Osborn stated that the loss was nearly compensated for by purchasing, with the proceeds from the sale of grain, the Company's depreciated bonds and cancelling them.     [118] *Annual Report*, 1862.

[119] *Illinois Farmer*, VIII, 41.

Shortly after the first experiment with corn had been made, wheat was also received by the Company in payment for its lands,[120] stated prices being guaranteed the farmers for brief periods.[121] As this grain was not grown on Illinois Central land to the extent that corn was, its collection was not of such importance.

Corn and wheat together, in spite of the losses sustained in their sale, helped to tide the Illinois Central over the dark days of 1861 and 1862. Without these collections in kind, which composed a large proportion of the entire collections, the income of the Land Department would have been exceedingly small. Towards the end of 1862, when conditions markedly improved, the grain collections were of less importance. It may be noted in passing that the Illinois Central in later years accepted ties in payment for its lands as it had previously taken wheat and corn.[122]

The improved economic conditions, with their attendant higher prices for agricultural products, made it easier after 1862 for the settlers on the railroad lands to meet their payments. Henceforth, for the remainder of the decade, the number of delinquencies was smaller and was confined mostly to that class of people who never desire to meet their obligations and upon whom pressure must be brought to bear.

By 1870 all but 500,000 acres of the Illinois Central grant had been sold, and most of the remaining land was of the poorer sort in southern Illinois. The great work of the Land Department in advertising and colonizing its lands was over, although there remains an interesting story of the colonization of Egypt after 1870.

There are a number of outstanding facts concerning the colonization work of the Illinois Central Railroad. First and most obvious is the lenient attitude of President Osborn and other officials of the Land Department towards the delinquent purchasers. Undoubtedly any other policy would have been disastrous for all parties, but Osborn felt a real bond of sympathy for the delin-

---

[120] J. M. Redmond to Walker, January 16, 1862, Ward's office.

[121] Thus from August 8 to September 10, the Company allowed 75 cents per bushel for No. 1 white winter wheat and 70 cents for No. 1 red winter wheat. See circular of William H. Osborn dated August 8, 1861, M. O.

[122] C. A. Beck to Peter Daggy, December 12, 1877, box: "Misc. Corr., No. 1," 16th St.

quents, and was willing to do practically anything within reason to assist them in eventually completing their payments. Another outstanding fact is the error which was made in the years 1855 to 1857 by Dupuy, Wilson, Griswold, and Osborn in encouraging overpurchasing. A more conservative policy, that of selling land in moderate amounts only to actual settlers, would have produced less spectacular but more constructive results, would have prevented the problem of enforced collections from arising, and might have minimized public criticism of the road. Other less important mistakes were made in the administration and sale of the Illinois Central's grant, but on the whole it would seem that most of the policies of the Land Department were wise and were well carried out.

# CHAPTER XIII

## PROMOTION OF AGRICULTURE

THE significance of the work of the railroads in promoting agriculture in the United States cannot have escaped the attention of any well-read citizen of thirty years ago or of today. The departments of agriculture of the various roads have done a great deal to diversify crops, to improve the grade of stock, and to teach better methods of tilling and enriching the soil. Their exhibition cars of blooded stock have been seen in most communities of the West, where they have stimulated wide interest in stock improvement, and their displays of other farm products have likewise done much to diversify the crops of different sections of the country. The railroads are much more public-minded today than they were even a generation ago, but their efforts to aid the farmers of the West are not wholly disinterested. These are undertaken for the purpose of building up the freight and passenger traffic of the roads by increasing at the same time the amount of farm produce going to market and the farmers' buying power. They are undertaken also with the idea of making the farmer more satisfied with his lot and less anxious to abandon the farm for the city. In other words, the railroads have come to realize that everything which benefits the farmer will directly or indirectly benefit them.

The credit for initiating this type of activity on the part of railroads has generally gone to James J. Hill, the promoter of the Great Northern Railroad. However, a full generation before Hill began his great work for the benefit of the farmers of the Northwest the Illinois Central Railroad, under the guidance of President Osborn, had undertaken practically all the kinds of work which were later carried on by Hill on a more extensive scale. Hill initiated no new policy, but simply enlarged upon the plans and ideas of Osborn and of others associated with him in the Illinois Central Railroad.

The Illinois Central Railroad, with its grant of 2,500,000 acres, had a great stake in Illinois. By 1857 a large body of settlers was living upon the Company's lands, most of whom had purchased their holdings upon the long-credit terms. The welfare of the Company depended, therefore, to a very considerable extent upon the welfare of its settlers and upon the farmers who were served by its line. Recognizing this, the officials of the Illinois Central, led by President Osborn, determined to assist the farmers by a broad program of agricultural promotion.

The first step taken in this direction was the assistance given the Illinois State Agricultural Society with its annual fairs. Reasoning that the dissemination of information concerning the agricultural possibilities of the State would not only assist the farmers but would also advertise the advantages of Illinois, the officials of the Illinois Central determined, in 1855, to make the Chicago fair of that year a great success. They gave reduced rates to visitors and provided free transportation for "cattle, stock, produce, and specimen articles" intended for exhibition at the fair. They instructed the station-agents to collect and forward to Chicago specimens of soil, wheat, coal and other minerals, and grasses and fruits found in the neighborhood. To win publicity for the fair, as well as for the Illinois Central, the officials, acting in cooperation with the State Agricultural Society, invited a large number of "eminent agriculturists," scientists, editors of rural and agricultural papers, and officials of local agricultural societies to visit the fair and then to participate in an excursion over the entire line of the road. One hundred and fifty invitations were sent out to persons in twenty-four states. Although some of those invited were unable to attend, many interested in agriculture accepted this opportunity of seeing Illinois. They were royally entertained by the city of Chicago during the days of the fair and were then taken over the Illinois Central. They were provided with literature and statistics by the Company and were generally encouraged to publish accounts of their experiences. Judging from the amount of publicity which this excursion received, its expense was well justified. Many of the agricultural weeklies and newspapers gave long descriptions of the fair, the excursion, and the crops and conditions in Illinois.[1]

The following year, the Illinois Central made an attempt to secure the state fair for southern Illinois. This region was being neglected by incoming settlers, and it was believed that if the fair were held there it would dispel the notion that Egypt was an infertile and unhealthy country. It was also felt that the location of the fair in southern Illinois would have a stimulating effect upon the settlers of the region by giving them a knowledge of new methods of farming and of the advantages of stock improvement. The Illinois Central subscribed $2000 to assist Jonesboro in securing the fair. Its efforts were unsuccessful, however; Alton rather than Jonesboro secured the coveted prize.[2] Bitter feeling was aroused and threats were made to start a rival fair. Although the threats came to nothing, agitation continued for the location of the fair in Egypt proper, and in 1858 success was attained; Centralia defeated its rivals, Jacksonville, Freeport, and Peoria, which were bidding for the location.[3]

The Illinois Central was especially generous in its efforts to assist the State Agricultural Society in making a success of this fair. This was the first time that the fair was to be held in Egypt proper, and without the cooperation of the railroad Centralia, then only a small town, would have been unable to provide sufficient accommodations to care for the exhibits and the crowds of people. To meet the needs, the Company volunteered to place at the disposal of the fair its large buildings in Centralia. It likewise furnished $2\frac{1}{2}$ miles of cars on its side-tracks to provide sleeping accommodations for the people who attended the fair. As in previous years, it transported exhibits, lumber, and fixtures free of charge and ran free special trains for a distance of 100 miles north and south of Centralia during the exhibition to enable as many people as possible to attend.[4] Such liberality was "unprece-

---

[1] For examples see *Country Gentleman* (November 15, 1855), VI, 320–321, which also quotes from the *Cincinnati Gazette*; *The Horticulturist* (1855), pp. 536–537, and the account in *Illinois Reports*, 1857, pp. 777–788. See also the letters of B. F. Johnson to Perkins, October 11, 12, 1855, M. O.

[2] *Prairie Farmer*, February 25, 1858.

[3] Illinois State Agricultural Society, *Transactions* (1857–1858), III, 76.

[4] *Illinois State Journal*, April 21, 28, 1858; *Prairie Farmer*, April 22, 29, 1858.

dented," as a resolution of the State Agricultural Society declared.[5]

Despite the advertising which southern Illinois received from the fair, its development, as we have already seen, continued to lag behind that of the rest of the State, a fact which caused the Illinois Central much concern. In the early 'sixties the Company's officials began to realize that the lands in Egypt were distinctly different from those in the central and northern parts of the State, and that to secure their settlement different means must be employed than were used for the other sections. The time was propitious for this change. With the outbreak of the Civil War and the stoppage of trade between the North and South, the North was forced to look elsewhere than to the slave states for its cotton, sugar, flax, and tobacco. Naturally people's eyes turned to the border communities whose climate and soil resembled those of the South most closely. President Osborn understood the situation and determined to make the best possible use of it.

At the opening of the nineteenth century, the early settlers in southern Illinois had raised cotton successfully but later comers had abandoned it almost entirely.[6] Under normal conditions the section could not compete with the Gulf States in cotton production, but now that trade with the South was cut off, Osborn thought that cotton could be grown profitably in Egypt. He interested prominent men in the production of this crop, notably William H. Seward, sent an agent to Maryland to procure seed, persuaded the Federal Government to forward through the Patent Office a large supply of seed, and gave wide circulation to an essay on cotton cultivation by an eminent agriculturist.[7] In sending out his annual passes to editors of agricultural papers in 1862, Osborn referred to his efforts to stimulate cotton-planting and suggested that they publish articles on the possibilities of cotton-growing in Illinois.[8] As a result of this correspondence, practically every prominent agricultural paper in the northern

---

[5] Illinois State Agricultural Society, *Transactions*, III, 98.

[6] *Prairie Farmer*, December 26, 1861.

[7] Osborn to J. A. Lewis, December 19, 1862; to W. H. Seward, January 3, 1862; to Robertson, January 15, 1862, "Osborn Letter Book," 1861–1862, M. O.

[8] Osborn to N. J. Coleman, January 15, 1862; to J. H. and Luther Tucker, January 15, 1862, *ibid.*

states published more or less material on the subject,[9] and wide publicity was obtained for Osborn's new project.

Osborn's efforts brought immediate results. A considerable amount of cotton was planted in 1862, one influential farmer preparing 1000 acres for this purpose.[10] The yield obtained that year was, of course, of little commercial importance, but as the result of an experiment it seemed to promise well for the future. One observer in southern Illinois wrote: "We are all in a fever, too, over cotton growing. The Illinois Central Railroad is foremost in fanning the flame to keep up the interests of their Egyptian lands." [11] The following year the Company procured 800 bushels of seed from Memphis and sold it at cost to farmers along its line between Cairo and Centralia. Similarly J. N. A. Griswold, former president of the Company, imported over 1½ tons of seed for distribution at cost.[12] Lack of seed had been one of the chief causes for the small amount of cotton planted in 1862, but now, with a more abundant supply, a larger acreage was planted and a substantial yield was expected. This did not prove to be the case, however, for the cotton suffered a severe setback from frosts in mid-season, which in many cases made picking unprofitable. Undiscouraged, the people of southern Illinois, spurred on by the high prices then offered, planted still larger areas in 1864 and 1865. Their efforts in these years were more successful, over 400,000 pounds of cotton being shipped from the section in 1864 and 1,500,000 in 1865.[13] With the return of peace, the reopening of trade with the South, and the consequent fall in the price of cotton, the production of this crop in Illinois, which could only be carried on profitably when prices were high, fell off at once; it amounted to only 465 bales in 1869.[14] Nevertheless, Osborn's

---

[9] For examples see *Illinois Farmer* (1862), VII, 6, 40; *Prairie Farmer*, November 15, 1862; *Country Gentleman* (February 6, 1862), XIX, 97.

[10] Osborn to Gen. W. K. Strong, March 27, 1862, "Osborn Letter Book," 1861–1862; *Prairie Farmer*, November 15, 1862.

[11] *Country Gentleman* (February 6, 1862), XIX, 97.

[12] *Illinois Farmer* (1863), VIII, 24; *Country Gentleman* (April 23, 1863), XXI, 267, 276.

[13] It is stated in *Sectional Maps* (1867 edition), p. 5, that about 15,000 bales of cotton were shipped from Illinois in 1865.

[14] *Ninth Census*, III, 132.

work in encouraging the production of cotton in this section was not lost. It had contributed much toward reviving interest in Egypt and had aided in its development.

Osborn's interest in southern Illinois was not limited to cotton production; he also endeavored, with more success, to develop the fruit industry there. Most of southern Illinois, particularly the Ozark ridge, was admirably adapted to fruit-raising, and as the Illinois Central possessed large amounts of land in this region, it sought to hasten its sale by appealing to persons interested in this industry. It published a pamphlet entitled *Illinois Fruit Industry, The Egyptian Basin and Its Contents*, and stressed the apple, peach, and small fruit industries in its advertisements and pamphlets.

The production of fruit was not new in Egypt, but hitherto there had been no market for it owing to the lack of transportation facilities. The Illinois Central, by connecting the region with Chicago, furnished a market for all available fruit. Furthermore, the road made all reasonable concessions to shippers of perishable commodities. At one time it gave a 33 per cent reduction in the freight tariff on fruit shipped from Egypt to Chicago.[15] This was a great boon to the industry. To expedite the transportation of fruit to Chicago, the Illinois Central put special fruit cars on its passenger trains. The business grew so rapidly that in 1862 it began running two- and three-car specials to Chicago, an innovation which, by 1866, had become an established policy. The train was run for berries and early vegetables for twenty days in June and for peaches, apples, and grapes from July 29 to September 29. By the late 'sixties southern Illinois had become an important fruit-producing section. In the height of the season ten to twenty carloads of peaches alone were transported daily to Chicago from this section, the total shipments for 1867 being 400,000 boxes to Chicago and 150,000 to St. Louis, besides smaller amounts of other fruits.[16]

This rapid expansion of the fruit industry led to the formation of the Southern Illinois Fruit Growers' Association, whose statis-

---

[15] *Prairie Farmer*, July 5, 1860, and May 1, 1869.

[16] Report of Dr. Meeker in *Illinois Farmer*, VII, 298–299; *Illinois Central Magazine* (1926), XV, 16.

tics on fruit-growing in this section are worthy of presentation. In 1866 the President of this organization reported the whole number of fruit trees set out in southern Illinois to be 816,375, of which 208,875 were apple, 78,000 were pear, and 439,500 were peach trees. These figures include only the number of trees set out by professional fruit-growers.[17]

As early as 1859 excellent profits were reported from this growing business, accounts of which were widely published in agricultural papers, no doubt with some exaggeration. The experience of the Evans brothers is a good example. They were reported to have sold 8000 baskets of peaches at an average price of $2 per basket in 1860. The net return was said to be well over $12,000, all from a farm which they had purchased the summer before from a rebel sympathizer for $10,000.[18] Somewhat later the Winter brothers of Du Quoin expected to market 20,000 boxes of peaches, on which they hoped to reap a small fortune.[19] So profitable did the expanding industry promise to be that, according to one observer, fruit-raising became "a mania." [20] One man in Washington County set out 3500 fruit trees in 1859 and 1860, another in Union County set out 2000 apple, 3000 peach, 200 pear and 100 cherry trees, and 2500 grape vines. Three years later orchards of 20,000 trees were common.[21]

The fruit industry in southern Illinois seems to have been largely developed by newcomers in the region, most of whom were Yankees.[22] As considerable initial capital was required to clear the lands, to set out seedlings, and to wait a number of years for returns, few of the older residents of Egypt were able to turn to fruit-raising, and indeed not many of the incoming settlers could engage in the fruit industry to any extent while they were paying for their land.

[17] There is considerable material on the fruit industry in Illinois in the 'sixties in the *Transactions* of the Illinois State Agricultural Society for 1865–1870, and in the *Annual Reports* of the United States Commissioners of Agriculture for the same years. See also *Sectional Maps, passim.*

[18] *Illinois Farmer*, VII, 279.        [19] *Prairie Farmer*, August 4, 1866.

[20] A. Babcock in *Country Gentleman* (March 27, 1862), XIX, 207.

[21] *Illinois Farmer*, VII, 101–104, 298–299; *American Agriculturist* (1863), XXII, 262; *New England Farmer* (1867), I, 469.

[22] Dr. Meeker in *Illinois Farmer*, VII, 298–299. The author is none too friendly to the natives of southern Illinois.

The Illinois Central made changes in its advertising pamphlets and cuts to make them conform to the new interest it was showing in its southern lands. Cotton, tobacco, and fruit were given attention, and to the enticing cuts hitherto picturing only corn, wheat, cattle, and hogs were added fine specimens of growing cotton and ripe fruit. The stimulus given to cotton- and fruit-growing in the southern part of the State revived immigration into that section, and henceforth it received a larger share of the incoming settlers than it had been receiving in the early 'fifties.

One of the great evils of American agriculture in the nineteenth century was the one-crop system, an evil which was particularly noticeable in Illinois in the 'fifties and 'sixties. Here many farmers raised the two staple crops, corn and wheat, on practically all of their arable land. When these crops failed, as happened in 1858, the farmers were in a bad way. With money scarce, it was difficult for the Illinois Central to collect from its purchasers, as we have seen. It was natural, therefore, that President Osborn should turn his attention to the problem of bringing about a more diversified system of farming.

The cultivation of the sugar-beet seemed to Osborn one means of solving the problem, at least for central and eastern Illinois, and in 1862 he began a campaign to induce farmers to plant beets instead of corn. He sent copies of a treatise on the sugar-beet by John M. Klippart to each member of the State Legislature and to many farmers in the State, as well as one hundred copies to the State Agricultural Society for distribution among its members.[23] Free transportation of all beets raised along the line of the road was promised.[24] Osborn made arrangements with the Germania Beet Sugar Company to establish a refinery on a large farm near Chatsworth which he owned personally; here 1500 acres were to be placed under beet cultivation as an experimental field.[25] The superintendent of the refining company went to Germany, where

---

[23] Osborn to Hoffman, February 11, 1863, "Osborn Letter Book," 1863–1865, M. O.; *Illinois Farmer*, VIII, 121.

[24] Osborn to William Miller, December 1, 1863, *ibid.*; *American Agriculturist*, XXII, 102.

[25] The letter book referred to in note 23 contains a great deal of information on Osborn's activities in promoting the cultivation of beets, cotton, flax, and other such commodities.

he secured the necessary machinery and 300 mechanics and laborers to operate the plant.[26] With an assured market for the product at good prices, many farmers took advantage of the opportunity offered them and planted beets in place of corn.[27]

At the same time sorghum culture became popular in Illinois, large quantities of land being devoted to its production, especially along the Chicago branch of the Illinois Central, and the sorghum mill soon became as ubiquitous in Illinois Central towns as the flour mill was in the wheat-growing district.[28] Osborn also sought to stimulate interest in the cultivation of flax and was successful in inducing many farmers on the branch line to take up flax culture.[29]

On his experimental farm at Chatsworth, Osborn also endeavored to show the farmers of the region what good management, crop rotation, and the use of fertilizers could do in increasing production and the profits of the soil. He was particularly interested in sheep-raising, and kept 1000 sheep on his farm.[30] It is interesting to note that Osborn's colleague and successor, J. M. Douglas, had a similar farm at Nora, in northern Illinois. Here he maintained a herd of pure-blooded shorthorn cattle which he had imported and of which he was extremely proud.[31] Both men were very much interested in farm problems, and hoped that their example in bringing in good stock and in maintaining model farms would have a good effect upon their neighbors.

President Osborn was most adept in the art of securing publicity for the activities of the Illinois Central in promoting agriculture. His efforts were never personal, and rarely did his name appear in the writeups. His policy was that which the Illinois Central had followed in the 'fifties — of keeping on friendly terms with the editors of agricultural papers. He furnished them with passes to enable them to travel free over the line of the road.

[26] *Prairie Farmer*, September 15, 1866; Cole, *op. cit.*, p. 381.
[27] *Sectional Maps* (1867), *passim*.
[28] *Prairie Farmer*, January 5, 1860. The pamphlet literature of the Illinois Central has many references to the beet-sugar industry and the sorghum mills.
[29] Osborn to Peter Sinclair, June 24, 1864, "Presidents Letters," 1864, box 48. See also *Sectional Maps*, p. 5.
[30] Osborn to Peter Sinclair, June 24, 1864, "Presidents Letters," 1864.
[31] Douglas to Osborn, November 12, 1866, and March 18, 1867, M. O.

When sending them these passes he would call their attention to some particular work which the Company was doing to promote agriculture and would suggest that they publish articles on these activities. He supplied them with material in the nature of pamphlets and reports of speeches, and filled his own letters to them with discussions of his policies.[32] The columns of the *Prairie Farmer*, the *Illinois Farmer*, the *Wisconsin Farmer*, the *Valley Farmer*, and such eastern periodicals as the *American Agriculturist* and the *Country Gentleman* were filled with items concerning the work of the Illinois Central in helping to promote the state fairs, in establishing the sugar-beet industry, in encouraging the growth of cotton and the production of fruit in southern Illinois, in stimulating the invention of farm machinery, in draining the wet lands, and in assisting its delinquent debtors to meet the payments on their land. Information concerning these activities was of course most valuable to the farmers of Illinois. Osborn was particularly successful in getting M. L. Dunlap, editor of the *Illinois Farmer* and contributing editor to the *Chicago Press and Tribune* (later the *Tribune*), to publish items concerning his agricultural promotion work, knowledge of which was thus widely disseminated among the people of the State. Dunlap was a farmer himself and could well appreciate the value of Osborn's work, and he was ready to assist him in every way possible.

From the date of his entrance into the Company, Osborn had been a powerful figure in its affairs. After he became President he kept his hands on everything: the financing, the operating departments, and particularly the Land Department. In order to supervise more closely the affairs of this department, Osborn determined to spend the major portion of his time in Illinois. He had a special car fitted up in which he and his family could live for weeks at a time while he was in Illinois.[33] He travelled continuously over the road investigating cases of non-payment, and persuading farmers to adopt his suggestions for the improvement of agriculture. His correspondence during these years was volumi-

---

[32] Osborn to J. H. and Luther Tucker, editors of the *Country Gentleman*, January 15, 1862; Osborn to N. J. Coleman, editor of the *Valley Farmer*, January 15, 1862, in "Osborn Letter Book," 1861–1862, M. O.

[33] Ferri Pisani, *Lettres sur les Etats-Unis D'Amérique* (Paris, 1862), pp. 336–337.

nous, and one can only be amazed at his broad grasp of detail, "his remarkable skill and executive ability, firm and unceasing devotion to the interests of the company, indomitable will and courage, and, above all, strict integrity of purpose." [34]

Osborn's activities in the interests of Illinois were appreciated by the editors of three of the more prominent agricultural papers in the Northwest. The *Illinois Farmer* commented upon the "commendable interest" which Osborn and other officials of the Illinois Central took in the introduction of new agricultural products, attributing their interest to a desire to forward the cause of agriculture, "to a personal love of it, and a desire to be generally useful." [35] "There is no enterprise in the state," declared the editor of this paper, "that has done so much to develop its resources as this road." [36] The *Prairie Farmer* spoke of the management of the Illinois Central as having won a "world-wide reputation for the liberality of its policy toward every agricultural interest. . . ." [37] The *Wisconsin Farmer*, in 1858, pointed to the liberality of the Illinois Central as an example for the Wisconsin roads to follow.[38] Somewhat later the same journal published an extremely favorable editorial on the Illinois Central which said, in part: [39]

We know of no railroad company in the United States whose example is so worthy of praise and imitation, as is that of the Illinois Central. By its liberal and far-seeing policy, its able managers . . . have really contributed more than any other one agency — perhaps more than any half dozen others — to the settlement, development and progress of the great state of Illinois. It promptly identifies itself with every movement that looks to the prosperity of the commonwealth and even originates ways and means for the promotion of that end. . . . To Messrs. Osborn and Arthur . . . we renew our cordial felicitations.

The Illinois Central's land grant had included a considerable quantity of fertile but wet lands which were situated for the most

[34] Ackerman, *Historical Sketch*, p. 68. See also Ferri Pisani, *op. cit.*, pp. 334 ff. Mr. Skeene, former Land Commissioner and intimate friend of President Osborn, in conversation with the writer, recalled many interesting details of the superior he so greatly admired.          [35] *Illinois Farmer*, VII, 363.

[36] *Ibid.*, VII, 90.
[37] *Prairie Farmer*, February 23, 1860.
[38] *Wisconsin Farmer* (1858), X, 208.
[39] *Wisconsin Farmer* (1865), XVII, 63.

part in eastern Illinois. The Company did not feel the necessity of draining its wet lands until the late 'fifties because it possessed sufficient dry land in central and eastern Illinois to meet the demands of incoming settlers. By 1859, however, when most of the dry lands had been taken up, attention was turned to the wet areas. The officials of the Land Department realized that settlers could do little with such lands until they were drained. In a dry year they might fare well, but otherwise their farming was certain to be a series of disasters. To secure a practical ditching machine the Illinois Central offered a prize of $250 for the implement which would best meet the needs of the region.[40] The prize was awarded, and a model of the machine was set up in the office of the Land Department.[41] This was helpful, but only the large land owners could afford such expensive machines, and consequently the problem of draining the wet areas was not solved. Osborn then induced the Illinois Central to undertake drainage in regions where it possessed considerable bodies of land, and a large sum was expended in 1863 in this work.[42] Somewhat later the Company cooperated with Solomon Sturges, one of the largest land owners in the State, in draining a tract of wet land in the vicinity of Gilman and Danforth, in Iroquois County. Here over 50 miles of ditching was dug and a considerable area of land was made available for farming.

Equally successful was the work of A. H. and G. W. Danforth. The Danforths were large owners of land in the Danville district, having purchased over 17,000 acres from the Government.[43] They bought from the Illinois Central at the minimum price of $6 an acre 10,000 acres additional, most of which needed draining.[44] The Danforths proceeded to lay out a town on the Illinois Central midway between Ashkum and Gilman, and the railroad established the new station of Danforth there to assist them.[45] Through their efforts a considerable number of immigrants came into the

[40] *Illinois Farmer*, VIII, 154; *Country Gentleman* (April 9, 1863), XXI, 241.
[41] Osborn to W. M. Phillips, October 17, 1863, "Presidents and Chairmans Letters," No. 18, box 48, 63rd St.
[42] *Annual Report*, 1863.
[43] Compiled from books of Danville land office, S. A. O.
[44] Computed from vol. 226, Land and Tax Commissioner's office.
[45] Ackerman, *Early Illinois Railroads*, p. 125; *Sectional Maps*, p. 68.

region and took up land. Within three years after the establishment of the new town, eighty farms had been laid out in the vicinity.[46] With the assistance of the new settlers, the Danforths endeavored to drain the district. They purchased a ditching machine and soon cut over 25 miles of ditches. A pond of 30 acres, where water always stood, was drained in 1866, and the entire area was broken up for crops in 1867. Altogether, a large tract of waste land was thus brought under cultivation. The Danforths' success served to stimulate others to follow their example, though slowly.[47]

The amount of capital necessary to drain large areas of land successfully was so great that the Illinois Central could do little more than make a start. Cooperation on the part of all land owners was necessary, and this could not be secured at that time. Notwithstanding the work of the Illinois Central, there were undrained swamp lands in eastern Illinois for years to come.

As a final means of selling its wet lands the Illinois Central reduced their price to $5.50 and then to $4 an acre, rates at which most of them were quickly taken up. In 1872 and 1873 the remaining lands in Kankakee, the most poorly drained county in eastern Illinois, were purchased by George Danforth.[48] The wet lands of Iroquois and Champaign Counties were also sold at reduced prices.

President Osborn watched with interest the changes which were taking place in agricultural machinery during the years with which we are dealing. Improved machinery meant that individual farmers could cultivate larger amounts of land and that they would have less idle, unimproved land than was normally the case, since in the past farmers had usually bought more land than they could use immediately. Osborn noted in 1864 that, whereas a few years previously a small farmer did not venture to plant more than 40 acres, the average being about 30, now, with improved machines, a man could take care of 60 or 70 acres of land in

---

[46] *Illinois Central Directory*, p. 45.

[47] *Prairie Farmer*, September 15, 1866.

[48] Danforth purchased 5300 acres for $5 and 1520 acres for $4 per acre. Daggy to J. M. Douglas, January 26, 1874, "Daggy Personal with officers I. C. R. R. Co.," 16th St.

crops.[49] During the Civil War, when man-power was scarce, the agricultural machinery which was developed enabled the North to produce ever-increasing amounts of corn and wheat with a diminishing labor supply. This was a source of much relief to Osborn. The wheat and corn planters and the cultivators which were brought on the market in 1863 and 1864 aided a great deal in replacing the men going to war. The reaper, of course, was not new, but its popularity grew rapidly in this period. The *Prairie Farmer* noted that 33,000 reapers were made for the trade in 1862 and 46,000 in 1863, and that over 70,000 were planned for 1864. As Illinois was the leading state in wheat production it seems fair to assume that a large number of these reapers was destined for farmers in that state.

Osborn was especially interested in the possibility of harnessing the steam engine to the plow. During the 'fifties continued improvements had been made upon the plow, but the task of breaking the tough prairie sod was still a slow and expensive operation and prevented the small farmer from making rapid progress in improving his land. The picture of the heavy breaking plow drawn by slow plodding oxen or by a number of laboring horses is enough to convince one of the difficulties of first bringing the land under cultivation. To encourage experiments with a steam plow the Illinois Central cooperated with the State Agricultural Society in offering a prize of $3000 for the invention and successful operation of a steam-driven plow. J. W. Fawkes, who had already experimented with such a machine, completed a model and took it to Illinois, where he exhibited it at Freeport and Chicago. The trials were only partially successful, but a tremendous amount of interest was shown in the exhibit and the judges felt justified in awarding a portion of the prize money to Fawkes.[50] The Illinois Central subsequently made a generous subscription to a "Steam Plow Manufactory."[51] These efforts, however, led to little result. More successful were the prizes offered for a ditching machine and a workable corn cutter and stacker.[52]

[49] Osborn to Heyworth, June 1, 1864, "Osborn Letter Book," 1863–1865, M. O.
[50] *Country Gentleman* (September 22, 1859), XIV, 193.
[51] Journal No. 7, Land Department, 16th St.
[52] *Illinois Farmer*, VIII, 154; *Country Gentleman* (April 9, 1863), XXI, 241.

The timely invention and development of practical farm machinery made possible the large-scale farming in Illinois which for a time probably surpassed anything of the kind in the United States. The low price of land in the early 'fifties had enabled men who planned to build up large farms to acquire great tracts of prairie soil. These large farms were most numerous in eastern Illinois, a region which was little settled prior to the coming of the Illinois Central Railroad. By 1870 there were 302 farms of 1000 acres or more in Illinois, of which 23 were in Vermillion County, 21 in McLean, 10 each in Iroquois, Christian, and Champaign Counties, and 9 in Shelby County.[53] Over one-half of the total number were in counties in which the Illinois Central had received land; in fact many had been bought from the railroad on the generous credit terms it offered. The first operations of breaking the prairie sod and fencing the land were slow and expensive, and in the 'fifties prevented most of these owners from carrying their operations far. In the following decade, with better prices, easier credit, and improved farm machinery, the era of large-scale farming reached its peak in Illinois.

One of the largest and most interesting of these great farms was Broadlands, owned by Michael Sullivant. Sullivant had purchased 80,000 acres in Champaign, Ford, Piatt, and Livingston Counties, the center of the corn belt, from the Government and the Illinois Central Railroad; 23,000 acres of his holdings were in one block in Champaign County. Employing a force of between one hundred and two hundred men, two hundred horses and mules, a large number of oxen, and a great amount of agricultural machinery, Sullivant proceeded to develop a farm on this tract. The entire area was fenced and subdivided into tracts of 640 acres or more; 1900 acres were planted to corn, 300 to winter wheat, and 40 to oats. In one year he was able to sell 22,000 bushels of corn after retaining a large amount for use on his farm. In addition to the production of crops, 5000 cattle and 4000 run-down government horses were pastured on the farm.[54] Sullivant soon got into

---

[53] *Ninth Census*, III, 349–350.
[54] *Chicago Weekly Democrat*, May 13, 1854; *Chicago Democratic Press*, March 6, 1855, quoting *Ohio Statesman*; *Prairie Farmer*, January 12, 1860; *Country Gentleman* (August 13, 1863), XXII, 105; *Wisconsin Farmer* (1866), XVIII, 93.

difficulties over payments due to the Illinois Central, and was finally forced to sell his estate to John T. Alexander, a wealthy cattleman and farmer of Morgan County, who continued to operate it on the same scale for some years.[55]

Sullivant then turned to a larger tract of 40,000 acres near Paxton which was still in his possession, and began putting it under cultivation. He commenced by planting 1000 acres of corn; within five years he had 18,000 acres in corn and 5000 in other crops. The yield of corn husked in one year was reported to be 450,000 bushels. The amount of farm machinery necessary to perform work on this large scale is almost staggering; 150 steel plows, 75 breaking plows, 142 cultivators, 45 corn planters, 25 gang-harrows, a ditching plow operated by 68 oxen and 8 men, an upright mower to clip the hedges, and numerous power shellers were employed; the motive power for the movable machinery was furnished by 350 mules, 50 horses, and 50 yoke of oxen.[56]

Alexander's management of Broadlands rivalled Sullivant's activities on his new farm. Additional land was acquired, so that the farm included 26,500 acres in 1869. It was maintained primarily as a stock farm, 4000 grazing cattle being kept on it in addition to 500 hogs; 150 acres were in grass, 400 in wheat, 140 in oats, 120 in rye, and 5000 in corn; to carry on operations on this large scale 160 men were employed, while 120 yoke of oxen and 100 head of horses and mules were worked. In 1869 the managers expected to clear from all operations a profit of $200,000.[57]

Both Sullivant and Alexander were attempting to apply modern methods of industry to farming by mechanizing operations and by carrying out the division of labor as far as possible. Tenant farming and crop sharing did not enter into their system. Their farms were the true forerunners of the highly mechanized farms of the Dakota and Kansas plains of today.

[55] Sullivant was reported to have sold Broadlands, including the stock, grain, hay, and farming implements, for nearly $500,000. *Prairie Farmer*, September 15, 1866.

[56] *Country Gentleman* (August 9, 1866), xxviii, 91, quoting *Cincinnati Inquirer*; *New England Farmer* (1867), i, 271; *Harpers Weekly*, September 23, 1871.

[57] *Prairie Farmer*, August 7, 1869; letter of C. L. Eaton, Alexander's agent, to Capt. J. Brown and Dr. H. C. Johns, August 27, 1866, in Illinois State Agricultural Society, *Transactions* (1870), vii, 135–136.

An equally interesting but less modern type of large-scale farm was E. E. Malhiot's 22,000 acre tract at Assumption, which has already been mentioned. Malhiot's plan seems to have been to pattern this colony partly after his plantation in the South and partly after the old Canadian seigniory. He found it difficult, however, to do this in Illinois, for the cheap lands and great opportunities for individual initiative caused the laborers to become dissatisfied. Instead of continuing as mere agricultural laborers or tenants, as Malhiot had planned, the French Canadians demanded the right to purchase the land. They finally secured this privilege, but in such a way that most of them were unable to acquire full title for many years. Moreover the land was not divided at once, but for the first few years was cultivated and managed as a unit. In response to the insistent demands of his tenants, Malhiot slowly turned the land over to them, although the estate was not completely settled for more than twenty years.[58]

Although Malhiot failed to adapt the Canadian seigniory to Illinois conditions, other capitalist-farmers were able to introduce tenant farming on a large scale. Indeed, in the future tenant farming was to be more important than the large-scale farming operations of such men as Sullivant and Alexander. The explanation for this development is that many capitalists who secured large blocks of land desired to retain their land though not to operate it themselves. This made tenant farming necessary. Frequently, in the beginning, the owner would open up the land, manage operations for a few years, and slowly turn the land over to the laborers, who would thus become his tenants.

Isaac and Jesse Funk, whose land holdings in McLean County, central Illinois, exceeded 30,000 acres, were among the first to introduce tenant farming in that region. These cattle kings were primarily interested in buying, fattening, and selling cattle and in raising sheep, hogs, and draft animals. Isaac Funk, who alone owned over 25,000 acres of rich land, had 1600 cattle, 500 sheep,

[58] Malhiot to Daggy, April 7, 1873; Abbott to Daggy, May 29, 1874; Trottier to Daggy, April 25, 1876; Paine to Daggy, March 24, 1879, 16th St.

500 hogs, and 300 horses and mules on his farm in 1861.[59] In 1863 he had 3000 acres in corn, besides smaller amounts in other grains.[60] Much of his land was rented to tenants on shares. If the tenant furnished his own tools he paid two-fifths of his produce as rent, but if Funk provided the tools the crop was divided equally between tenant and landlord. Both brothers were successful in their farming and cattle operations, but to Isaac came the greater profits. At his death in 1865 his estate was valued at $2,000,000, no small fortune to be built up in frontier Illinois.[61] The example of the Funks in introducing tenant farming in McLean County was widely followed by other large landholders. In 1880, the first year for which we have statistics on tenant farming, 36 per cent of the farms in that county were being operated by tenants.[62]

Perhaps the greatest impetus to tenant farming in the Middle West was given by William Scully, who owned 200,000 acres of land in the states of Kansas, Nebraska, Missouri, and Illinois. Scully bought 46,000 acres in Logan, Sangamon, Grundy, and Livingston Counties, Illinois, laid them out in tracts of 160 acres, and invited fellow Irishmen to settle upon them or made arrangements with squatters already upon them to become his tenants. Although part of the land in Illinois was subsequently sold, 30,000 acres were retained by the Scully family and have been farmed by tenants ever since on a cash basis. Scully's extensive holdings and his peculiar type of lease aroused much opposition in Illinois, and led to legislation directed against absentee ownership.[63] Although the legislation had little actual effect, it indicated the growing resentment at the concentration of land ownership.

The last of the larger capitalist-farmers to be mentioned here is Jacob Strawn, who owned and operated, either through tenants or laborers, over 20,000 acres in central Illinois. Like the Funks and

[59] *New York Tribune*, July 30, 1861.    [60] *American Agriculturist*, XXII, 263.

[61] *New York Tribune*, July 30, 1861; L. H. Kerrick, "Life and Character of Isaac Funk," McLean County Historical Society, *Transactions* (1903), II, 501–505.

[62] Computed from *Tenth Census.*

[63] *Illinois Central Magazine* (April, 1931), XX, 25–26; N. S. B. Gras, *History of Agriculture in Europe and America* (New York, 1925), pp. 269–272; Bogart and Thompson, *The Industrial State, 1870–1893* (*Centennial History of Illinois*, vol. IV, Springfield, 1920), pp. 220–221.

Alexander, Strawn was primarily interested in the cattle trade, but to provide grain for his stock he had to engage in large-scale farming. His chief grain crop was corn, to which he had planted 7000 acres in two fields.[64]

It should be emphasized that large-scale farming in Illinois was the exception, not the rule, and this was particularly true of these great farms of 20,000 or more acres. Usually the large farms did not exceed 4000 to 6000 acres. The most publicized of all the farms in this group was that of Benjamin F. Harris, another of the cattle kings of Illinois. The extraordinary size of Harris's cattle, which were offered to packers at Chicago and in eastern cities, won wide fame for him and led to the publication of frequent items on his farm and cattle in the agricultural journals and newspapers. Harris's chief interest was the fattening of cattle for market. The largest part of his 4000 acre farm at Urbana in the Grand Prairie was used for pasture, but grain crops were raised on a large scale. In 1855 Harris had 700 acres in corn, which averaged 65 bushels to the acre, besides smaller areas in oats and wheat.[65]

Another interesting farm in this group was that of Lemuel Milk of Chebanse. On a farm of 5364 acres Milk had 2500 acres in timothy, 1000 acres in other crops, and 40 acres in orchard. He pastured 3000 sheep, 1500 to 2000 cattle, and 1200 hogs.[66]

Less spectacular than the great farms of 4000 acres and over, but nevertheless a new phenomenon of interest to many people moving into the Prairie State, were the farms ranging in size from 1000 to 4000 acres. It seems probable that of the 302 farms in Illinois in 1870 of 1000 acres and over, the largest number was in this group. The operations of two individuals in this group

---

[64] *Illinois State Register*, March 2, 1854, quoting the *Chicago Democratic Press*; *Country Gentleman* (September 21, 1854), IV, 184; Prairie Farmer (1854), XIV, 427–430; *New York Tribune*, clipped in *Mining Register and Pottsville Emporium*, June 23, 1855.

[65] *Prairie Farmer* (1855), XV, 203; *Albany Knickerbocker*, clipped in *Freeport Bulletin*, May 29, 1856; *Illinois State Register*, March 20, 1856; *Chicago Press*, clipped in the *Horticulturist* (1856), XI, 240; Ferguson, *America by River and Rail*, pp. 376–377; Caird, *op. cit.*, p. 74; Harris, "Autobiography of Benjamin Franklin Harris," Illinois State Historical Society, *Transactions* (1923), pp. 72–101.

[66] *Sectional Maps*, p. 66.

are interesting because of the emphasis they placed on stock improvement.

On a farm of 2250 acres in Sangamon County, James N. Brown had 480 acres in corn, 120 in wheat and oats, 150 in grass, and 250 in timber. The remainder of the farm was in pasture on which were kept 350 sheep, 50 cows, 500 steers, and from 200 to 300 hogs. Brown was a thorough believer in keeping the best stock and following careful breeding methods. Shorthorns were his favorite breed, and to improve the strain he imported registered bulls from England.[67] He was one of the chief promoters of the Illinois Stock Importing Association, being its first president. Through the efforts of this organization there were purchased in 1857 in England and brought to Illinois 27 blooded cattle, which sold for as high as $3025, and in addition, a larger number of breeding sheep, hogs, and horses.[68]

Brown's activities were closely paralleled by the operations of John Wentworth at his Summit Farm in Cook County. This farm included 2500 acres, most of which were used for pasture and the raising of grasses for cattle. Wentworth was the chief promoter of the Illinois Breeding Association, Summit Farm being its headquarters. Pure-blooded Devon, Durham, and Shorthorn cattle, Merino sheep, and Suffolk hogs were imported and used to establish a breeding business. By 1863 there were on this farm 250 cattle, 200 sheep, 18 sows, 3 boars, and 60 horses, most of which were used for breeding purposes.[69] Farmers throughout the Northwest purchased stock from this farm.[70]

Sheep-raising in the Northwest had been branded as unprofitable by Horace Greeley, but James McConnell of Springfield proved that sheep could be raised successfully in Illinois. On his farm McConnell pastured between 17,000 and 21,000 sheep, and

[67] *Prairie Farmer*, January 3, 1856, quoting *Illinois State Journal*; Caird, *op. cit.*, pp. 59–61.

[68] An account of the activities of this Association may be found in the Illinois State Agricultural Society, *Transactions*, III, 301–304.

[69] *Boston Cultivator* clipped in *Country Gentleman* (August 6, 1863), XXII, 92–93.

[70] The *Prairie Farmer* frequently mentions sales of pure-blooded stock by the Illinois Breeding Association. See *ibid.*, January 1, July 23, 1857, February 2 and June 14, 1860.

was considered the greatest sheep-raiser in the country. He imported pure Merino rams from Germany and Spain to improve his flock.[71] Sir James Caird in his travel account gives considerable attention to this farm.[72]

Perhaps enough detail has been given to indicate the grand scale on which these capitalist-farmers were carrying on their activities in Illinois in the 'fifties and 'sixties. Their spectacular operations did much to influence Illinois agriculture; they opened up neglected sections of Illinois and hastened the agricultural development of the State. Generally they were the first to introduce new machinery and by extensive use helped to popularize such improvements. They did much to establish the one-crop system in the corn belt, as corn was necessary for the cattle trade, in which most of them were engaged. They imported pure-bred stock from England and the Continent, which the small farmer, with his meager capital, was unable to do. They were able to ditch and drain large areas of wet land, which the State and counties refused to develop and which it did not pay farmers operating 160 acre units to acquire. In many cases these large farms had a higher yield of corn and wheat per acre than the average, the result of better and more scientific methods.

It may be noted in passing that in spite of the somewhat alarming development of large-scale farming the average size of Illinois farms was declining in the period from 1850 to 1870. Thus the average size in 1850 was 158 acres, in 1860 146 acres, and in 1870 128 acres.[73] As we have already seen, it was the deliberate policy of the Illinois Central to persuade its purchasers to reduce the size of their farms if they were unable to meet their payments. These figures show that in general farmers were selling off those portions of their farms which they were unable to use to the best advantage.

The activities of the Illinois Central in popularizing the State, stimulating immigration, aiding agriculture, and developing markets, together with the high prices for agricultural products,

[71] *Illinois State Register*, June 29, 1854; *Country Gentleman* (December 11, 1856), VIII, 384.
[72] Caird, *op. cit.*, pp. 62–64.
[73] *Ninth Census*, III, 341.

the development and extensive use of farm machinery, and the large-scale farming by capitalist-farmers, led to a big increase in the number of farms and the amount of land under cultivation. Thus in the decade of the 'fifties 67,102 new farms were opened up in the State and 8,056,829 acres of land were first brought under cultivation.[74] Some idea of the contribution of the Illinois Central to this achievement may be gathered from the following estimates of the increase in the acreage under wheat and corn along its line during the years 1855 to 1859.[75]

NUMBER OF ACRES UNDER CULTIVATION

| | Wheat | | | Corn | | |
|---|---|---|---|---|---|---|
| | 1855 | 1858 | 1859 | 1855 | 1858 | 1859 |
| Dunleith to Sando-val .......... | 442,390 | 816,750 | 846,030 | 567,060 | 786,210 | 1,100,180 |
| Chicago to Cairo .. | 160,840 | 393,320 | 473,250 | 595,510 | 692,200 | 1,052,940 |

This tremendous expansion made Illinois the leading state in wheat and corn production by 1860.

Throughout the 'sixties Illinois maintained the position it had won during the previous decade. The number of new farms in the State increased by 59,000 and the number of acres under cultivation by 6,200,000. The corn crop increased from 115,000,000 bushels in 1859 to 201,000,000 in 1870. As this grain was not readily marketable, and in proportion to its bulk brought much less than wheat, the farmers found it more profitable to feed it to cattle and hogs than to ship it to market. This resulted in a proportionate though slower increase in the number of cattle and hogs in Illinois. By 1870 this State had definitely taken the lead in hog production and was second only to Texas in the beef-cattle industry. The production of wheat jumped from 24,000,000 bushels in 1860 to 33,000,000 in 1864,[76] the banner year for Illinois agri-

---

[74] Taken from the *Census Reports*, 1850, 1860.

[75] This table is taken from *Guide to the Illinois Central Railroad Lands* (1859), pp. 56–59. Though the statistics are not exact, they may be taken as an indication of the trend of agriculture during these years. It will be noticed that whereas the area under wheat production increased very little in the years 1858 to 1859, the area under corn during the same period increased tremendously. The State was already beginning to turn from wheat to corn as the surer and safer crop.

[76] Statistics taken from the *Census Reports* for 1860 and 1870 and the *Annual Reports* of the United States Commissioner of Agriculture for 1864 and 1870.

culture. In this year the State raised one-fifth of the entire wheat crop of the country.

The significance of this rapid expansion in wheat production has been pointed out elsewhere. During the Civil War England suffered from poor harvests and became more and more dependent on its imports from the United States. The export surplus of wheat, which the North controlled, greatly strengthened the financial and diplomatic position of that section. These wheat exports of the 'sixties marked the beginning of the great outpouring of American agricultural produce to Europe which has made such marked changes in the economic life of many of the European countries.

# CHAPTER XIV

## THE GRANGER PERIOD AND THE CLOSING ACTIVITIES OF THE LAND DEPARTMENT

UNTIL 1870 the Illinois Central was undoubtedly the most popular railroad in Illinois. Its officials had made constant efforts to retain the good will of politicians and editors of newspapers, particularly farm journals;[1] and by considerate treatment of its delinquent purchasers and readiness to help further the agricultural and industrial development of the State, the Company had succeeded in winning, to a substantial degree, the good opinion of the people of Illinois. Nevertheless, in the Granger period, when railroads became the target of bitter criticism on the part of the western farmer, the Illinois Central did not escape, and some of its policies, which in the 'fifties and 'sixties had won general approval, became the cause of bitter complaint. Numerous violations of the spirit and letter of the Company's charter had occurred, the fault of the purchasers of the railroad's grant rather than of the railroad itself, and the Legislature was now called upon to force the Illinois Central to carry out its agreement with the people of Illinois.

In the first place, that section of the charter which reserved the lands from taxation until the purchasers of those lands had received their patents from the Company,[2] although it caused little comment at the time the charter was drawn up, later led to much bitter feeling. By this provision, purchasers' lands were exempt from taxation until the final payment had been made, a feature which did not help the Company in making its collections but rather encouraged delay in payments. There were innumerable small holdings which had been under contract for years and which, under this provision, had been exempt from taxes. In handling such cases the Company was in a dilemma. If payments were strictly required, or if a policy of cancellation were carried out on a wide scale, an anti-rent war might ensue. On the other hand, if

[1] Osborn to William Tracy, October 10, 1862, "Osborn Official Letter Book," 1862–1865, box 48, 63rd St. archives.      [2] *Charter*, p. 30.

strict measures were not employed, purchasers would be lax in their payments, titles would not be acquired, and the towns and counties would resent the fact that such lands were untaxable. In either case, on account of the growing anti-monopoly and Granger feeling in the State, the Illinois Central could expect little public sympathy. Some of the contracts were allowed to run on interminably, and old residents, or people who had purchased their land from other large land owners, were forced to see purchasers of Illinois Central land escape taxation year after year. In some cases as much as one-third of the total area of a county was untaxable. As late as 1870, twenty years after the Illinois Central grant had been made, there still remained undeeded a million acres,[3] a large portion of which was in the southern counties.

Another unfortunate circumstance which involved an even more flagrant violation of the spirit of the charter was the failure to have deeds recorded when the title was passed. In the bitterness over this situation the Company was accused of "fraudulently and unlawfully"[4] agreeing with the purchasers. In the bitterness over this situation the Company was accused of "fraudulently and unlawfully" agreeing with the purchasers "that it would execute a written agreement to convey" some evidence of title, "upon the express contract and understanding that the purchasers should pay the purchase money, less a few dollars, so as to exempt the lands from the payment of state, county, and municipal taxes. . . ." The Company of course denied the accusation, with apparent justice.[5] It had nothing to gain but the ill-will of the people of Illinois by making such an agreement with its purchasers, and, on the other hand, it was to its own interest to have the contracts paid up in full when due, the title given, and the transaction closed.

The fact of the matter was that the Illinois Central was required to inform the State Auditor of all deed transactions, but was not required to inform the county officers. A large number of deeds had been issued which had been reported to the State Auditor but not to the county courts. As all these transactions were carefully

---

[3] *Annual Report*, 1870.     [4] *Journal of the Senate*, 1873, p. 105.

[5] The only reason why the railroad might have made such promises would be to give an additional inducement to purchasers.

recorded in separate books in Springfield, it would have been no great task for county officers to ascertain exactly what lands had been deeded.[6] This they failed to do, and not until the last decade of the century were steps taken to record the deeds and make the lands taxable. At that late period, the last land commissioner, Edward P. Skeene, prepared lists of all the lands which had been conveyed by the Company in each county and turned them over to the local officials to enable them to discover what persons were unlawfully avoiding taxes.[7]

In 1850 the people of Illinois had looked upon the central railroad as a means of opening up and settling regions previously neglected. They wanted the railroad lands, as well as the government lands, to be sold as quickly as possible in order that they might be taxed and that large areas of uncultivated land might not retard the development of the State. Under the leadership of John S. Wright, attempts were made to require immediate sale of the Illinois Central lands. As a result, a provision was included in the charter which reads as follows: [8] "All lands remaining unsold at the expiration of ten years after the completion of said road and branches, shall be offered at public sale, annually, until the whole is disposed of. . . ." This was interpreted to mean that in 1866 the Company was required to offer all its unsold lands at public auction for any price they might bring. The interval of ten years allowed the railroad, in which to dispose of its lands as it pleased, was displeasing to the forces opposed to land monopoly in Illinois, and the fear of legislation providing for forced sales of the lands at auction was ever before the officials of the road. In 1854 an attempt was made to force through the Illinois Legislature a bill which would require the sale of one-fifteenth of the lands each year and would deny to the Illinois Central the right to hold lands after the expiration of the fifteenth year. The measure won much popularity, and was defeated by only one vote after a violent debate and after strenuous efforts had been exerted by lobbyists in behalf of the railroad.[9]

[6] These books are still retained in the Public Auditor's office.
[7] Mr. Skeene was of much assistance to the writer in clearing up this matter.
[8] *Charter*, p. 27.
[9] Telegram, Joy to Burrall, February 27, 1854; letter of same to same, February 28, 1854, M. O.

Nevertheless, the feeling persisted that the lands should be disposed of as quickly as possible, and when it was seen that the Company had no intention of carrying out that provision in its charter which required annual auctions after 1866, steps were taken to force it to do so. In January, 1867, a resolution was adopted by the State Legislature, instructing the Judiciary Committee to ascertain what legislation was necessary to enforce this provision of the charter.[10] This second attempt was likewise defeated by the railroad officials, but was the cause of much anxiety and foreshadowed trouble in the near future.[11]

At the height of the Granger period, sentiment against the Illinois Central reached its climax and led to the passage of two acts concerning the lands of the Company. The first of these, approved March 30, 1872, provided that "Illinois Central Railroad lands and lots shall be taxable from and after the time the last payment becomes due." [12] This act, if enforced, would have rendered taxable lands on which payments had been extended, and would have thereby corrected one of the worst evils of the situation. The second measure was designed to force the Company to sell its remaining lands at auction. As the first move, the Attorney-General applied to the Supreme Court for a writ of mandamus for the purpose of forcing the railroad to carry out Section 17 of the charter. In reply, the court refused the mandamus, maintaining that further legislation was required to prescribe the terms and mode of conducting the sale.[13] At the next meeting of the Legislature the attack was resumed. A resolution was passed unanimously in the Senate asking the Governor what steps had been taken to force sales, and when his reply was returned, embodying the reports of the Attorney-General and the Supreme Court, it was ordered to be printed for distribution.[14] Somewhat later Thomas Casey, Senator from southern Illinois and a resident of Jefferson County, introduced in the upper House Senate Bill

[10] *New York Tribune*, January 14, 1867.

[11] J. M. Douglas to Osborn, February 11, 17, 1867, Ward's office.

[12] *Revised Statutes of Illinois*, 1874, p. 868. These two laws are found in *Charter*, 59–64.

[13] *Journal of the Senate*, 1873, p. 107.

[14] *Ibid.*, pp. 66, 104–107, 108.

No. 175, entitled "An Act to compel the trustees of the lands granted to the Illinois Central Railroad Company to execute their trust," or as it was more commonly called, the Casey Bill.[15] It was referred to the Judiciary Committee which reported favorably on it, and after some little opposition was passed unanimously by the Senate.[16] From there it went to the House, where it likewise passed unanimously and was signed by the Governor on March 28, 1873.[17] As finally passed, the act provided that the Illinois Central should offer at public sale in each county all the lands therein located twice a year till all had been sold; any bid of $2 or over was to be accepted; authority was given to the Attorney-General and the Supreme Court to enforce the act by issuing a writ of mandamus for that purpose.[18]

The State commenced action in 1874 by bringing suit against the trustees of the Illinois Central to compel them to sell the residue of the lands. The case went to the Supreme Court, which, speaking through Chief Justice Sidney Breese, handed down a decision favorable to the Company. The court held that a writ of mandamus was not a writ of right demandable by the State but that its issue was discretionary with the courts, acting upon the facts in the case, and that the facts in the present case did not warrant the issue of a peremptory mandamus to compel sales. The court added, however, that a bill in chancery might be brought which, if properly framed, would bring to light all collusive transactions in the future and compel the corporation to call in all deferred payments, close the contracts, and thus render the lands taxable.[19] Apparently this advice was lost, for no further action was taken to force the sale of the Illinois Central lands during the

---

[15] *Ibid.*, p. 181. Peculiarly enough, Casey was senior partner of a firm which was acting as land agent for the Illinois Central around Mt. Vernon. Five years later Daggy was urging Casey to organize a land company to take over the remaining lands of the railroad. The latter was interested and attempted to do so but was unsuccessful. Daggy to Casey and Wilson, July 27, 1878, "Land Dept., 1874," 16th St.; Casey to Daggy, September 22, 1878, box, "Land Dept., Misc. Corr., 1871–1895," *ibid.*

[16] *Journal of the Senate*, 1873, pp. 189, 231, 233, 263, 302.

[17] *Journal of the House*, 1873, p. 443; John Newell to William Tracy, March 29, 1873, Ward's office.

[18] *Revised Statutes of Illinois*, 1874, pp. 910–911.

[19] 72 *Illinois Reports*, 212–217.

'seventies. The officials of the road were delighted at such a satisfactory ending, and henceforth worried little about promoting sales.[20]

There were a number of factors which made if difficult for the Illinois Central to dispose of the 500,000 acres of its land still unsold in 1870. For one thing, competition for immigrants among western states, territories, railroads, and land companies was becoming keener. By the opening of the 'seventies, at least twenty-two states and territories had undertaken immigration promotion work and the trans-Mississippi railroads had their immigration campaigns well under way. The income of these roads, many of which had received larger land grants than had come to the Illinois Central, and whose lines were built through territory more undeveloped than eastern Illinois was in 1850, depended almost entirely upon their ability to settle their grants; consequently the competition among them for immigrants became very keen.

The immigration work of the trans-Mississippi railroads followed very closely the lines already laid down by the Illinois Central; in fact numerous requests came to the officials of the Land Department of the latter road asking for assistance in organizing the land departments of the new roads, and for advice as to the best methods of stimulating immigration. Among the railroads which sought assistance from the Illinois Central were the Vicksport, Shreveport, and Texas, the Kansas Pacific, the Vicksport, Pensacola, and Ship Island, the Memphis and Kansas City, the St. Louis and Iron Mountain, the Atlantic and Pacific, the Burlington and Missouri River, the Texas and Pacific, and the North Wisconsin.[21] Some of these railroads practically copied the

[20] John Newell to Wm. Tracy, April 15, 1874; J. M. Douglas to Osborn, October 6, 16, 1874, Ward's office.

[21] J. N. Perkins to Wilson, June 16, 1857, "J. N. Perkins, Treasurer," No. 12, box 48, introducing Mr. Young, President of the Vicksburg, Shreveport, and Texas Railroad; John P. Devereaux, Land Commissioner of the Kansas Pacific, to J. B. Calhoun, December 9, 1871; J. C. England, Land Commissioner of the Vicksburg, Pensacola & Ship Island R. R., to Daggy, April 11, 1872; W. G. Ford, President of the Memphis & Kansas City R. R., to Daggy, February 29, 1872; Jnos. Tildeskey to Daggy, November 7, 1872, asking for various forms to be given to Mr. Longhborough, Land Commissioner of the St. Louis and Iron Mountain R. R.; A. L. Deane, Deputy Land Commissioner of the Atlantic & Pacific R. R., to Land Commissioner, I. C. R. R., October 18, 1873; A. E. Touzalin of the Burlington and Missouri River

advertising literature of the Illinois Central, and many of them adopted the liberal credit terms and the "required improvements" plan of that road. The trans-Mississippi railroads, following the example of the Illinois Central, sent agents to the northern European countries who duplicated on a larger scale the work of Malmborg in Norway and Sweden, advertised widely in the newspapers and periodicals of the United States, and flooded the regions from which emigration was flowing with circulars, pamphlets, and other advertising literature.

Two of the trans-Mississippi roads which were later incorporated into the Chicago, Burlington, and Quincy even invaded Illinois in their advertising campaigns.[22] The Burlington and Missouri River Railroad had thirty-five local agents in the State, some of whom were located at Illinois Central towns such as Bloomington, Decatur, Urbana, Cairo, Centralia, Carbondale, and Galena. Their agents worked to stir up dissatisfaction with Illinois and to arouse interest in the regions in which their lands were located.[23] Such activities bear witness to the fact that Illinois was now considered an important emigration state, as the eastern states had previously been. The people who had been brought to Illinois by the efforts of the Illinois Central were now being importuned by other railroads to go yet farther west and to take up cheaper lands.

An example of the results of these activities is the movement of Germans from Will County. It will be remembered that the Illinois Central had been successful in colonizing a large number of Germans on its lands near Monee and Peotone in this county. But when the Kansas Pacific and the Santa Fe Railroads began to make known the advantages of their lands, a number of these Germans were induced to leave Illinois and to commence farming

R. R., to Daggy, November 23, 1873; W. H. Dewels to Daggy, October 3, 1876; Wm. Mahl of the Texas & Pacific R. R., to Daggy, August 14, 1873; Wm. H. Phipps, acting Land Commissioner of the North Wisconsin R. R., to Daggy, January 22, 1877, box, "Land Dept., Misc. Corr., 1871–1895," 16th St.

[22] See advertisement of the Hannibal & St. Joseph R. R. Co. in *Illinois State Journal*, August 19, 1859.

[23] In Harvard College Library there are three large volumes of advertising matter, blank forms, and newspaper clippings published or concerned with the Land Department of the Burlington and Missouri River, entitled "Railroads in Nebraska."

anew in Kansas.[24] Indeed, in 1874 Illinois was furnishing almost four times as many purchasers of land for the Santa Fe road as any other state and more than all the foreign countries together.[25]

The success which the trans-Mississippi railroads achieved in advertising for settlers in Illinois was alarming to the Illinois Central and to other groups interested in the continued growth of the State. By 1880 a total of 358,000 natives of Illinois had emigrated and settled in the four states of Missouri, Iowa, Kansas, and Nebraska,[26] besides thousands who had resided temporarily in Illinois and had then resumed their westward trek. With nearly 300,000 acres of its land still unsold and 16,000,000 acres of unimproved land in the State, the Illinois Central could not afford to remain inactive while such a heavy emigration was taking place.[27]

This movement of population from Illinois to the trans-Mississippi West was due not only to railroad and state emigration activities but also to the existence of free land available to all citizens under the provisions of the Homestead Law. This act, passed in 1862 after a long and bitter struggle, provided for the granting of free homesteads of 160 acres to citizens who had resided on the quarter section for a period of five years.[28] During the struggle over this measure, one of the major arguments presented by its opponents was the depressing effect which it would have upon the land sales of the land grant railroads.[29] How effec-

[24] Emil Mannhardt in *Deutsch-Amerikanische Geschichtsblätter* (1902), vol. II, No. 1, pp. 33–39; pamphlet, *Neustes von Kansas und seinen Hülfsquellen* (Hamburg, 1881), p. 41.

[25] Glenn Danford Bradley, *The Story of the Santa Fe* (Boston, 1920), p. 124. Ch. v, "Colonizing the Prairies," contains a good discussion of the colonization work of this road.

[26] *Tenth Census*, I, 480.

[27] A local agent of the Illinois Central became much disturbed about the emigration from southern Illinois to Nebraska. Accordingly, he determined to tell the "truth" about that state and its land agents and thus to check the emigration. He prepared an article to be published in German, English, and Polish papers in which he recounted the sad experiences of six Polish families who had been induced to go to Nebraska. In this tale of woe, they were swindled by a land agent, overtaken by a distressful epidemic and suffered terrible hardships until they returned to Illinois. The article also pointed out that in Nebraska contracts were arbitrarily cancelled if payments were not made when due. Letter of Klupp to Daggy, April 23, 1879, and an undated letter of February, 1879, box, "Land Dept., Misc. Corr., 1871–1895," 16th St.

[28] 12 *U. S. Stat.*, 392–393.

[29] Hibbard, *History of the Public Land Policies*, p. 368.

tive homestead competition was in reducing the sales of the Illinois Central is difficult to determine.

A number of important restrictions were incorporated into the Homestead Law before it was passed which reduced its immediate effect to an important degree. In the first place, the law applied only to surveyed lands; secondly, only 80-acre homesteads were permitted within the area reserved for the double minimum price along the land grant railroads; finally, there was the five-year provision, which was very unsatisfactory to many settlers, who would be on the move again before that period was up, and would thus lose the benefit of any improvements they might have made on the homestead unless they took advantage of the commutation privilege and purchased their quarter section, after six months, for $1.25 an acre.

There were a number of other considerations which made railroad lands more attractive to settlers than government lands available for homesteads. These latter lands were usually more than 15 miles from railroads, as the even sections within this distance from railroads were generally held by the transportation companies and the odd sections were owned by speculators. This was true of Illinois in the 'fifties, and became true of the trans-Mississippi states slightly later. Not infrequently, even beyond the indemnity areas, the best lands were in the hands of speculators and only the poorer tracts were open to homestead. Long distances from lines of communication meant high costs for transporting grain to market and consequently low net returns. In the second place, the liberal credit terms offered by railroads partly offset the attraction of free lands offered by the Government. For an initial payment of $40 a settler could secure possession of 160 acres of Northern Pacific Land.[30] This payment was only $30 more than the fee for entering a homestead.[31] Moreover, railroads generally placed no restriction on the amount of land sold to actual settlers, except that of required cultivation, whereas an individual could only homestead 160 acres of land held for the mini-

---

[30] James B. Hedges, "The Colonization Work of the Northern Pacific Railroad," *Mississippi Valley Historical Review* (December, 1926), XIII, 321.

[31] 12 *U. S. Stat.*, pp. 392-393.

mum price and 80 acres held for the double minimum. In semi-arid regions, 160 acres was too small a unit to be farmed profitably and there was much dissatisfaction at this limitation. Finally, railroad lands could be witheld from taxation longer than government lands.

The Illinois Central lands, in addition to possessing these advantages, had other features which made them even more attractive. As the Government possessed practically no lands in Illinois, settlers who were drawn to that state for some special reason had no alternative but to purchase from the railroad or from some other private holder. The fact that Illinois Central lands were unsurpassed in fertility, were easier to bring under cultivation than the timber lands of northern Michigan and Wisconsin, and were more profitable to farm than the semi-arid lands of Kansas, Nebraska, and the Dakotas made them especially attractive to immigrants. The desire to settle among friends and fellow-countrymen was an important consideration with many in inducing them to settle in Illinois instead of going father west, where free lands could be obtained but where population was sparse and educational and religious facilities rare. The Illinois Central lands, being nearer to eastern markets, had a distinct advantage in freight rates. A further advantage was given by the Company itself, which allowed substantial reductions in freight rates to its purchasers. Combined, these factors tended to diminish the effect which the Homestead Law had upon the sale of Illinois Central land.

It is apparent that free homesteads were not considered by the officials of the Illinois Central as important as the sales of rival land companies and railroads. Not a reference to the Homestead Law and its effects is to be found in the correspondence of its officials, but constant mention is made in the 'sixties and 'seventies of the activities of the trans-Mississippi railroads. Furthermore, the period of its most active sales to actual settlers began in 1863, the year the Homestead Law went into effect, and continued thereafter until 1868. In these years over one-half of the Company's grant was sold to 18,000 purchasers at annual average prices of $10 to $12 an acre.

Nevertheless, it does not seem unfair to assume that had the Homestead Law not been in effect the land sales of the Illinois Central in both the 'sixties and 'seventies would have been greater and even more profitable than they were. The competition of the trans-Mississippi railroads in disposing of their lands was without doubt more effective in diminishing the sales of the Illinois Central, but the competition of free lands cannot be disregarded. The ill success of the Illinois Central in disposing of its southern lands may have been partly due to Homestead competition but here, too, the western railroads were a more important factor. These southern Illinois lands, being covered with timber, were more expensive to bring under cultivation than the prairies of Iowa, Nebraska, Kansas, and Minnesota. With or without the Homestead Law settlers would have sought the more fertile prairies farther west rather than the wooded slopes of Egypt. The railroads popularized the prairies and plains of the trans-Mississippi West, and they, rather than the Homestead Law, must be regarded as the chief cause of the slow sales of Illinois Central land after 1870.

During the early 'seventies, when the threat of forced sales was hanging over it, the Illinois Central made strenuous efforts to dispose of its lands as rapidly as possible within the minimum prices established by the mortgage. Some of its officials favored reserving the lands for higher prices, but Osborn, Foster, Redmond, and Daggy realized that such action would be most unwise. In 1871, when unfriendly feeling towards the Company had accumulated sufficiently to make it certain that in the near future legislation requiring immediate sales would be enacted, the Land Department determined to forestall such action by holding auctions on its own terms. Accordingly advertisements in the newspapers and large handbills appeared announcing that such auctions would be held at Pana, Decatur, Maroa, El Paso, Wapella, Wenona, Kappa, and Mendota, at which all of the unsold lands between Pana and Mendota would be offered. The results obtained from these auctions were rather meager, an average of only $5.47 being received for the 5145 acres sold. Nevertheless, in the following year another auction was held at Kankakee, where all the vacant lands in the vicinity, over 9000 acres, were offered at a minimum valuation. This time the results were even less encouraging; only 760 acres were bought at the established price and the remainder were sold at private sale for as low as $4 an acre. Notwithstanding these results, pressure on the Company became so great that in 1873 it made another attempt to sell its lands at auction. At four towns in Jo Daviess and Stephenson Counties the 7000 acres remaining in that region were offered, of which but 1344 were taken for an average of $5.24 per acre.[32] Ten years later, in 1882, auctions were again attempted, but with even less success. To advertise an auction held in Effingham County $775 was spent, but the returns did not justify the expenditure. A total of 6722 acres was sold for an average of $2.63 an acre and some of the land sold for as low as $2.14. The auctions were well attended, but there was practically no competition in bidding.[33] Obviously, with such low prices prevailing the Illinois Central did not feel warranted in offering at auction its large amount of southern lands which had been less picked over than these more northern lands. Auctions brought no better results to the Illinois Central than they had to the Government twenty or thirty years earlier when it had attempted to dispose of its lands in this way.

Prior to 1870, the continued success of the Illinois Central in avoiding unfavorable legislation had made the officials of the Land Department somewhat over-confident, and they had made no serious effort to dispose of all the lands within the limited time allowed by the charter. The advertising appropriations had been gradually cut down from $16,251 in 1867 to $7684 in 1870 and $2591 in 1871.[34] With constantly declining appropriations, it was found impossible to continue the advertisements in the eastern papers, and gradually the local papers of Illinois, particularly of southern Illinois, were substituted for them.[35] Peter Daggy, who had been appointed Land Commissioner in the meantime, protested against such drastic reductions, pointing out that other land

---

[32] Daggy to Douglas, January 26, 1874, "Daggy Personal with officers I. C. R. R. Co.," 16th St.

[33] Daggy to Ackerman, August 18, October 4, 1882, *ibid.*

[34] Same to same, April 27, 1880, letter book, No. 252, 16th St.

[35] Land Department ledger, No. 13, 16th St.

grant roads were flooding the country with their advertisements and literature, that the Illinois Central was losing a great deal by its inactivity,[36] and that interference by the Legislature to force sales was imminent. When the agitation against the Company reached its peak, he secured permission to increase the advertising again. Pamphlet distribution was resumed, the local agents were urged to make greater efforts to dispose of the lands, prices were reduced to make the lands more attractive,[37] and finally attempts were made to close out the land business by selling the remaining lands to some groups of capitalists — which brings Andrew J. Galloway into the story again.

Galloway had made large profits from his contracts of 1855 and 1856 with the Illinois Central, and was now interested in Daggy's proposal that he take over its remaining lands. An appraisal of the lands was made by a local attorney, who reported that there would be little profit in handling them unless they could be purchased for $3 or $3.50 per acre. President Newell was loath even to consider such a low figure. Ultimately, however, he had no alternative but to agree to this price.[38] Galloway opened negotiations with parties in Europe who tentatively agreed to take over the lands south of the Terre Haute and Alton Railroad, and a conditional contract was executed between him and his associates on the one side and the Illinois Central on the other.[39] The group planned to organize emigration from Europe on a large scale and to settle the lands as rapidly as possible.[40] The Panic of 1873 intervened, however, and made it impossible to go on with the plan.[41]

[36] Daggy to J. M. Douglas, December 14, 1875, "Daggy Personal with officers I. C. R. R. Co."

[37] Ackerman to Osborn, August 14, 1873, green box, 63rd St.; Daggy to J. Q. Harmon, December 13, 1873, letter book, "General," No. 144, 16th St.; Daggy to J. M. Douglas, January 26, 1874, "Daggy Personal with officers I. C. R. R. Co."

[38] John Newell to Wm. Tracy, March 29, 1873, and copy of letter of C. Wahl to Galloway, n. d., Ward's office.

[39] Daggy to J. M. Douglas, January 26, 1874, "Daggy Personal with officers I. C. R. R. Co.," 16th St.

[40] Newell to Tracy, April 4, 1873, Ward's office.

[41] For purposes of comparison it is interesting to note that the Atchison, Topeka and Santa Fe Railroad, incorporated and constructed many years after the Illinois Central, disposed of its lands and closed out its Land Department first in spite of the

Pamphlet distribution and bill-posting were carried on somewhat sporadically during the 'seventies and 'eighties. Editions of the land pamphlets in English, Swedish, German, and Polish were prepared,[42] and were distributed by agents and through the mail. A quantity was also distributed to immigrants by the "German Society of the City of New York," [43] and by other immigration organizations. One of the travelling agents, John Turlay, travelled through Ohio, Pennsylvania, and Maryland in 1878, putting up posters at convenient and conspicuous places along the line of the Pennsylvania Railroad and posting over 5000 on one trip.[44] He reported much interest in western lands, but said that competition among the agents of the western roads was very keen. One of the Texas agents hired a brass band to parade the streets and to collect a crowd, which he harangued for two hours and a half, discoursing on the wealth, abundant crops, heavy rainfall, and other advantages of Texas while disparaging Illinois and its characteristics.[45] In the same year the collectors and timber agents of the Land Department attended twenty-two fairs in Illinois and distributed some thousands of pamphlets to interested persons.[46] Five years later an agent was distributing pamphlets in the southern states. About the same time the Illinois Central made a subscription to the Southern Illinois Immigration Society, the purpose of which, as its name indicates, was to undertake a campaign to induce immigration to that portion of the State.[47] Previously, the Company had made generous appropriations to assist immigrant protective associations in their work among the foreign immigrants in the eastern seaports. Perhaps

fact that it had a larger grant, much of which was in the region of semi-aridity. Bradley, *op. cit.*, pp. 136-137.

[42] Bill of *Svenska Amerikanaren* in Cash Book, No. 13, 16th St.; Daggy to P. H. Fitzgerald & Co., September 9, 1879, letter book, "General," No. 131, 16th St.

[43] Julius Hoffman to Daggy, April 23, 24, 1872, box, "Land Dept., Misc. Corr., 1871-1895," 16th St.

[44] Turlay to Daggy, January 5, 12, 16, 23, 1879, *ibid.*

[45] Same to same, January 12, 1878, *ibid.*

[46] Daggy to Ackerman, September 13, 1878, "Daggy Personal with officers I. C. R. R. Co.," 16th St.; T. F. Meagher to Daggy, September 28, October 12, 1878; D. B. Paine to Daggy, September 21, October 5, 1878, box, "Land Dept., Misc. Corr., 1871-1895," 16th St.

[47] A. F. White to Daggy, November 28, 1883, *ibid.*; Daggy to G. T. Meyer, May 25, 1882, "Daggy Personal with officers I. C. R. R. Co."

the largest amount so appropriated was $500 made to the Baltimore Emigrant Protective Union.[48]

Little was done after 1870 to promote immigration from abroad. A quantity of pamphlets was sent to Robert Benson for distribution in England, and they were also supplied to shipping companies.[49] Arrangements were also made with Michael O'Connell in Ireland and Timothy Gruaz, who planned to take a trip through Switzerland, France, and southern Germany, to make southern Illinois known as a field for immigration.[50] Such scattered efforts could accomplish little in the way of results.

In the meantime changes had taken place in the methods of selling the lands. Between 1855 and 1860 most of the sales had been made at the Chicago office by employees of the Land Department who were stationed at Chicago but who went with prospective purchasers over the line when necessary. Gradually the station-agents and other special agents took over the sales business, till, in 1872, the actual sales completed at the Chicago and Centralia offices were of slight importance compared with those made by outside agents.[51] Besides the seventy station-agents who were authorized to show the lands, make sales and accept the first payment, and who received 15 cents for each acre sold by them, there were three types of agents. The first was the resident agent, generally a local real estate dealer who handled the lands in a county or in a number of townships.[52] In 1874 there were twelve of these agents located at Chicago, Galena, Effingham, La Clede, Carlyle, Salem, Mt. Vernon, Murphysboro, Mound City, Cairo, Vandalia, and Cobden; others were appointed later at Bainbridge, Jonesboro, Makanda, Carbondale, Du Quoin, Marion, and Havana.[53] The second type of agent was the travelling employee of the Land

[48] *Annual Report*, 1869.

[49] Rand, Avery & Co. to Daggy, March 27, 1873; Henderson Brothers to Daggy, February 6, 1873, box, "Land Dept., Misc. Corr., 1871–1895."

[50] Michael O'Connell to Daggy, October 18, 1875; Timothy Gruaz to Daggy, February 19, March 4, 1876, *ibid.*

[51] Daggy to Newell, May 2, 1872, "Daggy Personal with officers I. C. R. R. Co."

[52] I. A. Church to Daggy, July 25, 1876, box, "Land Dept., Misc. Corr., 1871–1895."

[53] Daggy to Douglas, January 26, 1874; Daggy to Ackerman, April 6, 1878, "Daggy Personal with officers I. C. R. R. Co."; pamphlet, *Beautiful Homes in Southern Illinois* (1898), p. 24.

Department, whose chief duties were to secure payments from delinquent purchasers, to investigate causes for non-payment, and to protect the timber and incidentally sell the lands. Their activities will be discussed in more detail in connection with the problem of timber depredations. The third type of agent, and the most important in this period, was the person with whom a special contract was made. Galloway, Hoffman, and Augustana College, as well as others of less importance, had been of this type; in the period after 1870 there were two agents who belonged to this group — General John Basil Turchin, of military and literary fame, and George W. Fithian.[54]

Turchin, a Russian by birth, had been employed in the engineering service of the Illinois Central prior to the Civil War. After enlisting in the Union army he showed his ability as a disciplinarian and military strategist and was made a major-general.[55] In his later years he published accounts of some of the Civil War battles from the point of view of a military strategist. In 1872 he became interested in a project to establish a colony of Polish immigrants in southern Illinois. With a number of Polish and Russian friends, he opened negotiations with the McAlister and Markoe Land Company, a Philadelphia corporation owning 32,000 acres in Washington, Jefferson, and Franklin Counties, and was commissioned to sell its lands.[56] The Illinois Central, however, was the largest landed proprietor in these counties, and Turchin turned to

[54] Another type of agent might be included if there were any certainty that he accomplished anything. Under Daggy's administration of the Land Department much liberality was shown in the appointment of sales agents. In response to many letters from people in other states asking for appointments as land agents Daggy customarily replied by sending a small amount of advertising literature and promising the interested person a commission on all sales made by the Department as a result of his efforts. It is doubtful, however, whether anything of importance came from the efforts of such people. Letter of J. H. Bristor, Martinsburg, West Virginia, February 1, 1875, box, "Misc. Corr.," 16th St.; Daggy to Col. A. D. Hope of New York, March 6, 1882, "Daggy Letter Book," *ibid.*

[55] Turchin had seen considerable military service abroad and seems to have had an excellent military training. He incurred the ill-feeling of Buell and was demoted, only to be made a major-general by Lincoln. The *Chicago Tribune* had a warm feeling for Turchin and General Sigel, an Illinois German who likewise was the subject of much jealousy and ill-feeling, and was constantly puffing them. See especially *ibid.*, June 21, July 7, 15, 1862.

[56] Turchin to Daggy, November 23, 1872, May 19, 1875, box, "Land Dept., Misc. Corr., 1871–1895."

it and asked Daggy for a commission as agent.[57] After a short delay this was granted on the following terms: on sales made to persons whom Turchin introduced, who resided either outside of the State or in Illinois north of the Terre Haute and Alton Railroad, he was to receive a commission of 5 per cent; on sales made to persons whom he introduced who resided in the State south of the above-mentioned railroad a commission of 15 cents an acre would be allowed. This agreement was to run for one year, and if by that time Turchin had sold 4000 acres it was to be extended. The Company also agreed to establish a station on land which Turchin purchased from it at Radom, in Washington County. For six months Turchin's purchasers were to be permitted to transport all household effects, livestock, and lumber for building over the line at one-half the regular rate. Half-fare tickets were to be sold to prospective purchasers, and if they bought land this fare was to be applied on the first payment.

Turchin and Michalski, his associate, then organized the Agencyja Polskiej Kolonizacyi to promote immigration from Poland and from Polish centers in America. They visited various Polish colonies in America, had interviews with prospective immigrants,[58] and inserted advertisements in and wrote articles for the Polish papers in this country. Somewhat later, when the colony at Radom was well developed, a Catholic church was established there and a priest secured.[59] The latter spent much of his time in the interests of immigration, going to Chicago, Milwaukee, and Detroit to speak to his countrymen on the new colony.[60] A year later the new priest, John Wollowski, planned to visit Cleveland, Cincinnati, Pittsburgh, Chicago, Milwaukee, Detroit and other Polish communities, partly at the expense of Turchin, to collect money for a projected Catholic school for the colony and also to arouse interest in emigration.[61] To secure further publicity for the colony the editors of Polish newspapers were invited to visit the

[57] Same to same, October 25, 1872, *ibid.*
[58] Same to same, February 20, 1874, *ibid.*
[59] Same to same, November 12, December 2, 23, 1873, *ibid.*
[60] Same to same, October 11, 1875, *ibid.*
[61] Daggy to J. M. Douglas, June 30, 1876, "Daggy Personal with officers I. C. R. R. Co."

community,[62] in response to which invitation representatives from Polish papers in Chicago and New York came to the new settlement to view its development and prospects.[63] An elaborate exhibit showing the progress of the colony and the crops grown by it was shown at a Polish convention held in Chicago in 1874; the colony also sent a large delegation to attend the convention and to advertise the region.[64] To protect the Polish immigrants arriving from Europe an agent was stationed in New York [65] and agencies abroad were also established.[66]

Turchin, Michalski, Wollowski, and the other leaders were men of violent temper and strong language. They quarrelled among themselves, with other land agents, with the leaders of other colonization schemes, and with Polish editors at home and abroad. Articles inspired by their enemies appeared in a number of agricultural papers in Poland, in reply to which Father Wollowski wrote strong letters to their editors defending the colony in southern Illinois and denouncing its enemies.[67] At the same time the Polish papers of Chicago were championing colonization schemes in Texas, and vigorous action had to be taken against them because they were distracting attention from southern Illinois.[68]

Ill feeling also existed between Turchin and the local agents of the Philadelphia company which owned lands in the vicinity of Radom. Turchin had sold some few tracts for this company, but failing to get any satisfaction from them had severed his connection with them [69] and had become the agent of the Illinois Central. Thereupon cut-throat competition developed between Turchin and Henry Holbrook, the agent of the Philadelphia company. Following a quarrel with Turchin, Michalski deserted him and joined forces with Holbrook. These men employed every means

---

[62] Turlay to Daggy, April 25, 1874; Turchin to Daggy, April 6, 1874, box, "Land Dept., Misc. Corr., 1871–1895."

[63] Turchin to Daggy, October 6, 1874, *ibid.*          [64] *Ibid.*

[65] Daggy to Henry A. Hurlburt (n. d.), 1874, Land Dept. letter book, 1874, pp. 585–586, 16th St.

[66] Turchin to Daggy, July 12, 1874, box, "Land Dept., Misc. Corr., 1871–1895."

[67] Same to same, February 23, 1877, *ibid.*

[68] Gloskoski to Daggy, February 9, 1877, *ibid.*

[69] Turchin to Daggy, May 19, 1875, *ibid.*

to induce the incoming "Polanders" to purchase their lands from the Philadelphia firm instead of from the Illinois Central. By promising to build a church at Dubois, 4 miles from Radom, they secured the support of the Catholic priest who had been brought to Radom by Turchin. The latter met this move by stirring up the volatile Poles against their priest, and after a turbulent meeting, in which a petition asking for his removal was signed by 109 persons, succeeded in securing his dismissal.[70] Holbrook also offered to pay $10 to anyone who brought persons to him who purchased 40 acres of land. This offer, according to one observer, caused half the people in the community to become land agents or at least to act as such.[71] Turchin could not compete with Holbrook on such terms, and consequently lost many customers to the latter's agents, even though they had come into the district as a result of his efforts and by the aid of reduced fares on the Illinois Central.[72] Settlement of any of the lands in the vicinity of the road helped the Illinois Central, but Turchin received no return except on sales of railroad land.

As a result of this situation, Turchin determined to establish a new settlement at Kalish, not far from Tamaroa, in a locality where the Illinois Central had large amounts of land but where Holbrook had little or none under his supervision. But Holbrook was not to be outdone; he, too, planned to establish a new Polish colony, to settle which he organized a land company, secured the services of a number of prominent Poles, and planned to advertise in the Polish papers as Turchin was doing.[73]

Although the constant factional strife led to much confusion and division of effort, the results obtained were of real significance. In the short space of fourteen months passes on the Illinois Central were given to over two hundred and seventy Polish settlers. These people came to Radom from Pennsylvania, Ohio, Michigan, Wisconsin, Indiana, Kansas, New York, and Connecticut; Germans and Bohemians came directly from Europe.[74] Between 1873

---

[70] Same to same, April 2, August 1, 1876, *ibid.*
[71] Gloskoski to Daggy, December 13, 1875, March 18, 1876, *ibid.*
[72] Same to same, November 30, 1875; Turchin to Daggy, January 18, 1876, *ibid.*
[73] Turchin to Daggy, February 20, 1876, *ibid.*
[74] One group of seven families had a varied experience before reaching Illinois.

and 1878, 18,843 acres were sold for $152,560 to four hundred and forty-two purchasers.[75] Some of the sales were made to non-resident Poles who had not moved in by 1878, although they were planning to do so later. A large amount of land was also sold to Poles in this community by Holbrook and his agents, who profited in this way from Turchin's efforts.

The colonization of these people in southern Illinois had a number of results worth mentioning. First and most obvious, it opened up and developed an agricultural community hitherto largely unsettled. In 1878 the Polish community raised 80,000 bushels of wheat and smaller amounts of other commodities.[76] In the next place, the settlement of this group of people aided in the preservation of the Company's timber in that region, for the Poles would not steal nor would they permit others to do so.[77] Outside of this region, the timber agents were finding great difficulty in preventing depredations by the old settlers. The Poles, however, were disliked by the Americans, who refused to move into the same vicinity with them.[78] This was unfortunate for the Company, as the Polish immigration later fell off and the remaining lands around Radom and Dubois were long avoided by settlers.[79] Most important was the fact that a new racial element, somewhat difficult to assimilate, had come into a locality previously settled

They had embarked for Brazil but, instead, were fraudulently taken to Venezuela where they were in a destitute condition. They finally secured passage to the United States and landed at New Orleans. There they heard of the Polish village at Radom and proceeded thither. Gloskoski to Daggy, undated but written in February, 1879, *ibid.* Another group of six families was en route to Nebraska, but met with much misfortune and finally landed at Cairo, stranded, where means were provided for their transportation to Radom. Klupp to Daggy, undated but written in February, 1879, *ibid.*

[75] Daggy to Ackerman, April 17, 1878, "Daggy Personal with officers I. C. R. R. Co." In a letter to O. Ott of April 1, 1878, Daggy placed the sales at 19,505 acres. In February, 1877, it was said that there were three hundred and fifty Polish families residing at Radom. See resolution drawn up at a meeting of the residents of Radom and enclosed with letter of Turchin to Daggy, February 18, 1877, box, "Land Dept., Misc. Corr., 1871–1895."

[76] See the petition asking for lenient terms signed by sixty-seven Poles and presented to Daggy in January, 1879, *ibid.*

[77] Meagher to Daggy, January 9, 1875, *ibid.*

[78] Turlay to Daggy, July 25, 1874, *ibid.*

[79] Skeene to G. W. McGinnis, October 19, 1892, letter book with caption gone, 16th St.

by native Americans, and the presence of these newcomers, whose numbers were to be greatly augmented by the growing demand for coal miners in southern Illinois, gave rise to a series of bloody social conflicts whose echoes have not yet died away.

As late as 1876 Peter Daggy was pleased with the progress the Polish colony was making. He wrote concerning it:[80] "The most of the Polanders are industrious hard working people, and are doing well. I spent two days in the Radom colony among them, and was surprised at the improvements they have made in the last two years." He further observed that so far the Poles had met their payments quite promptly, as compared with other purchasers. His tone soon changed, however, for the Poles proved to be a most disagreeable people to collect from, and long and wearying were the complaints which they made to the Land Department of poor crops and low prices which prevented them from paying. Daggy became disgusted with them and was glad to cancel some of their contracts in order to get rid of their constant importunities.[81]

Somewhat later, successful attempts were made to colonize Negroes on the southernmost lands of the Illinois Central. Some of the leaders of the colored race in Mississippi and Alabama felt that their only chance of uplifting their people was by colonizing them in regions where they would have better economic opportunities than the southern states offered. They formed an organization at Cairo called "The Freedman's Relief Association" to assist Negroes in securing land. M. Gladden, the General Superintendent, secured an appointment as agent of the Illinois Central and set about colonizing his people on the Company's lands. He soon had a considerable movement of Negroes under way, and in the 'eighties a large quantity of land was brought under cultivation in Egypt by these people.[82]

[80] Daggy to J. M. Douglas, June 30, 1876, "Daggy Personal with officers I. C. R. R. Co."

[81] Daggy to Rev. D. Koziolek, March 18, 1886, "General," No. 138, 16th St.; Skeene to A. A. Hubbard, April 13, 1895, box, "Land Dept., Misc. Corr., 1871–1895." See also Meagher to Daggy, January 9, 1875, *ibid*.

[82] Grandison Colley to Daggy, November 22, 1877; James Clark to Daggy, February 22, 1878; Gladden to Daggy, September 25, 1879, August 16, 28, 1880, *ibid*., Daggy to Clark, May 8, 1885, "General I. C. R. R.," 16th St.

In the later 'sixties and during the following decade the demand for lumber in southern Illinois was increased by three factors which were in no small degree the result of the activities of the Illinois Central. In the first place, the population of that section was increasing and large amounts of lumber were required for building and fencing purposes. Second, the development of the fruit industry created a demand for boxes, baskets, and crates in which the fruit could be shipped to market. To supply this need the so-called "soft woods" of the region were utilized.[83] Third, and most important, there was a good market for railroad ties, owing to the rapid increase in railroad mileage during these years. Somewhat later, in 1880, Daggy reported that there was much demand for hickory for axe handles.[84] These factors made timber stealing profitable, and southern Illinois was overrun with plunderers.

The ravages of timber thieves and of squatters were by no means a new thing in Illinois, and they became a greater problem in the 'seventies, contrary to what might be considered the natural result of the coming of settlement and of the law. Cutting timber from government land and from the property of non-residents had never been considered a crime by the frontiersmen, and persons squatting on government land before it was open for sale incurred still less disapprobation. Both customs prevailed throughout pioneer days, and these manifestations of the lawless character of the frontiersmen lasted in southern Illinois long after the frontier had passed beyond that region.

The Illinois Central had first come into contact with the squatters when it carried out the provision of its charter with respect to them. The squatters had shown a preference for the timbered areas in the southern part of the State, a preference which was maintained in later years. During the remainder of the 'fifties and in the 'sixties the squatters gave little trouble, owing to

---

[83] Timothy Pickles of Lick Creek, Union County, writing to Daggy on February 21, 1877, said there were several sawmills in the vicinity which were furnished with poplar logs from railroad land and he offered to act as secret informant against the culprits, box, "Land Dept., Misc. Corr., 1871–1895." See Ina Cullom Robertson, "The Ozark Orchard Center of Southern Illinois," *Economic Geography* (July, 1928), IV, 255.

[84] Daggy to Ackerman, March 2, 1880, with comments on it, box, "Land Dept., Misc. Corr., 1871–1895."

the fact that the Company was not giving much attention to its southern lands and did not feel the necessity of adopting strict measures against them. But in the 'seventies the situation changed. The Illinois Central, having disposed of most of its land in central and northern Illinois, began to make more vigorous efforts to sell its southern land, spurred on, no doubt, by the fact that the demand for lumber was giving value to some of these lands which hitherto had been little prized.

Peculiarly enough, the number of squatters on Illinois Central land was increasing at this time. In 1875 their number was estimated at four hundred and fifty to five hundred. These people were a source of annoyance to the Illinois Central because, in addition to stealing the timber, they had, by their very presence, a depressing effect on the land sales. The squatters were a rough, turbulent, and shiftless lot who had no scruples against stealing from a neighbor or combining to prevent the law from taking its course against them.[85] One of the timber agents, commenting on a colony of squatters who in 1874 had come in from the West, where they had been eaten out by grasshoppers, said: [86]

> They swear they will kill any man who will buy the land they are on and each of them has laid claim to an eighty acre tract. I had a man there on Thursday last who wanted to buy eighty acres but who would not dare to buy any on the pieces the squatters are located upon without paying for their improvements and as they ask so much for whatever little they have done he declined taking any as he said he did not want to buy the land twice and they are as saucy and independent as if they had a government patent for the land.

Another agent writing from Du Quoin likewise reported that people refused to purchase lands on which squatters were located, being fearful of incurring their wrath and of the "Ku Klux now all through the country. . . ." [87] It was apparent that the southern lands could not be sold until the squatters had been removed.

---

[85] Daggy to J. M. Douglas, December 14, 1875; Daggy to Ackerman, December 28, 1877, "Daggy Personal with officers I. C. R. R. Co." One writer from Carbondale, after noting that the neighboring squatters had broken into his pear orchard and potato patch, offered to buy the land on which they were located to rid himself of their depredations. E. C. Palmer to Daggy, February 2, 1874, box, "Land Dept., Misc. Corr., 1871–1895."

[86] Meagher to Daggy, February 6, 1875, *ibid.*

[87] E. P. Phillips to Daggy, September 23, 1875, box, "S," 16th St.

The activities of the timber thieves, many of whom were squatters, were even more harmful to the Illinois Central than the mere illegal possession and cultivation of the soil by squatters. The former plundered the forests, cutting out in a reckless manner the most valuable trees, which they would use for firewood, fences, building purposes, and railroad ties. After such depredations the land was worth little, since it was too expensive to bring it under cultivation and since there was no demand for cut-over land. James Clark, timber agent of the Illinois Central, writing from Ullin on February 10, 1877, said despairingly, "The whole country is full of men cutting whatever they can find and on any and everybody's land. . . ."[88] He further observed that a man owning only 40 acres of land could not protect it and do any work besides.

In addition to the timber thief there was the person with similar morals who purchased a tract from the railroad, paid the advance interest, and perchance the first installment on the principal as required by the contract, and then proceeded to strip it of all marketable timber, after which he abandoned it. This practice was widespread.[89] In the early days of the Company it had not been possible, because cash was then required for timber lands. To require cash in the 'seventies for land in southern Illinois would have been unwise, but the more lenient terms which it was necessary to offer to secure purchasers further encouraged illegal methods of cutting timber.[90]

To prevent timber stealing, the Illinois Central found it necessary to maintain a number of agents in southern Illinois whose duty it was to visit the wooded tracts on the lookout for plunderers, secure evidence against them, and have the cases brought to trial and forced through the courts. It was no easy task, however,

---

[88] Clark to Daggy, February 10, 1877, box, "Land Dept., Misc. Corr., 1871–1895."

[89] Daggy to Ryan & Lawrence, February 4, 1874, "Land Dept. General," No. 4, 16th St.

[90] A writer from Mill Creek, in explaining why he could not meet the payments on his land, said that, unlike most of the Company's purchasers who had bought land in the neighborhood, made one payment, cut off the timber and then abandoned their tracts, he had purchased his land for a home. J. M. Whitlock to Daggy, December 19, 1884, box, "Land Dept., Misc. Corr., 1871–1895."

to suppress a practice which was so universal as timber stealing was in this section of Illinois, and it was rendered more difficult by the fact that the general public, which had little sympathy for railroads, connived at the practice. During the 'seventies, as has been seen above, the sentiment of the people toward the Illinois Central had been reversed. Once looked upon as an institution of much benefit to the State, it was now regarded as a plutocratic octopus which charged unfair rates to the small shippers, refused to sell its lands at auction in accordance with the provisions of its charter, held them for speculative purposes, and persecuted the poor farmers of Egypt by enforcing payments, cancelling unpaid contracts, and throwing them into jail for continuing the immemorial custom of taking timber from any non-resident's land.

Every possible obstacle was thrown in the way of the Company's agents in their attempts to prosecute timber thieves. Persons against whom warrants and subpoenas had been issued were forewarned, people refused to testify against their neighbors, county and state attorneys evinced little interest in helping the agents, judges quashed cases on mere technicalities, and juries refused to convict. In 1874 Meagher and Fox, timber agents, reported that the "fall campaign in ties has commenced rather lively in this region." [91] At the grand jury in Fayette County they presented eighteen cases, an equal number in Marion County, and had a number to put through in Effingham County. The one case tried in the latter county, in spite of irrefutable evidence as to the guilt of the accused, was decided against the Company on the technicality that the prosecuting attorney had neglected to ask if the tree was "standing and growing." [92] Meagher thought best to continue the others until the next term with the hope of securing a more impartial jury; concerning the cases he wrote: "I have plenty of evidence against them, but Justice in Effingham Co. to R.R.s is rather scarce." [93] Meagher remarked about another trial that he could not say how the case would end as the county

---

[91] Meagher to Daggy, September 19, 1874, *ibid.*
[92] Same to same, March 1, April 11, 1874, *ibid.*
[93] Same to same, July 11, 1874, *ibid.*

attorney was a farmer elected by the Grangers.[94]  In September, 1874, to his surprise, Meagher was able to secure indictments against five men.  He had not anticipated such success as he recognized some timber thieves on the jury itself.[95]  His elation was premature, however, for when the cases came up for trial one man under indictment had left the county, two were acquitted, one indictment was quashed on account of some technicality, and on the last case the jury failed to agree.  Meagher attributed his lack of success in part to a law just passed by the State Legislature, which permitted a prisoner to testify in his own behalf.  The accused in every case swore that he had never cut a tie on railroad property, which testimony "had considerable weight with a Granger jury the majority of whom have done more or less in the timber stealing line themselves. . . ." [96]  Contempt for the law and the connivance of juries and officials led to bolder efforts on the part of the plunderers.  Large-scale operations were underway, a gang of fifty men being reported at work on one section.[97]  It was impossible for the agents to be everywhere at once, and by employing lookouts to keep watch for them the gangs avoided arrest and continued work.[98]

These agents led strenuous lives in their efforts to suppress timber stealing on the Illinois Central lands.  Constant threats were made against them and it was necessary for them to go well armed.  Brown, "the King of Timber Thieves," sued Meagher for taking ties illegally and two other members of the same gang sued him for smaller amounts.[99]  After these cases were disposed of, the town authorities in Louisville, Clay County, arrested Meagher for rioting and inciting to riot.  To top this a firm of local dealers brought suit for fifty ties which they claimed he had no right to take.  The case was adjourned until he was out of town; then it was called, his appeal was dismissed, and judgment was rendered against him.[100]  Thus, while Meagher's efforts to secure judgment

[94] Same to same, January 24, 1874, *ibid.*
[95] Same to same, September 26, 1874, *ibid.*
[96] Same to same, December 19, 1874, *ibid.*
[97] Same to same, February 15, 1879, *ibid.*
[98] D. B. Paine to Daggy, August 30, 1879, *ibid.*
[99] Meagher to Daggy, October 19, 1873, June 13, 1874, *ibid.*
[100] Same to same, May 10, June 6, 1874, *ibid.*

against the thieves nearly always failed, his enemies were able to prosecute and convict him on a small technicality.

The agents were not wholly unsuccessful in their efforts to protect the property of the Illinois Central. In many cases they confiscated ties and boards already worked up, although in some instances the Company found itself purchasing ties which had been illegally cut on its own land. They also succeeded in frightening off some of the plunderers by securing indictments against them. Furthermore, many of the squatters were driven off by the burning of their cabins and by threats of prosecution. In some instances the agents brought pressure to bear upon persons whom they caught red-handed in the act of cutting illegally and forced them to purchase the tract upon which they had been trespassing.[101]

On the whole, despite the vigorous efforts of its agents, the Illinois Central failed to save its standing timber from plunderers; most of the more valuable timber lands were despoiled. These cut-over lands brought lower average prices each year until, by the turn of the century, they were selling for $2.50 an acre. To have met the situation successfully a much larger corps of agents and more vigorous enforcement of the laws by the State and county officials would have been necessary. Even then, considering the prevailing opinion of the Illinois Central held by most of the residents, it is doubtful if much could have been accomplished.

The problem of enforcing payments also continued to plague the Company throughout the remainder of the century. The archives of the Land Department are full of letters from delinquent purchasers, some of them offering the most ingenious excuses for non-payment, the most common being crop failures and low prices for farm commodities.[102] Anyone reading these letters would get the impression that every year was a disastrous one for the farmers on account of blight, wetness or dryness, grasshoppers, chinch bugs, and other parasites, whose ravages were greatly

---

[101] Wm. H. Green to Daggy, July 30, 1872, *ibid*. See also the file of letters of James Clark to Peter Daggy in box, "South Chicago," 16th St.

[102] In the Clock Tower of the Central Station, covered with the grime and soot of 20 years accumulation, there are thousands of letters of this nature, many of them written by illiterate persons.

magnified. All the threats of cancellations and of selling to the Poles made by the Company's collectors failed to produce results.[103] Discouraged by the small collections of 1875, Daggy wrote:[104] "The past year's experience has taught us that you may press farmers for payment in person or by letter as strongly as the English language will permit, yet they will be slow & will pay only when they get ready." Finally, in desperation, the Board of Directors passed a resolution in 1885 giving positive instructions to close out all past due contracts either by immediate payments or by forfeiture and cancellation.[105] The following year four hundred and sixty-seven contracts for 18,595 acres were cancelled, this being the largest amount cancelled since 1868.[106] Henceforth no further leniency was shown to the delinquents. Unfortunately cancelling and forcing the settlers off the land frequently led to their squatting on other sections, and thus further difficulties were created. It also brought the lands back on the market again, and unless some real improvements had been made on them they generally sold for less than the original price. The one thing that stands out above all others in this matter is the extreme leniency shown by the Company to purchasers of its lands.

In the decade of the 'seventies the Illinois Central sold land to approximately 5800 purchasers, and in the 'eighties to 3700.[107] As the average sale was small, ranging between 40 and 55 acres, the total amount of land disposed of was not large, and well over 100,-000 acres remained unsold as late as 1890. The sales of these two decades contributed largely to the upbuilding of Egypt, which was receiving more attention from immigrants than formerly. This section was now assuming a more modern aspect with its flourishing fruit industry, its lumber business, its coal mining, and its thriving towns.

In the decade of the 'seventies substantial additions were made to the agricultural resources of Illinois, as well as to its population.

---

[103] Turlay to Daggy, July 25, 1874, box, "Land Dept., Misc. Corr., 1871–1895."

[104] Daggy to Douglas, December 14, 1875, "Daggy Personal with officers I. C. R. R. Co."

[105] Daggy to Mrs. Michael Smolick, August 27, 1875, letter book, "I. C. R. R.," No. 138, 16th St.          [106] Annual Report, 1886.

[107] Compiled from Annual Reports, 1870–1890.

In this period more land was improved for the first time than in any previous decade with the exception of the 'fifties. This seems surprising indeed when one considers the great expansion which took place during and immediately after the Civil War. Between 1870 and 1880 52,938 new farms were opened up and 6,785,202 acres were added to the improved lands of the State.[108] This vast expansion enabled the State to retain the lead in wheat, corn, and oats production which it had previously acquired. The Illinois Central was an important factor in this continued expansion, both by bringing in and colonizing new settlers and by providing transportation facilities for large areas of land.

By this time, however, other north-south lines had been constructed, and the road was no longer the only means of transportation for the great prairie regions of eastern and central Illinois. The rapid period of railroad construction which followed the Civil War had brought all but $1\frac{1}{2}$ per cent of the total area of the State within fifteen miles of railroad lines and 73 per cent within five miles.[109] Under these circumstances it is not unnatural that Illinois surpassed all other states, with the exception of Ohio and Indiana, in the percentage of land in farms in 1880.[110] Nor is it surprising that the population of the State had a density of fifty-three to the square mile and was exceeded in actual population only by New York, Pennsylvania, and Ohio.[111]

By 1890 the Illinois Central had played its part in the settlement of Illinois, but there yet remained in its possession 135,000 acres of land, 100,000 of which lay south of the Ohio and Mississippi Railroad, and 385 town lots.[112] The Company did not wish to retain these lands any longer than was necessary, as they required much care and expenditure for the small income received from them; consequently in the 'nineties renewed efforts were made to dispose of them. A new pamphlet was published dealing wholly with southern Illinois, and advertising was renewed and carried on in connection with the Land Department of the Yazoo and Mississippi Valley Railroad, which had in the meantime come

---

[108] *Tenth Census*, III, pp. ix, xii.
[109] Railroad and Warehouse Commission, *Annual Report*, 1872, pp. 19–20, 168–169.  [110] *Tenth Census*, III, xi.
[111] *Tenth Census*, I, 4–5.  [112] *Annual Report*, 1891.

under the control of the Illinois Central.[113] Arrangements were made with George W. Fithian, ex-congressman, to undertake the sale of the land at a commission of one dollar an acre. Further price reductions were also put into effect. Fithian proved to be quite successful in his operations, and by 1905 the activities of the Land Department were practically ended.[114]

From 1854 to 1900 the Illinois Central made between 40,000 and 45,000 individual sales in disposing of its grant of 2,595,000 acres. Allowing for duplications caused by cancellations, these figures probably mean that between 30,000 and 35,000 heads of families purchased land from the railroad. In estimating the importance of the Illinois Central in colonizing Illinois, allowance must also be made for the numbers of people who, attracted to Illinois by the publicity of the railroad, purchased land from speculators, and also for those who made Illinois their temporary home before resuming their westward trek. The immigrants brought to Illinois by the railroad greatly changed the racial composition of the population. No longer were the southern uplanders of Scotch-Irish descent the dominant element; their places had been taken by the Teuton, the Celt, the Scandinavian, and the Yankee. These newcomers made the Republican party the dominant one in Illinois, and enabled the State to take a prominent part in national politics. Such names as Abraham Lincoln, Stephen A. Douglas, Lyman Trumbull, David Davis, William Jennings Bryan, John Logan, Joseph G. Cannon, and many others bear witness to the important role which Illinois has played in the affairs of the nation. And finally, the rapid growth of the population of Illinois brought about the tremendous agricultural and later industrial development of that State, made Chicago the world's greatest inland city and Illinois the third state in population and wealth in the country, developed many small urban centers, fostered educational institutions, and created wealth for a few and good living for many others.

---

[113] *Beautiful Homes in Southern Illinois*, 1898.
[114] Sales Blotter, 1891, 16th St.; vol. vi, Illinois Central books, S. A. O., for deeds issued to Fithian; Skeene to Fithian, June 16, 1905, box, "Land Dept., Misc. Corr., 1871–1895."

# BIBLIOGRAPHY

# KEY TO BIBLIOGRAPHY

The location of material used in the preparation of this study which is not to be found in most research libraries is designated by the key letters shown below. No attempt has been made to list all known copies of the books and pamphlets but only to locate those which the writer himself has used. Buck, *Travel and Description*, cited below, gives the location of many of these references.

| | |
|---|---|
| Augustana Book Concern, Rock Island, Illinois | T |
| Augustana College and Theological Seminary | A |
| Boston Public Library | B |
| Chicago Historical Society | C |
| Chicago Public Library | D |
| Crerar Library | E |
| Dominion Archives, Ottawa, Canada | Z |
| Essex Institute, Salem, Massachusetts | F |
| Harvard University | |
|     Arnold Arboretum | G |
|     Baker Library | H |
|     Bussey Institute | I |
|     Harvard College Library | K |
|     Law School Library | J |
| Illinois Central Archives | S |
| Illinois State Historical Society | L |
| Illinois State Library | M |
| Library of Congress | Y |
| McCormick Library | CC |
| Massachusetts Historical Society | N |
| Massachusetts Horticultural Society | U |
| Massachusetts State Library | O |
| Newberry Library | P |
| New York Historical Society | X |
| New York Public Library | V |
| Ontario Archives, Toronto, Canada | AA |
| Provincial Library, Toronto, Canada | BB |
| University of Chicago | Q |
| University of Wisconsin | R |
| Wisconsin Historical Society | W |

# BIBLIOGRAPHY

## A. SOURCES

### I. UNPUBLISHED

#### (a) *Illinois Central Railroad Company Archives*

The chief source for a study of the colonization activities of the Illinois Central Railroad is the archives of the Company. The writer was given complete access to them and to all available material in the various offices of the Central Station. Unfortunately many of the early records, particularly the correspondence of the Land Department, were destroyed in the Chicago Fire of 1871. The losses of the Department were less than they might have been owing to the fortunate circumstance that an empty freight car was available during the fire, which enabled the officials of the Department to remove many of the account books, plat books, and ledgers before the flames destroyed the so-called "fire-proof" building which had been recently constructed. This material, however, was not sufficient for the present study and without further records the scope of the work would have been somewhat limited. A second saving factor was the "President's Correspondence," which from the beginning of the Company's existence had been preserved in the New York office. In the early days of the road the main offices were maintained in New York, and there the President, the Chairman of the Board of Directors, the Treasurer, the Secretary, and other officers were located. To them came daily and weekly letters from the resident officers in Illinois reporting the various occurrences which came under their supervision. There are thousands of these letters, including many from the officials of the Land Department and many from President Osborn, who spent much of his time in Illinois. They were of prime importance for this study. Equally important were the impression letter books of the New York officials in which were kept copies of all letters sent out. A huge chest of these books furnished much help.

The "President's Letters" were preserved in the New York office until recently, when they were taken to Chicago for use in the preparation of the evaluation records which were required by the Interstate Commerce Commission. There this collection was broken up and scattered in various locations; parts of it were lost. A large number of the original letters were taken to a storehouse in the freight terminal at South Water Street, where they remained in danger of fire until quite recently. Mr. C. J. Corliss of the *Illinois Central Magazine*, in search of items of historical interest to publish, discovered this mass of letters and, recognizing their value, had the bulk of them transferred to his office in the Central Station, where they still remain. A second trip by Mr. Corliss and the present writer led to further discoveries in this storehouse, but not all the newly found documents were removed, some books and other bulky materials being left there.

Two chests of the President's Correspondence were left in Mr. Ward's office in the Dowie Building, where the writer was permitted to use them. The remainder and by far the larger part of this collection, which had first been taken to the Dowie Building, was removed to another place and temporarily forgotten. No one seemed to remember where it had gone. The Dowie Building, the Central Station, and the South Water Street storehouse were ransacked, but with no result. Finally permission was granted to take a gang of roustabouts furnished by the Company to its 63rd Street storehouse and there examine some large chests which were known to be in existence. As a result of this search the missing correspondence, the impression letter books, and tons of other documents were found in these chests. They have been preserved in a dry place and are in excellent condition. These four parts of the same collection are referred to respectively as Magazine office or M. O., South Water Street storehouse, Ward's office, and 63rd Street.

The original plat books containing the location, sales, cancellations, and other information about the lands are to be found in the Land and Tax Commissioner's office, Central Station. This was at first closed to the writer by the then commissioner, but access was later gained as a result of his demise and subsequent replacement by Mr. Hogberg, who furnished every possible assistance in locating further material. In the "6th floor vault" under the control of this same office was found a file of correspondence on A. J. Galloway's relations with the Company, as well as some other material. In the "Clock Tower," likewise under the same office, are copies of several thousands of the land contracts with the files of correspondence concerning them. The later contracts with their correspondence are kept in the office of the Land and Tax Commissioner.

All the files and books of the old Land Department which have been preserved and are not in use or in the Clock Tower are either in a storehouse addition to the Dowie Building or in the 16th Street storehouse, in that portion allotted to the Land and Tax Commissioner's office. Most of the material is at 16th Street. It has suffered greatly from dampness and from rough handling. Some of the impression letter books are in wretched condition, the ink having run or rotted the paper. Letters are jumbled up in a pile and many are lost. The material is, however, now kept in a dry place and is subject only to fire and loss by irresponsible and unthinking caretakers and truckmen. Upon information gathered from this material the last chapter was largely based, and further light was also thrown by it on the earlier period.

(b) *Office of the Auditor of Public Accounts, Springfield*

i. *Records of the government land offices* are deposited here and were of invaluable assistance in the preparation of this work. For a list of the material available see Alvord and Pease, *The Archives of the State of Illinois*, cited below.

ii. *Semi-Annual Reports of Sales of Illinois Central Lands*, 7 volumes. These volumes include each transaction which was completed, giving the names of the purchasers, the location of the land, the price and number of acres, and the date the deeds were given. Of particular importance is the volume containing the records of conveyances of town lots, as the Company's records of this business were partially destroyed in the fire of 1871.

iii. *Tract Books* containing the records of the original sales of most of the land in the State. These books are convenient for tracing the records of original purchasers.

### (c) *Illinois State Library*

*Manuscript returns of the state census of 1855 and 1865.* These were not officially published but the figures for 1855 were given considerable publicity by the local newspapers.

### (d) *Augustana Book Concern, Rock Island*

*Hasselquist Manuscripts.* These include original letters to, and impression copies of letters from, T. N. Hasselquist. This collection is combined with the *Norelius Manuscripts*, some of which were also used for this study.

### (e) *Baker Library, Harvard University*

*Neal-Rantoul Manuscripts.* They include a Journal and Autobiography of David A. Neal, plat books, impression letter books, and other documents dealing with the activities of the Associates Land Co. The Autobiography and Journal contain much of interest on the early development and financing of the Illinois Central. They were originally in possession of Miss Edith Rantoul, of Salem, Massachusetts, who kindly gave the writer access to them, but have been recently deposited in the Baker Library.

### (f) *Chicago Historical Society Library*

i. *Brayman Manuscripts.* The most important collection, next to the archives of the Company itself, for the early history of the Illinois Central. While Solicitor of the Road, Brayman apparently planned to write its history some day. Accordingly he saved every document, published and unpublished, concerning it which came into his hands. Forms, blanks, copies of deeds, pamphlets, and advertisements are found here which are nowhere else available. But more valuable is the correspondence. Brayman's plan to write a history of the Illinois Central never materialized. At his death the collection passed into the hands of a St. Louis dealer from whom it was purchased by the Chicago Historical Society.

ii. *Ackerman Manuscripts.* Almost from its inception William K. Ackerman was connected with the Illinois Central as clerk, Secretary, Vice-President, and finally President. By this means he became familiar with its history, and in later life he decided to write it. He corresponded with early officials yet living, and in the replies secured much information of real value even though it was written twenty years or more after the events had occurred. A considerable amount of the material used in the preparation of Ackerman's two works on the Illinois Central is available in this collection.

iii. *Swift Manuscripts.* The letters of E. S. Prescott, Land Agent of the Illinois and Michigan Canal, to W. H. Swift contain useful information on the affairs of the Illinois Central.

iv. *Andreas Manuscripts.* Material used in Andreas, *History of Chicago.*

v. *Gillespie Manuscripts.* Correspondence from W. H. Bissell concerning the Illinois Central.

vi. *Miscellaneous Manuscripts.*

### (g) *Newberry Library*

i. *Ackerman Manuscripts.* Contain several extended sketches of the early promoters of the Illinois Central, of which Ackerman used only small portions in his published works. The sketches were prepared in most cases by intimate associates.

ii. Pamphlet: *Letter on the Value of the Public Lands of Illinois* (Boston, 1851), by Robert Rantoul, Jr., with corrections in his hand in the margin. The pamphlet also contains two letters from Rantoul's son and some newspaper clippings.

### (h) *Harvard College Library, Harvard University*

i. *Haven Manuscripts.* Mostly concerned with the finances of the Illinois Central. The collection contains a number of published documents.

ii. *Davis Diary.* "Diary of a journey to Illinois in 1843 and 1844, etc.," by John Davis. Of considerable interest for those years.

iii. *Transcripts of material in the office of the Chief Accountant, General Land Office, Washington.* Volume of transcripts and photostats entitled, "Purchase-Money Received and Acreage Transferred in the Sale of Public Lands by the United States Government, 1806-1860," prepared under the direction of Arthur Harrison Cole. The statistics here contained can be found mostly in the *Annual Reports* of the Commissioner of the General Land Office. The collection was of use for its photostat copies of maps of the land districts as they existed at different periods.

### (i) *Massachusetts Historical Society*

i. *Woodman Manuscripts.* Contain a letter descriptive of Cairo in the Civil War.

ii. *Haven Manuscripts.* The material bearing on the Illinois Central was deposited in Harvard College Library.

### (j) *Wisconsin Historical Society*

*Fairchild Manuscripts.*

### (k) *Dominion Archives, Ottawa, Canada*

*Baring Manuscripts.* Valuable for the financial history of the Illinois Central.

### (l) *Library of Congress*

*Lyman Trumbull Manuscripts.*

(m) *McCormick Library*

*Letters of the McCormick agents in Illinois*, giving details concerning sales of reapers, collections of debts, crops, etc.

## II. PUBLISHED

### BIBLIOGRAPHICAL GUIDES

Alvord, C. W., and Pease, T. C., "The Archives of the State of Illinois," American Historical Association, *Annual Report*, 1909, pp. 383–463.

Bowker, R. R., *State Publications. A Provisional List of the Official Publications of the several States of the United States from their Organization.* 2 vols., 4 parts. New York, 1899–1908.

Buck, Solon J., *Travel and Description, 1765–1865, together with a List of County Histories, Atlases, and Biographical Collections and a List of Territorial and State Laws* (Illinois State Historical Library, *Collections*, vol. IX). Springfield, 1914.

Hasse, Adelaide R., *Index of Economic Material in Documents of the States of the United States, Illinois, 1809–1904.* Washington, 1909.

Pease, Theodore Calvin, *The County Archives of the State of Illinois* (Illinois State Historical Library, *Collections*, vol. XII). Springfield, 1915.

Sabin, Joseph, *A Dictionary of Books relating to America, from its Discovery to the Present Time.* 19 vols. New York, 1869–1891.

Scott, Franklin William, *Newspapers and Periodicals of Illinois, 1814–1879* (Illinois State Historical Library, *Collections*, vol. VI). Springfield, 1910.

United States, Superintendent of Documents, *Tables of and Annotated Index to the Congressional Series of United States Public Documents.* Washington, 1902.

University of Illinois, *Materials for Historical Research Afforded by the University of Illinois* (University of Illinois, *Bulletin*, vol. XX, No. 1). September 4, 1922.

Weber, Jessie Palmer, *Alphabetic Catalogue of the Books, Manuscripts, Maps, Pictures, and Curios of the Illinois State Historical Library* (Illinois State Historical Library, *Publications*, No. 5). Springfield, 1900.

### (a) OFFICIAL DOCUMENTS

#### (1) *Federal and State*

United States, *Census Reports*, 1840–1920.

—— Commissioner of the General Land Office, *Annual Reports*, 1835–1925. These reports were issued separately and in both the *Senate* and *House Documents*.

—— *Congressional Globe*, 29th Cong. to 36th Cong., 1845–1860.

—— Department of Agriculture, *Annual Reports*, 1862–1870.

—— *Senate Documents*, 15th Cong. to 36th Cong., 1818–1860.

United States, *House Documents*, 15th Cong. to 36th Cong., 1818-1860.
—— *Statutes-at-Large*, vols. v, ix, x.   Boston, 1850-1855.
Illinois, *Law Reports*, vol. 72.   Springfield, 1877.
—— *Journal of the Convention, Assembled at Springfield, June 7, 1847 . . . for the Purpose of Altering, Amending, or Revising the Constitution of the State of Illinois.*   Springfield, 1847.
—— *Journal of the House of Representatives*, 9th to the 29th General Assemblies, 1835-1875.
—— *Journal of the Senate*, 9th to the 29th General Assemblies, 1835-1875.
—— *Laws of Illinois*, 1835-1890.
—— *The Public and General Statute Laws of the State of Illinois.*   Chicago, 1839.
—— *Reports made to the General Assembly of the State of Illinois*, 1840-1880.
—— Railroad and Warehouse Commission, *Second Annual Report*, 1872.   Springfield, 1873.
Michigan, *Messages of the Governors of Michigan*, George N. Fuller, editor.   4 vols.   Lansing, 1925-1927.
—— *House Journal*, 1845.
—— *Senate Documents*, 1848-1850.
—— *Senate Journal*, 1845.
New Brunswick, *Journal of the Legislative Council of New Brunswick*, 1857, 1861.
New York, Commissioners of Emigration of the State of New York, *Annual Reports, 1847-1860*.   New York, 1861.
Wisconsin, *Appendix to Assembly Journal*, 1854.
—— *Governor's Message and Accompanying Documents*, 1852-1855.

### (2) *Corporation Documents*

The *Annual Reports* of the Illinois Central Railroad constituted the most important published source for the present study. In the 'fifties the Land Commissioner was given considerable space in these reports for a review of activities of his department, and he presented in detail a great deal of valuable information such as itemized lists of expenditures of the department, the amount, size, location, and price per acre of the sales, the cancellations, the methods employed in advertising the lands, the agricultural and business conditions in the State, and immigration prospects.   The Presidents' and Trustees' reports in the same documents likewise contain valuable information for these years.   In the 'sixties the *Annual Reports* contain less material on the activities of the Land Department, but still present valuable information.   After 1870, however, aside from the records of sales, cancellations, and locations of lands remaining unsold, the reports are more barren for the purposes of a study of colonization.

The Illinois Central has at least two files of these reports: one in the office of the Land and Tax Commissioner, which includes the reports from 1853 to 1870, and the other in the Secretary's office, which contains the reports for the years 1855 to date.   The Baker Library has an almost complete file of the *Annual Reports*, and there are scattered numbers in the libraries of the University of Wisconsin and the Chicago Historical Society.

Augustana College and Theological Seminary, *Catalogue of the Officers and Students of Augustana College and Theological Seminary, Rock Island, Illinois, for XXVth Academic Year, 1884–1885*. Rock Island, 1885. Contains some information not otherwise available on the net income from the agency which the college had for the sale of Illinois Central lands. K

Augustana Synod, *Protokoll Ballet wid Skandinaviska ev. Lutherska Augustana Synodens*, 1862–1870. T

Cairo Company, *Engineers' Reports and other Documents Relating to the Cairo City Property at the Confluence of the Ohio and Mississippi Rivers, Illinois*. New York, 1847. K

—— *The Past, Present and Future of the City of Cairo in North America: with Reports, Estimates and Statistics. By a Committee of Shareholders*. Portland, 1858. K

—— *Prospectus of the Cairo City and Canal Company with the Act of Incorporation and Documents relating to the City of Cairo*. New York, 1838.

Chicago, Burlington and Quincy Railroad, "Railroads in Nebraska." 3 volumes of pamphlets, circulars, advertisements, and other documents of the Burlington and Missouri River Railroad and other roads which were consolidated into the Chicago, Burlington and Quincy system. Concerned entirely with the activities of the land departments. A unique collection. K

Chicago Board of Trade, *Annual Statements of Trade and Commerce of Chicago*, 1859–1870. It is impossible to discuss adequately the economic development of Illinois in the 'fifties and 'sixties without a study of these reports. K

Illinois Central Railroad, *Documents Relating to the Organization of the Illinois Central Railroad Company*. New York, 1852.

—— *Ibid.*, third edition. New York, 1855.

—— *Charter of the Illinois Central Railroad Company and other Documents*. Chicago, 1878.

Illinois and Michigan Canal, *Annual Reports*, 1848–1871. These reports are also available in the *Reports to the General Assembly*. Contain much information of interest on the disposal of the land grant. C

Illinois State Agricultural Society, *Transactions*, 1853–1870, vols. I–VIII, continued as: Department of Agriculture, *Transactions*, 1871–1881. These were published separately and also bound in *Reports to the General Assembly*.

Michigan Central Railroad, *Circular of the Treasurer of the Michigan Central Railroad, to Stockholders, December 26, 1855*. Boston, 1855. K

—— *Laws and Charters in Michigan, Indiana, and Illinois under which the Michigan Central Railroad, and its connections with Chicago have been constructed*. Detroit, 1856. K

—— *Statement and Replies in Reference to the compensation for the Use of the Road of the Illinois Central R. R. Company, From Calumet to Chicago, by the Michigan Central R. R. Company*. Boston, 1860. Contains some valuable information on the relations of the two roads in 1851 and 1852. H

—— Miscellaneous collection of circulars and leaflets issued by the Michigan Central Railroad in envelope: "Michigan Central Railroad, Misc. Pamphlets." K

Michigan Southern Railroad, *Exhibit of the Condition and Prospects of the Michigan Southern Railroad.* New York, 1850. K

Board of Directors of the Michigan Southern & Northern Indiana Railroad, *Report.* New York, 1853. K

### (b) Correspondence, Speeches, Diaries, and Reminiscences

Calhoun, John C., "Correspondence of John C. Calhoun," American Historical Association, *Annual Report*, 1899, vol. II.

Chetlain, Augustus L., *Recollections of Seventy Years.* Galena, 1899.

Chiniquy, Father (Charles), *Fifty Years in the Church of Rome.* Chicago, 1888. Contains some information on French Canadian colony in Kankakee County.

Gillespie, Joseph, *Recollections of Early Illinois and her Noted Men (Fergus Historical Series*, No. 13). Chicago, 1880.

Greene, E. B., and Thompson, C. M., Governors' Letter-Books, 1840–1853 (Illinois State Historical Library, *Collections*, vol. VII). Springfield, 1911.

Hamilton, Luther, *Memoirs, Speeches and Writings of Robert Rantoul, Jr.* Boston, 1854.

Hughes, Sarah Forbes, editor, *Letters and Recollections of John Murray Forbes.* 2 vols. Boston, 1899.

Johns, Jane Martin, *Personal Recollections of Early Decatur, Abraham Lincoln, Richard J. Oglesby, and the Civil War.* Decatur, 1912.

Linder, Usher F., *Reminiscences of the Early Bench and Bar of Illinois.* Chicago, 1879.

McIlvaine, Mabel, editor, *Reminiscences of Chicago During the Forties and Fifties. The Lakeside Classics.* Chicago, 1913.

—— editor, *Reminiscences of Chicago During the Civil War. The Lakeside Classics.* Chicago, 1914.

Marsh, Charles W., *Recollections, 1837–1910.* Chicago, 1910.

Matson, N., *Reminiscences of Bureau County.* Princeton, Illinois, 1872.

Mattson, Hans, *Reminiscences, The Story of an Emigrant.* St. Paul, 1891.

Mills, Abel, "Autobiography of Abel Mills," Illinois State Historical Society, *Journal* (April–July, 1926), vol. XIX, Nos. 1–2, pp. 95–239.

Pease, T. C., and Randall, J. G., editors, *The Diary of Orville Hickman Browning* (Illinois State Historical Library, *Collections*, vol. XX). Springfield, 1925. Vol. I, 1850–1864.

Rantoul, Robert S., *Personal Recollections.* Cambridge, 1916.

Sparkes, Edwin Erle, editor, *The Lincoln-Douglas Debates of 1858* (Illinois State Historical Library, *Collections*, vol. III). Springfield, 1908.

Stephenson, George M., editor, "Hemlandet Letters," Swedish Historical Society of America, *Year-Book* (1923), VIII, 56–152.

Stomberg, A. A., editor, "Letters of an Early Emigrant Agent in the Scandinavian Countries," *Swedish-American Historical Bulletin* (June, 1930), vol. III, No. 2, pp. 7–52. The editing is done very loosely and many errors appear in these valuable letters. The document on page 11 was never forwarded to Malmborg, as the Executive Committee reversed its previous action in appointing him agent for Norway and Sweden.

Tillson, Christiana Holmes, *A Woman's Story of Pioneer Illinois*. M. M. Quaife, editor. *The Lakeside Classics*, Chicago, 1919.

Van Tyne, C. H., editor, *The Letters of Daniel Webster from Documents owned principally by the New Hampshire Historical Society*. New York, 1902.

Webster, Fletcher, editor, *The Writings and Speeches of Daniel Webster*, National Edition, 18 vols. Boston, 1903. Vols. XVII and XVIII, containing the private correspondence, were of some assistance.

Wentworth, John, *Congressional Reminiscences, Adams, Benton, Calhoun, Clay, and Webster (Fergus Historical Series*, No. 24). Chicago, 1882.

(c) NEWSPAPERS

| | |
|---|---|
| *Boston Daily Advertiser*, November 14, 1855. | K |
| *Boston Herald*, January 26, 1929. | K |
| *Boston Transcript*, May 9, 1851. | K |
| *Cairo City Gazette*, July 2, 1858. | C |
| *Champaign Union*, December 3, 1868. | K |
| *Chicago Daily Democratic Press*, 1852–1858. | CDW |
| *Chicago Daily Journal*, 1850–1854. | P |
| *Chicago Democrat* (daily and weekly), 1850–1861. | C |
| *Chicago Press and Tribune* (daily and weekly), 1858–1860. | CW |
| *Chicago Times* (weekly), 1850–1853, 1857–1859. | P |
| *Chicago Tribune*, 1857, 1860–1862. | CW |
| *The Citizen*, Cairo, December 22, 1887. | K |
| *Freeport Journal* (daily and weekly), 1856–1857, 1859. | KW |
| *Freeport Weekly Bulletin*, 1854–1856. | K |
| *Green Mountain Freeman*, Montpelier, Vermont, 1855. | K |
| *Hemlandet Det Gamla och Det Mya*, 1863–1866. | A |
| *Herald of the Prairies*, January 26, 1848. | K |
| *Illinois Staats Zeitung* (Taglische Ausgabe and Sonntags Zeitung or *Sonntags Ausgabe der Illinois Staats Zeitung*), 1862–1863. | P |
| *Illinois State Journal* (daily and weekly), 1857–1860, 1862. | KL |
| *Illinois State Register* (weekly edition), 1851–1862. | KLW |
| *Lockport Telegraph* (weekly), scattered. | K |
| *Mining Register and Pottsville Emporium* (Pottsville, Pennsylvania, weekly), 1856. | K |
| *New Yorker Criminal Zeitung und Belletristisches Journal* (weekly), 1859–1860. | K |
| *New York Times*, 1853–1865. | K |
| *New York Tribune*, 1850–1870. | K |
| *Philadelphia Morning Times*, August 27, 1855. | K |
| *Philadelphia Public Ledger*, August 27, 28, 1855. | K |
| *Toronto Globe*, 1859–1860. | BB |
| *Toronto Leader*, 1859. | BB |

#### (d) Contemporary Periodicals

*American Agriculturist*, vols. XVI–XXIX, 1857–1870.  K
*American Journal of Science and Arts*, vols. I–XC, 1818–1865.  K
*American Railroad Journal*, 1850–1861.  R
*American Railway Times*, 1860–1870.  K
*Atlantic Monthly*, vols. I–XIV, 1857–1864.  K
*Canadian Agriculturist and Journal and Transactions of the Board of Agriculture of Upper Canada*, vols. XI–XV, 1859–1863.  K
*Commercial and Financial Chronicle*, vols. I–XI, 1865–1870.  HK
*Country Gentleman*, vols. I–XXII, 1853–1863.  B
*De Bow's Review of the Southern and Western States*, vols. X–XXV, 1850–1861.  K
*Gardener's Monthly and Horticultural Advertiser*, vol. I, 1859.  K
*Hillyer's American Railroad Magazine*, 1859–1860.  W
*Home Missionary*, vols. XIX–XXXVI, 1847–1864. There is much information on the economic development of Illinois during these years to be found in the extracts from letters of missionaries stationed in Illinois.  K
*Horticulturist*, 1850–1865.  G
*Illinois Farmer*, vols. VI–VIII, 1861–1863.  U
*London Spectator*, March 19, 1859. Contains a review of Caird's *Prairie Farming in America*.  K
*New England Farmer*, 1853–1862, 1867–1870.  I
*Prairie Farmer*, 1850–1858, 1860, 1866, 1869.  KWUB
*Railway Times* (London), 1850–1864. This is the most valuable railroad periodical used in the preparation of this study. Large extracts were published in it from the *Annual Reports* of the Illinois Central, from letters of the officials of the Company, from Satterthwaite's circulars and other documents. The editors during most of the period were unfriendly to the Illinois Central, and consequently their items and articles are frequently unfair.  E
*Wisconsin Farmer*, 1855–1856, 1858, 1862–1866.  · BK

#### (e) Maps

*Railroad Map of Illinois. One Million Acres of Land for Sale by the Illinois Central Railroad Company.* . . . Chicago, 1865. An advertising map issued by the Illinois Central.  W
*New Map of Chicago.* . . . Hall and Co., October, 1855.  K
*A Map of a part of the Southern & Western States showing the contemplated route of the New Orleans & Ohio Railroad and Central Railroad of Illinois . . . together with a view of Fort Massac, the site selected by the United States for the "Western Armory," and the probable future site for the seat of Government of the United States or Western District of Columbia, etc.* Wm. McBean, Projector, 1850.  C

(*f*) Miscellaneous Guides and Pamphlets issued by Land Companies, "Emigration Agents," and Professional Writers of Gazetteers and Guides.

A vast amount of more or less ephemeral material has been consulted in the preparation of this monograph. Some of this gave hints for further investigation, but is not mentioned in the footnotes because other and more authentic references were found. Many of the county histories are cases in point. Dozens of these were consulted and leads were found in them which were traced down in other sources. Hundreds of pamphlets were also consulted, but none of these are included in the footnotes or bibliography unless definite material or ideas are taken from them. To list all the works used would have been an interminable task, and would have cluttered up the bibliography with titles which would be of little or no use to anyone but persons studying settlement and colonization.

(Almy and Bostwick), *State of Michigan, 1845. To Emigrants.* Issued in 1845 by the immigration agents of the state of Michigan. This is the first pamphlet issued by state immigration agents which the writer has seen. K

Anon. *How to Get a Farm and Where to Find One.* New York, 1864. K

Anon. *Our Suburbs. A Résumé of the Origin, Progress and Present Status of Chicago's Environs.* Chicago, 1873. K

Cram, T. J., *Basin of the Mississippi, and its Natural Business Site, at the Confluence of the Ohio and Mississippi Rivers.* New York, 1851. K

Campbell, A., *A Glance at Illinois, Her Lands, and their Comparative Value.* La Salle, Ill., 1856. C

*Emigration to Canada. Canada: A Brief Outline of her Geographical Position.* ... Quebec, 1860. K

*Ibid.* Quebec, 1861. Contains additional matter. K

*The Canadian Settlers Guide.* 10th ed. London, 1860. K

*Letters from Canada.* London, 1863. K

*Caird's Slanders on Canada Answered and Refuted.* Toronto, 1859. This pamphlet was written in reply to Caird's *Prairie Farming in America.* The four preceding pamphlets also bitterly criticize Caird for his unfair treatment of Canadian agriculture. K

*Central Illinois Farm, Coal and Lumber Co.* Philadelphia, 1856. K

Cowan, William Bowie, *A Description of Grand Tower, on the Mississippi, with Letters from distinguished Individuals containing a Description of the Country.* New York, 1839. K

*The Present Advantages and Future Prospects of the City of Freeport, Illinois.* Freeport, 1857. K

Gerhard, Fred., *Illinois As It Is.* ... Chicago, 1857. CWK

*Illinois Central Directory. Containing Brief Historical Sketches of the Various Towns Located on the lines of the Illinois Central Railroad.* Pittsburgh, 1869.

Illinois Land Company, *The Illinois Land Company offers for Sale 30,000 acres, rich selected Prairie Farm Lands, in Tracts of any Size, to suit Purchasers, on long Credits, and at low Prices.* Illinois, 1855. E

Illinois Staats Zeitung, *Übersicht der Geschichte und des Handels von Chicago.* Chicago, 1856. K

*Kankakee, Illinois, A Steady Growth, Not a Creation.* 1913. K

Lindsey, Charles, *The Prairies of the Western States. Their Advantages and their Drawbacks.* Toronto, 1860. Another one of the numerous pamphlets written to refute Caird's account of Canadian agriculture. Lindsey wrote parts of the other pamphlets cited above. K

(Mitchell, S. A.), *Illinois in 1837.* . . . Philadelphia, 1837. Published in the interests of John Grigg, of Philadelphia, who owned over 100,000 acres of land in Illinois. CK

New York and Boston Illinois Land Company, *For Sale, The Following Parcels of Land, Situate in the Military Tract, State of Illinois, and Belonging to the New York and Boston Illinois Land Company.* No date, but 1835–1837. K

——— *Annual Report to the Board of Trustees of the New-York & Boston Illinois Land Company, 1837.* New York, 1837. K

Peck, J. M., *A Gazetteer of Illinois, in three parts: Containing a general view of the State; a general view of each County; and a particular description of each town, settlement.* . . . Jacksonville, 1834. K

Peyton, Jesse E., *Report of Jesse E. Peyton, Esq., to the Eastern Stockholders of the Emporium Real Estate and Manufacturing Company of Mound City.* Philadelphia, 1860. K

Spence, Thomas, *The Settlers Guide in the United States and British North American Provinces.* . . . New York, 1862. K

Wright, John S., *Chicago: Past, Present, Future.* Chicago, 1868.

——— *Chicago the Center of Commerce and Manufactures, of 150,000 Square Miles and of 3,000,000 People, Fast Increasing.* Chicago, 1861. K

——— *Grants of Land to Illinois. Plans for using the lands donated by Congress to Illinois under the "Chicago & Mobile Railroad Bill."* Chicago, 1850. EX

(g) Pamphlet Literature Issued by Railroads

Atchison, Topeka & Santa Fe Railroad, *Neuestes von Kansas und seinen Hülfsquellen mit besonderer Berucksichtigung der Landerien der Atchison Topeka & Santa Fe Eisenbahn.* Hamburg, 1881. K

Great Western Railway Company, *Great National Thoroughfare From the West and South-West into New England, by the Northern, or Lake Route, from New Orleans to New York, Boston and Portland.* December, 1847. H

Hannibal and St. Joseph Railroad Company, *The Hannibal and St. Joseph Railroad Company, Farming & Wood Lands.* Hannibal, 1859. K

Caird, James, *Letter on the Lands of the Illinois Central Railway Company.* London, 1859. K

——— *A Brief Description of the Prairies of Illinois . . . 1,300,000 acres of the nearest and best of these are for sale, in tracts of 40 acres and upwards, to suit purchasers either for cash or on long term credit.* London, 1859. C

Davis, J. C. Bancroft, *Report upon the Condition, and Sources of Business of the Illinois Central Railroad.* New York, 1855. K

Fisher, Joseph, *Report of Joseph Fisher to British Shareholders, June 1858.* A report of one of the numerous investigating committees representing British investors in the Illinois Central.     C

Foster, J. W., *Report upon the Mineral Resources of the Illinois Central Railroad.* New York, 1856.     K

Illinois Central Railroad, *Sectional Maps, Showing 2,500,000 acres Farm and Wood Lands, of the Illinois Central Rail Road Company in All Parts of the State of Illinois, with the Line of their Rail Road and other intersecting Roads.* Chicago, 1854 or 1855, 1857, 1861, 1865, 1866. Various editions with slightly different titles containing varying material. Show the location of all the lands which the Illinois Central received from the Government, whether the lands are flat, rolling, or broken, whether they are timber or prairie lands, and also show all the lands which have been sold to the date of publication.     K

—— *Sectional Maps . . . 850,000 Acres Yet for Sale. . . .* Chicago, 1867. This edition contains much valuable information concerning sales and settlements. Though exaggerated, it is the most valuable pamphlet used in this study. It shows the location of all lands sold to October, 1866.     CHWS

—— *Guide to the Illinois Central Railroad Lands. 800,000 Acres of the best farming lands for sale.* Chicago, 1868. Includes text of *Sectional Maps* (1867 edition) but not the plates.     S

—— *Ibid., 340,000 Acres for Sale.* Chicago, 1872.

—— *Two Million Five Hundred Thousand Acres of Land in Illinois Belonging to the Illinois Central Rail Road Company.* Prepared by David A. Neal. Salem, 1854. This was the first of a long series of land pamphlets issued by the Illinois Central Railroad.     CHS

—— *The Illinois Central Rail Road Company offer for Sale over 2,500,000 acres Selected Prairie, Farm and Wood Lands, in Tracts of any size, to suit Purchasers. . . .* Chicago and New York, 1855. Numerous editions were published in 1855.     CHKS

—— *The Illinois Central Rail-Road Company offers for Sale over 2,000,000 acres Selected Farming and Wood Lands. . .* New York, 1856. Numerous editions.     CEHKS

—— *The Illinois Central Railroad Company offers for Sale over 1,500,000 Acres. . . .* Boston, 1857.     CHK

—— *A Guide to the Illinois Central Railroad Lands. The Illinois Central Railroad Company offers for sale over 1,400,000 acres. . . .* Chicago, 1859.     HK

—— *Ibid.,* Chicago, 1860.     S

—— *Ibid.,* Chicago, 1861.     CW

—— *Illinois Fruit Region, The Egyptian Basin and its Contents.* Chicago, 1867. Contains an eight-page reprint of an article in the *Chicago Times.*     B

—— *Beautiful Homes in Southern Illinois.* Prepared by Edward P. Skeene, 1898.     S

—— *100 Cities and Towns Wanting Industries in the States of So. Dakota, Iowa, Wisconsin, Illinois, Kentucky, Tennessee, Mississippi, and Louisi-*

*ana on the Lines of the Illinois Central Railroad and Yazoo & Mississippi Valley Railroad.* Cedar Rapids, 1893.    S

—— *Illinois Central Railroad Co.* Chicago, 1857. Prepared by Judge Ebenezer Lane for distribution in England.    CHW

—— *The Illinois Central Railroad. Its Position and Prospects.* Published in 1851. This pamphlet was prepared by David A. Neal.    K

—— Robert Rantoul, Jr., *Letter on the Value of the Public Lands of Illinois.* Boston, 1851.    CK

—— *To the Directors of the Illinois Central Railroad.* New York, 1851. A report of Robert Schuyler.    CKS

—— Robert J. Walker, *Examination of the Value of the Bonds of the Illinois Central Railroad Company.* London, 1851. The pamphlets of Neal, Rantoul, Walker, and Davis were published to secure financial aid for the Company.    K

Pacific Railroad Company, *The Pacific Railroad Company offers at Public Sale 125,421 Acres of Selected Farming, Timbered and Mineral Lands.* . . . St. Louis, 1859.    K

(*h*) TRAVEL ACCOUNTS

Birkbeck, Morris, *Extracts from a Supplementary Letter from the Illinois; An Address to British Emigrants; and a Reply to the Remarks of William Cobbett, Esq.* London, 1819.    K

Buckingham, J. S., *The Eastern and Western States of America.* 3 vols. London, 1842.    K

Caird, James, *Prairie Farming in America. With Notes by the Way on Canada and the United States.* New York, 1859. This booklet went through a number of editions.    BCDKLOVWYS

Dicey, Edward, *Six Months in the Federal States.* 2 vols. London, 1863. K

Dickens, Charles, *American Notes for General Circulation.* Boston, 1867.

Fearon, Henry Bradshaw, *Sketches of America. A Narrative of a Journey of Five Thousand Miles through the Eastern and Western States of America; Contained in Eight Reports addressed to the Thirty-Nine English Families By Whom the Author was deputed, in June, 1817, to ascertain whether any, and what part of the United States would be suitable for their Residence. With Remarks on Mr. Birkbeck's "Notes" and "Letters."* London, 1818.    K

Ferguson, William, *America by River and Rail; or Notes by the Way on the New World and its People.* London, 1856. Ferguson came to America to investigate the affairs of the Illinois Central. He was a member of the firm of Robert Benson and Co., which was acting as financial agent of the Illinois Central in London.    K

Ferri-Pisani, *Lettres Sur Les Etats-Unis d'Amérique.* Paris, 1862.    K

Flower, Richard, *Letters From Lexington and the Illinois, Containing a Brief Account of the English Settlement in the latter Territory and a Refutation of the Misrepresentations of Mr. Cobbett.* London, 1819.    K

Fordham, Elias Pym, *Personal Narrative of Travels in Virginia, Maryland, Pennsylvania, Ohio, Indiana, Kentucky; and of a Residence in the Illinois Territory: 1817–1818.* Frederic Austin Ogg, editor. Cleveland, 1906. K

Hancock, William, *An Emigrant's Five Years in the Free States of America.*
London, 1860. K
Kohl, J. G., *Reisen im nordwesten der Vereinigten Staaten.* New York, 1857.
CK
Russell, William Howard, *My Diary North and South.* 2 vols. London, 1863.
K
Shaw, James, *Twelve Years in America: Being Observations on the Country,
the People, Institutions and Religion; with notices of Slavery and the late
War; and facts and incidents illustrative of Ministerial Life and Labor in
Illinois, with Notes of Travel through the United States and Canada.*
London, 1867. K
Steele, Mrs. (E. R.), *A Summer Journey in the West.* New York, 1841. K
Thwaites, Reuben Gold, editor, *Early Western Travels, 1748–1846.* 32 vols.
Cleveland, 1904–1907. WK
Trollope, Anthony, *North America.* New York, 1862.


(*i*) MISCELLANEOUS SOURCES

*Cairo Business Mirror and City Directory.* Cairo, 1864. X
*Chicago Directory, 1859–1860.* Chicago, 1860. C
"Farming in the Great West," *Harpers Weekly* (September 23, 1871), xv,
897–898, 900–901.
"The Prairie State," *Atlantic Monthly* (May, 1861), vii, 579–595. Taken
mostly from Gerhard's work cited above and the *Prairie Farmer.*
*The Tribune Almanac and Political Register.* New York, 1856–1861. K


B. SECONDARY WORKS

I. BIOGRAPHY

Adams, George M., "Franklin Haven," sketch of, *New England Historical
and Genealogical Register* (1894), xxxxviii, 474–475.
Ander, Oscar Fritiof, *T. N. Hasselquist, The Career and Influence of a Swedish-
American Clergyman, Journalist and Educator* (Augustana Library,
*Publications,* No. 14). Rock Island, 1931. An excellent study of a prom-
inent Swedish-American.
Barrett, Walter, *The Old Merchants of New York City.* First series, New
York, 1862. Second series, New York, 1863.
Beveridge, Albert J., *Abraham Lincoln, 1809–1858.* 2 vols. Boston, 1928.
Carriel, Mary Turner, *The Life of Jonathon Baldwin Turner.* 1911.
Coffin, William, *Life and Times of Hon. Samuel D. Lockwood.* Chicago, 1889.
Harris, Mary Vose, "Autobiography of Benjamin Franklin Harris," Illinois
State Historical Society, *Transactions,* 1923, pp. 72–101. The title is a
misnomer, for the work is not an autobiography but rather a sketch pre-
pared from what may be a brief autobiography.

Johnson, Allen, *Stephen A. Douglas; A Study in American Politics*. New York, 1908.

Morehouse, Frances Milton I., *The Life of Jesse W. Fell* (University of Illinois, *Studies in Social Sciences*, vol. v, No. 2). Urbana, 1916.

Parish, John Carl, *George Wallace Jones*. Iowa City, 1912. The chapter on the Illinois Central in the autobiographical portion is unreliable.

Parker, William Belmont, *The Life and Public Services of Justin Smith Morrill*. Boston, 1924.

Pearson, Henry Greenleaf, *An American Railroad Builder, John Murray Forbes*. Boston, 1911.

Pyle, Joseph Gilpin, *The Story of James J. Hill*. 2 vols. New York, 1917.

Sheahan, James W., *The Life of Stephen A. Douglas*. New York, 1860.

Snyder, John Francis, *Adam W. Snyder, and his Period in Illinois History, 1817–1842*. Virginia, Illinois, 1906.

—— "Charles Dickens in Illinois," Illinois State Historical Society, *Journal* (October, 1910), vol. iii, No. 3, pp. 7–22.

*Complimentary Dinner to Jonathon Sturges. 1867*. New York, 1868.        K

Thwaites, Reuben Gold, "Cyrus Hall McCormick and the Reaper," State Historical Society of Wisconsin, *Proceedings*, 1908, pp. 234–259.

Weed, Harriet A., *Life of Thurlow Weed, Including his Autobiography and a Memoir*. 2 vols. Boston, 1884.

## II. LOCAL HISTORIES

Andreas, A. T., *History of Chicago*. . . . 3 vols. Chicago, 1884–1886.

Bateman, N., and Selby, P., editors, *Historical Encyclopedia of Illinois and History of Champaign County*. 2 vols. Chicago, 1905.

Blanchard, Rufus, *Discovery and Conquests of the Northwest with the History of Chicago*. 2 vols. Chicago, 1898–1900.

Bogart, E. L., and Thompson, C. M., *The Industrial State, 1870–1893* (*Centennial History of Illinois*, Clarence Alvord, editor, vol. iv). Springfield, 1920.

Breese, Sidney, *The Early History of Illinois, from its Discovery by the French, in 1673, until its cession to Great Britain in 1763, including the narrative of Marquette's discovery of the Mississippi*. With a biographical memoir by Melville W. Fuller. Edited by Thomas Hoyne. Chicago, 1884.

Brinkerhoff, J. H. G., *Brinkerhoff's History of Marion County, Illinois*. Indianapolis, 1909.

Buck, Solon Justus, *Illinois in 1818* (*Illinois Centennial Publications*, Introductory Volume). Springfield, 1917.

Colbert, E., *Colbert's Chicago, Historical and Statistical Sketch of the Garden City*. Chicago, 1868.

Cole, Arthur Charles, *The Era of the Civil War, 1848–1870* (*Centennial History of Illinois*, vol. iii). Springfield, 1919. An excellent study of Illinois during this period.

Davidson, A., and Stuvé, B., *A Complete History of Illinois from 1673 to 1873*. . . . Springfield, 1874.

Duis, E., *The Good Old Times in McLean County*. . . . Bloomington, 1874.

Erwin, Milo, *The History of Williamson County, Illinois.* . . . Marion, Illinois, 1876.

Ford, Thomas, *A History of Illinois From its Commencement as a State in 1818 to 1847. Containing a Full Account of the Black Hawk War, the Rise, Progress, and Fall of Mormonism, the Alton and Lovejoy Riots, and other Important and Interesting Events.* Chicago, 1854.

Johnson, William J., *Sketches of the History of Stephenson Co., Illinois, and Incidents connected with the early Settlement of the Northwest.* Freeport, 1854.

Lansden, John M., "Cairo in 1841," Illinois State Historical Society, *Journal* (April, 1912), vol. v, No. 1, pp. 25–41.

—— *A History of the City of Cairo, Illinois.* Chicago, 1910. Contributes some interesting points to the discussion of the passing of the land grant and the charter. Lansden takes a more friendly attitude toward Breese than do most writers.

Pease, Theodore Calvin, *The Frontier State, 1818–1848 (Centennial History of Illinois,* vol. II). Chicago, 1922.

Perrin, William Henry, *History of Effingham County.* Chicago, 1883.

Reynolds, John, *The Pioneer History of Illinois containing the Discovery in 1673, and the History of the Country to the Year 1818, when the State Government was organized.* Chicago, 1887.

Tillson, Gen. John, *History of the City of Quincy, Illinois.* Chicago.

*History of Champaign County, Illinois.* . . . Philadelphia, 1878.

*History of Christian County, Illinois.* . . . Philadelphia, 1880.

*Historical Atlas of Ford County, Illinois.* . . . Chicago, 1884.

*History of Jo Daviess County, Illinois.* . . . Chicago, 1878.

*History of McLean County, Illinois.* . . . Chicago, 1879.

*History of Will County, Illinois.* . . . Chicago, 1878.

## III. MIGRATION, IMMIGRATION, AND IMMIGRANTS

Appel, L., and Blegen, T. C., "Official Encouragement of Immigration to Minnesota During the Territorial Period," *Minnesota History Bulletin* (August, 1923), v, 167–203.

Blegen, Theodore C., "The Competition of the Northwestern States for Immigrants," *Wisconsin Magazine of History* (September, 1919), III, 3–29.

—— "An Early Norwegian Settlement in Canada," Canadian Historical Association, *Annual Report* (1930), pp. 83–88.

—— *Norwegian Migration to America, 1825–1860.* Northfield, Minnesota, 1931. An excellent study.

Boggess, Arthur Clinton, *The Settlement of Illinois, 1778–1830* (Chicago Historical Society's *Collection,* vol. v). Chicago, 1908.

Everest, Kate Asaphine, "How Wisconsin came by its Large German Element," Wisconsin Historical Society, *Collections* (1892), XII, 299–334.

Faust, Albert Bernhardt, *The German Element in the United States with Special Reference to its Political, Moral, Social, and Educational Influence.* 2 vols. Boston, 1909.

Hansen, Marcus Lee, "Emigration from Continental Europe, 1815–1860, with Special Reference to the United States." A doctoral dissertation submitted at Harvard in 1924. An original and valuable study.

—— "Official Encouragement of Immigration to Iowa," *Iowa Journal of History and Politics* (January, 1921), XIX, 159–195.

Hedges, James B., "Promotion of Immigration to the Pacific Northwest by the Railroads," *Mississippi Valley Historical Review* (September, 1928), XV, 183–203.

—— "The Colonization Work of the Northern Pacific Railroad," *Mississippi Valley Historical Review* (December, 1926), XIII, 311–342.

Janson, Florence Edith, *The Background of Swedish Immigration, 1840–1930*. Chicago, 1931.

Johnson, E., and Peterson, C. F., *Svenskarne i Illinois*. Chicago, 1880.

Körner, Gustav, *Das deutsche Element in den Vereinigten Staaten von Nordamerika, 1818–1848*. Cincinnati, 1880.

Mannhardt, Emil, "Deutsche und Deutsche Nachkommen in Illinois und den östlichen Nord-Centralstaaten," Supplement to *Deutsch-Amerikanische Geschichtsblätter*, vol. VII, 1907.

Mathews, Lois Kimball, *The Expansion of New England*. Boston, 1909.

Monckmeier, Wilhelm, *Die deutsche überseeische Auswanderung*. Jena, 1912.

Olson, Ernst Wilhelm, editor, *History of the Swedes of Illinois*. 2 vols. Chicago, 1908.

Onahan, W. J., "Irish Settlements in Illinois," *Catholic World* (May, 1881), XXXIII, 157–162.

Pooley, William Vipond, *The Settlement of Illinois from 1830 to 1850* (University of Wisconsin, *Bulletin*, "History Series," vol. I). Madison, 1908.

Russell, John Andrew, *The Germanic Influence in the Making of Michigan*. Detroit, 1927.

Schockel, B. H., "Settlement and Development of the Lead and Zinc Mining Region of the Driftless Area with Special Emphasis upon Jo Daviess County, Illinois," *Mississippi Valley Historical Review* (September, 1917), IV, 169–192.

—— "Settlement and Development of Jo Daviess County," Illinois State Geological Survey, *Bulletin* (Urbana, 1916), No. 26, pp. 173–228.

Stephenson, George Malcom, "The Background of the Beginnings of Swedish Immigration, 1850–1857," *American Historical Review* (July, 1926), XXXI, 708–723.

—— *The Religious Aspects of Swedish Immigration*. Minneapolis, 1932.

Tassé, Joseph, *Les Canadiens de l'ouest*. Montreal, 1878.

## IV. TRANSPORTATION

Ackerman, William K., *Early Illinois Railroads (Fergus Historical Series*, No. 23). Chicago, 1884.

—— *Historical Sketch of the Illinois Central Railroad.* . . . Chicago, 1890.

Ambler, Charles Henry, *A History of Transportation in the Ohio Valley*. Glendale, California, 1932.

Bradley, Glenn Danford, *The Story of the Santa Fe*. Boston, 1920.

Brownson, Howard Gray, *History of the Illinois Central Railroad to 1870* (University of Illinois, *Studies in the Social Sciences*, vol. IV, Nos. 3 and 4). Urbana, 1915.

Dunbar, Seymour, *A History of Travel in America*. . . . 4 vols. Indianapolis, 1915.

Gates, Paul W., "The Railroads of Missouri, 1850–1870," *Missouri Historical Review* (January, 1932), XXVI, 126–141.

Gordon, Joseph Hinckley, *Illinois Railway Legislation and Commission Control since 1870* (University of Illinois, Studies in the Social Sciences, vol. I, No. 6). Urbana, 1904.

*History of the Illinois Central Railroad Company and Representative Employees*. Chicago.

Hulbert, A. B., *Historic Highways of America*. . . . 16 vols. Cleveland, 1902–1905.

*The Illinois Central Railway, Historical sketch of the undertaking with statistical notes on the state of Illinois, the cities of Chicago, Cairo, etc., and a description of the railway, its route and lands*. London, 1855.

Joy, James F., "James F. Joy tells how he went into the Railroad Business," *Detroit Free Press*, May 1, 1892, reprinted in Michigan Pioneer and Historical Society, *Historical Collections* (1894), XXII, 297–304.

Lee, Judson Fiske, "Transportation. A Factor in the Development of Northern Illinois Previous to 1860," Illinois State Historical Society, *Journal* (April, 1917), X, 17–85.

MacGill, Caroline E., *History of Transportation in the United States Before 1860*. Washington, 1917.

Martin, William Elejius, *Internal Improvements in Alabama* (Johns Hopkins University, *Studies in Historical and Political Science*, vol. XX, No. 4). *Baltimore*, 1902.

Mathews, Lois Kimball, "The Erie Canal and the Settlement of the West," Buffalo Historical Society, *Publications* (1910), XIV, 189–203.

Million, John W., *State Aid to Railways in Missouri*. Chicago, 1896.

Paxson, Frederic L., "The Railroads of the 'Old Northwest' before the Civil War," Wisconsin Academy of Sciences, Arts and Letters, *Transactions* (October, 1912), XVII, part 1, pp. 243–274.

Putnam, James William, *The Illinois and Michigan Canal; A Study in Economic History* (Chicago Historical Society's *Collection*, vol. x). Chicago, 1918.

"The Railroad System of the United States," clipped from some British periodical, about 1852.        K

*The Railroads, History and Commerce of Chicago*. Chicago, 1854.     W

Riegel, Robert Edgar, *The Story of the Western Railroads*. New York, 1926.

Sanborn, John Bell, *Congressional Grants of Land in Aid of Railways* (University of Wisconsin, *Bulletin*, No. 30). Madison, 1899.

Starr, John W., *Lincoln and the Railroads; a Biographical Study*. New York, 1927. The author repeats many stories of doubtful authenticity.

## V.  MISCELLANEOUS

Adams, Ephraim Douglass, *Great Britain and the American Civil War.* 2 vols. London, 1925.

Baker, N. M., "The Pioneers of Macon County," Illinois State Historical Society, *Journal* (1921), vol. XIV, Nos. 1–2, pp. 92–106.

Barrows, Harlan H., *Geography of the Middle Illinois Valley* (Division of the State Geological Survey, *Bulletin,* No. 15). Urbana, 1925.

Bidwell, P. W., and Falconer, J. I., *History of Agriculture in the Northern United States, 1620–1860.* Washington, 1925.

Burnham, J. H., "How the Normal was Located," McLean County Historical Society, *Transactions* (1903), II, 170–175.

Cameron, Jenks, *The Development of Governmental Forest Control in the United States.* Baltimore, 1928.

Channing, Edward, *History of the United States.* 6 vols. New York, 1905–1925.

Craven, Avery Odelle, *Soil Exhaustion as a Factor in the Agricultural History of Virginia and Maryland, 1606–1860* (University of Illinois, *Studies in the Social Sciences,* vol. XIII, No. 1). Urbana, 1926.

Curti, Merle E., "Robert Rantoul, Jr., The Reformer in Politics," *New England Quarterly* (April, 1932), V, 264–280.

Cutts, J. Madison, *A brief Treatise upon Constitutional and Party Questions, and the History of Political Parties, as I received it orally from the late Senator Stephen A. Douglas, of Illinois.* New York, 1866. This work must be used with caution.

De Motte, Harvey C., "Illinois Soldiers' Orphans' Home," McLean County Historical Society, *Transactions* (1903), II, 187–200.

*Deutsch-Amerikanische Geschichtsblätter.* 31 vols. Chicago, 1901–1931.

Dodd, William E., "The Fight for the Northwest, 1860," *American Historical Review* (July, 1911), XVI, 774–788. A suggestive article.

Donaldson, Thomas, *The Public Domain.* Washington, 1884.

Dondore, Dorothy Anne, *The Prairie and the Making of Middle America; Four Centuries of Description.* Cedar Rapids, 1926.

Dowrie, George William, *The Development of Banking in Illinois, 1817–1863* (University of Illinois, *Studies in the Social Sciences,* vol. II, No. 4). Urbana, 1913.

Evans, Paul Demund, *The Holland Land Company* (Buffalo Historical Society, *Publications,* vol. XXVIII). Buffalo, 1926.

Fite, Emerson David, *The Presidential Campaign of 1860.* New York, 1911.

—— *Social and Industrial Conditions in the North during the Civil War.* New York, 1910.

Gjerset, K., and Hektoen, L., "Health Conditions and the Practice of Medicine among the Early Norwegian Settlers, 1825–1865," Norwegian-American Historical Association, *Publications,* "Studies and Records" (1926), I, 1–59.

Gras, Norman Scott Brien, *A History of Agriculture in Europe and America.* New York, 1925.

Greeley, W. B., "The Relation of Geography to Timber Supply," *Economic Geography* (March, 1925), I, 1-14.

Hibbard, Benjamin Horace, *A History of the Public Land Policies*. New York, 1924.

Hubbard, George D., "A Case of Geographic Influence upon Human Affairs," American Geographical Society, *Bulletin* (1904), XXXVI, 145-157.

Huntington, Ellsworth, "The Handicap of Poor Land," *Economic Geography* (July, 1926), II, 335-357.

*Illinois Central Magazine* (1911-1928), vols. III-XVII.

Illinois Central Railroad Company, *Abraham Lincoln as Attorney of the Illinois Central Railroad Company*. 1905.

Jacobson, J. N., "A Pioneer Pastor's Journey to Dakota in 1861," Norwegian-American Historical Association, *Publications*, "Studies and Records" (1931), VI, 53-65.

Jenks, Leland Hamilton, *The Migration of British Capital to 1875*. New York, 1927.

Kellar, Herbert A., "The Reaper as a Factor in the Development of the Agriculture of Illinois, 1834-1865," Illinois State Historical Society, *Transactions* (1927), 105-113.

Leverett, Frank, *The Illinois Glacial Lobe* (*Monographs of the United States Geological Survey*, vol. 38). Washington, 1899.

McLean County Historical Society, *Transactions* (1899-1903), vols. I-III.

Merk, Frederick, *Economic History of Wisconsin During the Civil War Decade* (Wisconsin Historical Society, *Publications*). Madison, 1916.

Nevins, Allan, *The Emergence of Modern America, 1865-1878* (Schlesinger, A. M., and Fox, D. R., editors, *A History of American Life*, vol. VIII). New York, 1927.

—— *Illinois*. New York, 1917.

Orfield, Matthias, *Federal Land Grants to the States with Special Reference to Minnesota* (University of Minnesota, *Studies in the Social Sciences*, No. 2). Minneapolis, 1915.

Paine, A. E., *The Granger Movement in Illinois* (University of Illinois, *Studies in the Social Sciences*, vol. I, No. 8). Urbana, 1904.

Patterson, Robert W., *Early Society in Southern Illinois* (*Fergus Historical Series* [1880], No. 14, pp. 103-131).

Paxson, Frederic Logan, *History of the American Frontier, 1763-1893*. Boston, 1924.

Pickels, G. W., and Leonard, F. B., *Engineering and Legal Aspects of Land Drainage in Illinois* (Illinois State Geological Survey, *Bulletin*, No. 42). Urbana, 1921.

Powell, Burt E., *The Movement for Industrial Education and the Establishment of the University, 1840-1870* (*Semi-Centennial History of the University of Illinois*, vol. I). Urbana, 1918.

Ridgley, Douglas Clay, *The Geography of Illinois*. Chicago, 1921. A convenient handbook.

Riley, Elmer A., *The Development of Chicago and Vicinity as a Manufacturing Center Prior to 1880*. Chicago, 1911.

Robertson, Ina Cullom, "The Ozark Orchard Region of Southern Illinois," *Economic Geography* (July, 1928), IV, 253–266.

Rose, James A., *Counties of Illinois, Their Origin and Evolution.* Springfield, 1906.

Sandham, W. R., "A Lost Stark County Town," Illinois State Historical Society, *Journal* (April, 1920), vol. XIII, No. 1, pp. 109–112.

Sauer, Carl Ortwin, *Geography of the Upper Illinois Valley and History of Development* (Illinois State Geological Survey, *Bulletin*, No. 27). Urbana, 1916.

Schafer, Joseph, *Four Wisconsin Counties, Prairie and Forest* (*Wisconsin Domesday Book*, "General Studies," vol. II). Madison, 1927.

—— *A History of Agriculture in Wisconsin* (*Wisconsin Domesday Book*, "*General Studies*," vol. I). Madison, 1922.

Schmidt, Louis Bernard, "The Influence of Wheat and Cotton on Anglo-American Relations During the Civil War," *Iowa Journal of History and Politics* (1918), XVI, 400–439.

—— "The Westward Movement of the Corn Growing Industry in the United States," *Iowa Journal of History and Politics* (1923), XXI, 112–141.

Smith, Donnal V., "The Influence of the Foreign-Born of the Northwest in the Election of 1860," *Mississippi Valley Historical Review* (September, 1932), XIX, 192–204. Amplifies the thesis of Professor Dodd.

Stanwood, Edward, *American Tariff Controversies in the Nineteenth Century.* 2 vols. Cambridge, 1903.

Stephenson, George Malcom, "The Founding of the Augustana Synod: Illustrative Documents," Swedish-American Historical Society, *Bulletin* (1928), I, 1–52.

Stewart, Charles Leslie, *Land Tenure in the United States with Special Reference to Illinois* (University of Illinois, *Studies in the Social Sciences*, vol. V, No. 3). Urbana, 1916. Neglects the early period of Illinois agriculture.

*Minnesalbum Sv. Ev. Luth. Forsamlingen Paxton, Illinois, 1863–1903.*

Thompson, John Giffin, *The Rise and Decline of the Wheat Growing Industry in Wisconsin* (University of Wisconsin, *Bulletin*, No. 292). Madison, 1909.

Turner, Fred H., "Misconceptions concerning the Early History of the University of Illinois," Illinois State Historical Society, *Transactions* (1932), 63–90.

University of Illinois Agricultural Experiment Station, *Soil Reports*, Nos. 1–40. Urbana, 1911–1929. Of value for a knowledge of the soil content of the various counties.

Vose, Reuben, *Wealth of the World Displayed.* New York, 1859.

# INDEX

# INDEX

Ackerman, William K., author, *An Historical Sketch of the Illinois Central Railroad*, states Government sold reserved sections at high prices, 106

Adams County, growth of, 15

Advertising. *See* Farm journals, Illinois Central Railroad, Newspapers, Wisconsin

Agencyja Polskiej Kolonizacyi, Polish colonization agency, 319 ff.

Agriculture, Caird authority on British agriculture, 215; his criticism of Canadian farming, 217; decline of, in New England, 226; one-crop evil, 287, 300; development of, in eastern Illinois, 240–241; in southern Illinois, 282–286; expansion of, in Illinois, 301–303, 330–331

Promotion by Illinois Central: assistance to agricultural fairs, 281–283; urges cotton cultivation, 283 ff.; encourages fruit development, 285 ff.; urges cultivation of sugar-beet, 287; aids drainage movement, 291; stimulates development of agricultural machinery, 292–293; appreciation of work of, 290

Crops: high prices for, in 1855–1857, 225; decline of prices for, 256, 274; poor yields of, 256–257; received as payment for lands, 276 ff.; cotton, 283–284; fruit, 285–286; sugar-beet, 287–288; sorghum, 288; corn, 301, 331; wheat, 301, 331

Farm machinery: improvements in plow, 14; experiments with steam plow, 293; in ditching machine, 291; in planters, 293; in cultivators, 293; in reapers, 293; farmers' productivity increased by, 292; large-scale farming made possible by, 294

Livestock: on Sullivant's farm, 294–295; the cattle kings, 296–298; Illinois Stock Importing Association, 299; Wentworth's Illinois Breeding Association, 299; J. M. Douglas, shorthorn breeder, 288;

Osborn, sheep breeder, 288; McConnell, great sheep raiser, 299–300; Illinois cattle exhibited in Great Britain, 233; increase in number of, 301

Drainage: necessity for, 9, 239, 292; failure of Swamp Land Act to accomplish, 102; ditching machine for, 291; Illinois Central drains its lands, 291; Danforths drain large area, 291–292

Large-scale farming: by Sullivant, 294–295; by Alexander, 295; Malhiot's attempt at, 296; the Funks' operations, 296–297; Scully promotes tenant farming, 297; Strawn's cattle farm, 297–298; other large farms, 298 ff.; a passing stage, 300

Ague, in southern Illinois, 8; retards railroad construction, 95

Alexander, John T., large-scale farming operations of, 295

Alsop, J. W., becomes interested in central railroad, 50

American Emigration Association, 231

American Land Company, owned land in Illinois, 39

Appleton & Co., publish Kohl's book, 199; publish Caird's booklet, 218

Ashmun, George, connection with tariff bargain story, 34–35; supported land grant, 36 n., 37; Beveridge on connection with land grant, 34 n.

Associates Land Co., town-site company, 122; lands of, 123; Illinois Central stations located on its lands, 124; rapid growth of its towns, 124–125; encourages industrial development, 125–126; standardized town-site promotion, 126–127; rivalry with Illinois Central after 1855, 131–132; Neal's interest in, produces criticism, 166; interest in Pera, 206–207

Assumption, developed by Malhiot, 131

Atchison, Topeka & Santa Fe Railroad, draws immigrants from Illinois, 309–310

nal, 19; promoters of Michigan Southern come to support of, 45; opposed by Illinois & Michigan Canal, 46; aids in development of large area, 86; permits Michigan Southern to use its Chicago entrance, 91

*Chicago Democrat*, opposes Wadsworth proposal, 53; acclaims Robert Rantoul, 54; official paper of Illinois Central, 63

*Chicago Democratic Press*, criticizes land sale to Douglas, 268

*Chicago Press & Tribune*, corrects Caird's errors, 216

Chiniquy, Father, draws French Canadians to Kankakee County, 235

Cholera, prevalent in Illinois, 10; in construction camps, 95, 98

Civil War, aids Cairo development, 144; reduces immigration from abroad, 194–195, 223, 259; reduces immigration from East, 197; delays Lutheran plans for college, 205–206; forces cessation of immigration work, 223; copperheads in Southern Illinois, 249; refugees from, flee to Illinois, 248; outbreak of, reduces land sales and collections of Illinois Central, 258; severs trade routes, consequences of, 274–275; induces cotton cultivation in southern Illinois, 283; produces inflation and expansion, 260; revives demand for lands, 261–262; forces higher land prices, 262–263; agricultural machinery replaces man power, 293; significance of exportable surplus during, 302

Closter, Christopher, Canadian immigration agent, 193–194

Coal mining, encouraged by Illinois Central, 133–134

Cobden, Richard, investor in Illinois Central, 82 n.; investigates its affairs, 81; his report used for publicity purposes, 81–82, 214–215; interested in land company, 222

Coles County, speculators retard settlement of, 155

Colleges. *See* Augustana College, Normal College, University of Illinois

Colonies. *See* Group migration

Congregational Church, evidence of New England settlement, 229–230, 232

Corcoran, W. W., Washington banker, held land in Illinois, 118

Corning, John, in charge of travelling agents of Illinois Central, 178–179

Cotton. *See* Agriculture

Daggy, Peter, opposes advertising reduction, 314–315

Danforths, A. H. and G. W., large land owners, 291; drain large area, 292

Davis, David, speculator-politician, 59, 112; aids development of Bloomington, 138

Decatur, 25

Dement, John, Receiver of Dixon land office, large speculator, 113

Democrats, declining importance of, 242; Douglas's control of Illinois endangered, 243; new immigrants largely Republican, 241, 243–244; Pyrrhic victory of, in 1858, 245 ff.; lose control of State in 1860, 247

Devaux & Co., underwrite Illinois Central loan, 73

Dickens, Charles, 28

Dodge, John C., buys land for Associates Land Company, 123–124; land agent of Illinois Central, 165–166

Dodge, John W., leader of Ohio colony at Rantoul, 230–231

Douglas, J. M., 288

Douglas, Stephen A., favors land donation for central railroad, 27–28; moves to Chicago, 28; broadens central railroad project, 31–34; favors bondholders' plan, 49; later opposes same, 53; speculations of, 112, 268–269; profits from sale of right-of-way to Illinois Central, 64; opposed plan to deflect Illinois Central to Indiana border, 92; subordinates land interests to political ambitions, 113; election of 1856 alarming to, 243; debates with Lincoln, 244; accused of corrupt bargain, 245; relations with Illinois Central, 269 n.; wins election by gerrymander, 245–246; loses State in 1860, 247

123; proprietor of Dunleith, 127–128; in charge of Illinois Central lands, 149; selects lands, 150; deals with preemption claimants, 157; arbitrary method of pricing lands, 158; credit plan of, 158–159; credit plan encourages speculation, 159–160; appoints Gridley as land agent, 161; policies criticized, 163–166; favors immigration work abroad, 189–190; resignation of, 126, 166; modification of policies of, 167 ff.; interested in land contracts, 267, 268; death of, 127.

Neal, Theodore A., succeeds to management of Association Land Co., 127

Neal-Griswold group, seeks land grant for central railroad, 49; Billings, chief lobbyist for, 50; other lobbyists for, 51; fights Wadsworth plan, 52–53; Rantoul aids, 54; bargain with Holbrook, 56; secures land grant and charter, 61

Negroes, settlement of, in Southern Illinois, 323

Neoga, Swedes settling in, 197; considered as site for Augustana College, 206

New England, emigration from, 226; newspapers alarmed at same, 227; decline in land values in, 226

New York & Boston Illinois Land Co., offers land for sale in Military Tract, 38

New York-New England element, first appearance of, in Illinois, 12; in northern Illinois, 19; group immigration of, 28, 226 ff.; individual immigration of, 231 ff.; political importance of, 241 ff.

*New Yorker Handels Zeitung*, advertises for Illinois Central, 198–199

Newspapers, Illinois Central advertises in, 172, 185; expenditures for, 181; Malmborg advertises in, 190 ff.; Wisconsin advertises in, 170; German newspapers advertised in, 198, 213. See *Barometern, Chicago Democrat, Chicago Democratic Press, Chicago Press & Tribune, Hemlandet, Illinois State Register, London Times, New Yorker Handels Zeitung, Spring-*

*field Journal, Toronto Leader, Wexjö Bladet*

Normal College, located at Normal by Fell, 117, 134

Northwest Land Co., advertises land for sale, 116

Norwegians, immigration promotion among, by Illinois Central, 189; Malmborg's work among, 190 ff.; prospects for immigration of, 194; results of Malmborg's work among, 196 ff.; settle in compact area, 212

O'Connell, Michael, 317

Odell, Waldensian colony in, 251

Ohio & Mississippi Railroad, aids in opening central Illinois, 87

Onarga, Associates seek to make county seat, 126

Osborn, William H., president of Illinois Central, 77; characterized, 77–78; recognizes error concerning stock assessments, 78; advocates assessments, 79; restive under criticism of investigators, 80; wins Cobden's friendship, 81; gains confidence of British investors, 82; critical of Neal's management, 163; opposes local sales agents, 164; critical of personnel of Land Department, 165; reform of land administration by, 166; admits advertising pamphlets were exaggerated, 177; opens "intelligence office" in New York, 181; protests at reduced advertising,182; begins second advertising campaign, 184 ff.; sends Malmborg to Norway and Sweden, 190; skeptical of results of Malmborg's work, 196; begins larger campaign to promote immigration to Illinois, 200–201; appoints Hoffman, land agent, 203; gives Augustana College land agency, 208; ships cattle exhibit to England, 223; gives publicity to German colonies, 233; aware of political changes in Illinois, 242; alarmed at small collections, 257–258; favors higher land prices, 259, 262–263; leniency to delinquent debtors, 278; aids agricultural fairs, 281 ff.; urges cotton cultiva-